Dreams of Freedom

A RICARDO FLORES MAGÓN READER

Dreams of Freedom: A Ricardo Flores Magón Reader
Edited by Chaz Bufe and Mitchell Cowen Verter

ISBN 1-904859-24-0
ISBN-13 9781904859246
Copyright 2005 AK Press

AK Press	AK Press U.K.
674-A 23rd Street	PO Box 12766
Oakland, CA 94601-1163	Edinburgh, EH8 9YE
USA	Scotland
510.208.1700	0131.555.5165
www.akpress.org	www.akuk.com
akpress@akpress.org	ak@akedin.demon.co.uk

The addresses above would be delighted to provide you with the latest complete AK catalog, featuring several thousand books, pamphlets, zines, audio products, video products and stylish apparel published and distributed by AK Press. Alternatively, visit our websites for the complete catalog, latest news and updates, events and secure ordering.

Library of Congress Control Number: 2005929131
Library of Congress Cataloging-in-Publication data
A catalog record for this title is available from the Library of Congress

Printed in Canada

Front cover portrait by Jesus Barraza
Cover and interior design, layout, and typesetting by Josh Warren-White

Dreams of *Freedom*

A RICARDO FLORES MAGÓN READER

EDITED BY CHAZ BUFE AND MITCHELL COWEN VERTER

AK PRESS

EDINBURGH, WEST VIRGINIA, OAKLAND

1990   15 YEARS   2005

CONTENTS

CHAPTER 1: LETTERS

CHAPTER 2: DOCUMENTS OF THE PLM

CHAPTER 3: THE REVOLUTION

CHAPTER 4: EXPROPRIATION

CHAPTER 5: CLASS WAR

CHAPTER 11: PHILOSOPHICAL

CHAPTER 12: WAR

CHAPTER 13: STORIES

ACKNOWLEDGEMENTS

Mitchell Cowen Verter

The Russian anarchist Peter Kropotkin explains that no work can be considered the "intellectual property" of one author or set of authors. In *The Conquest of Bread*, he proclaims, "There is not even a thought, or an invention, which is not common property, born of the past and the present." Before an author can express himself, he must first recognize the authority of others, acknowledging his allegiance to those who have guided him towards knowledge.

I first learned about Ricardo Flores Magón on a Oxazacan beach from the anarcho-punk Luis Cárdenas who, decked out in his *Revolución X* t-shirt, urged me to seek out this great "poet, philosopher, and prophet." I unfortunately lost Luis' contact information in the Cleveland Greyhound terminal years ago, so if anyone ever meets him, please tell him I say thanks.

I am also indebted to the numerous scholars who have given their advice and support. My thanks go out to Lillian Castillo-Speed, Ward S. Albro, Colin McLachlan, Mona Cowen, Richard Swartz, Lyle Brown, Reggie Rodriguez, Juan Gomez Quiñones, Dana Ward, George Salzman, Eric Rauchway, Fermin Rojas, Omar Córtes, Chantal López, and Alfonso Torua Cienfuegos.

In *The Conquest of Bread*, Kropotkin teaches that the revolution must first supply adequate food and shelter before it can progress any further. In that spirit, I would like to thank Wade and Lewis Jones and Hiroko and Koichi Tamano for granting me refuge during the writing of this book.

Most especially, I would like to express my gratitude to two individuals who aided and abetted me throughout this project, supporting me materially, intellectually, emotionally, and spiritually through its darkest hours. Without reservation, I can safely state that this volume would not have been possible without the comradeship of Barry Pateman (and the whole gang at the Emma Goldman Papers Project) and my golden palamino Benjamin Ehrenreich.

Lastly I dedicate the book to the people who got me walking down the anarchist path in the first place: Food Not Bombs, Homes Not Jails, and the Lucy Parsons Center.

TRANSLATOR'S NOTE

Chaz Bufe
Tucson, Arizona

This book is largely the result of the mule-headed persistence of Ramsey Kanaan of AK Press. For several years, seemingly every time I talked with him, Ramsey would ask me, "When are you going to start on the Magón book?" My answer was invariably, "Never." There were two reasons for this: 1) I didn't want to go to the time and trouble of selecting and translating tens of thousands of words of Ricardo Flores Magón's writings; and 2) I already had a Magón biography in the works (written by another author) that I was planning to publish as a See Sharp Press title.

Last fall, I had to cancel that title after investing more time, money, and effort into it than I care to recall. Shortly after that painful decision, Ramsey caught me in a moment of weakness and I agreed to produce this volume for AK.

However, I'm not an authority on Mexican history nor on Ricardo Flores Magón. So, I suggested that Mitch Verter, who had already translated a number of Magón's writings and who is much more knowledgeable about Mexican history than I am, be involved in the project. It's worked out well. Mitch and I worked assiduously for more than six months to produce the book you hold in your hands. Mitch was responsible for writing the chronology and the historical introduction, for compiling the bibliography, for selecting the bulk of the translated materials, and for translating perhaps 20% of them. I had the relatively easy tasks of translating the bulk of the writings and of editing this volume.

As for my translations, I did my best to preserve Magón's meaning, though at times my translations are far from literal, and in a few places I even did some minor copy editing (where there were incomplete sentences, glaring grammatical lapses, etc.). The reason for this is that many of Magón's writings were produced under duress—the difficulties of producing an under-funded, under-staffed weekly newspaper while simultaneously fomenting a revolution and being viciously persecuted are hard to overstate—so, it's not surprising that even as good a writer as Ricardo Flores Magón made a number of grammatical errors in the pieces reproduced here. Under the circumstances, I've done what I think that Magón would have wanted me to do: I've preserved his meaning but fixed the errors.

The end result of Mitch's and my hard work is this volume: the largest compilation of English-language translations of Ricardo Flores Magón's writings ever published. We are proud to make many of these valuable works available in English for the first time.

I hope that you find them as inspiring as Mitch and I do.

Finally, I would like to thank Benjamin Maldonado for graciously and on short notice writing his illuminating Introduction; Chuck Morse of the Institute for Anarchist Studies for fact checking the historical information in this volume; and Earl Lee and Randy Roberts of Pittsburg State University's Axe Library for their help with research materials.

INTRODUCTION

by Benjamin Maldonado

(Author of *La utopía de Ricardo Flores Magón. Revolución, anarquía y comunalidad india*)

(Translated by C.B.)

When dawn broke on Leavenworth Penitentiary on November 21, 1922, it found Ricardo Flores Magón dead. With his death, the historical Magonist movement lost its principal figure, but in reality it had ceased to exist years before with the imprisonment of Ricardo Flores Magón and Librado Rivera, the suppression of the newspaper, *Regeneración*, and the abandonment of the struggle by Enrique Flores Magón and many others.

But the influence of Ricardo Flores Magón was so powerful that despite the failure of the revolutionary struggles of Magón's Partido Liberal Mexicano (PLM), Mexico's anarchists and many other leftists still identified with Magón's ideology, his ethical qualities, his vigor, his consistency and coherence, and his explosive style. These thinkers and social activists engaged in activities that coincided with Magón's proposals, and they gave them a direction and dynamic all their own.

Despite the death of Ricardo Flores Magón, the historical Magonist movement lived on with the little-studied activities of the survivors of the PLM, such as Librado Rivera, Magón's longtime comrade, who had been imprisoned with him in Leavenworth. Until his death in 1932, Rivera was extremely politically active in Tamaulipas. Among other things, he edited several periodicals, maintained ties with the labor movement, and kept up a correspondence with Sacco and Vanzetti (Rivera 1980). For his part, the youngest of the Magonistas, Nicolás T. Bernal, continued to play an active role in the Mexican and international anarchist movements until his death in the 1980s (Bernal 1982; Iparrea 1982). Like Librado Rivera, Bernal died in poverty. For her part, Magón's *compañera*, María Brousse, and a group of friends, undertook the publication of a good part of Magon's articles and speeches, even though Brousse had running disputes with Rivera and Bernal (Bernal 1982, pp. 141–144).

Others made worse use of Magón's legacy. On the day following his death, a disagreeable legend arose: that the Magonist movement was "the precursor of the Mexican Revolution." An ex-Magonist, Antonio Díaz Soto y Gama, at the time a member of congress, delivered an emotional speech in which he notified the other deputies of Magón's death and then, undoubtedly with good intentions, exalted Ricardo Flores Magón, praising him as the precursor of the revolution. The political class, which had benefited from the Mexican Revolution—which in reality resulted in only a change of those in power—saw in this estimation of Magón an opportunity to co-opt the legacy of an inconvenient national hero, and at the same time to claim him as its own antecedent.

So it was that Magonism was incorporated into the official history as the precursor of the revolution, in other words as the precursor of the brutal, corrupt, authoritarian Partido Revolucionario Institucional (PRI). The PRI appropriated the ideas and actions of Magonism's first epoch (1900–1910), and propagated the false idea that these things comprised the whole of Magonism. That is, the PRI presented Magonism as only a liberal ideology and movement, leaving to one side the radicalism of post-1910 Magonism. For the state, there were no figures such as Zapata, Villa, Carranza, and Obregón to fill the void at the beginning of the twentieth century, and as an agitator Francisco I. Madero was an insignificant figure. It was the Magonists who revolted in 1906 and 1908, who had done tireless agitational work with *Regeneración*, who had organized the PLM in 1905–1906, put forward its program, and who had participated in the strikes in Cananea and Rio Blanco in 1906 and 1907. But all these things were *not* preparation for the limited political revolution of 1910. Rather, they were preparation for a radical economic revolution, which ultimately failed, and whose final important armed uprising took place in 1911 in Baja California. And, it's important to note, this final uprising was suppressed not by the forces of the old Díaz dictatorship, but by Madero's "revolutionaries" (utilizing troops from the old Díaz regime, for fear that their own troops would join the actual revolutionaries).

The attempts by government officials to appropriate Ricardo Flores Magón have, however, contributed—contrary to the original intentions of the appropriators—to keeping this difficult-to-assimilate person in the public eye. In 1945, the transfer of his remains to the Rotunda of Illustrious Men (Hernández 1950) stirred in the public the memory of this polarized figure, who on the one hand was painted as a self-abnegating leader of the anti-Porfirista movement by the government, and on the other hand who was still believed by a large part of the population to be guilty of "filibusterism," of conducting a military adventure in Baja California in 1911 with the goal of annexing Baja to the United States.

Later, around 1973, the centenary of the birth of Ricardo Flores Magón, an important group of academics published many books and articles on Magón and Magonism with the support of three government agencies: the Secretary of

Housing and Public Credit, in its *Boletín Bibliográfico* (Maldonado 1988); the National Institute of Historical Studies on the Mexican Revolution, a dependency of the Secretary of the Interior; and the Center for Historical Studies on the Labor Movement, under the auspices of the Secretary of Labor and Social Forecasts.

But even more important since the end of the historic Magonist movement have been what we can call Magonist narratives or histories, which come in many forms and in which one of several aspects of historic Magonism have influenced the activities of persons, collectives, and organizations. These narratives constitute the tracks of the dying movement radiating outward in the free expression of every one of the protagonists of "the idea."

The explosive tenant farmer movement in Veracruz in the 1920s, tied to the radical campesino movement in the area, had amongst its activities the presentation of the theater works of Ricardo Flores Magón (Agetro 1942; Fowler 1979). The campesino movement in Michoacán had among its primary leaders Primo Tapia, who had been involved with the PLM Junta in Los Angeles (Friedrich 1984). The Nueva Leon anarchist Ricardo Treviño, a key worker in the unfolding of revolutionary syndicalism in the workers' movement of Tampico, had been part of the Magonist group in San Antonio. In the same part of Tampico, the agrarian mobilization was headed by another Magonist, Higinio Tanguma (González 1987). And the reading of *Regeneración* influenced the social policies of post-revolutionary state governors, such as Felipe Carrillo Puerto (Yucatán), Emilio Portes Gil (Tamaulipas), and Adalberto Tejeda (Veracruz). In 1937, Efrén Castrejón began publishing *Regeneración*, with his edition being taken over by the Federación Anarquista Mexicana in 1941 (López y Cortés 1999).

But the greatest work in spreading awareness of the thoughts and actions of the Magonist movement has been done since the 1970s by Omar Cortés and Chantal López through their indispensable Ediciones Antorcha, which has printed dozens of books comprising collections of articles from *Regeneración*, speeches by Ricardo Flores Magón, the letters and manifestoes of Emiliano Zapata, etc., etc. More recently, Omar and Chantal have with great care and commitment put a great many of these works on line in nicely produced, free editions on their web site: www.antorcha.net/index/catalogo/catalogo.html.

Beyond this, in the context of workers and campesino struggles, the figure of Ricardo Flores Magón and the various Magonist slogans were present in the second half of the twentieth century in important social movements which were not anarchist. In this regard, it's worth mentioning that several outstanding Marxist intellectuals of the Mexican left, such as José Revueltas, have turned their eyes toward Magonism to lend its support to contemporary social struggles.

More recently, Magonism has inspired the formation and activities of several collectives of young people in Mexico City and in other parts of the country. In large part these groups have ties to the Biblioteca Social Reconstruir (Social Reconstruction Library), an organization formed by Spanish exiles in the 1940s following the defeat of the Spanish Revolution in 1938–39, and which, following the death of its leading member, Ricardo Mestre, has had to exert extraordinary effort simply to survive.

In the case of Oaxaca, Magonism has been forcefully reborn in the land of Ricardo Flores Magón's birth, in the municipality of San Antonio Eloxochitlán. Over the last ten years, Magonism has been reaffirmed there, consisting of discussion of the historical movement, a mass visit to Ricardo's tomb, the orientation of the community assembly toward Magonism, and the forging of ties with anarchist collectives in different parts of the country and throughout the world.

Also in Oaxaca, since the end of the 1990s the social movement that has most openly confronted the state has been propelled by the Consejo Indígena y Popular de Oaxaca "Ricardo Flores Magón" (CIPO-RFM), with, obviously, clear Magonist orientation. This group, in addition to being the driving force behind many popular initiatives, has also created ties with several European collectives.

The examples of Magonist "narratives" are multiplying, and without doubt the most eye-catching is found in the Zapatista movement in the indigenous villages of Chiapas. In this movement two important elements are tied together: the appropriation which the Zapatistas are making of the figure of Ricardo Flores Magón and the political/social discussion which implies the presence of Magonism in the Zapatista movement.

One of the first and largest municipal rebellions in Chiapas took the name of Ricardo Flores Magón, and it's one of the 29 municipalities located in the territory controlled by the Ejército Zapatista de Liberación Nacional (EZLN—Zapatista National Liberation Army). It was begun in the Tzeltal community of Taniperlas on April 9, 1998, and since then has endured governmental harassment. Within 24 hours of the rebellion's constitution, the Mexican army invaded the community and destroyed its seat of government. But it wasn't able to destroy the community council. (This same municipal council is one of the four municipal councils which since August 2003 have constituted the Junta de Buen Gobierno "El camino del futuro" [the Council of Good Government, The Way of the Future]. These four communities all belong to the "Resistance to Bring a New Dawn," which was established in La Garrucha.) In this rebel municipality, Ricardo Flores Magón, the Tzeltals rule themselves without depending on the Mexican government. They have their own systems of justice, health, education, and production, based in their own customs and supported by Mexican and foreign activists.

As well, the presence of Magonism in the present-day Zapatista movement leads us to examine the mutual presence in both historic movements. This has led us to discover that there was an approach between the two movements between 1912 and 1914. This approach implies that the Zapatistas were familiar with the anarchist objectives of the Magonist struggle, expressed in the slogan ¡Viva Tierra y Libertad!, which since 1910 was the principle Magonist slogan. And the struggle for Tierra y Libertad was a libertarian revolution, not a "revolution" for a change in government, but a revolution whose aim was the destruction of the capitalist socioeconomic model and the reconstruction of Mexico based on a libertarian schematic nourished by the historical experience of indigenous community organization. (The formulation of this proposal to turn one's eyes toward the forms of indigenous life had three central proponents within Magonism: Ricardo Flores Magón, Voltairine de Cleyre, and William C. Owen, all of whom from the beginning of the decade in 1910 developed and published these ideas.)

In sum, Magonism is certainly close enough to Zapatismo in the present epoch; this much is certain, and it implies that Magonism has an important role in these moments when the nation-state model is reaching exhaustion, propelling us toward a new social compact.

Historical Magonism reaches its centenary in 2006. Following Armando Barta (1977), we can say that Magonism consisted of three elements: 1) an ideology; 2) a periodical; and 3) an organization. The ideology was formed with the input of, among others, Ricardo Flores Magón, Librado Rivera, Práxedis Guerrero, William C. Owen, and Voltairine de Cleyre, with Ricardo Flores Magón standing above the rest in clarity and forcefulness in expressing the ideology. The periodical, *Regeneración*, first appeared in 1900 and for the next 18 years would be the instrument of diffusing Magonism in Mexico and the United States. And the organization was the Partido Liberal Mexicano, which through an exemplary process of creation and elaboration of its plan and program saw light in July 1906 (López and Cortés 1985).

Even though historical Magonism has long since disappeared, it has continued and will continue to nourish Magonist "narratives" in many distinct locales, which certainly are playing and will continue to play a substantial part in the transformation of Mexico.

PREFACE

Mitchell Verter, 2005

In Ricardo Flores Magón's 1917 play, "Víctimas y Verdugos" (Victims and Executioners), the worker José defends his companion Isabel from a judge who arrives with a group of gendarmes to throw her and her sick, dying mother out on to the street. After José proclaims that the bourgeoisie have prostituted the concepts of "justice" and "rights" to forward their own interests and to whip down the poor, the judge furiously demands, "Are you an anarchist?" José responds, "I am a friend of justice, of human justice, of the justice that is not written in the codes, of the justice that prescribes that all human beings have the right to live without exploiting and without being exploited, without ordering and without being ordered." Falsely believing that he has uncovered the underlying reason for José's revolutionary awareness, the judge shouts to his gendarmes, "This man is a magonista"—a follower of Ricardo Flores Magón—"Search him!" However, José, restrained and patted down by the authorities, indignantly responds "I am not a magonista: I am an anarchist. An anarchist does not have idols."

Flores Magón was quite clear about this: about placing principles above "leaders." A prison letter to his brother Enrique and his comrade Praxedis Guerrero explains that they must work as "anarchists, even from those who take us as their leaders." Rejecting all forms of coercion, Flores Magón believed that a true anarchist would neither order others around nor prescribe a doctrine for others to follow. Rather than leading a set of followers, true revolutionaries would inspire others to action. He explained, "Let us then, those who are conscious, prepare the popular mentality for when the moment arrives." This notion of the anarchist intellectual as one who points the way rather than commands echoes the classical, Socratic idea of the philosopher as one who frees shackled slaves from false ideas.

Throughout his writing, Ricardo Flores Magón repeatedly describes himself as a prophet of emancipation. Traditionally, a prophet does not merely call others to justice; his own prophecy is also a response to a calling from beyond himself. Flores Magón describes his own inspiration in a similar manner: "'Onwards!' says a mysterious voice that appears, uprooting the innermost core of our being. It spurs on all those who are weary, spiritually burdened; whose swollen feet have been bled dry by the long, hard road; we who intend to rest for a while. … 'Onwards, onwards!' the voice orders us." Similarly, Flores Magón asserts his prophetic role in human history in the essay, "Utopians": "Nevertheless, at all times, the progress of humanity is indebted to the dreamers and the utopians. This thing called civilization: what is it if not the result of utopian efforts? The visionaries, the poets, the dreamers, the utopians, so disdained by 'serious' people, so persecuted by the 'paternalism' of governments: lynched here, shot down there, burnt to death, tortured, imprisoned, torn to pieces in all epochs and all countries, nevertheless, have been the engines of all movements forward, the prophets who have pointed the blind masses towards luminous paths leading to glorious summits."

Those who knew or observed Ricardo Flores Magón attested to his spiritual force. Their descriptions of him tend not to focus on his personal qualities, but rather on his ability to beckon others to the struggle for human liberation. On hearing of his death, Flores Magón's old Liberal Party comrade, Antonio Díaz Soto y Gama, eulogized him by saying, "he was the inspiration, the clear vision that impelled the people to revolution ... Ricardo Flores Magón saw the Revolution totally, integrally, with the vision of a prophet." Similarly, Flores Magón's closest comrade for over half his life, Librado Rivera, praised him because, "his great steadfastness and heroic courage even transformed a people enslaved, downtrodden, and humiliated by the greatest of despots into a proud, valiant, and respected people, resplendently uplifting faces imbued with terror and horror towards their exploiters and torturers. Indeed, Ricardo Flores Magón was the soul of that great libertarian epic who, in the manner of Prometheus of mythological legend, infused that divine fire that impelled the people to rebellion; rebellion, the creative well of all liberties." Even Thomas Furlong, the detective who made a career out of pursuing Flores Magón and other members of the Partido Liberal Mexicano, described him in spiritual terms. In his 1906 report to the Mexican government, he stated that Flores Magón had "a very resolute and energetic character and is fanatical about the cause he pursues ... Ricardo is the soul of all, and without him the other people would do nothing."

As a revolutionary prophet, Ricardo Flores Magón attempted to awaken the enslaved masses of the world from their nightmares through a dream of social, economic, and political justice. As is still the situation today, in Flores Magón's time most people accepted their misery and degradation as part of the normal order of things. As an apostle of anarchism, Ricardo Flores Magón taught that misery and degradation are not natural, but rather that they are produced by the thievery of the rich, the manipulation of religion, and government repression. He taught that these three forces conspire to uphold the very basis of injustice: the institution of private property.

Indeed, one can look at the history of Mexico as one example, among countless others, of how private property rights have enslaved millions. In 1511, Fernando Cortés and his conquistadors invaded Central America, irrevocably disrupting the life of the populace; they declared the land to be the property of Spain and subjected the natives to foreign domination and exploitation. Although Mexico eventually cast off the Spanish yoke, a tiny but powerful minority within the country continued to steal the land from beneath the feet of the people. Even after what would now be called "national liberation," plantation owners seized the ejidos, native communal holdings, as their personal property, forcing the masses who had lived on them into perpetual debt slavery. Other natural resources met nearly the same fate, though in the cases of oil and minerals they often passed into the hands of foreign capitalists and corporations.

In contrast to this wallowing at the trough, this pushing aside and trampling of the weak by the cunning, ruthless, and dishonest, Ricardo Flores Magón proposed economic, social, and political equality. Not an enforced "equality" in which the naturally gifted are beaten down, but an equality of opportunity, an equality of access to the world's wealth, an equality of access to Land and Liberty.

In almost all of Ricardo Flores Magón's writings, one can detect an underlying current of empathy for the downtrodden, empathy for those called The Other by the philosopher Emmanuel Levinas. Indeed, this is the mark of the man: Ricardo Flores Magón keenly felt the suffering of others, and he dedicated his life to alleviating it. He dedicated his life to inspiring others to cast off their chains by denouncing the horrors the Mexican people were subjected to by what he referred to as the "three-headed hydra": capitalism, the state, and the clergy. But he went further and offered a vision of a much brighter tomorrow, a libertarian, achievable vision—if the people would but seize it.

His libertarian, humanistic, empathetic vision is Ricardo Flores Magón's legacy. A scene in a recent film,[1] "The Fourth World War," profoundly explores this idea of empathy as a call to justice. In it, an Argentine grandmother passionately denounces the government that has so savagely murdered so many young political dissidents. She says, "We must fight so that more children do not die. It cannot be a thing of pity. It cannot be that, in this country, 100 children die every day. We can not allow it. We must participate in the struggles. Each of us must feel, at last, that I am 'the other'. I am 'the other'. I am 'the other'. I am the unemployed worker. I am the revolutionary. I am those who take over the factory. I am those who do not eat. I am all of us." At the end of the film, the Zapatista, Subcomandante Marcos likewise urges, "Listen to the word of the other. You shall no longer be you; now you are us."

A man may die, yet his noble ideals shall live on in the minds and hearts of others. Even though Ricardo Flores Magón, the apostle of anarchism, was martyred for his prophecy, he spread his dreams of freedom through his writing and his actions. Across the infinity of time, hope shall spring eternally from his words and his life.

An early photo of Ricardo and Enrique Flores Magón taken in 1900.

HISTORICAL BACKGROUND
[by M.V.]

MIGUEL HIDALGO AND THE WAR FOR INDEPENDENCE

In order to comprehend Ricardo Flores Magón's anarchist vision of social and economic justice, one must understand the struggle for liberalism that
preceded him in 19th-century Mexico. The Spanish conquest of Mexico in 1519
brought extraordinary misery to the native population: it subjugated them politically to the Spanish king, dominated them spiritually via the Catholic religion,
and enslaved them economically on the Spanish plantations. In the early 1800s,
dissidents began to receive books bearing the European libertarian ideas that had
inspired revolutions in France and the United States. Posing as a literary club, a
group in Dolores, Mexico began to plot the nation's independence from Spanish
rule. This group included the radical parish priest Miguel Hidalgo. Before the club
could inaugurate its uprising planned for December 8, 1810, Spanish colonial
authorities discovered the plot and arrested several members on September 13.
Three days later, Hidalgo received news of this capture.

Fearing that authorities might soon descend upon him as well, Hidalgo
rang his church's bells early on the morning of September 16, 1810, summoning his parishioners to mass. He confronted them with the words that are now
famously remembered as El Grito de Dolores ("The Cry of Dolores"): "Will you
free yourselves? Will you recover the lands stolen three hundred years ago from
your forefathers by the hated Spaniards?"[1] The congregation responded enthusiastically, and Hidalgo led them toward San Miguel. Hundreds more Mexican patriots joined them on their march. Over the course of its struggle, the rebel army
swelled to several thousand. In San Miguel, Guanajuato, and other towns, the impoverished masses following Hidalgo rioted, burning and pillaging the homes,
businesses, and political edifices of the privileged Spanish oppressors. Worried
about his followers' uncontrollable rage, Hidalgo decided not to attack Mexico
City. It was a bad decision. Hidalgo's elitist distrust of the popular will caused
many brave Indians to abandon his struggle. His hesitation also gave the government an opportunity to organize its military force and quash the uprising. As a
result of Hidalgo's indecision, the War for Independence raged on for another
eleven years.

Hidalgo ultimately met defeat on the fighting fields of Guadalajara. During the battle, a Spanish artillery shell hit the rebel army's munitions wagon. Fires
spread quickly in the tall, dry grass surrounding the revolutionaries, impelling

them to flee. Hidalgo was captured shortly afterwards and executed by firing squad. As a warning against other revolutionary attempts, his head was impaled upon a pole in the middle of Guanajuato.Yet, the popular will that had awoken so furiously on the morning of September 16, 1810 could not so easily be put back to rest. Under the leadership of José María Morelos, Vicente Guerrero, Guadalupe Victoria, and others, the insurgents continued fighting valorously. Finally, on February 24, 1821, the Spanish Colonel Augustín de Iturbide met with the rebel leader Vicente Guerrero, agreeing to the Plan de Iguala that asserted Mexico's independence from Spain.

Even though this document established autonomy for the nation of Mexico, it preserved the structures that had subjugated the people of Mexico since the Spanish conquest. It organized the country politically as a monarchy. The Catholic Church still maintained its authority over the people's spiritual life. Socially, the Plan de Iguala benefited only those who were already near the top of the ladder: the criollos. For the first time in history, criollos, white Mexicans directly descended from pure European ancestry, would be granted the same rights as gachupines, Spaniards living in Mexico. In contrast, the indigenous and mestizo (mixed race) populations would be relegated to the same misery they had endured for three centuries.

BENITO JUÁREZ AND THE STRUGGLE FOR REFORM

For the next 35 years, Mexico continued to suffer under a succession of emperors, monarchs, and military tyrants. Although the rebel leader Vicente Guerrero briefly became president and abolished slavery, he was soon overthrown by his vice-president, Anastasio Bustamante, who was in turn toppled by General Antonio López de Santa Anna. Against the popular will for liberation, Santa Anna centralized power under himself and promoted the dominance of the Catholic Church. Further, he sold Mexico's natural resources—its precious mines—to foreign investors, making himself a millionaire. Although he defended Mexico against an invasion by the French, he lost the territory that is now California, Texas, New Mexico, Nevada, Utah, and Arizona to the United States, when the U.S. government, pursuing its policy of Manifest Destiny, invaded Mexico and seized half its territory in 1846–1847.

In the 1850s, a new group of revolutionaries began to plot the overthrow of Santa Anna's military dictatorship. Like their predecessors, they read widely from classic liberal thinkers such as Voltaire and Rousseau. In addition, they studied newer libertarians, such as the anarchist Pierre Joseph Proudhon.The inspirational leader of this group was Benito Juárez, an Indian from the state of Oaxaca who, after being orphaned at a young age, walked to Oaxaca City, where he worked and studied law. He donated his legal services to the impoverished, largely indigenous masses of Mexico. After defending many poor villagers without much success, Juárez realized that improving their lives required political engagement. He served in various government posts, including governor of Oaxaca. Still frustrated by the lack of progress, Juárez and his supporters issued the Plan de Ayutla and fomented a revolution against Santa Anna, driving him from the country.

The movement inaugurated by Juárez and his liberal cohorts, known in Mexico as The Reform, profoundly changed the country by wresting power away from traditional sources of authority. The Ley Juárez required members of the church and the military to stand trial in civil courts for civil offenses. The Ley Lerdo required ecclesiastical and civic institutions to forfeit property they did not need for their daily functioning. Unfortunately, the law considered ejidos, the traditional communal lands of native Mexicans, to be civil corporations. In the end, this resulted in many villagers being forced to sell their homes and lands to the rich and the politically powerful. The Constitution of 1857, incorporating these two laws, further constrained the power of the Church and established a wide range of liberal legal protections for the Mexican people. It included a bill of inalienable rights that prescribed such fundamental liberties as the freedoms of press, speech, and assembly. After a long, hard military struggle against the conservatives, the liberals emerged victorious in 1861 and elected Juárez to the presidency.

Not long after the liberals attained power, however, French armies invaded Mexico. Emperor Napoleon III had committed himself to extending his empire throughout the world. Not only did he desire to expand his imperial territory, he also wanted Mexico to repay its debts and he wished to reassert the Church's influence over its people. The Mexican army repelled the Napoleon's invasion on May 5, 1862 in a battle now commemorated in Mexico as the holiday Cinco de Mayo. The brilliant maneuvering of the young Oaxacan brigadier general Porfirio Díaz was primarily responsible for this victory. Nevertheless, the French returned to conquer Mexico and installed the Austrian archduke, Ferdinand Maximillian of Hapsburg, as emperor. Although Maximillian was not a particularly tyrannical ruler, liberals resented the foreign domination. In reaction, Juárez and his supporters led a revolt against Maximillian and ultimately regained control of Mexico in 1867.

As before, Juárez was elected to rule over the process of reform, and implemented changes to improve the lives of the Mexican people. As one who had risen to prominence through his learning, Juárez placed the utmost emphasis on improving education. To dispute the Catholic Church's monopoly of the schools, Juárez commissioned Gabino Barreda to design a curriculum inspired by the positivist philosophy of Auguste Comte. This would replace belief in God with an emphasis on science. Even more important for Juárez, the law made primary education free and compulsory for all Mexican children. It also mandated the building of schools throughout the country.

Along with positivism, anarchist philosophy began to influence Mexican social movements during this period. One of the leaders of the Reform, Melchor Ocampo, became enthralled by the thought of the French anarchist Pierre Joseph Proudhon while he was traveling in Europe in the 1840s. He translated many of Proudhon's works into Spanish and published them in Mexico City. Although Ocampo's desire to divide large plantations into small peasant proprietorships was probably influenced by Proudhon, he did not seriously question the fundamental basis of government as a true anarchist would. Nevertheless, through the efforts of various educators and activists, anarchism became the leading ideology of Mexican radicals for many years.

Like Ocampo, the Greek-born scholar Plotino Rhodakanaty was also deeply affected by the writings of Proudhon. While studying medicine in Berlin in 1850, he traveled to Paris to meet the great anarchist thinker. In 1861, Rhodakanaty moved to Mexico City intending to set up a utopian socialist system of agrarian communes. In 1863, he formed a small study group to discuss libertarian socialist thought with students such as Francisco Zalacosta and Santiago Villanueva. These disciples helped deliver anarchist ideas to both agrarian peasants and industrial proletarians, inspiring movements in villages and cities.

Rhodakanaty and Zalacosta founded and directed a school in Chalco, a town near Mexico City. There, they inspired a young student, Julio Chávez López. In response to this libertarian teaching, Chávez López led a series of agrarian insurgencies in 1868-9, raiding various plantations and redistributing the land to the local peasantry.

Although peasant uprisings had occurred throughout Mexico ever since the Spanish conquest, Chávez López's movement was the first that consciously articulated an ideology. Ever loyal to his anarchist ideals, he issued a manifesto on April 20, 1869 that specifically indicted the exploitation of landowners, the indoctrination of the church, and the repression of the government for causing the misery of the peasants. Chávez López's movement grew to over 1500 partisans, and inspired uprisings in various Mexican states. However, after he was captured in his hideout, he was executed by federal troops on September 1, 1869.

He cried out "Long live socialism" as the firing squad discharged its fatal bullets. Even though the peasant movement lost a great leader with Chávez López's death, uprisings continued throughout Mexico. The ideology he propounded and the movements he started ultimately influenced Emiliano Zapata's agrarian program of expropriating haciendas (plantations) during the Mexican Revolution of 1910–19.[2]

While Francisco Zalacosta spread anarchist ideals among the rural population of Mexico, Santiago Villanueva and other activists organized industrial workers along anarchist-collectivist lines and spread their radicalism through a variety of labor organizations and newspapers. In 1865, Villanueva helped organize textile workers in Mexico City and Tlalnepantla who fought the first labor struggles in Mexican history. Although these protests were brutally repressed, Villanueva helped to organize another textile strike three years later in nearby Tlalpan that won better working conditions and shorter hours for female laborers.[3] As with the agrarian spokesmen, Villanueva and other radical labor activists passionately advocated anarchist-collectivism, repudiating the malign impact of capitalism and government. These union movements, like the peasant movements, greatly affected the Mexican Revolution, influencing the formation of the Casa del Obrero Mundial, an explicitly anarcho-syndicalist labor federation, in 1912.

THE DICTATORSHIP OF PORFIRIO DÍAZ

Although Juárez did much to liberalize Mexico and to improve the lives of its campesinos, his repeated reelections provoked opposition from Porfirio Díaz, the military officer who had repulsed the French Invasion on Cinco de Mayo and who ran unsuccessfully against Juárez the second time Juárez was reelected in 1867. After serving his third presidential term, Juárez decided to run for a fourth in 1871. Two candidates opposed him: Sebastián Lerdo de Tejada, the brother of the man who had authored the Ley Lerdo, and Porfirio Díaz. The election did not produce a clear majority for any of the candidates. Following the Mexican constitution, the Congress cast ballots to appoint their new leaders, electing Juárez as president of the nation and Lerdo as the president of the Supreme Court. In reaction, an embittered Díaz issued his Plan de Noría, which lashed out at the principle of reelection and specifically against the ascent of Juárez to a fourth term. Following his military instincts, Díaz subsequently led a coup against the government that federal troops quickly crushed.

Undeterred, Díaz continued to plot. On July 18, 1872, Juárez died of a heart attack, and Lerdo succeeded him to the presidency. When Lerdo ran for re-election in the presidential campaign of 1876, Díaz issued his Plan de Tuxtepec, criticizing Lerdo for a variety of alleged misdeeds, and again promoting the principles of "no reelection" and "free suffrage." As before, Díaz led a military coup against the government. By this time, he had amassed enough ammunition and manpower to defeat the federal forces of President Lerdo, who had alienated many of Juárez's supporters. Díaz's victory established him as the military dictator of Mexico—a position he would hold for the next thirty-five years, but for one hiatus. As he had rallied forces under a banner of "no reelection," Díaz stepped aside in 1880 to allow his lackey, Manuel González, to rule for four years. After González changed the constitution to allow for reelection, Díaz maintained his iron grip over Mexico until the Revolution of 1910.

The notoriously corrupt Díaz tyranny combined the brutality of military barbarism with the exploitation of capitalism, bringing tremendous suffering to the Mexican people. Díaz ruled by the principle of *pan o palo*, the bread or the stick. Noting that a dog with a bone in his mouth does not bite or steal, Díaz lavished favors upon his political friends and neutralized his political enemies with bribes, kickbacks, land concessions, and sweetheart contracts. He was particularly concerned with subduing the ambitions of military officers who could mount a coup against him, as he had against Juárez. Powerful army figures received large land grants and tended to dominate government posts. Those who were not placated by these gifts were routinely assassinated.

Many of the gifts the dictator doled out to friends and potential rivals were political appointments. Under his autocratic rule, Díaz created a feudal system of governors, *jefes políticos* (district political bosses), and mayors. He manipulated elections, circulating lists to his underlings of future appointments. These officials made sure Díaz's candidates won political offices. A few times, the tyrant made the mistake of including on these lists names of candidates who had died. Other times, he made sure that particular opposition candidates joined the deceased before an election could take place.

Díaz's primary concern in establishing this hierarchy was to ensure that none of his political rivals could grow powerful enough to challenge him. He skillfully manipulated officials against each other, so that they would be too busy with their internal statewide or interstate struggles to confront his federal authority. As the dictator only attended to threats to his own national position, he cared little about how his subordinates lorded over their local domains. Many oppressed and exploited their subjects with regimes far more murderous and thieving than even that of Díaz. Governors and political bosses routinely used their power to enrich themselves, seizing natural resources and selling them off to foreign investors. For example, Enrique Creel, the governor of Chihuahua, personally owned almost two million acres of land, and directed the most influential bank in the state. His clan, the Terrazas-Creel family, owed 70 million acres and controlled many industries, including mines, steel and iron mills, sugar refineries, breweries, granaries, meat packing plants, telephone companies, and railroads.

In this feudal dictatorship, all shreds of political justice were sacrificed to preserve the authoritarian order. The people of Mexico were subjected to the whims of the landowners, industrial bosses, and government officials. The local overlords had unrestrained license to murder male subjects and to rape the females.[4] Just as Díaz controlled the elections of local leaders and legislative representatives, he and his underlings directly appointed most of the judges throughout Mexico. To promote the economic and political interests of the regime, they routinely rendered verdicts that protected the interests of foreigners and wealthy, prominent Mexicans. Peasants and proletarians rarely found justice in the courts.

The verdicts of the courts and the mandates of the rich and powerful were enforced by the police, the army, and the *rurales* that terrorized the disenfranchised. The *rurales* were bandits recruited by Díaz to control the rural population; as police officers, they had free reign to subject villagers to their depredations. The ranks of the Mexican army consisted mostly of humble people who were forcibly conscripted into its ranks. However, the government professionalized the military and spent one-quarter of its budget to maintain it, spending every resource to train the soldiers or to intimidate them into following the dictator's ruthless orders.

The Díaz regime routinely ignored the most basic human and political rights. The Ley Fuga (Fugitive Law) allowed police to execute citizens freely with the excuse that their victims were trying to flee from prosecution. Opponents of the dictator and those who challenged the whims of their local overlords were frequently assassinated. Uprisings, protests, and strikes were drowned in blood. Officials rarely enforced and regularly violated the mandates of the 1857 Constitution. The Catholic Church had free reign in the country, reappropriating its property and extorting money from the peasants. Additionally, the government routinely silenced voices of dissent by suppressing opposition newspapers. Díaz's lackey Manuel González reversed the constitutional order that had guaranteed journalists and newspapers the right to a jury trial, forcing them to accept the decisions of judges appointed by the dictator. As a result, Filomena Mata, the publisher of the opposition journal *El Diario del Hogar*, received prison sentences 34 separate times for criticizing the government.

The dictatorship subjected the indigenous masses to the same spiritual degradation that they had suffered under the Spanish. Although Díaz came from a humble, mostly native family, he was determined to fit into the European high society that had dominated the nation since its conquest by Cortés. Indeed, when one compares pictures of the tyrant over the course of his rule, it appears that his skin and his hair get lighter, and his features more continental. His wife Carmen Rubio not only taught him the social graces that would endear this primitive warrior chieftain to aristocratic society, but also encouraged him to embrace the Catholic Church. Under her influence, Díaz ignored the laws of reform. In return, the church dutifully preached submission to the dictator.

As the regime became a modern bureaucratic-capitalist state, it advanced an ideology that complemented the Catholicism that had promoted feudal hierarchy for so long. Díaz assembled around him a cabinet of advisors who called themselves *científicos*, or scientists. They supplemented the authoritarianism of Church ideology by justifying the oppression of the masses in scientific terms. They explained Mexico's social inequality as a function of Darwin's theory of the survival of the fittest. According to these so-called scientists, the Indian and mixed-blood population of Mexico consisted of a primitive and brutal race of men that required the rule of the more advanced Europeans to guide it. In these terms, this social and racial disparity between white aristocrats and the indigenous masses seemed to be the proper consequence of natural laws.

Emboldened by this racist ideology, Díaz allowed foreign capitalists to freely exploit the native masses. He seized the Indian communal lands, or ejidos, from peoples who had lived on them for centuries, and sold them for a pittance to foreign land speculators and white aristocrats within Mexico. While the seizure of these ejidos began under the 1856 Ley Lerdo, Díaz severely aggravated this situation by eliminating all legal limits on land ownership, resulting in an extraordinary concentration of ownership among a small elite. By 1910, half of the nation's land belonged to fewer than three thousand families. The dictator waged long and bloody wars against native populations that resisted this encroachment, such as the Maya in the Yucatan and the Yaqui in Sonora.

As well as selling off the land of Mexico, Díaz promoted foreign capitalists' seizure of natural resources and industries. He lavished favors upon foreign investors, granting them contracts to build railroads and drainage systems, and giving them control over textile, coffee, tobacco, petroleum, mining, and other industries. Along with local aristocrats, foreign capitalists owned almost everything of value in Mexico. United States capital alone controlled over a billion dollars' worth of Mexico's natural resources. The Arizona rancher, Colonel William Greene, acquired enormous mines in Sonora from the governor's widow for only 47,000 pesos, roughly $25,000. He exploited this national resource to become one of the largest copper magnates in the world.[5]

This combination of brutal military rule and foreign exploitation reduced Mexico's people to the most desperate misery. Their lands stolen from them, half of the rural population was forced to work on enormous haciendas (plantations). Landowners paid them the same salaries as a century before, even though inflation had quadrupled the prices of most basic commodities. These starvation wages were often even further reduced: many peons did not receive payment in actual currency, but rather in script that could only be redeemed at the plantation's *tienda de raya* (company store). In addition, these poor villagers had to pay rent to the landowner, taxes to the government, and exorbitant fees to the church for religious services. This extraordinary impoverishment, combined with the lack of decent shelter, clean water, and adequate health care, produced a high mortality rate among peasants. However, even death did not permit release from this system of exploitation. Landowners forced peasants to work long hours on fields and farms by keeping them in perpetual debt. When they died, this debt was passed on to their descendants, enslaving a new generation to the plantation.[6] Although the industrial laborers did not suffer the same kinds of exploitation as the rural peasantry, they too faced brutal conditions, working long hours for miserable salaries in extremely unsafe factories and mines.

RICARDO FLORES MAGÓN

EARLY DAYS IN MEXICO

Ricardo Flores Magón was born during Porfirio Díaz's first presidential term on Mexican Independence Day, September 16, 1874, in the village of San Antonio Eloxochitlán in the district of Teotitlán del Camino, Oaxaca. He was the second of three brothers, preceded by Jesús three years before, and followed by Enrique three years after. His father Teodoro Flores may have been a full-blooded Oaxacan Indian.[7] Whether he was or not, the villagers respected his position in their community, referring to him as "tata" (elder). He supported his family modestly as a farmer. He had also served for many years in the Mexican Army fighting for his fellow Oaxacan Benito Juárez in the War of Reform. Flores helped Juárez beat back the French invasion under the command of another Oaxacan, Porfirio Díaz. When Díaz rallied patriotic Mexicans to his cry of "No Reelection" in his Plan of Tuxtepec, Flores unfortunately believed in Díaz's sincerity and supported his grab for power.

An idealistic, principled man, Teodoro Flores impressed upon his sons the nobility of Juárez's mission to free the natives of Mexico from the oppression that still reigned under the Díaz dictatorship. He explained to his sons that, in contrast to the brutal competition of Mexico City, the villagers of Oaxaca practiced a form of mutual aid. No rich and no poor existed in their communities: each person produced what she or he could and each took what she or he needed for survival. The villagers did not need judges, jails, or policemen to govern them: "We live with peace, respect, and love towards one another as friends and brothers."[8] During Porfirio Díaz's reign, however, local aristocrats and foreign capitalists were quickly appropriating these effectively anarcho-communist ejidos as their own private property. Ricardo's mother, Margarita Magón, a mixed-blood Mexican whose grandfather had emigrated from Cartagena, Spain, also fiercely supported the legacy of Juárez. Furthermore, she realized that Juárez became capable of improving the lives of himself and the Mexican people by receiving a good education. A strong willed woman, she moved her family to Mexico City so that her three sons could attend the best schools in the country.

Ricardo Flores Magón began his struggle against tyranny while he was still in school. On May 16, 1892, when he was only seventeen years old and in his final year of preparatory education, he and his two brothers participated in mass student demonstrations against the second re-election of Díaz. Police arrested Ricardo and his brother Jesús along with many others. Thanks to subsequent protests denouncing the incarceration of demonstrators, Ricardo was released after a brief detention. However, the authorities sent Jesús to the dark, musty, spider- and rat-infested cells of Belen prison, a frequent destination for opponents of Díaz's regime. Ricardo continued his struggle when, emulating Juárez, he entered the School of Jurisprudence in 1893 to train for a legal career. Here, he embarked on his life's work as a journalist, founding the opposition newspaper *El Demócrata*. In its pages, he criticized the plantation system that the dictator's policies supported so vigorously and that so dramatically impoverished the peasants. The *porfiriato* suppressed the paper after only three months. The government used a legal technicality to close it down, raiding its offices and arresting many of the staff. Flores Magón escaped by jumping out of a window.

After these heady beginnings as a student activist, Flores Magón disappeared from the political scene for several years. He seems to have gone into hiding—or at least to have curbed his dissident activities—for the remainder of the nineteenth century. His father passed away in 1893. Some scholars believe that Flores Magón avoided political activity during the following years so that he could focus on earning money to provide for his mother.[9] Apparently, he spent some of these years working for a liberal lawyer in Pachuca, Hidalgo,[10] and perhaps as a bookkeeper in a Oaxacan town near his birthplace.[11]

REGENERACIÓN AND THE LIBERAL PARTY

Ricardo Flores Magón returned to the political struggle in 1900, writing for the journal with which he would be identified for the rest of his life. On August 7, 1900, he, along with his brother Jesús and Antonio Horcasitas, both recent graduates of law school, founded the newspaper *Regeneración*. Declaring itself to be a *"Periódico Jurídico Independiente"* ("Independent Juridical Journal"), the paper focused on exposing miscarriages of justice, violations of rights guaranteed by the constitution, and corruption in courts under the *porfiriato*. Although its tone was basically reformist rather than revolutionary, criticism of the judiciary ultimately constituted attacks on Díaz and his underlings. They responded with typical repression. Horcasitas resigned from the staff after authorities jailed him for an article he had written.

When Ricardo Flores Magón assumed many of Horcasitas' duties, *Regeneración* became more militant. Beginning with its December 31, 1900 issue, it assumed the motto *"Periódico Independiente de Combate"* ("Independent Journal of Combat"). Now the paper attacked the regime directly, criticizing corruption among specific governors and cabinet members. It also discussed atrocities such as slavery in Sonora and the Yucatan. Although it dared to confront political injustices more stridently, the paper remained ambivalent about revolution. In certain articles, it proclaimed its desire for true democracy, claiming that it is only a dictator, not the masses, who foments a revolution. However, other articles celebrated the legacy of the Jacobins, the most radical leaders of the French revolution, as well as that of Miguel Hidalgo, whose Grito de Dolores initiated Mexico's struggle for independence against the Spanish.

Soon after Regeneración appeared, the wealthy engineer and occasional politician Camilo Arriaga issued a statement calling for the formation of a liberal party. Arriaga was the nephew of one of the framers of the liberal Constitution of 1857 that, among other things, wrested power away from the Catholic Church.

Díaz, under the influence of his devout wife and other conservative aristocratic interests, did not enforce any of these provisions.

Arriaga's call for a liberal party was largely a reaction to a statement made by his local bishop. While returning from a trip to the Vatican, the priest bragged to a Paris newspaper that Díaz allowed the church to carry out its activities unimpeded and that it would soon control Mexico.[12] The infuriated engineer, Arriaga, demanded that Mexico return to Juárez's legacy and enforce the civil rights guarantees and the anti-clerical provisions of its constitution. In response to this call, liberal clubs sprang up throughout the nation. On the anniversary of the constitution, February 5, 1901, the Liberal Party held its first congress to discuss reforms. Army officers patrolled the streets outside the meeting hall. Fifty-six delegates from 50 different clubs attended. Ricardo Flores Magón was invited to represent a liberal student group and also acted as an emissary of his dissident newspaper. At this conference Flores Magón met many of the people who would work with and support him in the future, such as Librado Rivera, Juan Sarabia, and Antonio Díaz Soto y Gama.

The congress began with Diódoro Batalla citing the individualist anarchist Max Stirner: "Tyrants appear great because we come to them on our knees. Let us rise!"[13] Most of the speeches, however, critiqued only the misdeeds of the church, a relatively safe and indirect condemnation of the government. In contrast, Flores Magón gave a fiery speech detailing the evils of the dictator's regime, concluding with "the administration of Porfirio Díaz is a den of thieves." The shocked, timid representatives hissed his speech, yet Flores Magón bravely repeated himself. After the audience received him with more hisses and nervous murmuring, he again repeated, "Yes gentlemen, the administration of Porfirio Díaz is a den of thieves." After this third declaration, that many delegates knew in their hearts to be true, the buzzing transformed into a round of applause.[14]

Soon after the conference, *Regeneración* became an important outlet for the Liberal Party, publishing its manifestoes and spreading its message through its pages. It glorified Juárez and the constitution. It promoted classical liberal values such as freedom of the press, detailing Díaz's frequent attacks on dissident voices. *Regeneración* demanded that neither should Díaz run for re-election nor should he manipulate one of his underlings into his office as he had in 1880 with Manuel González. Instead, it declared, a Liberal should be elected as the next president. Along with these political statements, *Regeneración* continued to condemn various administrators, judges, and representatives in the government. It also drew attention to social and economic issues, criticizing exploitation by

U.S. capitalists, detailing the abuses of plantation owners, and supporting a strike among carriage drivers.

The paper's outspoken stances soon earned it official retribution. On May 23, 1901, Ricardo and Jesús Flores Magón were arrested for an article discussing kickbacks in a road construction project. This piece allegedly defamed the character of a Oaxacan political boss. While the two brothers languished in Belen prison for over eleven months, their youngest brother Enrique assumed the responsibility of publishing *Regeneración*. From jail, Jesús and Ricardo continued to write stories for the paper, including one criticizing their own imprisonment. The authorities finally shut down the press on October 7. During their imprisonment, the beloved mother of the two dissidents, Margarita Magón, passed away. Reportedly, *científico* government officials offered to grant her sons freedom if she would convince them to give up their struggle. As strong willed as ever, she replied that she would rather die alone than make her sons back down.[15] Years later, Ricardo Flores Magón wrote of his profound regret that "I could not be at her bedside: I could not give her a last kiss nor could I hear her last words."[16]

Throughout Mexico, Díaz attacked the growing opposition. Federal and state police swept through liberal clubs in every part of the nation, closing them down and imprisoning their leadership. Antonio Díaz Soto y Gama was arrested for a fiery speech opposing the dictator that he delivered in commemoration of Benito Juárez.[17] Similarly, Díaz suppressed various dissident journals, including Filomena Mata's *El Diario del Hogar*, whose press had printed *Regeneración's* allegedly libelous article. Yet the liberals continued to organize clubs and publish newspapers. In November 1901, Camilo Arriaga issued a call for a second party congress on the next anniversary of the constitution, February 5, 1902. However, on January 24 soldiers invaded a planning meeting for the convention, arresting important leaders such as Arriaga, Juan Sarabia, and Librado Rivera.[18]

EL HIJO DEL AHUIZOTE

When Ricardo and Jesús Flores Magón emerged from Belen on April 30, 1902, they took diverging paths. An exhausted Jesús left the movement, retiring to pursue his legal career; he set up a law office and married Clara Hong, his fiancée of 11 years. In his stead, the youngest Flores Magón brother, Enrique, joined Ricardo to continue the fight against the dictatorship. Together, the two brothers took over *El Hijo del Ahuizote*, a paper best known for artist Jesús Martínez Carrión's brilliant caricatures that ridiculed government officials. They soon landed in trouble again. After publishing a critical article about General Bernardo Reyes, sometimes governor of Nuevo Leon, Díaz's Minister of War, and his possible successor to the presidency, Ricardo and Enrique were arrested on the orders of a military judge. The paper was closed down. Even though Ricardo testified that the elderly editor of *El Hijo del Ahuizote*, Daniel Cabrera, had no control over the journal anymore, Cabrera was also taken in. Enrique and Ricardo languished in prisons, first military and then civil, until the end of January 1903.

Despite this repression, the liberals were by no means defeated. As various leaders emerged from jail, they recommenced the publication of opposition newspapers and the formation of liberal clubs. Juan Sarabia and Antonio Díaz Soto y Gama, then Camilo Arriaga, then the Flores Magón brothers revived *El Hijo del Ahuizote* several times as it was repressed again and again by the government. On the anniversary of the constitution, February 5, 1903, the editors draped a banner from the balcony of the newspaper's office boldly pronouncing "LA CONSTITUCION HA MUERTO" ("THE CONSTITUTION HAS DIED").[19] As Ricardo Flores Magón explained in the next issue of the paper, the tyrant Díaz had prostituted the cause of justice and had subjected the Mexican people to the domination of the church, murdering the great liberal document of 1857. On April 2, a holiday commemorating one of Díaz's victories against the French, Ricardo and Enrique, along with the liberal Club Redención, marched to the dictator's palace carrying signs proclaiming "No reelection." Only the crowds around them saved them from execution. Soon after this demonstration, *El Hijo del Ahuizote* also publicized General Bernardo Reyes' bloody suppression of a rally in support of his challenger for Nuevo León governor.

In the wake of all this, the dictatorship took drastic measures to silence the persistent dissident voices of Ricardo Flores Magón and the Liberal Party. On April 16, police invaded the offices of *El Hijo del Ahuizote* and arrested the staff, including the Flores Magón brothers, Juan Sarabia, and Librado Rivera. Courts accused them of criticizing officials for fulfilling their duties. They were again sent to Belen, this time for a month and a half. The final blow, however, came shortly after they were released from prison. On June 9, Mexico City courts decreed—and the Supreme Court later ratified the decision—that it would be illegal for any periodical to carry anything written by either Flores Magón brother.

EXILE IN THE USA

TEXAS

Even though the Mexican Supreme Court forbade the Flores Magóns from writing articles of dissent, the brothers refused to halt their revolutionary mission. Unable to pursue their vocation in their native country, Ricardo, along with his brother Enrique, fled to the United States, never to return to Mexico during his lifetime. They arrived virtually penniless in Laredo, Texas in January 1904. The brothers' trip to Laredo was funded by Camilo Arriaga who had fled to El Paso, Texas along with Antonio Díaz Soto y Gama shortly before the final raid of *El Hijo del Ahuizote*. Other liberals fleeing from the dictatorship, such as Juan Sarabia and his cousin Manuel, soon joined them. Ricardo Flores Magón hoped to set up dissident newspapers in New York City and along the Mexico-U.S. border to foment the inevitable revolution. Although he never made it to the East Coast, he was able to set up an impressive network of revolutionary cells that in the coming years incited several unsuccessful uprisings against Díaz.

As soon as they arrived in Texas, the Flores Magóns immediately began organizing to resume publication of Regeneración. They took jobs as farm laborers and dishwashers,[20] surviving off the vegetables they could bring back from harvests. Ever a vigorous writer, Ricardo sent letters to liberals throughout Mexico asking for money and requesting that readers solicit friends to contribute and provide leads to other potential supporters. Liberals in Mexico, such as Ricardo's brother, the lawyer Jesús Flores Magón, helped raise money. *El Colmillo Público* ("The Public Eyetooth"), the Mexico City liberal newspaper that cartoonist Jesús Martinez Carrion founded after the suppression of *El Hijo del Ahuizote*, advertised their efforts in its pages. Wealthy liberals such as Arriaga and Francisco I. Madero, the wealthy landowner who would ultimately topple the *porfiriato*, also contributed substantial funds. After some initial setbacks, the liberals finally moved to San Antonio and bought a press.

Regeneración resumed publication on November 5, 1904. In its first issue, it introduced itself with a long history of the persecution of the press and the Liberal Party in Mexico. The editors explained their reasons for moving to the United States, vowing to struggle for political change in Mexico. The paper resumed its criticism of Porfirio Díaz and his vice president Ramon Corral. It also broadly criticized the social and economic injustices of the nation, citing exploitation by foreign capital, debt slavery on plantations, and oppression of poor workers in the cities.

SAINT LOUIS, MISSOURI

Even though they had exiled themselves to the United States, the Flores Magóns' efforts soon attracted the repression of the Mexican government. The local consulate maintained its surveillance upon them. In December 1904, a Mexican agent entered their residence and attempted to stab Ricardo in the back. Luckily, Enrique was standing nearby and wrestled the attacker to the ground. The police, however were conveniently stationed outside. They arrested and fined Enrique for disturbing the peace, allowing the assailant to go free. Worried by this attack, the brothers decided to move farther from the border.

Through Camilo Arriaga, they contacted Francisco I. Madero, who contributed $2000 for the liberals' trip to the heart of the United States: Saint Louis, Missouri. Juan Sarabia and Ricardo Flores Magón arrived on February 2, 1905, and others followed soon after. *Regeneración* was published again from Saint Louis beginning on February 27, eventually acquiring 30,000 subscribers. As before, the paper was widely distributed in border towns in Texas, Arizona, New Mexico, and California. It was smuggled into Mexico through a variety of means, such as by sending copies within hollowed-out Sears catalogues. Railroad workers and other volunteers aided in this effort. The publishers solicited additional subscribers through lists of names submitted by current readers. Publication agents and newsstands distributed the paper in their local communities. As before, *Regeneración* attacked prominent people in the Diaz administration such as General Bernardo Reyes and the *científico* financial minister José Ives Limantour. Aware of its new situation in a new country, the paper also encouraged people to send in reports about exploitation by local officials, judges, and Masonic lodges.

In Saint Louis, Ricardo contacted the local anarchist and socialist community, mostly composed of refugees from Russia and Germany. Here, he may have first met the most prominent anarchist of the age, Emma Goldman, a dissident who had fled from czarist Russia.[21] Even if this encounter did occur, it may not have had much impact, because Ricardo was not yet fluent in English, and Goldman didn't speak Spanish. Ricardo's close friendship with the Spanish anarchist Florencio Bazora, one of the founders of the IWW and a comrade of the Italian anarchist Errico Malatesta, was probably the most important political relationship he developed.

Although the influence of the Saint Louis anarchists upon Ricardo Flores Magón's political opinions is uncertain, scholars believe that they might have reinforced ideas that were already fermenting in Flores Magón's mind. However, when he first adopted the radical anarchist ideals that superseded his reformist liberal views remains an open question.[22] Many scholars believe that Flores Magón embraced anarchism as early as 1901, if not even earlier. Indeed, fellow activist Antonio Díaz Soto y Gama later proclaimed that, at that time, "We were all completely anarchists."[23] The Liberal leader Camilo Arriaga owned a huge library of political thought, and it seems that, by 1901, Ricardo had used this resource to become familiar with the writings of Maxim Gorky, Peter Kropotkin, Errico Malatesta, Karl Marx, Mikhail Bakunin, and Max Stirner. Flores Magón also encouraged the opposition Mexico City newspaper *Vesper* in 1902 to serialize Kropotkin's anarchist classic, *The Conquest of Bread*.

Flores Magón's 1905 encounters with Bazora and other anarchists in Saint Louis undoubtedly influenced his thinking, but scholars do not possess much documentation about these discussions. Even though Flores Magón had not yet proclaimed any political philosophy, the Mexican dictator Porfirio Díaz began referring to him as a "dangerous anarchist" in 1906. Ricardo Flores Magón's first recorded mention of anarchism was in a secretive 1908 letter to his brother Enrique and his comrade Práxedis Guerrero. However, he warned them to avoid using the term explicitly to avoid alienating potential supporters, because many people wrongly associated anarchism with random violence. Although Flores Magón's writings during the following years clearly invoked anarchist concepts, he never used the word "anarchism" in any published document until after his 1914 release from prison. Because he was so reluctant to espouse publicly his commitment to anarchism, scholars can not be entirely sure of when he finally embraced the philosophy. Nevertheless, they agree that his writings and political analyses were always far more class conscious than those of most of the other liberal leaders. At all stages of the movement, Ricardo was its most radical spokesman, emphasizing the need for social and economic changes as well as political reforms.

Flores Magón's passion for revolutionary social and economic justice frightened away moderate and wealthy liberal factions who generally wanted only political reform. Throughout the history of the liberal movement, his radical views often alienated former allies. Ricardo's brother Jesús sent him letters warning him that he did not approve of Ricardo's revolutionary tone. And as soon as Ricardo Flores Magón arrived in the United States to join the wealthy, influential founder of the Liberal Party, Camilo Arriaga, the two began to have disagreements about the group's philosophy and tactics. Over time, their disagreements became more pronounced. Francisco I. Madero, a friend of Arriaga who had praised Flores Magón for "inflaming Mexicans to righteous indignation against the tyrant,"[24] sent him $700 to forward to Arriaga for promoting the cause of the Liberal Party. Rather than doing so, Flores Magón sent a letter to Madero denouncing Arriaga as a "false liberal." In turn, Arriaga wrote Madero telling him that the Saint Louis group was defrauding contributors.[25] As a result of these philosophical and personal disagreements, Arriaga, along with several other moderates, moved back to Mexico.

THE ORGANIZING JUNTA OF THE MEXICAN LIBERAL PARTY

To distinguish themselves from the moderate wing of the Liberal Party, Ricardo Flores Magón, along with Juan Sarabia, Antonio I. Villarreal, Enrique Flores Magón, Librado Rivera, Manuel Sarabia, and Rosalío Bustamante, formed the Junta Organizadora del Partido Liberal Mexicano (Organizing Junta of the Mexican Liberal Party), or PLM, on September 28, 1905. In their declaration of purpose, they explained that, even though they were now living in a foreign country, they would fight for Mexico using all available means against the dictatorship of Porfirio Díaz. They explained that *Regeneración* would be the official organ of the Junta, but also urged others to publish opposition newspapers to foment revolution. They called for the formation of secret groups to meet periodically and to maintain communication with the Junta. These cells would send political notices, revolutionary plans, funds, and membership lists to Saint Louis. The Junta also asked members to show solidarity among their ranks by supporting poor, imprisoned, and otherwise oppressed members of the movement.

Newspapers spread the ideas of the Junta. When *Regeneración* was delivered to a plantation or an industrial center, peasants and proletarians would gather eagerly and the few literate members of the community would read to the rest. Long discussions followed these readings, and news of the insurgent movement soon spread. The Junta also made strong connections with other dissident papers on both sides of the border. Texas and Arizona papers printed their incendiary propaganda alongside stories about local struggles. In Mexico City, *El Colmillo Público* published the Junta leaders' invitation to join the new movement.

In response to this call, an impressive network of between 40 and 70 revolutionary cells sprouted up all over Mexico and the southwestern United States. In both countries, people were eager to overthrow the tyrant. Some Mexicans were so inspired that they even left their homes to join the Junta leaders in the United States. Some clubs had hundreds of members; some only a few. Local groups sent in their membership applications, pledged their dues, submitted the names of their officers, announced the mottoes of their clubs, and gave the Junta leads to other interested liberals.

Groups wrote to the Saint Louis Junta from every state in the Mexican republic. In the mining town of Santa Barbara, Chihuahua, liberals formed a union and held rallies calling for revolution and criticizing their exploitation by mine owners. The peasants in Zacatecas sent in 25-cent contributions, a substantial amount for these severely impoverished people.[26] In Hidalgo, Prisciliano Silva led a well organized group with 75 men ready to revolt.

Far away from the border, the Veracruz cells were very powerful. Underground organizations formed throughout the state, small newspapers were founded, and public demonstrations were held. The Puerto México PLM cell had grown so vocal that police arrested its leader, Cipriano Medina, for speaking out against Díaz.[27] The state of Veracruz remained one of the major centers of PLM activity throughout the following years.

The PLM also spread throughout the United States along the Mexican border, where a ready audience of immigrant and U.S.-born Mexicans hoped to overthrow Díaz. Along the Texas border, Mexican-American farm laborers and new workers from Mexico resented having to work on ranches owned by Americans who had stolen the land from them. The PLM made affiliations with activist institutions already within San Antonio, such as the newspaper *La Humanidad*, which criticized the oppression of farm workers. El Paso had a large club of over 200 people that published three newspapers. In Del Rio, the newspapers *El Mensajero* ("The Messenger") and *1810*, founded by the longtime agitator Cresencio Villarreal Márquez, decried injustice along the border, criticized corrupt Mexican and U.S. officials, and spread the liberal message in their pages.

In contrast to the primarily agricultural membership of the Texas groups, clubs in Arizona and New Mexico were composed mostly of mine workers. Mining companies operated freely in Arizona and New Mexico and in the northern Mexican states of Chihuahua and Sonora, treating the border as a legal formality. Labor also moved back and forth, with mine owners forcing workers to endure long hours and to suffer terrible working conditions. Collapses occurred frequently, crushing hapless miners, and ventilation was rudimentary. In response, several union groups, such as the radical Western Federation of Miners, attempted to organize the laborers.

Douglas, Arizona was perhaps the most powerful liberal center. Its clubs contained at least 300 members, and it distributed *Regeneración* along with local opposition papers such as *El Demócrata*. As with other groups, the Douglas clubs formulated plans for smuggling weapons across the border and for attacking the Mexican government.

As the Junta had requested, most of the clubs in Mexico and United States operated as secretive organizations. Despite this secrecy, they were often infiltrated and betrayed by spies, and they consistently had to eject members. The liberal clubs often operated through front groups such as social centers, union halls, and even Masonic lodges. In certain cases, after meetings of the general group, select people would be invited to the secret meeting of the liberal organization. In one instance, the liberals even posed as a Mexican-American political club, and local politicians actually contributed money to win their votes.[28] At meetings of the PLM clubs, members agreed to the resolutions of September 28, 1905, pledging allegiance to the Organizing Junta of the Mexican Liberal Party and its objectives. They elected officers, decided upon a motto, and maintained regular correspondence with the leaders in Saint Louis. The groups developed their own local initiatives, while also developing plans for the revolution, acquiring arms and ammunition, and identifying targets to attack.

Coordinating this network of revolutionary cells was a major challenge. Some scholars have claimed that the lack of centralization and standard procedures led to the downfall of the PLM.[29] Whether or not this is so, reliable correspondence was essential to the development of the party. Liberal groups sent their revolutionary plans and all other information to Saint Louis, and the Junta leaders responded with advice and instructions. Both the Mexican and the U.S. governments intercepted much of this correspondence, which certainly impaired the revolutionaries' efforts.

Many of the most important members of the liberal movement, such as Práxedis Guerrero, Antonio de P. Araujo, and the Mayo Indian Fernando Palomarez,[30] functioned as Special Delegates, coordinating the activities of various branches of the party. They spread the message of the Saint Louis Junta far and wide, recruiting new members and carrying correspondence between groups. They moved back and forth along the border, helping to smuggle arms and maintaining a watchful eye on military buildups. Such an important job was also an extremely dangerous one. With police, soldiers, detectives, and spies stationed on both sides of the border, Special Delegates ran a very real risk of being arrested and extradited to Mexico, where they would face imprisonment or execution.

CHASED FROM THE HEARTLAND

Not long after the Junta issued its call for the formation of liberal clubs, it encountered repression once again, this time in Saint Louis. The Mexican government had been trying to stop the circulation of *Regeneración*. It had instructed the postal service to intercept all communications with the Junta and to forward them to a Mexico City post office. Postal authorities then sent copies of these intercepted letters to the government. Mexican officials also hired Pinkerton spies and Thomas Furlong from the Furlong Detective Agency to monitor the Junta in Saint Louis. It even employed a spy, Ansel T. Adams, to wrangle a position inside *Regeneración* as its advertising manager. U.S. officials, particularly postal authorities, aided the Mexican government by confiscating donations to the group and intercepting correspondence. They also withdrew *Regeneración's* fourth-class mailing permit. The Saint Louis postmaster even invited a private detective to his meeting with Flores Magón so the agent could identify the liberal leader in an upcoming trial.[31]

On October 12, 1905, Ricardo and Enrique Flores Magón, along with Juan Sarabia, were arrested in their office by three Saint Louis detectives and two private detectives hired by the Mexican government. The authorities closed down the office of *Regeneración* and sold its property. Manuel Esperón de la Flor, the district political boss of Pochutla, Oaxaca, traveled to Missouri to charge the three with criminal libel for a defamatory article. This scathing indictment in *Regeneración* had detailed the brutality of Esperón de la Flor's rule. It further alleged that the governor of Oaxaca had given him his office as repayment for his wife's sexual favors.

News of the arrest spread quickly, engendering protest in both the United States and Mexico. In Mexico City, *El Colmillo Público* encouraged letters and donations to support the Junta, raising 600 pesos, about $300, in one month. In Saint Louis, anarchists, socialists, and liberals, especially among the German and Russian populations, spoke out against the arrests. Local newspapers, such as the *Saint Louis Post Dispatch* and the *Saint Louis Globe Democrat*, condemned the trial. One individual even took out a full-page ad in the Sunday magazine section of the *Post Dispatch* to decry the injustice.[32]

The Flores Magón brothers and Juan Sarabia were finally released on bond in January 1906. However, legal proceedings had cost over $4000, completely draining their resources. Fearing that they would be extradited to Mexico and executed, and knowing that spies were following them, most of the Junta leaders fled to Toronto. In Canada, they changed their names, posed as Italians, and worked for construction companies. However, they were unable to evade the spies of the Mexican government, who soon began interrogating their neighbors and co-workers. After a female Pinkerton agent seduced Manuel Sarabia into divulging the Junta's secret hiding place, they fled to Montreal. Even there, agents pursued them, so they eventually returned to the United States.

1906 PROGRAM AND MANIFESTO

In April 1906, while they were in Canada, the Mexican exiles formulated the Program and Manifesto of the Organizing Junta of the Mexican Liberal Party. As many scholars have pointed out, this was perhaps the most important, most comprehensive, and most far-reaching document of the Mexican Revolution. It formed the basis of many other revolutionary documents, yet surpassed them in scope and ingenuity. It inspired the relatively mild reforms of Francisco I. Madero as well as the revolutionary agrarian program of Emiliano Zapata. The framers of today's Mexican Constitution also borrowed heavily from it.[33] Francisco J. Mújica, who began his political career writing for *Regeneración* about injustices in his state of Michoacán,[34] led the group that drafted the constitution in 1917. In particular, he helped to formulate article 123, probably the most radical labor code at that time, which took most of its proposals from the earlier PLM document.

Even though the 1906 Program and Manifesto was one of the most progressive works in Mexican history, Ricardo Flores Magón's own political views soon became even more radical. Despite his realization by 1908 (at the latest) that the revolution should be anarchist rather than reformist, he continued for years to use the 1906 document as the foundation for his struggle.

The drafting of the Program and Manifesto was an intensely collaborative process. Ricardo's brother Jesús had advised him to present the views of the majority. The avid writers of the Junta engaged in a phenomenal amount of correspondence to solicit the ideas of liberal club members and other readers of *Regeneración*. Through letters, as well as in the pages of *Regeneración* and *El Colmillo Público*, people were asked to send their complaints and ideas for reform to Saint Louis. Because most of the Junta leaders had already fled this city, one of the few members remaining in Saint Louis, Librado Rivera, would then forward letters to the Junta leaders doubly exiled to Canada. Throughout the United States, Canada, and Mexico, in letters and the pages of newspapers, as well in the Mexican prisons of Belen and San Juan de Ulúa, dissidents discussed the possibilities and submitted them to the liberal leaders. These suggestions seem to have been compiled mostly by Juan Sarabia and Antonio I. Villarreal as the text of the Program. Ricardo Flores Magón wrote the introductory Exposition and the concluding Manifesto.

Once the 1906 Program and Manifesto was completed, papers such as *Regeneración* and *El Colmillo Público* publicized it and they, along with the Junta, requested money for its publication. At least 15,000 copies were sent to and circulated among liberal clubs in Mexico and the United States. Special Delegates also helped transmit it. Práxedis Guerrero brought it to the mineworkers in the southwestern U.S. And across the border to mineworkers in Chihuahua and Sonora; Antonio I. Villarreal brought it to Texas and Mexico; Manuel Sarabia to Arizona; Ricardo Flores Magón to El Paso, Texas.

Declaring its motto to be *"Reforma, Libertad, y Justicia,"* the Program and Manifesto laid out a detailed plan that the party would instate once it had overthrown the dictator. The Exposition explained that, "Any political party that struggles to attain real influence in its country's public realm is obligated to declare before the people, in a clear and precise form, what ideals it struggles for and what program it proposes to put into practice if it is favored by victory. In consequence, the Partido Liberal declares that its aspirations are those that are recorded in this present program, whose realization is strictly obligatory for the government that will be established after the fall of the dictatorship, also being the strict obligation of the members of the *Partido Liberal* to watch over the fulfillment of this program."[35]

The Partido Liberal would curb the powers of the executive branch, limiting the president to a four-year term with no possibility of re-election. It would require that all officials be honest and fair. The plan would curtail the injustice of the military: compulsory service would no longer be required of citizens; military tribunals would be abolished. To bring justice back to Mexico, the PLM would reform the courts. Agricultural penal colonies would replace prisons, and the death penalty would be eliminated. The 1906 Program also promoted human rights. It stipulated that women would be considered equal to men in all regards. It would enforce the 1857 Laws of Reform, especially Juárez's prescription of free and universal secular education for all children. The PLM would also ensure liberty of speech and of the press.

Whereas the 1857 Constitution had only dared to institute political reforms, the 1906 Program proposed radical changes to better the working conditions of the urban proletariat and the rural peasant. It proposed to limit the working day to eight hours, observe Sunday as a day of rest, and ensure each worker a minimum wage with pension benefits. The Program promoted unions, forbade child labor, and required decent working conditions. Along with these industrial reforms, the Program would also restore lands illegally confiscated from native tribes and other peasant communities. Lands appropriated from these seizures would be distributed among peasants. Loans from an agricultural bank would help them procure the lands. In addition to confiscating illegally obtained property and unused land, the PLM program also proposed making Mexican citizenship a mandatory condition of property ownership.

This far-reaching, farseeing document concluded with a manifesto authored by Ricardo Flores Magón. Echoing the biblical prophets, the manifesto began by alerting Mexicans to the horror of their country's enslavement. It beckoned them to redeem their country through rebellion against the tyrant. Flores Magón stated, "I have here the program, the banner of the Partido Liberal, under which all of you should unite who have not renounced being free men, all of you who are smothering in this ignominious atmosphere which has enveloped you for thirty years, all of you who are ashamed of the enslavement of the country (which is your own slavery), all of you who hold against your tyrants the rebellion—blessed rebellion—of those restless under the yoke, because that feeling of rebellion is the signal that dignity and patriotism have not died in the heart that shelters them."[36]

The manifesto concluded by calling upon Mexicans to assert their human dignity, urging them to choose between the humiliating, miserable shackles of the dictatorship and the liberating vision of the PLM. "Between that which despotism offers you and that which the program of the Partido Liberal offers you, choose! If you want shackles, misery, humiliation before foreigners, the gray life of the debased outcast, supporting the dictatorship gives you all of this; if you prefer liberty, economic improvement, the raising up of the Mexican citizenry, the noble life of the man who is master of himself, come to the Partido Liberal that fraternizes with the noble and the virile, and join your efforts with those of all of us who fight for justice, to hurry the arrival of the radiant day on which tyranny will fall forever and the awaited democracy will surge forth with all the splendor of a star which never ceases shining brilliantly on the clear horizon of our country."[37]

As can be seen from the citations above, the 1906 Program and Manifesto had a deeply nationalistic character. It repeatedly referred to the land of Mexico as a *patria* (literally "fatherland") and mentioned the people inhabiting it as a *raza* ("race"). The Manifesto fed off this nationalistic resentment, "look at our country now, oppressed, miserable, abject, the booty of foreigners, whose insolence has grown gigantic thanks to the cowardice of our tyrants; see how the despots have trampled national dignity, inviting foreign forces to invade our territory."[38] Indeed, liberals had good reasons for resenting foreign influences. As mentioned before, European imperialism had dominated the natives of Mexico from the 1511 Spanish invasion to the 1864 imposition of Austrian archduke Maximilian as Emperor. The PLM particularly objected to Porfirio Díaz's government that permitted, even encouraged, foreigners to seize Mexican natural resources and to exploit Mexican labor.

One might be able to excuse the PLM's nationalism as a natural reaction against imperialism. However, it manifested itself in one particularly ugly way in the 1906 Program and Manifesto: the PLM proposed eliminating Chinese immigration to Mexico. Appealing to economic jingoism, the Manifesto explained, "The prohibition of Chinese immigration is, before all else, a measure to protect the workers of other nationalities, principally the Mexicans. The Chinese, disposed in general to work for the lowest salary, submissive, with meager aspirations, is a great obstacle to the prosperity of other workers. His competition is baneful and must be avoided in Mexico. In general, Chinese immigration does not produce the least benefit for Mexico."[39]

As Flores Magón's politics became more radical and more openly expressed his anarchist beliefs, he largely abandoned this nationalist rhetoric for an internationalist ideology that emphasized the liberation of all mankind. Years later, Magón wrote an essay about the same problem that confronted Mexican liberals in 1906: what should one do when the labor market is flooded by foreign workers whom capitalists can use to lower wages. Rather than advocating economic nationalism, he explained "the cause of the wage-slave against his master has no frontiers; it is not a national problem but a universal conflict; it is the cause of all the disininherited of the world over, of every one who has to work with his hands and his brains to bring his family a loaf of bread."[40] The First World War and the jingoistic rhetoric that propelled it seem especially to have taught him the dangers of nationalism. In a 1917 essay, Flores Magón warned against the patriotism that "puts a bloody blindfold over your eyes when you see a foreigner; this patriotism that teaches you to hate everyone who wasn't born in the land you were born in."[41]

CANANEA

The network of cells organized by the PLM took the Program and Manifesto of July 1, 1906 as its working document. Corresponding with Junta leaders in the U.S. And Canada, local groups crafted plans to foment revolution in Mexico and to install a government that would enact the PLM Program's wide-ranging reforms. Only a few months after its publication, groups throughout Mexico and the southwestern United States rose up against the dictator. In addition, the enthusiastic reception that greeted the Program and Manifesto was in part fostered by an event that occurred a month before its publication. The June 1 strike in Cananea, Sonora, considered by many scholars to be the first major strike in modern Mexican history,[42] inspired people to consider the imminent need to dethrone the dictator.

The PLM found many supporters among the economically and racially oppressed miners in Cananea, Sonora, about 100 miles south-southeast of Tucson, Arizona and 40 miles southeast of the twin cities of Nogales, Arizona and Nogales, Sonora. Along the borders of Arizona and New Mexico in the United States and Sonora and Chihuahua in Mexico, U.S. capitalists freely exploited mostly Mexican and Mexican-American labor. Investors from the United States owned about three-quarters of the mines in Mexico. As mentioned above, one of those exploiting cheap labor, Colonel William C. Greene, owner of the Cananea Consolidated Copper Company, had acquired his mine through Porfirio Díaz's policies favoring foreign capital and via corrupt officials in the state of Sonora.

As in other instances of foreign exploitation, the Mexican mine workers suffered from both economic misery and racism. The workers simply did not make enough money to survive. They had to pay for commodities in dollars, yet were paid in pesos, a much weaker currency. Instead of even earning proper wages, they often received only credit at the company store. Additionally, most had to live in overpriced company housing. As in most Mexican haciendas and many Mexican industrial towns, the company owners kept workers as virtual slaves by maintaining them in perpetual debt. To make matters even worse, Greene decided to slash the wages of Mexican workers, because the worldwide drop in copper prices was threatening the financial stability of his enterprise. Further, the governor of Sonora, Rafael Izábel, encouraged him to lower wages so that fewer agricultural laborers would leave the fields to work in the mines.

In addition to this economic strife, most of the Cananea miners were Mexican, whereas the vast majority of the foremen and managers were from the United States. These supervisory workers worked much shorter hours and were paid in dollars rather than pesos, making two to four times as much as the Mexicans. This combination of economic and racial oppression combined to produce a volatile revolutionary sentiment fueled by financial desperation and patriotic pride.

Cananea was typical of the industrial centers where a receptive audience welcomed the radical vision of the PLM. Three months after the PLM had initially called Mexicans to form revolutionary cells in September 1905, organizers in Cananea created the Unión Liberal Humanidad. This group drafted bylaws that declared its support for the Junta and exchanged correspondence with the exiled leaders. At the same time, it also focused on local issues, awakening workers to labor grievances and attempting to create a miner's union. The club helped develop the 1906 Program and Manifesto by suggesting reforms in labor practices and the restoration of native lands. Members of the cell also maintained newspapers, such as *El Centenario* ("The Centennial"), which criticized mine policies, urged the creation of a union, and reprinted articles from *Regeneración*. On May 5, the holiday celebrating Díaz's 1862 defeat of the French invasion, the Union Liberal Humanidad organized an alternative rally. The principal speaker, socialist lawyer Lázaro Gutiérrez de Lara, exhorted workers to contribute to Mexican history by forming a union and securing their liberty. He further urged them to create a united miners' movement with other Mexican workers in coalition with the PLM.[43] After this rally, Gutiérrez de Lara organized a second group, the Club Liberal de Cananea, in the working class neighborhoods of the town. Members of this cell discussed the plans of the Junta as well as immediate concerns such as wages, hours, discrimination, and working conditions.

There is still a great deal of controversy about precisely how the strike in Cananea started and how much the PLM-affiliated clubs influenced it. They certainly raised the workers' consciousness of their need for a union and propelled them to think and talk about their oppression. However, it is unclear what specific roles various liberals played during the development of the strike. It began on June 1, 1906 when Mexican laborers gathered in front of the Oversight Mine to prevent the 7:00 a.m. shift from going to work. Soon, other mines closed and over 2000 miners gathered on the Mexican side of town chanting "five pesos, eight hours."[44] The mine owner, William C. Greene, decided to forestall any possible confrontation by selecting a representative group to present their demands to him in writing. This group, many of whom were also prominent members of the two liberal clubs, asked, among other things, for better wages and for more

Mexicans to be appointed as foremen and managers. In response, Greene wrote a letter refusing each request.

Greene's delay of the inevitable confrontation between capital and labor only exacerbated the tension. During this period, agitators spread a circular around town filled with inflammatory declarations against the mine owner's oppression and against the dictator who allowed foreign capital to exploit Mexican labor. It is unclear who authored this piece, whether it was a liberal leader, an unaffiliated individual, or even a company provocateur. Eventually, strike agitators fomented a general walkout, inspiring all Mexicans to leave their posts. They began to march toward the side of town where white workers lived, carrying banners and chanting "five pesos, eight hours." The march was peaceful until the manager of the company lumberyard began hosing them down and then commenced shooting at them. In response, the workers clubbed him to death. The manager's brother attempted to save him by firing at workers. The workers killed him as well and set the lumberyard ablaze. After this, the strikers armed themselves and continued to town, dynamiting company property and engaging in rifle battles with white workers. The fighting abated as Mexican army regiments came to town, disarming people and forcing them either to return to work or to enlist in the war against the Yaqui Indians, who had rebelled against the dictator's theft of their lands.

During the confrontation, Greene made a critical misstep that greatly increased patriotic resentment against foreign capitalist exploitation in Mexico. When he saw Mexicans cross over to the white area of Cananea, he and the U.S. consular agent sent alarmed telegraphs to the U.S. Department of State and to Sonora Governor Izábel. Additionally, Greene sent messages to friends and newspapers in Arizona saying that the Mexicans were killing men, women and children. He warned of an imminent race war. Izábel then allowed a group of Arizona volunteers under the command of Ranger Captain Thomas Rynning to enter Sonora. By the time they arrived in Cananea, the situation had already calmed down to a state in which they were no longer needed. Given this somewhat chaotic but not at all critical condition, Governor Izábel asked the foreign fighters to return to the United States. Even though they had not fired a single shot, this violation of Mexican territorial sovereignty reflected poorly on the regime of Porfirio Díaz. Throughout the country, people regarded it as tantamount to a dictator-approved U.S. invasion of Mexican territory to protect U.S. capital from the threat of Mexican labor. For many, the Cananea strike inspired revolutionary awareness by explicitly connecting workers' rights with deep patriotic feeling.

The strike led to harsh repression against liberals in both Cananea and in the United States. Greene and Governor Izábel blamed the local PLM groups for fomenting the uprising; they believed that the strike was intended to be the first stage of an all-out revolution against Díaz. Further, when authorities raided the clubs, they found letters from the Saint Louis Junta urging them to fight for better working and living conditions. Many liberal club members were imprisoned or conscripted into the army as retribution. However, both the liberals in Cananea and the leaders of the Junta denied responsibility for the strike. Antonio I. Villarreal told a Los Angeles newspaper that the Junta was striving for a revolution, but Cananea was merely a labor dispute.[45] Nevertheless, Díaz informed the U.S. Ambassador to Mexico, David Thompson, that events in Cananea were part of a revolutionary effort to overthrow the government. A reporter stationed in Washington, DC for the Mexican paper, *The Herald*, learned of this communication and published it, embarrassing both the United Sates and Mexico.[46] Díaz also warned the ambassador about the PLM Junta and asked him to suppress both the movement and its newspaper, *Regeneración*. In response, Thompson presented the U.S. Department of State with the journal, warning them that "[Díaz] has told me that the publishers of the paper are anarchistic in all that they advocate."[47]

THE 1906 REBELLIONS

Whether or not the Cananea strike was part of the general strategy intended to bring about the great PLM revolution, coordinated uprisings did begin soon afterwards. More than 40 secret clubs formed in every state of Mexico and the southwestern U.S., and many of them developed plans for local uprisings. Ricardo Flores Magón realized that, if the revolution were to meet with success, all of the groups would have to work together, and he wanted to delay the rebellion until all were prepared so that it would be more powerful. Díaz could easily quash isolated revolts, but simultaneous insurgencies would divide federal forces and would inspire local communities to join the struggle. The liberal leaders decided to initiate the revolution around September 24. However, clubs would immediately execute their plans before then if either another strike broke out in Cananea, if another club had begun its struggle, or if a Junta leader was arrested.

Once victorious, the revolution would immediately institute the reforms of the 1906 Program. It would enact changes such as limiting the working day to eight hours and guaranteeing a minimum wage for all. Ousted officials would be put on trial and punished for their crimes. Free elections would follow. Successful groups would try to procure money and munitions—generally from government institutions—to help the revolution continue, and the PLM would establish its headquarters in Mexico City. Fearing U.S. intervention, the Junta warned its partisans to leave foreigners alone except in self-defense. In September, the members of the Junta telegrammed President Theodore "Teddy" Roosevelt about its plans, assuring him that they intended only to provoke the overthrow of Porfirio Díaz, and meant no harm to the United States. The Junta emphasized that the dictator violated principles Americans hold dear: his government was undemocratic, did not respect its constitution, and upheld the institution of slavery. The PLM leaders assured the U.S. president that Mexico would become a true democracy that would establish friendly relations with its northern neighbor. Roosevelt seems to have ignored this communication, but J. B. Scott, a Department of State solicitor, assured the Department of Justice and the Missouri governor that these ideas could be expressed freely in the United States.[48]

Although Flores Magón realized how essential it would be to initiate simultaneous uprisings, organizing the revolts was a major challenge. Local clubs were to communicate their plans to the Saint Louis Junta, who in turn would coordinate the struggles and write back to the cells. To ensure security, individual groups generally did not know about each other, and the PLM used secret code names and code scripts in its correspondence. However, maintaining communication was difficult, especially because much of the Junta leadership had fled Saint Louis. Additionally, both Mexican and U.S. postal authorities were intercepting the PLM's mail. This enabled police to imprison agitators and to thwart revolutionary plans of various groups before they commenced. Realizing that the governments of both the U.S. And Mexico were monitoring them, the members of the Junta utilized traveling Special Delegates to handle much of the communication between cells, to promote the movement, to recruit new fighters, and to procure arms and ammunition. However, the PLM did not have enough couriers. Many were arrested performing this extremely dangerous job, as soldiers and police forces on both sides of the border tried to suppress the revolution they knew was brewing.

PLM UPRISINGS AND DOWNFALLS

Because the governments of two countries were preparing for the PLM insurrections, they effectively suppressed most of them. The rebellion did not get off to a propitious start. One of the first groups that was apprehended was the powerful, well-organized cell in Douglas, Arizona. It had planned to lead expeditions into Mexico and proceed to Cananea, about 50 miles to the southwest. Along the way, the expeditions would have captured customs houses at the border, blown up railroads, cut telegraph wires, and raided stores for weapons. Acquiring arms and ammunition without attracting attention had been quite difficult, although the Douglas group had managed to smuggle rifles across the border. Additionally, it had commissioned Javier Huitemea to rally the support of his brothers in the ruthlessly oppressed Yaqui tribe, promising the return of land that had been seized from them.[49]

However, this ambitious plan was foiled before it could begin. U.S. And Mexican authorities knew that an uprising was developing, as they had noticed arms being smuggled across the border. Furthermore, Governor Izábel of Sonora hired a spy, Trinidad Gómez, to infiltrate the group. On September 4, 1906, the Ranger captain who had intervened during the Cananea strike, Thomas Rynning, led his troops and immigration officers to a meeting of the Douglas group. Officers arrested seven members of this club for violating the neutrality law and deported others back to Mexico. Their raid also uncovered dynamite, pistols, and banners, as well as volumes of correspondence with the Saint Louis Junta. In the towns of Mowry and Patagonia, Arizona, about 75 miles to the west, police raided other cells, finding more maps and letters that revealed the PLM's plans.

In contrast to the Arizona groups, the Del Rio, Texas club met with some success. Its members had planned for months to lead a revolt in Jiménez, Coahuila, and began smuggling weapons to the city and surrounding towns. On September 25, they launched a surprise attack on Jiménez, apprehending the mayor, the treasurer, and the tax collector. The insurgents left a receipt from the PLM for the $108.50 they withdrew from the treasury. Taking arms, ammunition, and horses to continue their struggle, the 80 rebels left Jiménez, cutting wires to prevent local officials from communicating with federal forces. However, a counsel in Eagle Pass, Texas had already reported the attack, and troops were already mobilized. Soon after they left Jiménez, soldiers from nearby Ciudad Porfirio Díaz pursued the rebels. The PLM fighters dispersed, seeing that they had neither enough manpower nor sufficient ammunition to confront the army.

Far south of the border, powerful clubs throughout the state of Veracruz had developed detailed plans for their uprisings. They had recruited at least a thousand insurgents across the state. As in Sonora, many of PLM fighters were dispossessed Indians fighting to take back lands the dictator had stolen from them. The liberal groups intended to initiate their revolts simultaneously throughout the state, but they were unable to do so. On September 30, Hilario Salas, who had met Ricardo Flores Magón in Mexico City years before, attacked Acayucán with over 200 followers. They seemed to be winning the battle until a bullet punctured

Salas' stomach, at which point he and his troops retreated. On September 29, liberals held a demonstration in Pajapán at a plantation. Protestors cut wires and recruited fighters for their uprising. The next day, they seized money going to treasury officials from the mails, and continued gathering fighters and ammunition. On October 1, a few hours after Salas attacked Acayucán, Román Marín led a force crying, "Long Live the Liberals!" and "Death to General Porfirio Díaz!"[50] They imprisoned city officials, took funds from the mayor and the secretary, and appointed new officials in city hall. After this, they proceeded to Puerto México to continue the struggle, but, short of ammunition, they had to retreat when they saw federal troops coming to the city.

Enrique Novoa delayed his soldiers' attack on nearby Minatitlán until October 1 when he saw federal troops approaching. He suggested an ambush, but the proud Indians who composed most of his army felt this would be cowardly. In disgust, they deserted his command, leaving his army too weak to continue.[51] Liberals led a successful assault on Ixhuatlán on October 1, imprisoning the justice of the peace, the city attorney, and the police. They looted treasury funds and destroyed municipal and treasury records. However, a local citizen fleeing the invasion flagged down a ship. Unfortunately, this vessel was carrying the Minatitlán political boss and a lieutenant leading a contingent of 25 soldiers. The troop heeded the citizen's cry for help, expelling the insurgents from the city.[52]

As in Douglas, Arizona, treachery caused the collapse of the final Veracruz uprising. A few days after the failed assault on Acayucán, rebel forces regrouped outside of San Pedro Soteapán and successfully ambushed federal soldiers. The government troops waved the white flag of truce, promising to join the insurgents in an attack on the town. However, when they reached San Pedro Soteapán, the mayor signaled the army soldiers, who then plunged their bayonets into the flanks of the rebel fighters.[53]

As retribution for these insurgencies, the Mexican government made arrests throughout Veracruz in October. It executed and imprisoned most of the leaders of the uprisings. About 200 individuals were sent to jail, including many who had not even participated in combat. Worst of all, the dictatorship brutally attacked several Indian villages in retaliation for their contributions to the revolts. The last major PLM attack was supposed to have been launched from El Paso, Texas. Ricardo Flores Magón and Juan Sarabia had arrived there on September 2 from Montreal, and Antonio I. Villarreal joined them soon afterwards. They organized the local population of unemployed migrant farm laborers and railroad workers to cross the Rio Grande and attack Chihuahua. From there, they would control the states of Sonora and Coahuila through train lines. The Junta leaders coordinated the revolt from El Paso, gathering Winchester rifles, guns, ammunition, cartridges, bombs, and dynamite.

The PLM intended to attack Ciudad Juárez, the city that Madero's general, Pascual Orozco, would eventually capture in 1911, finally prompting Porfirio Díaz to resign. The liberals had prepared a detailed plan. They would begin by seizing the army's warehouse to acquire weapons and by taking the customs house to get money. They would then attack the police station, the army barracks, the post office, city hall, various banks, and several haciendas.

Unfortunately, spies betrayed this detailed agenda. To muster a formidable fighting force against the dictatorship, Ricardo Flores Magón not only had reached out to industrial laborers and peasant farmers, but also had solicited members of the Mexican military for support. Under the dictatorship, many poor people were drafted into the army against their will, so Flores Magón expected at least some support from within the military. The PLM promised to promote Mexican military personnel two ranks when they joined the Junta's battalions and guaranteed them a more generous salary. Flores Magón believed that many soldiers would fight to overthrow the government that had forcibly enlisted them.

Unfortunately, Mexican politicians cleverly used Flores Magón's strategy against him. The Chihuahua governor instructed General José María de la Vega, commander of the 18th garrison in Ciudad Juárez, to use PLM's solicitation to the military to defeat its revolutionary effort. The general sent two officers to infiltrate the El Paso movement with promises of directing PLM forces to weapon caches throughout Ciudad Juarez. On October 16, authorities arrested liberal leaders meeting in nearby Rio Grande City. Three days later, just before the intended invasion, the PLM office in El Paso was raided and the rebels were arrested. El Paso police found weapons and bombs, as well as stacks of letters and documents. They arrested many of the prominent PLM leaders. In Ciudad Juárez, Mexican police apprehended Juan Sarabia. Luckily, however, Ricardo Flores Magón successfully escaped, fleeing to the house of a local supporter, Modesto Díaz.

PERSECUTION OF THE PLM

The dictatorship sternly punished the PLM for its rebellions. In public, Porfirio Díaz denied the revolutionary import of the uprisings, claiming that they were caused by bands of dissatisfied Indians joined by unemployed railroad workers.[54] U.S. Ambassador Thompson informed Secretary of State Elihu Root that the attacks had no political significance whatsoever. Nevertheless, the Mexican government stepped up its efforts to destroy the PLM, arresting members all over the country. Seventeen were arrested in Ciudad Juárez. Liberal clubs, Indian tribes, and even many innocent civilians were brutally treated in the state of Veracruz. Over 200 PLM fighters were sentenced to the Mexican prison San Juan de Ulúa. The governor of the state of Chihuahua, Enrique Creel, had the most success cracking down on the movement. He worked with Mexican Vice President Ramon Corral to round up all of the liberals in his state, ultimately bragging to President Díaz that he had cleared Chihuahua of conspirators.

The documents and correspondence that Mexican officers had seized in raids of various clubs aided authorities in their pursuit of PLM members. The Mexican government opened and copied letters, retaining the names and addresses listed in them. They even forged letters and sent them to sympathizers to collect more information. Mexican authorities swept through the country arresting liberal combatants as well as unaffiliated persons. Not only were PLM members attacked, their supporters were as well. San Antonio, Texas authorities closed the PLM-affiliated journal *La Humanidad*. In Mexico City, police suppressed the newspaper *El Colmillo Público*. Police so severely beat the paper's old and sick director, the brilliant caricaturist Jesús Martínez Carrión, that he died in prison soon afterwards.

The Mexican government was most concerned with stopping revolution at its source by apprehending the leaders of the PLM. Juan Sarabia had been arrested with other liberal fighters near Ciudad Juárez, Chihuahua right before the El Paso club was about to attack. Porfirio Díaz instructed judges to make sure Sarabia was sent to prison. Sarabia was indicted for murder, robbery, insults to the president, and rebellion. He denied the first three trumped-up charges, and defended himself brilliantly against the last accusation of rebellion. Rather than denying it, he asserted that the Constitution of 1857 empowered him with the political right to revolt against a tyrant. He stated, "While the Republic is a fact, while the venerable democratic institutions remain inviolate, while the majesty of the law is not offended, while authorities comply with their lofty mission to watch over the good and to guarantee the rights of citizens, rebellion will be a crime perfectly punishable that no one could justify; but when the Republic is a myth, when its institutions are iniquitously tattered, when the law only serves the derision of despotism, when authority is stripped of its character .... rebellion must not be a political crime punishable by the Penal Code, but a right conceded to the oppressed by article 35 of [the] Constitution."[55] The unsympathetic court sentenced him to seven years in San Juan de Ulúa.

The Mexican government also attempted to apprehend and extradite to Mexico PLM leaders living in the United States. After Antonio I. Villarreal was arrested in the raid on the El Paso club, he was charged with violating the United States neutrality law. This statute forbids the initiation of combat on foreign territory from U.S. soil. However, the Mexican government preferred to bring Villarreal back over the border for punishment rather than putting him on trial in the U.S. After he was delivered to immigration authorities to face deportation, he requested permission to send a wire to his father and his sisters, who had been organizing a campaign for his freedom. Once he entered the Western Union office, he knocked out a guard and escaped out the back door, running away to the El Paso home of a liberal partisan.[56]

Authorities were most concerned about stopping the PLM's inspirational leader and its newspaper, *Regeneración*. Worried by Ricardo Flores Magón's escape, Chihuahua Governor Creel employed private detective Thomas Furlong to track him throughout the United States. William Greene, owner of the Cananea mine, became so obsessed with destroying the liberal movement that he filed a libel suit against the Junta. Saint Louis police arrested the last Junta leader remaining in the city, Librado Rivera, along with the typesetter of *Regeneración*. The two were detained three weeks in an Ironton, Missouri jail while the Mexican government attempted to manufacture charges against them. To guarantee extradition to Mexico, Mexican authorities accused them of murder and robbery. However, local supporters as well as newspapers like the *Saint Louis Post Dispatch* and the *Saint Louis Globe Democrat* ardently condemned these miscarriages of justice. On November 30, 1906, United States Commissioner James R. Gray held a public hearing in Saint Louis. He ruled that the offense committed by Rivera was "entirely of a political nature" and freed the men.[57] A frightened Rivera left St. Louis to reunite with Ricardo Flores Magón in Los Angeles, which at that time and for the next decade would be the most heavily socialist city in the United States.

RIO BLANCO

Soon after the PLM uprisings, a major textile strike occurred in Rio Blanco, Veracruz, further threatening Díaz's dictatorship. In turn, the conflagration impelled the tyrant to crush dissent even more vigorously. In the summer of 1906, the Gran Circulo de Obreros Libres ("The Great Circle of Free Laborers") formed to organize workers, recognizing the leadership of the Saint Louis Junta and circulating *Regeneración*. The textile workers in Veracruz suffered terrible injustices. They worked 13-hour shifts, yet earned only 40 cents a day. Workers' salaries were quickly devoured by exorbitant prices at the company store and outrageous rents for company housing. Young children were forced to work in the mills. The situation grew even worse after the declining cotton market prompted the owners' federation, the Centro Industrial Mexicano, to slash wages. Aware of the rising tide of discontent, the owners also restricted workers' access to reading materials.

In December 1906, strikes broke out all over the nearby states of Puebla and Tlaxcaca. The workers submitted demands for shorter hours, higher wages, safer working conditions, and the elimination of child labor and company stores. The owners decided to ignore these demands, preferring instead to starve the workers into submission. However, laborers in other states showed great class solidarity by collecting money to support the strikers. In response, the owners' federation decided to close down all of the mills throughout the region. On January 4, 1907, Díaz ordered that all textile factories be reopened and that all strikers return to work. Beyond the empty gesture of forbidding children younger than nine from working in the mills, the dictator made no attempt to respond to the strikers' demands. However, he granted all the wishes of the owners. Additionally, he required all workers to carry identification notebooks at all times.

Whereas most strikers were so worn down that they had to return to the factories, those in Rio Blanco, Veracruz rejected the settlement and remained on strike. After the French manager of the company store refused to sell a worker food for her starving family, people in the city rioted, looting the store and burning it down. Federal troops responded to the uprising by shooting down laborers, but the crowd was too powerful for them. The rioters stormed the municipal palace and then proceeded to the nearby village of Nogales. After the army turned them back, they returned to Rio Blanco. While they were gone, government forces sent from Veracruz and Puebla arrived in the city. When the workers arrived back home, federal forces engaged in a massacre of civilians, shooting down men, women, and children in the streets, and pursuing them through the surrounding towns. Many innocent people were ruthlessly murdered. Many others were jailed or conscripted into the army.[58]

As with the Cananea strike six months before, the brutal repression in Rio Blanco provoked strong reactions throughout Mexico. The nation was shocked by the amount of innocent blood spilled by federal troops. People once again became aware of the need to overthrow the dictator, making them more receptive to the message of the PLM. Enrique Creel, now serving as the Mexican ambassador to the United States, warned the U.S. Secretary of State Elihu Root that Ricardo Flores Magón and the other exiled Junta members were damaging political relations with Mexico. He further warned that they would hurt U.S. economic investments in Mexico as well. Root contacted Attorney General Charles J. Bonaparte, asking him to help maintain friendly relations with Mexico by apprehending the PLM leaders. Already concerned by the Cananea strike and the various uprisings of 1906, the U.S. Department of Justice was convinced by this last message to pursue Ricardo Flores Magón and the other Junta members.

MANUEL SARABIA KIDNAPPED

On June 30, 1907, Arizona Ranger Sam J. Hayhurst arrested Manuel Sarabia in Douglas. Sarabia had been organizing local mine workers and coordinating PLM activity in the area while working under the pseudonym "Sam Moret" as a printer and reporter for the Douglas *International American*. Authorities apprehended Sarabia while he was depositing PLM correspondence on a train, confiscating his letters and taking him to the city jail. That evening, a constable and the jailer took a resistant Sarabia from his cell, put him in a car, and drove him across the border, delivering him to Mexican rural police. These officers bound his hands and led him on a mule to a prison in Cananea. After spending two days in jail, he again rode a mule to Imuris, from where he was taken by train to the Sonora capital, Hermosillo.

Luckily, a Douglas laborer noticed Sarabia screaming for help and struggling against his captors. People throughout the city spoke out against his apprehension and an active campaign of protests drew attention to his case. Several groups of concerned citizens, including the Citizens Committee of Douglas, wrote letters and sent telegrams to the state and federal governments. Local newspapers such as the *Douglas Daily Examiner* and the *Douglas Industrial* denounced the kidnapping. Mary "Mother" Jones, the renowned labor activist, happened to be in Douglas to organize copper smelters. After learning about Sarabia, she powerfully condemned his arrest at a labor rally and then went to Phoenix to speak to the governor about it. The intense pressure put upon the Arizona and U.S. governments secured Sarabia's release. Arizona rangers and public investigators traveled down to Hermosillo, Sonora to bring him back to Douglas on July 12. This incident dramatically revealed to U.S. citizens, especially to leftists, that Mexico abused its dissidents, and that the U.S. government was aiding and abetting this repression.

RICARDO FLORES MAGÓN IN LOS ANGELES

Despite these assaults on the PLM leadership, the most important Junta member, Ricardo Flores Magón, still remained free, encouraging liberals throughout the U.S. And Mexico to continue the struggle. Although El Paso, Texas police raided the PLM club before it commenced its invasion of Ciudad Juárez, Flores Magón managed to escape. He fled first to the home of a local supporter, then to California. Concerned about capturing this inspirational figure, Mexican Ambassador Enrique Creel posted signs offering $20,000 for his capture throughout the U.S. And Mexico, and hired Thomas Furlong to pursue him. Furlong unsuccessfully tried to find Flores Magón in El Paso and Austin, Texas, Toronto and Montreal, Canada, and New York City before looking in California. Years later, Flores Magón related in a prison letter to his friend Nicolás Bernal that these were grinding times for him: he hid himself away, often not eating for days, terrified that he would be deported to an execution in Mexico. He first arrived in Los Angeles, but soon realized that an agent was following him. Ricardo Flores Magón, somehow concealing his prominent moustache, evaded capture by dressing up as a woman and fleeing to San Francisco. Fearing pursuit there, he left for Sacramento, and then departed that city to settle back in Los Angeles.

Even while he was running for his life, Ricardo Flores Magón continued to plot the Mexican revolution. Sensing that the dictatorship could no longer sustain its repressive regime, he continued to write to individuals and clubs, urging them to continue the fight. One letter insisted, "One must not lose faith or be dismayed. Great causes are not lost nor won in a day."[59] After another circular explained the causes of previous failures, it exhorted PLM members to collect money and weapons to prepare for the imminent insurrection. This document proposed essentially the same revolutionary agenda as before: federal soldiers would be promoted and paid better in the liberal army; corrupt officials would be put on trial; and the 1906 Program would be instituted, providing reforms such as a minimum wage and an eight-hour working day. Even though police crackdowns after the 1906 rebellions had destroyed or severely damaged many groups, various clubs developed plans for uprisings. As before, PLM cells hoped to invade border towns, blow up bridges, cut telegraph wires, and raid treasuries, thereby initiating the revolution. Junta leaders also planned to assassinate a high official in Chihuahua.[60] However, U.S. And Mexican authorities were aware of the possible revolt, so they stationed troops along the border. Soon rumors spread that the rebellion would occur on Mexican Independence Day, September 16, 1907. Fearing a catastrophe even worse than the 1906 attempts, the PLM held back for another year.

Once Flores Magón and other prominent PLM members arrived in Los Angeles, they began publishing another newspaper. Along with Librado Rivera, Antonio I. Villarreal, Lázaro Gutiérrez de Lara, and Modesto Díaz, Flores Magón published the first issue of *Revolución* on June 1, 1907. It was distributed throughout California and the southwestern United States and smuggled into Mexico. In contrast to the *Regeneración* of previous years, this paper made much more passionate, abrasive calls for revolution. Certain articles echoed German philosopher Friedrich Nietzsche in their criticism of a Christian slave morality that teaches humility and obedience.[61] For example, the essay "Clarion Call of Combat" declared, "It's a lie that virtue resides in the suffering, pious, and obedient spirits! … Never has altruism budded in these morbid, terrified temperaments; altruism is the patrimony of strong characters, of those abnegating individuals who love the others too much to forget about themselves."[62] Similarly, Magon's article "Go Towards Life" seems inspired by Nietzsche's reflections on the death of god and metaphysics: "Religions are dissolving in the shadows of indifference. The Koran, the Vedas, the Bible no longer radiate glory: in their yellowing pages, sad gods are dying like the sun in a winter's twilight. … Social inequality died in theory when metaphysics died during the revolution in thought."[63] Other essays in *Revolución* urged soldiers to join the revolution and citizens to procure weapons and become guerillas. The paper as a whole focused a great deal on labor issues and the class struggle. Although he did not explicitly state his philosophical leanings, Flores Magón's writings began clearly to evoke anarchist notions, repeatedly stressing the importance of expropriating the land and distributing it to all. For example, he urged, "We do not fight for abstractions, but for material realities. We want land for everyone; for everyone, bread. Insofar as blood must necessarily flow, it will be so that the conquests we secure will benefit everyone and not just a certain social caste."[64]

RICARDO FLORES MAGÓN AND OTHER JUNTA LEADERS APPREHENDED

After having pursued the Junta leaders throughout the United States and Canada, Thomas Furlong finally apprehended them on August 23, 1907. Even though they had no warrant to do so, he and several Mexican detectives arrested Ricardo Flores Magón, Librado Rivera, and Antonio I. Villarreal, dragging them from their house and seizing their correspondence. Flores Magón was beaten unconscious. Rivera cried out that they were being kidnapped. Because they attracted so much attention, the Mexican government could not easily bring the prisoners across the border as they had Manuel Sarabia. Instead, the three men were brought to the Los Angeles jail on charges of "resisting arrest." Although both the Mexican and the U.S. governments wanted the Junta leaders behind bars, neither had decided what charges to lodge against them. Various libel suits had been filed against them, so there were many possible venues for a trial. Authorities tried to connect the prisoners with the planned El Paso invasion of Ciudad Juárez, but these charges would not have led to their deportation. Instead, the Mexican government accused them of murder and robbery to ensure extradition, but soon admitted it had no evidence for this claim.

Luckily, the PLM cause had drawn sufficient political attention in the U.S. to prevent deportation. The imprisoned men retained excellent, committed lawyers to dispute the specious charges of the Mexican government. The Mexican socialist lawyer Lázaro Gutiérrez de Lara, who had previously organized unions and a PLM club in Cananea, was joined by two U.S. socialist lawyers, A. R. Holston and Job Harriman. The prominent Harriman had run for the vice-presidency in 1900 on the Socialist Party ticket, and would almost win the Los Angeles mayoral seat in 1911 as a Socialist. The lawyers wrote to Washington to prevent the deportation of the Junta leaders, eventually taking the case to the Supreme Court. Various concerned citizens groups also sent letters to Congress and the President to fight the extradition. Soon, Attorney General Charles J. Bonaparte realized that the case had become politically sensitive and warned against any illegal deportations.

Authorities eventually decided to try the three men for violating the neutrality law by initiating a military offensive across the Mexican border from Douglas, Arizona. Flores Magón, Rivera, and Villarreal were released from the Los Angeles County Jail on September 24, 1907, and immediately rearrested on federal charges. They were moved to Arizona, but the trial was delayed another 20 months, finally beginning on May 12, 1909. By this time, the U.S. had grown so concerned with growing leftist movements in both the U.S. And Mexico, especially the anarchist movement, that the trial became an indictment of radicalism. Porfirio Díaz informed prosecutor Joseph L. B. Alexander of the PLM's anarchist tendencies. In turn, he insulted the defendants as "rank anarchists" to Attorney General Charles J. Bonaparte and as parasitic "grafters" before the jury.[65]

Even more than the prosecution, the PLM's defense attorneys focused on the general issue of radicalism. Because their Los Angeles lawyers could not follow them to Arizona, the Western Federation of Miners (WFM) and the Political Refugee Defense League of Chicago hired new advocates to represent them.

Unfortunately, the WFM was more concerned with recruiting Mexican labor than with fomenting the Mexican revolution. Its lawyers employed a basically ineffective and specious argument to defend the liberal Junta.[66] Ignoring the PLM's struggle against Porfirio Díaz's dictatorship, the advocates portrayed the case as an attack on a group that ardently supported workers' rights. Even if the attorneys had chosen a more effective and more honest defense strategy, the evidence against Flores Magón, Rivera, and Villarreal was overwhelming. The raid on the Douglas PLM club had uncovered too many incriminating letters and detailed battle plans. Although the defense tried to overturn the case on various technicalities, the three men were found guilty and sentenced to 18 months in federal prison at McNeil Island, Washington.

Along with the Junta leadership, the newspaper it had founded in Los Angeles, *Revolución*, was also repressed. On September 27, 1907, police arrested on libel charges the paper's printers and its editor, Lázaro Gutiérrez de Lara, who was also defending the Junta in court. Although the printers were soon released, authorities kept Gutiérrez de Lara in prison for three months as they tried to create a case to extradite him to Mexico. Eventually, they charged him with stealing wood in 1903. The value of this lumber was placed at $28, a sufficient amount to guarantee deportation. He and Job Harriman appealed the charges, and luckily succeeded in getting the case dismissed on a technicality.

In Gutiérrez de Lara's stead, Práxedis Guerrero and Enrique Flores Magón went to Los Angeles to help Modesto Díaz and Manuel Sarabia continue publishing the paper. However, the Mexican government was still determined to shut it down. Like Flores Magón, Rivera, and Villarreal, Manuel Sarabia was arrested for conspiring in the Douglas, Arizona raids. The printers continued putting out the paper, but authorities soon incarcerated them for libel. After they were freed on bail, they were arrested yet again and the presses of *Revolución* were seized. Modesto Díaz died in his Los Angeles jail cell. Manuel Sarabia had become very sick with tuberculosis by the time he was released on bond. Afraid that he too might die if he returned to prison, Elizabeth Darling Trowbridge, a wealthy supporter of the PLM, married him and they fled together to England. After the suppression of *Revolución*, the PLM was unable to establish a sustained publishing effort until Ricardo Flores Magón emerged from prison in 1910. Práxedis Guerrero periodically issued his newsletter *Puntos Rojos* ("Tracer Bullets"). Liberals and supporters in Los Angeles briefly put out the journal *Libertad y Trabajo* ("Liberty and Work"), but this soon ended when its editors left to fight in the revolutionary uprisings of 1908.

THE 1908 REBELLIONS

While they were behind bars, the Junta leaders plotted a new set of uprisings in 1908. Despite the suppressions of PLM members and newspapers, they still communicated to liberals throughout Mexico and the United States. Even though he was being held incommunicado in jail, forbidden to write letters or publish articles, Ricardo Flores Magón continued to incite opposition through his pen. He smuggled out his writings by passing them to attorneys as well as by sewing them within his undergarments. A PLM supporter who worked in the prison laundry would then help route them to eager readers. *Libertad y Trabajo* published his articles under the names of his common law wife, María Brousse Talavera, and her daughter Lucía. The letters he wrote instructed various PLM figures to plan revolts in Mexico, especially along the Texas and Arizona Borders.

In addition to writing letters, the Junta members spread revolutionary fervor from their prison cells by writing a manifesto in December 1907. This document explained that they were still plotting the overthrow of Díaz and that PLM members should continue the struggle. This document was to be printed on broadsheets, distributed as pamphlets, posted on billboards, and even sent to officials in the U.S. And Mexican governments.[67]

Flores Magon called for a general uprising to occur on June 25, 1908. He communicated his general battle plans and propaganda ideas to his brother Enrique and his comrade Práxedis Guerrero. They would then coordinate the insurgencies in detail. The country would be divided into five zones of activity, and the 60 or so PLM groups in Mexico and the U.S. would be responsible for fomenting rebellions in their respective zones. Additionally, PLM delegates would disseminate propaganda to recruit new members and form new clubs. The clubs would then gather weapons and develop new plans of attack.

As most of the liberal cells were still along the Texas and Arizona borders, traveling Special Delegates were responsible for coordinating much of the activity. They carried messages across the line between different groups, attempting to coordinate their activities with each other. Armed with credentials signed by Ricardo Flores Magón and lists of people to contact, they traveled all over Mexico and the southwestern U.S. On these tours, they raised money, gathered arms and ammunition, and recruited people to join the fight against the dictator. As before, liberals in the Mexican state of Sonora contacted the local Indian tribes to solicit their help. Yet the role of Special Delegate was as dangerous as ever, and many emissaries were arrested.

In addition to coordinating the revolution from prison, Ricardo Flores Magón also communicated his vision for its ultimate goal. In a June 13, 1908 letter to his brother Enrique and his comrade Práxedis Guerrero, Ricardo stated explicitly that the forthcoming rebellion must be anarchist in nature. Warning that revolutions are always betrayed by leaders and bourgeois pressures that co-opt and corrupt the will of the people, he explained that the PLM fighters must strive for an anarcho-communist society in which peasants and workers themselves will directly own and control the land and the industries. However, Flores Magon further warned that various Junta leaders, including Antonio I. Villarreal and Manuel Sarabia, were too reformist to accept such radical ideas. He also feared that many PLM members might be intimidated by libertarian terminology "because they are so accustomed to hearing anarchists talked about in disparaging terms."[68] Authorities and the press had libeled this movement as one that merely advocated violence rather than as an idealistic struggle for human liberation.

In his 1908 prison letter, Ricardo Flores Magón instructed Enrique and Práxedis to avoid the anarchist label. He advised, "To obtain the great benefits for the people, real benefits, it is necessary to work as well-disguised anarchists, even from those who take us as their leaders. Everything boils down to a mere question of tactics. If from the start we would have called ourselves anarchists, no one, not even a few, would have listened to us."[69] According to Flores Magón, the PLM should still fight under the aegis of liberalism, yet act like anarchists. He stated "We will continue calling ourselves liberals in the course of the revolution, but in reality we will go on propagating anarchy and carrying out anarchist acts. We will continue expropriating from the bourgeoisie and making restitution to the people with what we seize."[70] Some scholars have claimed that Ricardo Flores Magón made a tactical error in deceiving his supporters about his true political goals. In their view, not only did he forestall and aggravate rifts that were inevitable, he mistakenly underestimated the radical commitment of many Mexicans.[71]

After the previous revolutionary attempts, Mexican and U.S. Authorities prepared themselves for the imminent uprisings. Ambassador Enrique Creel wrote to the U.S. Secretary of State to warn that liberal groups were gathering weapons and money. The governments of both nations added troops along the border. Political officials went into hiding. By June 1908, Mexico placed its northern states under martial law and stationed soldiers in villages and garrisons.

Intercepted PLM communications aided authorities in their repression of liberal clubs. When the Mexican Consul in Los Angeles, Antonio Lozano, learned that Ricardo Flores Magón was sewing letters in his prison laundry, he photographed them and sent copies to U.S. And Mexican authorities. Similarly, incoming letters were photographed and distributed. As a result, both governments arrested hundreds of PLM activists, many of whom were murdered. Detectives followed Práxedis Guerrero throughout his travels, yet never apprehended him. The Mexican government even employed a spy to pose as Antonio I. Villarreal and visit various liberal clubs. This impostor gathered details of the clubs' plans and solicited names of other revolutionaries. Having gathered sufficient information, federal authorities raided PLM clubs throughout Mexico on June 23, seizing their arms and imprisoning their members.

Ironically, perhaps the most important revolutionary attempt was foiled not by government vigilance, but by incredibly bad luck. As in 1906, the PLM club in El Paso hoped to capture Ciudad Juárez. Its members had readied between 200 and 800 men, collected arms, made bombs, and identified strategic points of attack. They also developed plans about what they would do once they achieved victory. However, the club's neighbor grew suspicious about the crates arriving next door, about the armed guards surrounding the house, and about the shots he heard at night. Fearing that he was living next to smugglers or thieves, he informed local police. On June 25, a city detective stopped the leaders of the club, and officers raided their headquarters. Inside, El Paso police found many guns, dynamite sticks, bombs, and thousands of rifle cartridges. Additionally, they uncovered stacks of correspondence and maps indicating locations of banks, prisons, and municipal centers. Officers apprehended the PLM members, again charging them with violating the neutrality law.

Revolts did break out in northern Mexico, but they were not well coordinated. Because they did not occur simultaneously, the Mexican government was able to defuse one after the other. On June 25, PLM fighters in the farming and rubber-producing city of Viesca, Coahuila rose up in arms. Two hundred or more fighters, including over 60 from a local hacienda, successfully captured the city, cheering "Down with the Dictatorship!" and "Long live the Liberal Mexican Party!" They took over the municipal palace and bombed the house of the district political boss. The PLM army ransacked offices and haciendas for money, food, horses, and weapons. They also opened the jails and freed the prisoners. The victorious liberals then instituted the 1906 program. To prevent federal forces from retaking the city, insurgents tore up railroad tracks and cut telegraph wires. After they had controlled the city for a day and a half, the PLM fighters moved on to attack the town of Matamoros. On the way, however, they encountered a large force of soldiers sent from the federal and state capitals. After an unsuccessful fight in the mountains, the liberal forces scattered. Government troops advanced to Viesca, driving liberals from the city. They executed or imprisoned some 30 insurgents.[72]

None of the subsequent uprisings met with as much success as the Viesca revolt. Rebels had planned to attack Las Vacas, Coahuila from Del Rio, Texas on June 26. To prepare for the struggle, liberals had carefully hidden arms and ammunition along the river in Mexico. However, the attack did not happen as planned. Although the leader of the rebel infantry, Encarnación Díaz Guerra, had his 60 troops ready for the early morning assault, the cavalry did not show up for many hours. After waiting a while, Díaz Guerra ordered an attack, and his fighters, chanting "Long Live Liberty!" and "Long Live the Liberal Club!", entered the city. They fought soldiers, attacked the military barracks, even engaged in hand-to-hand combat against Díaz's forces. However, the superior federal troops drove them from the city. Six hours later, the PLM cavalry finally showed up. A smaller force attempted another attack on the city, but it soon ran out of ammunition. PLM insurgents retreated again to the mountains, taking horses and ammunition from a local hacienda, dogged by troops tracking them.

The rebels confronted additional problems when they crossed the border to return to their Texas homes. Citizens in Del Rio had heard the shooting in nearby Las Vacas. Local authorities performed a census of the population to determine who had left for the struggle and to look for literature and weapons. One wounded leader made a full confession to the Del Rio police. Soon after this attempt on Las Vacas, remaining partisans from the failed El Paso attack on Ciudad Juárez regrouped to capture Palomas, Chihuahua. However, a U.S. citizen noticed 11 liberal soldiers armed with rifles and cartridges marching toward Mexico on June 29. El Paso police notified Mexican authorities, so Palomas was prepared for the attack on July 1. A close friend of Práxedis Guerrero, Francisco Manriquez, was slain in the battle. The insurgents fled towards Casas Grandes, but when they got lost after their guide deserted them, they returned to El Paso.

FALLOUT OF THE 1908 REBELLIONS

As in 1906, PLM fighters and supporters were severely punished for the uprisings of 1908. The Mexican government hunted down leaders throughout the country, imprisoning and murdering them. Furthermore, the dictatorship made false promises of amnesty for PLM fighters, and some foolishly returned to Mexico where they were immediately arrested. U.S. Authorities also chased liberals, charging them with violating the neutrality law. Waco, Texas police and Thomas Furlong arrested the Special Delegate Antonio de P. Araujo, one of the travelers so important to maintaining contact between various sectors of the movement. He was sentenced to two-and-a-half years at the federal penitentiary in Leavenworth, Kansas for violating neutrality laws. Acting on information from Furlong, the U.S. Secret Service captured Encarnación Díaz Guerra, commander of the Las Vacas assault, brutally fracturing his skull. On November 11, 1908, he was also sent to Leavenworth for the same crime as Araujo.

As before, the Mexican government tried to downplay the revolutionary significance of the uprisings. Porfirio Díaz claimed that the fighting was merely the work of bandits and had no political significance. The Mexican Ambassador to the U.S., Enrique Creel, similarly denied that the uprisings grew out of a revolutionary movement. However, both the Mexican and the U.S. governments knew that this was a political attempt to overthrow the despot, not mere banditry. The U.S. Consul in Las Vacas noted that the insurgents neither robbed nor stole, and had the sympathy of the people. An editorial in the *El Paso Times* even more directly averred that this was a revolutionary attempt to topple an oppressive tyrant.

Even though the uprisings of 1908 had ended so poorly, Enrique Flores Magón, Práxedis Guerrero, and Jesús María Rangel continued to organize another rebellion. María Rangel, a leader of the Las Vacas attack, had escaped from U.S. Authorities after his initial arrest, changing his identity and concealing himself among the sizable San Antonio Mexican community. He continued collecting weapons and coordinating PLM cells throughout Texas until his capture on August 10, 1909. When they raided his home, authorities found many important documents that indicated the general plan for future uprisings during September 1909 as well as a list of liberals throughout the U.S. Soon after María Rangel's apprehension, San Antonio police also arrested liberal organizer and publisher Thomas Sarabia, cousin of Juan and brother of Manuel. Although many protested against the apprehension of the two activists, only Sarabia was freed because of lack of evidence. María Rangel joined other PLM fighters in Leavenworth prison incarcerated for violating the neutrality laws.

Despite these further reductions in the PLM leadership, several important figures remained active. On Mexican Independence Day, September 16, 1908, Fernando Palomarez, the Mayo Indian who had joined the PLM cause in Cananea, attempted to assassinate Porfirio Díaz when the dictator ascended the steps of the National Palace to invoke the Grito de Dolores. Unfortunately, the tyrant's bulletproof vest deflected the shot. Luckily, the crowd helped Palomarez to escape.[73] Práxedis Guerrero, the scion of a wealthy Guanajuato landowner who had abandoned his privilege to live among the poor workers of Mexico, successfully avoided arrest throughout his busy organizing career.[74] Working sporadically as a lumberjack to support himself, he traveled around the U.S. border and into Mexico, spreading PLM ideas and talking to Mexicans and Mexican-Americans about the goals of the Junta. Encouraging people to arm themselves, he gathered money and weapons, and even smuggled rifles over the border. He helped many different clubs develop their revolutionary plans and coordinated strategies between groups. Throughout his travels, various detectives, police, and military authorities pursued Guerrero, yet none ever caught him. In one instance, Houston police invaded his house and seized his documents, yet Guerrero managed to escape by tying together bed sheets and climbing out the back window.[75]

In addition to his indefatigable organizing work, Guerrero spread the liberal message through his essays and poetic epigrams, such as "It is better to die on your feet than to live on your knees." He and Enrique Flores Magón published circulars and manifestoes that urged collective solidarity against the injustice of capitalism, exhorting the world's poor to rise up against the rich and powerful. After publishing these statements, Guerrero put together the newspaper *Puntos Rojos* with Thomas Sarabia and Jesús María Rangel. Its pages passionately urged people to overthrow the Mexican tyrant, exhorting them to purchase weapons and to organize militias. *Puntos Rojos* also discussed other radical themes. It highlighted the role of female soldiers in the liberal struggles, recommended the formation of a Pan American Labor League, and condemned the execution of the influential Spanish anarchist philosopher and educational reformer Francisco Ferrer Guardia.

SUPPORT AMONG THE U.S. LEFT

Although the PLM was severely weakened by the arrests and murders of so many of its Mexican and Mexican-American members, many white leftists in the U.S. came to its aid. Rather than contributing to the development of another rebellion, most of these radicals assisted the PLM through legal support. Anarchists, socialists, and labor activists wrote letters to protest the persecution of PLM captives and helped fund legal defense. However, substantial rifts occurred with several labor and socialist groups. After telling his brother that "this is truly a country of pigs,"[76] Ricardo Flores Magón lamented to his wife María that many U.S. leftists condescended to the PLM because "we are poor Mexicans. ... This is our fault. Our skins are not white."[77] U.S. support for the Mexican movement was uneven at times, and many labor and socialist leaders deserted Ricardo

Flores Magón and perhaps even harmed him over the years. Nevertheless, Flores Magón's dream could not have survived without the aid of North American leftists, especially as his opportunities in Mexico collapsed and his legal troubles in the U.S. mushroomed.

Flores Magón actively encouraged PLM members to associate with radical groups in their country of exile. Whereas he had previously regarded his revolutionary mission as the liberation of the Mexican peasantry and proletariat, he realized that his struggle was part of the international fight against the exploitation of capitalism, tyranny of government, and brainwashing of religion. In the wake of his philosophical rifts with prominent Junta leaders such as Manuel Sarabia and Antonio I. Villarreal, Ricardo urged PLM members to affiliate with socialist groups and spread their message at socialist meetings.

As a journalist, Flores Magon understood the importance of support among the U.S. press. Newspapers in Saint Louis, Missouri and Douglas, Arizona had vigorously denounced the apprehensions of Junta leaders, helping to secure their freedom. Flores Magón knew that the backing of radical journals would be essential to the survival of the PLM. There was already much controversy in the U.S. press about the PLM. The radical press heartily supported the PLM cause, but many mainstream papers attacked the group. One San Francisco newspaper fired journalist Ethel Mowbray Dolson for her sympathetic interviews with Flores Magón, Villarreal, and Rivera.

Left-wing Spanish-language papers supported the PLM's struggle and protested its political persecution, but conservative papers mocked and insulted the PLM leaders. While newspapers in Texas generally supported the PLM's efforts, the daily press in Los Angeles was hostile. L.A. newspaper moguls had acquired substantial interests in Mexico from the corrupt policies and cronyism of Porfirio Díaz's dictatorship. General Harrison Gray Otis, publisher of the *Los Angeles Times*, owned 850,000 acres of land in Mexico. E.T. Earl, owner of the *Los Angeles Express,* was president of Sinaloa Land and Water, which possessed three million acres. William Randolph Hearst, owner of the *Los Angeles Examiner,* controlled mines, ranches, and railroads in Mexico.[78] These three papers ruthlessly attacked the PLM leadership, and left-wing journals defended them against these calumnies.

One of the reasons why U.S. leftists supported the exiled Mexican dissidents was because they themselves were encountering harsh repression from the government. In the wake of massive labor protests in the 1890s, Congress had passed a law in 1902 making it illegal to advocate changes in property ownership. Almost a century before George W. Bush proclaimed his War on Terror, President Theodore Roosevelt declared a War on Anarchists.[79] Just like Bush fuels his current campaign with barely disguised racism and xenophobia, Roosevelt similarly targeted aliens living in the U.S. In 1903, he signed a law that stipulated the deportation of any immigrant anarchist who had been in the U.S. for less than three years. After sundry anarchist activities in 1908 and 1909, such as the murder of a Denver priest, the explosion of a bomb in New York City's Union Square, and an assassination attempt on the Chicago chief of police, the government stepped up its efforts to suppress anarchist papers and deport foreign anarchists.[80] Given this brutal political climate, the PLM garnered significant sympathy among the socialist, labor, and anarchist movements.

Local, national, and even international socialist organizations rallied against the imprisonment of the Mexican radicals, raising money for their defense and passing resolutions calling for their release. In response, members of these groups sent letters soliciting pardons to presidents Roosevelt and Taft and other important government officials. Los Angeles organizations often discussed and publicly protested against the evils of the Mexican dictatorship. As mentioned above, the prominent L.A. socialist attorneys Job Harriman and A. R. Holston represented the PLM leaders in court. The North American socialist leader Eugene V. Debs passionately defended the Mexican dissidents, speaking about their cause at rallies, publishing articles about their fate in socialist newspapers, and distributing a pamphlet about them, *Political Prisoners Held in the United States*. He even made their liberty an issue in his 1908 run for the U.S. presidency.

The most important socialist newspaper in the states, *Appeal to Reason* (prior to WWI the largest-circulation periodical—of any sort—in the world), devoted the entirety of its March 13, 1909 issue to the PLM cause. It printed a letter from Ricardo Flores Magón explaining the reasons for the arrest of the PLM leadership and describing the abuse inflicted upon him and the others in prison: their visitors were harassed; they were forbidden to receive books or magazines; and Librado Rivera's wife was even molested by jailers in a search of her person. In a later issue of *Appeal to Reason*, the editors wrote and published a manifesto on the front page that exhorted its readers to solidarity between the U.S. And Mexican working class, instructing them that supporting the PLM would further the international revolutionary movement.

The PLM was especially helped by several prominent socialists who came to Los Angeles to involve themselves deeply in the liberal struggle. The young journalist John Kenneth Turner and his wife Ethel Duffy Turner supported

Ricardo Flores Magón through many phases of his life and even after his death. The Turners first met the Junta leaders while interviewing them in their Los Angeles prison cells. The convicts' tales of Díaz's brutal oppression horrified them. Determined to expose these evils, John Kenneth Turner recruited PLM member and socialist Lázaro Gutiérrez de Lara to guide him through Mexico. In reaction to his discoveries, he wrote an influential series of articles detailing the evils of the tyrant's Mexico. These essays described the systematic extermination of the Yaqui Indians and the perpetuation of slavery in Oaxacan tobacco plantations and Yucatan hemp fields. They also explained how the dictator systematically destroyed all voices of political protest. Pointedly, these articles further implicated the U.S. government and businesses for giving the Díaz regime financial and moral support. First published in *American Magazine* in 1909, these essays were collected and published as the book *Barbarous Mexico* in 1911. In later years, the Turners helped the PLM organize revolutionary attempts, and even smuggled arms across the border. To mourn Flores Magón's passing, Ethel Duffy Turner wrote one of the most thorough histories of his life and his movement, *Ricardo Flores Magón and the Mexican Liberal Party*, which was later translated and published as *Ricardo Flores Magón y El Partido Liberal Mexicano*.

Like the Turners, socialist John Murray was outraged by the injustice in Mexico and by the imprisonment of its dissidents in the U.S. He contacted a Pennsylvania congressman to investigate the political persecution, which resulted in a 1910 congressional investigation.[81] He helped found the socialist newspaper *The Border* to reveal the atrocities committed by the Mexican dictator, especially detailing injustice along the frontier. It called attention to the fate of the PLM and its leaders, calling them "The Men Díaz Dreads." Like John Kenneth Turner, Murray decided to travel through Mexico to investigate conditions firsthand. Carrying a letter of introduction from Ricardo Flores Magón that contained the date for the upcoming revolution, he contacted PLM clubs and imprisoned members throughout Mexico. His reports detailed harsh labor conditions in places such as the textile factories of Rio Blanco, as well as brutality in prisons such as San Juan de Ulúa and Belen. In addition to the Turners and Murray, the wealthy Boston libertarian socialist Elizabeth Darling Trowbridge came to Los Angeles to help the persecuted Junta leaders. She wrote letters to various government officials requesting pardons, funded the publication of pamphlets and newspapers, financed Turner and Murray's trips to Mexico, and supported the families of Ricardo Flores Magón and Librado Rivera.

These engaged supporters also helped form special committees to secure the freedom of the imprisoned Junta leaders. John Kenneth Turner, Murray, and Trowbridge created the Mexican Revolutionist Defense League to publicize their plight and solicit aid. The Defense Committee of Los Angeles also collected funds for attorney fees and transcript requests. John Murray contacted the Chicago Political Refugee Defense League. This group, which had typically fought for Russian exiles, protested against the persecution of the PLM, holding rallies, releasing bulletins, and sending letters of protest to the U.S. Secretary of State.

Like the socialists, labor unions organized substantial support for the PLM. Because they were generally quite militant and their membership contained a high proportion of Mexican-American workers, miners' unions were particularly vocal. The miners' magazine *Labor Literature* publicized the plight of the Junta leaders. As discussed previously, the tireless labor activist and IWW organizer Mother Jones first became aware of the PLM when she protested against Manuel Sarabia's arrest at a Douglas, Arizona rally for a copper smelter's union. She toured the country discussing the PLM leadership's plight to unions, raising $1000 from the United Mine Workers and $3000 from other unions. The UMW also passed a resolution to help the persecuted Mexicans. The radical Western Federation of Miners, one of the primary participants in the formation of the syndicalist Industrial Workers of the World, had encountered the PLM before and continued to support them. The WFM had actively recruited Mexican-American and Mexican laborers in Arizona and Sonora mines, and its members may have been key organizers of the 1906 Cananea, Sonora strike. It raised over $1500 to fund Flores Magón, Villarreal, and Rivera's legal defense. As mentioned above, the WFM also hired the union lawyers who represented the men in their 1909 Arizona trial.

Not just the miners, but also the entire labor community spoke out against the persecution of Mexican dissidents. The Los Angeles Labor Council issued a statement decrying the U.S. government that condemned these men for helping the working class. At every level, from small locals to national federations, unions rallied to the PLM cause. As one small example, Shreveport, Louisiana Local 215 of the Women's International Labor League wrote a letter of protest to the U.S. Attorney General.[82] On November 13, 1908, the American Federation of Labor, the largest union organization in the U.S., passed a resolution that pledged sympathy and solicited support for the PLM leaders. When the president of the AFL, Samuel Gompers, later met with President Roosevelt, he also delivered to him a letter about the unjustly locked-up Junta members.

Whereas the labor and socialist movements eventually broke with the PLM, anarchists supported the PLM throughout its struggle. Emma Goldman and Alexander Berkman protested the treatment of Flores Magón and his cohorts. They solicited funds at massive protests and speaking engagements. Goldman published articles about the PLM and the Mexican revolution in her journal, *Mother Earth*, and Berkman did so in his paper, *The Blast*. *Mother Earth* also published Ricardo Flores Magón's "Manifesto to the American People" that detailed the persecution of the PLM to citizens of "the free fatherland of Washington" and exhorted them to support the Mexican struggle in the name of international working-class solidarity.[83] Similarly, the prominent U.S. anarchist Voltairine de Cleyre spoke out at rallies against the imprisonment of the PLM leaders and even became the Chicago correspondent for *Regeneración*. Internationally, figures such as the great Russian anarchist Peter Kropotkin came to the defense of Ricardo Flores Magón.

THE OPENING YEARS OF THE MEXICAN REVOLUTION

The PLM prisoners feared that the Mexican dictator Porfirio Díaz might still attempt to apprehend or murder them even after they got out of jail. To prevent any such intrigue, John Kenneth Turner and members of the Western Federation of Miners met Ricardo Flores Magón, Librado Rivera, and Antonio I. Villarreal on their August 3, 1910 release from prison in Arizona and guided them to the railroad station. A large crowd, cheering and throwing flowers, greeted them when they disembarked in Los Angeles. A few evenings later, over 2000 supporters attended a fundraiser for the men at the Los Angeles Labor Temple. John Kenneth Turner and Los Angeles lawyers Holston and Harriman discussed the persecution of the PLM and aspects of the legal case. Antonio Villarreal stated that the fight for freedom would continue. An exhausted and sick Ricardo Flores Magón spoke briefly, leading rousing chants of *"¡Viva la Revolución Social!"* With the $414.66 raised from this event, the Junta leaders restarted their newspaper, *Regeneración*.

Almost a decade after its first issue was published in Mexico City, the first Los Angeles edition of *Regeneración* appeared on September 3, 1910. It achieved a circulation of over 12,000 by early November. In the lead editorial of its premiere issue, Ricardo Flores Magón bravely asserted "here we are again at our combat posts," vowing to foment armed revolution against Porfirio Díaz.

Additionally, Flores Magón seems to have developed his radical political views during his years in prison. His essays in this new version of *Regeneración* did not merely address the situation in Mexico, but also proposed a vision of an international anarchism. In contrast to the 1906 slogan of "Reform, Liberty, and Justice," Flores Magón proclaimed a motto that had originated with the Russian narodnik movement and was employed by Spanish anarchists: Tierra y Libertad, Land and Liberty.[84]

As he could feel the Mexican Revolution quickly approaching, Flores Magón filled the pages of *Regeneración* with passionate exhortations to violent rebellion. "Workers, my friends, listen: it's necessary, it's urgent that you carry the revolution to the point where it reflects the consciousness of the epoch; it's necessary, it's urgent that it incarnates the great spiritual battle of the century."[85] He denounced the oppression of the dictator and the exploitation of capitalism. Explaining that economic equality is the basis of liberty, he urged Mexican workers and peasants to foment the revolution themselves, taking possession of the factories and the land. "We ought to keep in mind that what is needed is that the people have bread, shelter, and land to cultivate; we ought to keep in mind that no government, no matter how good its intents, can declare the abolition of misery. It's the people themselves, the hungry, the dispossessed who must abolish misery, taking, in the first place, possession of the earth which, by natural right, cannot be monopolized by a few, but is the property of every human being."[86]

In other essays, Flores Magón envisioned the revolutionary not as a political or military leader, but as one who sows the seeds of ideals.[87] On a philosophical note, he imagined the force of discord as the one that propels humanity forward. "Always revolutionary, discord makes disgust ferment in proletarian breasts until, their nerves pulled tight until they are ready to snap, desperation makes hands search for rocks, bombs, daggers, revolvers, rifles, and men cast themselves against injustice, intending each one to be a hero."[88]

In addition to its Mexican focus, *Regeneración* also addressed the concerns of its readers in the North America. The Junta was especially worried that the U.S. government might intervene to support Díaz against the coming uprising. It also addressed social and economic problems faced by Mexicans in the U.S., criticizing widespread racism and lamenting the lack of schools for brown children. "Everyone knows the contempt in which Mexicans in general are treated; everyone knows that in Texas Mexicans are treated worse than blacks. Mexicans are not admitted to hotels, restaurants, and other public establishments in Texas. The public schools close their doors to children of our race. North American semi-savages take target practice on Mexicans. How many men of our race have died because a white-skinned savage decided to prove his ability with firearms by shooting at us—and without having any dispute with us! In the so-called courts of justice, Mexicans are judged, generally without bothering with legal formalities, and are sentenced to hang or to suffer other horrendous penalties without there being proof, or even the suspicion that they actually committed the crimes for which they are sentenced."[89]

For the first time in its history, *Regeneración* reached out to U.S. leftists by including a page written entirely in English. Fearing that socialist and labor supporters would abandon him if he were too open about his anarchism, Flores Magón initially filled these pages with reformist rather than radical proclamations. While Spanish readers were exhorted to expropriate the land, English ones read proposals for incremental change taken from the 1906 Program. However, the developing revolution in Mexico required Flores Magon to clearly distinguish his dreams for human freedom from less idealistic ones. He could no longer afford to conceal his true political intentions. His radicalism alienated the first editor of the English-language page, the Los Angeles socialist Alfred Sanftleben, as well as the second editor, Ethel Duffy Turner. Only in April 15, 1911, when the British anarchist William C. Owen took over this responsibility, did the newspaper honestly declare its guiding ideology to all of its audiences.

Soon after *Regeneración* began its publication in Los Angeles, the Mexican Revolution erupted, finally ousting Porfirio Díaz. Wealthy Coahuila landowner and former Flores Magón supporter Francisco I. Madero had tried to run for the presidency against the dictator, vowing to abolish the laws that permitted re-elections. After he was arrested by the tyrant before the June 21, 1910 vote, and then released through the influence of his powerful family, Madero fled to the United States. On October 10, 1910, he issued his Plan de San Luis Potosí calling for a revolution. Unlike Flores Magón's radical focus on social and economic changes, the privileged Madero only argued for the political reforms of "effective suffrage" and "no re-election," the same changes that Díaz had called for in his Plan de Tuxtepec. Rather than envisioning true social liberty, Madero only sought a well-ordered electoral democracy.

On November 20, Madero's supporters fomented an uprising in the state of Chihuahua. Citizens throughout Mexico followed their example. Ironically, in contrast to Flores Magón and most other leaders in the Mexican Revolution, Madero—whose mild reformist call had been the immediate spark that ignited the revolution—was timid about confronting the dictatorship. As an example, Madero refused to attack Ciudad Juárez, the border city that the PLM had targeted so many times, for fear that stray bullets might fall on U.S. soil and thereby provoke U.S. intervention. Nevertheless, his general Pascual Orozco and former bandit leader Francisco "Pancho" Villa ignored his orders, taking the city on May 13, 1911. Porfirio Díaz fled for Europe on May 25. [90]

PLM REBELLIONS DURING THE MEXICAN REVOLUTION

Ricardo Flores Magón had tried many times before to foment the rebellion that would overthrow Porfirio Díaz and bring justice to the Mexican peasant and proletariat. Because he had been free only a few months before its eruption, he did not have sufficient time to coordinate PLM activities before the outbreak of the revolution. Nevertheless, Flores Magón formulated several attempts to inaugurate a true social, economic, and political revolution before and during the course of the great insurrection. He instructed PLM fighters to forestall their uprisings until the presidential election to take advantage of growing dissent and chaos. Knowing that Madero would begin his military struggle on November 20th, Flores Magón instructed many clubs to delay their attacks until this date. In the pages of the November 16th *Regeneración*, he urged his readership to rise up alongside Madero's partisans, but not to join Madero's forces.

Although Flores Magón tried his hardest to rally his supporters, he made several critical mistakes that doomed the PLM struggle. Perhaps fearing political persecution if he returned to the centers of the 1906 and 1908 uprisings, he remained in California rather than going back to Texas, where many Mexican revolutionary leaders were congregating. As well, several critics, such as Antonio Villarreal and the French anarchist journal *Les Temps Nouveaux*, would later criticize him for remaining in the U.S. rather than moving to Mexico to personally lead the insurgency. [91] Additionally, Magon's three years imprisonment and the persecution of the other PLM leaders had taken its toll on the PLM as a whole. The organization was severely debilitated by its lack of organization and poor administration. Arrests and executions had drastically reduced its membership, and government infiltration had fractured its network of cells.

Despite this organizational weakness, PLM groups initiated struggles against Díaz in several Mexican states. On June 26 in Bernardino Contla, Tlaxcala, 300 campesinos took over the town hall and arrested the political boss in the name of the PLM, but the army soon suppressed the uprising. Along the U.S.-Mexico border and in the state of Veracruz, PLM groups had been consistently corresponding with the Junta leaders and planning uprisings. On October 17, 1910, Santana Rodríguez Palafox, or "Santanón," a former bandit leader who converted to liberalism, tried to capture San Andrés Tuxtla, a city near the capital of Veracruz. However, he and his 59 troops were defeated by a rural police force and Santanón was mortally wounded.

On December 9, Práxedis Guerrero, the tireless PLM organizer, its most capable military leader, and one of its most poetic voices, went to El Paso, Texas to organize the veterans of the Las Vacas and Palomas attacks for a new assault on Chihuahua. They entered Mexico, commandeering trains and blowing up bridges. They continued recruiting soldiers and captured the village of Corralitos. Guerrero telephoned the town of Casas Grandes, ordering it to surrender immediately. After taking the village of Janos on December 29, federal troops arrived from Casas Grandes, driving out the PLM rebels and murdering Guerrero.

BAJA CALIFORNIA

Amidst its long history of failures, the PLM achieved one major success in the Mexican Revolution. It inaugurated a significant military campaign in the Mexican state of Baja California. The Junta had a number of reasons for choosing this target. Because it was relatively close to Los Angeles, Flores Magón and his cohorts could more easily coordinate an attack. As this territory was sparsely populated and contained few federal troops, the liberal movement, even in its weakened state, had a good chance of succeeding. Flores Magón also believed that the Baja peninsula had great strategic importance as a base for future attacks on the Mexican mainland.

Ricardo Flores Magón demonstrated his understanding of the international struggle against exploitation by inviting non-Mexican fighters to join in the Baja campaign. Lacking sufficient Mexican troops, especially ones with much military experience, the PLM turned to U.S. radicals for help. Flores Magón urged his supporters in Los Angeles and throughout Southern California to take up arms with the PLM. Asserting that all workers share the same struggle against authority and capitalism, he explained that one did not need to have Mexican blood to fight for the liberation of Mexico. In a manifesto directed to the Industrial Workers of the World, Flores Magón described the Mexican Revolution as the first stage in smashing tyranny and exploitation worldwide. The manifesto stated, "This formidable struggle of the two social classes in Mexico is the first act in the great universal tragedy which very soon will break upon the scene all over the planet, and whose final act will be the triumph of the magnanimous formula of Liberty, Equality, Fraternity which the bourgeois political revolutions have not been able to translate into physical reality, because these revolutions have not dared to break to pieces the dorsal spine of tyranny: capitalism and authoritarianism. ... Our cause is your cause. If you remain inactive when your brothers go to their deaths clutching the red flag, you'll give, through your inaction, a rude blow to the proletarian cause."[92]

In response to this call, the IWW and John Kenneth Turner gathered arms and ammunition and smuggled them to Mexico every way possible. Of the 500 soldiers assembled for the battle, about one-fifth were IWW members. Many U.S. socialists and members of unions such as the AFL and the WFM joined the struggle. So did several soldiers of fortune and drifters. From Europe, several Italian and Spanish anarchists came to fight for Mexican liberation. PLM emissaries also enlisted local Baja Indians from the Tarahuma tribe to rise up with them. On January 29, 1911, the PLM army captured the border city of Mexicali. From there, it continued, taking the towns of Algodones and Tecate. It eventually achieved a major victory by taking Tijuana.

Unable to tolerate the international thrust of Flores Magón's mission, various individuals used nationalistic arguments to discredit this struggle. U.S. And Mexican officials and newspapers spread the rumor that the motley crew of fighters was composed of mere "filibusters" (foreign mercenaries), fighting in Mexico to seize territory for the U.S. Los Angeles newspapers, especially the *Los Angeles Times*, published by H. G. Otis who owned the San Ysidro Ranch in Tijuana and land throughout Baja, denounced the combatants as traitors. He urged first Díaz then Madero to crush the rebellion that so greatly threatened his financial interests. Porfirio Díaz attacked the uprising as an invasion by foreigners. Madero likewise criticized the Baja fighters as "filibusters." Using such propaganda, the Mexican Counsel in Los Angeles organized reactionary Mexicans to fight against PLM supporters.

Although Flores Magón definitely did not want to seize Baja for Yankee capitalists or for the U.S. government, his struggle was embarrassed by the few who did. The Baja campaign attracted combatants with a variety of motives. Radicals who wanted to bring justice to the Mexican people or to foment worldwide anarchist revolution composed the vast majority of the PLM army. However, the struggle also attracted a few opportunists whose desires were not so noble. Some profiteers sold day passes to San Diego tourists who freely looted Mexican shops. Actor, charlatan, and adventurer Dick Ferris attempted to plant a banner in Tijuana declaring Baja to be an independent, U.S.-affiliated republic. Some have speculated that Ferris conducted his campaign at the behest of the *Los Angeles Times* publishers.[93] Similarly, soldier of fortune Carl Rhys Pryce stole funds from the PLM struggle and tried to claim the land for the British Empire. Impelled by the propaganda of the Mexican government and suspicious of the odd assortment of individuals in the PLM army, some of Baja's local population began to fight against their liberators in June 1911. Soon afterwards, Madero sent a brigade of federal troops inherited from Díaz—rather than revolutionary soldiers who might have refuse to fight, or might even join, the PLM—to capture Tijuana, thereby cementing his rule over the Mexican nation.

PLM BETRAYED BY MADERO AND U.S. LABOR AND SOCIALISTS

Madero's defeat of the PLM in Baja represented the culminating stage in the war between these two philosophically opposed camps and put an end to Flores Magón's hopes for military success in the Mexican Revolution. The two men had a long history. Madero had originally supported Flores Magón and other Junta leaders when they were first exiled to the U.S. in 1904. However, as Flores Magón's views became more radical and as he called for social and economic change, Madero and other moderate, wealthy liberals withdrew their support. In 1906, Madero, a committed vegetarian and spiritualist, repudiated Flores Magón's call for revolution, stating that it would be a "crime to stain the fatherland in blood."[94] Ironically, he himself was now leading the military struggle. In September 1910, barely two months before he inaugurated his battle, Madero, realizing the strength of the PLM along the border, sent a representative to Los Angeles asking Ricardo to support his election and to work with him to unseat Díaz. In return, a contemptuous Flores Magón demanded money from the privileged aristocrat to fund the PLM struggle. Madero refused and Flores Magón denounced him. After Díaz fled for Europe on May 25, 1911, soon-to-be President Madero approached Flores Magón to offer him the vice-presidency. Ricardo rebuffed this request by making the counteroffer that all revolutionary leaders should direct Mexico together until peace was finally established. Again, Madero refused.[95]

Flores Magón adamantly rejected Madero's grab for power. From the beginning of the revolution, he repeatedly attacked the Coahuilan aristocrat in all possible forums. In the pages of *Regeneración*, Flores Magón criticized the *personalismo*, the cult of personality, behind Madero and other revolutionary leaders. He emphasized that the Mexican workers and peasants must not rally behind a leader. Instead, as the sole creators of wealth, they must make the revolution themselves for their own well-being. In a circular, Flores Magón criticized Madero for fighting for only political liberty, whereas the PLM desired to expropriate plantations and factories and distribute them to the Mexican populace. In *Regener-*

ación, he asserted that, by only forwarding a reformist plan of "effective suffrage" and "no-reelection," Madero remained an advocate of the capitalist exploitation that oppressed the Mexican people.

Although events in the Mexican Revolution would prove Flores Magón's analysis to be fundamentally correct, much of the U.S. left abandoned him in favor of Madero. Leftists in the U.S. Agreed that Porfirio Díaz was a tyrant, but did not clearly understand the political situation in Mexico. As well, many were themselves too reformist to dare to dream the anarchist vision of Ricardo Flores Magón. Many powerful labor leaders among the Junta's former supporters withdrew their endorsements of the PLM. On March 11, 1911, Flores Magón solicited aid from Samuel Gompers, president of the American Federation of Labor. However, Gompers, wary of Flores Magón's radicalism, refused to provide any support until the PLM clearly articulated its revolutionary agenda to him. In any case, the AFL was already planning to establish labor deals with the Madero regime.[96] Mother Jones, a key organizer of the United Mine Workers and the Western Federation of Miners, traveled to Mexico where Madero gave her the right to organize Mexican miners. When she returned in October 1911 to speak to Flores Magón, she ardently praised Madero. She asked Flores Magón to return to Mexico and make peace with him. A shocked, hostile Flores Magón proudly stated that he refused to betray his disinherited brothers. In turn, Mother Jones denounced him as an unreasonable fanatic.[97]

Not only the labor movement, but also the socialist movement became alienated from Flores Magón. The anarchist tone of his Manifesto to the Workers of the World drove many away. A socialist group in Los Angeles asked Ricardo to state clearly his political views. Although he hemmed and hawed, questioning why one would argue over "isms," Flores Magón could not conceal his libertarian ideals. In a July 1911 *International Socialist Review* essay, the socialist leader Eugene V. Debs proclaimed distinctly, "Reading between the lines I can see nothing but anarchism in this program."[98] Indeed, Debs doubted that such a total social and economic revolution would ever succeed in Mexico. Arguing that Mexicans were not class conscious, he promoted a program of political reform that would gradually propel the nation towards socialism. Even though Debs criticized the PLM ideology, he still spoke out against the unjust persecution of the PLM. In contrast, certain other socialists were downright vicious. *The New York Call* openly attacked the anarchist Junta leaders. It mocked Flores Magón for remaining secure in his Los Angeles newspaper office rather than personally joining the fight in Baja.

In the wake of so much abandonment by labor leaders and socialists, only anarchists rallied to Ricardo Flores Magón's cause. The Manifesto to the Workers of the World that had alienated so many socialists attracted many in the syndicalist IWW with its proclamation of the Mexican Revolution as the first act of the international uprising of the disinherited. Influential Russian-American anarchists Emma Goldman and Alexander Berkman spoke and wrote articles endorsing the PLM and Flores Magón's critique of Madero. Voltairine de Cleyre also contributed to these issues as the newspaper's Chicago correspondent. She continued to speak and solicit funds for the PLM, but her vigorous efforts were cut short by her untimely death on June 20, 1912. British anarchist William C. Owen became the editor of the English-language page of *Regeneración*. Owen attacked socialists for deserting Flores Magón. Goldman similarly allowed Flores Magón to defend himself in issues of her magazine, *Mother Earth*. She excoriated socialists for abandoning his cause, calling the attitude of the Socialist Party towards the Mexican Revolution "an attitude so cowardly, contemptible, and disgusting as to deserve the severest chastisement by the entire international revolutionary proletariat. Not enough that the party leaders ridicule and slander the rebels of Mexico, but they are actively playing into the hands of capitalism by their treachery to the brave fighters for Mexican liberty."[99] In addition to defending stridently the PLM's engagement in the Mexican Revolution, anarchists supported Junta leaders most fervently when they were sent to prison. Owen rallied people to fight for the liberation of these martyrs of McNeil Island. Goldman continued to remind readers and audiences of these class war convicts.

Although anarchists generally agreed with Flores Magón's political views, several criticized him harshly for his tactical decisions. Some of the Italian anarchists who had fought in Baja California complained that the campaign was not clearly guided by any anarchist principles. They further chastised Flores Magón for failing to join the troops on the peninsula. The prominent French anarchist publication *Les Temps Nouveaux* ("New Times") echoed this complaint, attacking Flores Magón for not personally leading the military campaign in Baja. Similarly, the paper attacked him because he did not clearly and unequivocally declare the anarchist nature of his struggle. Most seriously, the journal accused him of misusing donations to foment factionalism. In response, the Russian anarchist Peter Kropotkin wrote a letter to the journal, roundly condemning it for abandoning Ricardo Flores Magón. Goldman and Owen also spoke out in his defense.

Flores Magón's struggle was also debilitated by the defection of many PLM members, including several Junta leaders. In the pages of *Regeneración*,

Flores Magón warned against moderates blunting the impact of the Mexican Revolution. He urged fighters not to support Madero, for he would only bring political reform and would leave intact the oppressive structure of capitalism. Conversely, the PLM would fight for the working class and expropriate the land for the people. However, by the time the Mexican revolution broke out, Flores Magón had been so secretive about his anarchism that many Mexicans had not clearly distinguished his goals from reformist ones. Many PLM members did not plainly understand the differences between Flores Magón and Madero. The chaos of the Revolution prevented them from receiving issues of *Regeneración* that would have clarified this distinction.

Many people only saw that Madero—like Flores Magón—was fighting to overthrow Porfirio Díaz. Because Madero possessed the most powerful armies, they decided to join his struggle. Aquiles Serdán, whose father had been assassinated by the dictatorship for being an anarchist activist, probably held views as radical as Flores Magón's. Nevertheless, he fought for Madero, whose movement was stronger in his state, Puebla.[100] Madero exploited Mexicans' confusion by pretending that he was working together with the PLM. Even though there were many battles between Madero's supporters and the PLM's, rumors spread that they had joined together. More insidiously, Madero published and distributed a manifesto listing him as president and Flores Magón as vice-president. Many PLM members were fooled and enlisted as his soldiers.

In addition to this desertion by many naïve PLM troops, certain key members of the Junta broke with Flores Magón for more ideological reasons. Throughout his political career, Ricardo Flores Magón alienated many of his former comrades and supporters. One gets the impression that he was so driven by his radical vision for human liberation that he repeatedly estranged himself from people with more moderate views. He had broken with the reformist Liberal Party founder Camilo Arriaga in 1905. While he was imprisoned in Los Angeles, he began to have disagreements with other prominent Junta leaders. As mentioned above, he wrote to Práxedis Guerrero and his brother Enrique on June 13, 1908, instructing them to conceal the anarchist nature of his revolutionary plans from Manuel Sarabia and Antonio I. Villarreal, because they would not be radical enough to accept it. His partisanship became even more explicit in an October 1908 letter to his common-law wife's daughter, Lucía Norman. He wrote, "Antonio is no longer a member of the Junta, and shortly Manuel will not be either"[101]

Not only philosophical differences, but also pragmatic considerations prompted several Junta leaders to part ways with Flores Magón. Juan Sarabia,

Manuel Sarabia, and Antonio I. Villarreal all hoped to be involved personally in the rebuilding of Mexico after Díaz's ouster. They realized that they would have to abandon Flores Magón for the victorious Madero if they wanted any influence over that process. After Madero freed Juan Sarabia from the Mexican prison San Juan de Ulúa, Sarabia wrote an open letter to the socialist *New York Call* denouncing Ricardo for forcing anarchism on Mexico. He further claimed that Flores Magón's politics were too personal, and that he was too moody and too unstable to be an authentic revolutionary. Similarly, Sarabia's cousin Manuel wrote an article denouncing Ricardo for being too authoritarian a leader.

On a February evening in 1911, Antonio I. Villarreal and Ricardo Flores Magón discussed the Mexican Revolution at the Turners' home in Los Angeles. As the discussion progressed, their disagreements became more heated and they soon began denouncing each other. After a few minutes, an enraged Villarreal leapt to his feet, put on his hat, raced down the stairs, and stormed out of the house to join Madero's movement.[102] Once in Mexico, Villarreal published nasty articles denouncing Flores Magón for not actively fighting in the revolution. He further insulted him as a "blackguard, swindler, coward and degenerate" who "shared his mistress with all men of bad taste." Villarreal challenged Flores Magón to a fight, saying "if I capture him, I will spit in his face and send him to a madhouse."[103]

Rather than trying to restore any sense of dignity to these squabbles, Flores Magón's responses sustained the baseness of this partisan conflict. In an open letter in the July 2, 1911 issue of *Regeneración*, he denounced Juan Sarabia as a Judas who had sacrificed the welfare of the humble people of Mexico for the gold of Madero. Even more savagely, he heaped accusations upon Villarreal, calling him an assassin and a homosexual with a particular penchant for young boys.[104]

In addition to the vicious denunciations by former comrades who had left him for Madero, Madero himself employed a number of treacherous tactics to undermine Flores Magón's revolutionary efforts. During February 1911, Madero entered Mexico from his exile in Texas. He tried to capture Zaragoza, Chihuahua, but soon became lost and confused in the harsh desert. He asked PLM general Prisciliano Silva, who had recently seized nearby Guadalupe, for help and for troops. Silva sent emissaries and food to assist Madero. Silva's lieutenant Lázaro Gutiérrez de Lara also arrived in Guadalupe with reinforcements from the border. When Madero came with his troops to meet them, he arrogantly demanded that the two men and their armies join his forces. Gutiérrez de Lara, a socialist, joined Madero's cause. When Silva refused to betray his principles, Madero arrested him.

Madero not only undermined the PLM's military efforts, he used several underhanded schemes to attack Flores Magón personally. On June 13, 1911, Madero sent Juan Sarabia and Ricardo's own brother, the lawyer Jesús Flores Magón, to negotiate a peace with Ricardo and Enrique. The two emissaries asked them to terminate the PLM's independent struggle, to join forces with Madero, and to end the conflict in Baja. Enrique exploded with rage, and Ricardo flatly rejected their proposal. According to Ricardo, Sarabia then threatened them "If you do not cooperate with us, *I will do all the harm that is possible.*"[105] Indeed, Madero had already indicated to U.S. Authorities that he approved of the apprehension of Ricardo Flores Magón. By this time, the U.S. government wanted to eliminate anarchism by apprehending or exiling all anarchist leaders such as Flores Magón and to shut down all anarchist media outlets such as *Regeneración*.[106] The day after Juan Sarabia and Jesús Flores Magón's visit, U.S. Authorities raided the offices of the paper, arresting Ricardo Flores Magón, Enrique Flores Magón, Librado Rivera, and Anselmo L. Figueroa on seven counts of violating the neutrality laws in Baja.

To add insult to injury, Madero's supporters co-opted the radical message of Ricardo Flores Magón in a most dramatic way. A few of Flores Magón's former collaborators in the liberal party and the PLM, such as Juan Sarabia, Antonio I. Villarreal, Jesús Flores Magón, and Camilo Arriaga, published a newspaper entitled *Regeneración* in Mexico City during August 1911. This paper, which Ricardo mocked as "Degeneración," did not last long. Nevertheless, it indicated that Madero still needed to claim the legacy of Ricardo Flores Magón to forward his own agenda. This process of appropriating a radical tradition to forward a moderate, even conservative, agenda was repeated throughout the Mexican revolution. It is still being perpetuated in Mexico today.

MANIFESTO OF SEPTEMBER 23, 1911

Reacting to the many attacks on the PLM, Ricardo Flores Magón issued the radical Manifesto of the Organizing Junta of the Mexican Liberal Party on September 23, 1911. Thousands of copies were distributed throughout Mexico. For too long, the PLM had been fighting under the banner of the 1906 Program. Because this document proposed only making reforms to the government, many PLM members mistakenly associated their party's goals with the moderate aims of Madero. The French anarchist journal *Les Temps Nouveaux*, among others, had criticized Flores Magón for employing this document instead of one that more clearly proclaimed his anarchism. By authoring the Manifesto of 23 September 1911, Flores Magón seems to have been trying to answer his critics and to stake out the most radical position for Mexico's revolutionary future. Yet, even in this document whose concepts are unmistakably anarchist-communist, Flores Magón, perhaps concerned about intimidating his potential audience, refrained from using the word "anarchism."

In the Manifesto of September 23, 1911, Flores Magón and the other PLM spokesmen laid out a remarkable vision for a utopian future. They began by explaining how the institution of private property is the source of all inequality and therefore the cause of all injustice and human misery. The Manifesto began, "The Organizing Junta of the Partido Liberal Mexicano views with sympathy your efforts to put into practice the lofty ideals of political, economic, and social emancipation, whose reign upon the earth will finally put an end to the long battle of man against man, which has its origin in the inequality of wealth born of the principle of private property."[107] The Manifesto vowed to annihilate all the institutions that serve to protect that principle: the exploitation of capitalism, the tyranny of government, and the manipulation of the church. As the Manifesto declared, "The Partido Liberal Mexicano recognizes that Authority and the Clergy are the support for the iniquity of Capital, and therefore the Organizing Junta of the Partido Liberal Mexicano has declared solemn war upon Authority, Capital, and the Clergy."[108] With the overthrow of this three-headed beast, economic equality, political liberty, and peace between men would reign. Urging Mexicans not to support an individual leader or government, the manifesto exhorted them to take back the land and the industries that rightfully belong to the people, the sole producers of all wealth.

Much of this document's model for a future society was borrowed from Peter Kropotkin's *Fields, Factories and Workshops*. Like this work, the Manifesto instructed revolutionaries to expropriate all property and to take a careful inventory of all produce and industrial goods. These resources would be distributed to all for survival until the next harvest. During this time, workers from each industry would meet with each other and with farmers to plan future production. Agricultural produce and manufactured wares would then be deposited in huge storehouses from which all could take what they needed.

Unfortunately, Flores Magón issued the Manifesto too late in the Mexican Revolution to prevent the dissipation of his radical hopes. With Madero's defeat of the PLM in Baja, the PLM military effort had essentially gasped its last breath. Around this time, Ricardo Flores Magón received positive attention from an ally who could have greatly helped him realize his utopian dream. In the state of Morelos, Emiliano Zapata revolted against Madero because Madero would not do anything to restore lands stolen from the people. Zapata had been aware of Flores Magón's crusade for a long time. He had first read *Regeneración* in 1905. Many PLM members and readers of its newspaper had joined his army. Additionally, delegates from the PLM visited him several times to discuss the revolution. Further, Zapata's Plan de Alaya, which insisted on expropriating the land for the people, borrowed many ideas and phrases from the pages of *Regeneración*. In 1912, Zapata offered Flores Magón and other PLM leaders the opportunity to move to his state of Morelos where they could freely publish and distribute their newspaper. Unfortunately, by the time he made this offer, these men were facing legal prosecution from the United States government.

THE LAST TRIALS OF RICARDO FLORES MAGÓN

The Mexican Revolution finally achieved the goal that Ricardo Flores Magón had envisioned over a decade before in Mexico City: at last, the dictator Porfirio Díaz had fled the country. However, the revolution fell far short of the ideals that Ricardo now dreamed. In stark contrast to his hopes for social and economic justice for all people, the revolution seemed only to strive for political reforms, leaving the oppression of capitalism fully intact. The privileged Madero refused to redistribute land to the virtually enslaved populace of Mexico. Additionally, because Madero's prominent family was close to a number of Díaz's ministers, especially the powerful cientifico leader José Limantour, his government retained many corrupt officials from the previous regime. Among the revolutionary chieftains, only Emiliano Zapata remained loyal to the impoverished masses of Mexico, fighting to restore land stolen from them by local aristocrats and foreign capitalists. Not only did the aims of the Mexican Revolution fall short of Flores Magón's hopes, but its fundamental orientation was deeply misguided. The masses of Mexico were tricked again and again into the mystique of *personalismo*, the cult of personality, choosing to follow one leader or another rather than fighting for their own liberation. In Flores Magón's opinion, the generals were creating a Mexico that would be fundamentally authoritarian and bourgeois-capitalist rather than anarchist and communist as it should be.

After the PLM's failure in Baja, it could no longer muster sufficient military force to fight for the liberation of all Mexicans. Although Porfirio Díaz had worried about Flores Magón's threats to his dictatorship, the corrupt, bourgeois leaders of the new regime were no longer concerned about his movement. Perhaps Flores Magón, who had regenerated the PLM struggle so many times before, could have established a significant anarchist-communist presence in the following years of the revolution. However, legal problems in his country of exile prevented him from doing much of anything. Whereas Mexico's chieftains no longer worried about Flores Magón's radical dream, the U.S. government forcefully repressed his passionate voice of dissent.

THE TRIAL OF 1912

The U.S. intended to suppress the PLM's radicalism through its June 1912 trial of Ricardo and Enrique Flores Magón, Librado Rivera, and Anselmo L. Figueroa. At the time that the four were apprehended, the political situation in Los Angeles and around Southern California was quite volatile. On June 1, 1910, metal workers in Los Angeles went on strike for the right to unionize. Harrison Gray Otis, the reactionary publisher of the *Los Angeles Times,* used his paper as a forum to attack these labor struggles. Several months later, the offices of the newspaper were bombed, killing and injuring many innocent workers. Six months later, two union officials were charged with the crime, casting a long shadow upon radical movements. In addition to this tension in Los Angeles, members of the IWW—many of whom had fought with the PLM in Baja—were dramatically confronting the authorities in San Diego. In an attempt to clean up the business district, San Diego police were attempting to suppress IWW orators who railed against the evils of government, god, and capitalism. In reaction to the city council's January 8, 1912 ordinance that prohibited all public speeches downtown, IWW members flocked to San Diego to protest and to clog up the courts. Alarmed by the massive influx of itinerant radicals, groups of San Diego citizens—often organized by business interests—formed vigilante groups which, working with local police, viciously beat the IWW out of their city. One group kidnapped Emma Goldman's lover, the bold and flamboyant Ben Reitman, using cigars to burn "IWW" in his buttocks, twisting his genitals, and covering his body with tar and sagebrush.

To confront the U.S. government's determination to quash leftist movements and to imprison anarchists, many radicals protested the arrests of the PLM spokesmen. The Turners and the IWW organized rallies and coordinated support. Emma Goldman sent copies of *Regeneración* and The Manifesto to the Workers of the World to sympathizers around the globe, soliciting their help. A Chicago support group contributed funds for the PLM defense and sent letters to Washington, DC. It also organized international support in England and Canada. In the U.S., many immigrant and U.S.-born Mexicans rallied around the imprisoned Junta leaders. Ricardo Flores Magón's wife and daughter spoke out at Los Angeles' very first public square, the Placita de Los Angeles, a popular site for Mexicans and Mexican-Americans to proclaim their views during the early history of Los Angeles. These speeches motivated crowds to attend the June 1912 trial of the persecuted Junta leaders.

Radicals boldly pronounced their support for the PLM at the Los Angeles trail. The courtroom was filled with Mexican, Mexican-American, and white radicals wearing red and black to display their solidarity. Vocal women wore banners proclaiming anarchist slogans across their breasts. Men also declared their anarchism and derided the U.S. flag. Every day, supporters outside the court clashed with police.[109] The U.S. used a number of devious tactics to convict the Junta leaders. It manufactured witnesses and utilized spies from the Mexican government. Government agents arrested most defense witnesses before they could appear in court. Attorneys also intimidated and bribed participants in the Baja revolution for their false testimony. They offered a $200 base payment plus $5 a day to Baja fighters for their perjury, and offered to drop whatever previous legal indictments they may have been facing. Flores Magon's adopted daughter Lucia grew so outraged that she interrupted one of one witness's many lies to slap him across the face. Even more dramatically, the prosecution's key witness, Jack Mosby, an IWW member and a general in Baja, bravely asserted his radical beliefs and denounced the treachery of the corrupt prosecution when called to the stand. Despite this heroic act, the court found Ricardo Flores Magón and the other defendants guilty and sentenced them to 23 months imprisonment at the federal penitentiary in McNeil Island, Washington.

This miscarriage of justice sparked one of the wildest riots in Los Angeles history.[110] Thousands of radicals demonstrated in front of the jail and courthouse chanting "Down with Taft and the USA." Magón's daughter Lucía led a group of over 2000 men and women to follow the guards who were taking the convicts to a county jail. Hundreds of policemen attacked this crowd. They beat down protesters for over an hour, arresting many. Authorities later claimed that the protest was an effort to free the prisoners.

1914: THE STRUGGLE CONTINUES

When Ricardo Flores Magón and his associates were released from jail on January 19, 1914, mass meetings in Tacoma, Seattle, Portland, San Francisco, and Southern California greeted them. Even though most of their supporters were terribly poor, they still managed to raise some money at these fundraisers. However, the military possibilities for a PLM revolution had been demolished by this time. Many fighters had been arrested or killed or died in prison. Many others had joined the forces of Madero or another leader. With no other prospects, Flores Magón returned to the role he knew best: the publisher of the newspaper *Regeneración*. While the paper had appeared sporadically under the editorship of Antonio P. Araujo while Flores Magón was in jail, it had not come out on any consistent basis.

In the first issue the Junta spokesmen published on January 31, 1914, they vowed yet again to continue their fight. By this time, Madero had been executed, but new bourgeois, reactionary "revolutionary" leaders such as Victoriano Huerta and Venustiano Carranza had taken his place. *Regeneración* opposed each new figure, typically employing the same arguments it had used against Madero. In late 1914 or early 1915, Ricardo, his brother Enrique, his wife María, her daughter Lucía, Librado Rivera, and several others founded a communal five-and-half acre farm at Edendale, known today as "Echo Park," in northeastern Los Angeles. Here they put into practice their anarchist ideals, living and working communally, growing vegetables and publishing their newspaper. Ricardo toured the area speaking about the Mexican revolution, his experiences, and his dreams for an anarchist utopia. He also extended the literary forms of anarchist discourse by writing plays and didactic stores for children and uneducated peasants.[111]

In all venues, Ricardo spoke and wrote vigorously against the Mexican tendency towards personalismo, the act of identifying a movement of liberation with a certain individual. To prevent the U.S. And Mexican PLM from dividing into different factions, he asserted that PLM members must not follow any leader, but instead must fight together for the social and economic liberation of all. When Venustiano Carranza took control of Mexico, Flores Magón exhorted his readers not to follow him, but to continue their expropriation of the land. Anarchists such as Emma Goldman supported his analysis of the Mexican Revolution as well as his desire for a worldwide social and economic revolution.

In the April 1915 issue of her journal *Mother Earth*, Goldman published Ricardo's "Manifesto to the Workers of the United States." This prophetic document foresaw many of the ultimate effects of global capitalism and of trade accords like NAFTA and the FTAA. Warning that wage slavery does not recognize national borders, the Manifesto urged all to struggle in solidarity against hunger and poverty. It stated, "To deny solidarity to the Mexican workingmen who are struggling to conquer their economic freedom is to stand against the Labor cause in general, because the cause of the wage-slave against his master has no frontiers." The Manifesto explained that a Mexico controlled by a government rather than the people would flood the U.S. with cheap labor, lowering wages. It further warned that U.S. companies would relocate their factories below the border. "The wealth of the magnates of American industry will flow into Mexico, for all the adventurers and all the exploiters; the manufacturers of the United States would be transplanted to Mexico, that would become an ideal land for business because of the cheapness of salaries, and the American workingmen will find their factories and firms in this country closed down because it will be more profitable to their bosses to open their business where they will pay twenty-five to fifty cents a day for the same kind of work for which they would have to pay two or three dollars a day in this country."[112]

While anarchists understood Flores Magón's prophetic message, many other leftists believed that he was jealous that another individual was now ruling Mexico. Just like Francisco I. Madero had done years before, President Venustiano Carranza duped many U.S. labor and socialist leaders with false promises of reform. After Carranza allowed AFL president Samuel Gompers to make strategic alliances with Mexican labor, the union leader wrote President Woodrow Wilson declaring Carranza a friend of labor and democracy. Even John Kenneth Turner, one of the few who had defended Flores Magón against Madero, claimed that Carranza's regime was a victory for socialism and labor. Similarly, within Mexico, many people, including many PLM members, were tired of four years of bloody fighting and supported the new president.

Carranza cleverly manipulated unions into supporting his regime. His government implemented several labor reforms, most of which were taken directly from the 1906 PLM manifesto. He legalized unions, increased wages, limited working hours, and decreed Sunday as a day off. Carranza allowed the anarcho-syndicalist Casa del Obrero Mundial to organize Mexican labor and even granted it the use of a former Jesuit convent. Tragically, the Casa returned the favor by drafting working-class men into "Red Battalions" to fight as soldiers of Carranza against the armies of Zapata, the defender of agrarian peasants. As before, Flores Magón saw through the reforms that naïve unionists and socialists embraced. Six months after Carranza came to power, he ruled that it would be treason to strike against government interests and began cracking down on unions. On August 1, 1916, he signed a law threatening striking workers with the death penalty and brutally repressed on charges of "rebellion" a general strike called by the Casa del Obrero Mundial. [113]

The U.S. government refused to tolerate Flores Magón's condemnation of Carranza and Magón's other radical statements, in part because business and political leaders were eager to establish normal working relations with the new Mexican president. Carranza further leveraged his influence by exploiting racial tensions against Ricardo Flores Magón. Economic tensions in both the white and Mexican populations in several Texas counties along the Mexican border had been polarizing both of these groups. This soon erupted into violence: In the tumult of the Mexican revolution, bandits were crossing into Texas to execute border raids. White Texas rangers and vigilante groups reacted by freely attacking Mexicans and other ethnic groups living in the United States. In turn, these oppressed people responded with similar violence. Amidst this chaos, a dissident group published a document called the "Plan de San Diego." This manifesto declared that immigrants should fight to retake the former Mexican territories of Texas, Arizona, New Mexico, and Southern California. In this land, they would establish an independent territory that would eventually rejoin the rest of Mexico. Later versions of the document encouraged blacks and Japanese to join in the struggle against the Yankee oppressor.

Carranza complained to the U.S. government and postal service that *Regeneración* was creating disruptions along the border, prompting Mexicans and Mexican-Americans to revolt against his rule. He further accused Flores Magón of being behind the raids on U.S. territory and of conspiring to create the Plan de San Diego. Several conservative newspapers, such as *The Los Angeles Times*, spread these rumors that the PLM was scheming to retake Mexican territory. Indeed, certain authors of the Plan de San Diego may very well have been inspired by *Regeneración* and other PLM propaganda. In the midst of their anti-imperialist yet nationalist declarations, they employed anarchist terminology that urged the "proletariat" to "expropriate" the land. [114] One member of the group, Aniceto Pizaña, had met Flores Magón in Laredo in 1904. He had been organizing local PLM cells before vigilante brutality drove him to join the San Diego group.

As an internationalist, Flores Magón was at best ambivalent towards the Plan. He declared that it was a "hoax" invented by the bourgeois press to distract people from the racial injustice that was the true source of the violence. However, Flores Magón used extremely incendiary rhetoric to decry the brutality of the Texas Rangers. He asserted, "Justice, not gunshots, is what should be given to the revolutionaries in Texas. And, of course, everyone should demand that these persecutions of innocent Mexicans should cease and, in regard to the revolutionaries, we should also demand that they not be shot ...Those who should be shot are the rangers and the mob of bandits who accompany them on their depredations."[115] Already concerned that the PLM might be responsible for the Plan de San Diego, government officials soon became convinced that Flores Magon intended to incite an insurrection against the United States.

THE TRIAL OF 1916

Flores Magón's insults to Carranza and his advocacy of decent treatment for Mexican-Americans again landed him in a U.S. court again. Ricardo Flores Magón had long known that the U.S. Post Office was monitoring him. A few weeks before his arrest, a postal inspector had requested copies of the September and October 1915 issues of *Regeneración*. On February 18, 1916, Ricardo Flores Magón, Enrique Flores Magón, and William C. Owen were indicted for defamation of character and for sending indecent materials through the mail, a violation of article 211 of the 1910 penal code. In particular, the U.S. government reacted against two articles by Ricardo that used inflammatory language to attack Carranza, as well the essay cited above that criticized the Texas rangers' violence towards Mexicans. Not only did President Wilson fear *Regeneración's* poisoning of U.S. relations with Mexico, but he was also concerned that its radicalism might corrupt his Preparedness Campaign, a plan to send U.S. troops to fight in World War I.

Ricardo and Enrique were apprehended on their Edendale commune. A policeman pistol whipped Enrique so severely that he had to be rushed to a hospital to stitch up his skull. Owen escaped, fleeing to Washington State. Soon after their arrests, the U.S. Post Office also denied the publishers their fourth-class newspaper mailing privileges.

As before, anarchists rallied to the aid of their Mexican comrades. In Los Angeles as well as other places, organizations such as the International Workers Defense League protested this persecution. William C. Owen decried Carranza as a lackey of Wilson who was only safeguarding the interests of U.S. capitalists in Mexico. Emma Goldman and Alexander Berkman, who criticized Wilson as a lackey of Carranza, once again spoke out against the arrests at rallies, organized meetings to free the convicts, and wrote against the injustice in their papers, *Mother Earth* and *The Blast*. Goldman and Berkman further linked these arrests to the U.S. government's repression of all radicals. After several bombings and the discovery of various bomb plots, the frightened U.S. government had stepped up its attacks on anarchists. A few months previously, Goldman herself had been arrested. Also, the ninth and tenth issues of Berkman's *The Blast* had been pulled from the mails for printing Goldman's "indecent" articles on birth control.[116]

In this repressive environment, the courts stridently attacked anarchism and anarchists. Courtroom observers were thoroughly searched for weapons. The prosecuting U.S. Attorney, Mansel G. Gallaher, directly insulted the ideals of anarchism, claiming it was tantamount to violence. He argued that the Flores Magón brothers were advocates of murder who were a threat to the nation. According to him, they were merely leeching off of poor people with their false revolutionary promises. Additionally, the judge in the case, Judge Trippet echoed the prosecution's argument by averring that the government must be able to protect itself. The brothers were found guilty on May 21. However, the judge sympathized with the poor health of Ricardo, who was so sick he could not even speak during the trial. Trippet sentenced Ricardo to a year and a day in prison, whereas his brother Enrique received three years. The judge set bail at the steep price of $3000 for Ricardo and $5000 for Enrique. Luckily, Emma Goldman was speaking against the First World War in Los Angeles at that time. Learning of the Flores Magón brothers' fate, she declared that her visit would be a failure unless they were both released. She miraculously raised the necessary funds and, on June 26, secured their release on bond pending appeal. Ricardo published an article in *Regeneración* thanking Goldman and Berkman for their numerous acts of anarchist solidarity. He then continued to speak against his persecution before the International Workers Defense League and the Severance Club, a group of prominent Southern California liberals.

THE TRIAL OF 1918

Although Enrique eventually served his sentence once all appeals were rejected, Ricardo's case never reached the court. While he was out on bail, Ricardo issued a statement that would land him in jail for the rest of his life. He believed that the outbreak of World War I indicated the downfall of the old society and that the Russian Revolution signaled the collapse of capitalism. On March 16, 1918, Ricardo Flores Magón and Librado Rivera published their Manifesto to the Members of the PLM, the Anarchists of the World, and the Workingmen in General. This document discussed the masses' discontent with the repression of government and the exploitation of capitalism, beckoning the workers to overthrow their bourgeois masters. It declared that "the death of the old society is close" and that "the death of bourgeois society won't be long in coming." It summoned people to struggle: "Comrades, the moment is solemn; this moment is the precursor of the greatest political and social cataclysm recorded in history: the insurrection of all peoples against existing social conditions."[117] Opposing the fights between working class soldiers on the battlefields of Europe, Flores Magón exhorted revolutionaries around the world to rise up against the old order to inaugurate a society that would be truly free. He urged intellectuals to prepare the masses, but again warned them against supporting any leader or government.

This statement profoundly alarmed the U.S. government. By 1917, the fighting of the Mexican Revolution had abated, so Flores Magón's agitation no longer concerned Mexico's president. However, U.S. officials worried that Flores Magón's passionate voice of dissent would impair the security of the United States. Furthermore, federal authorities feared that it would interfere with the country's engagement in World War I. President Wilson was deeply concerned that a radical U.S. working class might undermine industrial production and military expansion.

In much the same manner that George W. Bush has attempted to silence protest through the Patriot Act and other repressive measures, President Wilson embarked on a campaign to quash radicalism. In the media, he intimidated people with patriotic propaganda. In 1917, he signed the Espionage Act and the Trading with Enemies Act to suppress any and all possible voices of dissent. As a result, Emma Goldman and other anarchists were deported to Soviet Russia. The U.S. War Department further attacked "seditious" acts that might damage the nation's "vital interests." Soldiers put down strikes and raided meetings of radicals and IWW offices. All protests against the war were suppressed, and demonstrators were arrested for disloyalty and for advocating anarchy. Thousands of dissenters were thrown behind bars. Socialist and anarchist newspapers were banned.

As Mexicans, Ricardo Flores Magón and Librado Rivera had yet another strike against them. In 1917, the U.S. learned of the so-called Zimmerman telegram. In this document, the German government offered the Mexican government the return of its former territory in the U.S. in exchange for its aid in World War I. Although the PLM was definitely not involved in this scheme, this communication prompted U.S. Authorities to pay special attention to Mexican dissidents.

For writing and distributing the Manifesto to the Members of the PLM, the Anarchists of the World and the Workingmen in General, Ricardo Flores Magón and Librado Rivera were indicted for violations of the Espionage Act on March 21, 1918, less than a week after the Manifesto's publication. The government accused the two of participating in a conspiracy to foment insubordination and disloyalty, and of obstructing the recruitment of soldiers. They were also arraigned for violating the Trading with Enemies Act. This edict made it illegal to print any news item or editorial in a foreign language without first filing a translation. The U.S. postmaster, who had been monitoring *Regeneración* for a long time, averred that no translation had been received. Finally, the men were again charged with violating section 211 of the 1910 penal code that made it illegal to distribute indecent materials through the mail.

The government argued that the Manifesto's declaration of the death of the old society would cause dissension among the working class. It feared that the document's proclamation that the working class has no interests in protecting a nation owned by the rich would create strikes that would paralyze the industrial production necessary for the war. U.S. Authorities believed it would further reduce recruitment with its poignant lament over the "son sent off to war ... [who] will be yanked from the loving breast of the family to confront, gun in hand, another youth who is, like him, the light of his home, and whom he does not hate and cannot hate, because he does not even know him."[118] Prosecuting attorneys argued that Flores Magón and Rivera intended to overthrow the U.S. government and to disrupt the war effort, thereby aiding the enemy's cause.

To corroborate this image of the defendants as a threat to national security, government attorneys introduced a speech pronounced by Flores Magón on May 27, 1917 in defense of two comrades. These two men, Raul Palma and Odilon Luna, were being threatened with deportation for being anarchists who dared to speak out against the war. Therefore, both men—like so many others during this period—were being persecuted for violating two separate articles of anti-radical legislation. President Wilson's 1917 Espionage Act had effectively forbidden any public statements opposing the First World War. President Roosevelt's 1903 decree had stipulated the deportation of foreign anarchists.

In his speech, Flores Magón boldly defended the right of all to speak freely. "It is precisely because the country is engaged in a war ... that we must talk, and must talk high and loud, hurt whom it may and no matter what the consequence of our words may be." Indeed, Flores Magón used this discourse as a forum to declare his opposition to the war and to question the objectives and values that motivated it. After asserting that Carranza was merely the "lackey of Wilson and of the bandits of Wall Street," Flores Magón explained how the working class was being slaughtered to serve the interests of the vampiric capitalist class: "We shall give our blood in the trenches so that our masters may debauch in banquets, the product of our sacrifice."[119] Given this additional piece of inflammatory evidence, the prosecution argued that Flores Magón and Rivera would threaten the war effort and that their anarchism would be a direct threat to the US government.

The presiding judge, Benjamin F. Bledsoe, inveighed even more vigorously against the defendants. Bledsoe had already disclosed his reactionary tendencies by banning the Hollywood movie *The Spirit of '76*, which explored the revolutionary conflict between the American colonies and their current ally, England. The judge openly ridiculed anarchism before the jury, praising the great Anglo-Saxon system of law as the proper ideal.[120] Echoing the current Patriot Act, Judge Bledsoe explained that national security took precedence over free speech. He affirmed that dangerous times require extraordinary measures to safeguard the state and society. The jury only needed two hours to render its guilty verdict. Unlike the judge in his 1916 trial, Bledsoe felt no concern for Flores Magón's frail health, sentencing him, a dangerous radical with a long criminal record, to 20 years in prison. Ricardo immediately realized that he would not survive prison to see the light of day ever again. Although the defense filed an appeal, it was denied by the court, which affirmed its disdain for the Mexicans' calls for violent revolution.

The U.S. government not only desired to silence the Mexican and Mexican-American radical voice, but also to dissuade the many women who had joined dissident groups. On June 13, 1918, just as the court was concluding its case against Flores Magón and Rivera, Judge Bledsoe ordered the arrest of Ricardo's wife María. She had replaced Enrique Flores Magón after he had resigned from the editorial board of *Regeneración*. In this position, according to the Bledsoe, she had violated the same laws as her husband: she had placed copies of the indecent foreign-language newspaper in the mails without first filing a translation. Furthermore, she had included one of her own statements along with the mailed copies of the 1918 Manifesto. This letter had asserted that the war was being waged in the interests of capitalists and tyrants, and was therefore meaningless to the working class. Her statements had freely mocked the U.S. government, its flag, and its military. According to the judge, María had additionally violated the Trading With Enemies Act by sending copies of the 1918 Manifesto to Peru and Cuba. After her initial arraignment, María was released on bail. Luckily, the government never brought her to trial. Once the allied forces won the war and her husband was safely behind bars, the government no longer cared about prosecuting her.

FLORES MAGÓN'S FINAL DAYS IN PRISON

Ricardo Flores Magón and Librado Rivera were initially sent back to McNeil Island, but Flores Magón was soon transferred to the drier climate of Leavenworth Penitentiary because of his failing health. Rivera followed soon afterwards. Suffering profound emotional desolation and suffering from headaches, rheumatism, bronchitis, and encroaching blindness, Flores Magón turned to the only pursuit that had ever brought him joy: expressing himself through writing. Through his voluminous correspondence, he remained engaged in historical, political, and literary developments. Flores Magón encouraged anarchists to join the syndicalist movement, which would be the nexus of production in the ideal world of the future. He discussed current events, condemning the Russian revolution for erecting a communist dictatorship. In many of his letters, he reflected on his life and his ideals. Although his ambitions had been frustrated many times, Flores Magón never regretted his oftentimes tragic role as a prophet of liberation. "My former comrades are practical men, while I am only a dreamer, and this, therefore, is my own fault. They have been the ant and I the cicada; while they have counted dollars, I have spent time counting the stars. I would like to make a man out of each human animal; they, more practical, have made an animal out of each man and have made themselves pastors of the flock. Nevertheless, I prefer to be a dreamer than a practical man." [121]

Flores Magón continued to hope that true social and economic liberty would soon be achieved. "History is already writing the last lines of the period which had as its cradle the ruins of the Bastille, and is about to open a new period, whose first chapter will be known by generations to come as the groping of the human race upon the road to freedom." [122] In one of his last letters, he again asserted his faith in a utopian future of worldwide freedom, brotherhood, equality, and peace. "Not a prison, not a courthouse, not a capital building offend the sweet, tranquil beauty of the City of Peace. ... Its wondrous vernacular is full of words capable of expressing the subtlest and most elusive emotions, there is no meaning for the words Master and Slave, Charity and Piety, Authority and Obedience." [123] He described the life in this ideal world, "I watch the happy throngs of the City of Peace. ... These blessed people have found the way of making a pleasure out of work by suppressing the parasites and by becoming themselves the owners and the workers at the same time. Some of them are going to work, some of them are going merry making, but all of them bear the same radiant countenance, for work and play are now synonymous." [124]

Just as Flores Magón expressed his passionate beliefs to his distant correspondents, he engaged other prisoners in profound historical, political, and literary discussions. He helped educate other convicts and remained close to literature by working quietly as the prison librarian. Flores Magón was widely revered by the many PLM and other Mexican convicts in Leavenworth. According to Gilbert O'Day, they would have done anything to ease the suffering of this slowly dying man, this man who had so bravely fought for their dignity through his words and actions. "There was not a Mexican worker in that prison—and there were many—who would not have laid down his life to give Magón a free and easy hour."[125] The many white U.S. radicals in Leavenworth also deeply respected this profoundly sincere anarchist. The great IWW organizer and songwriter Ralph Chaplin stated that Flores Magón impressed all as being "the highest type of revolutionary idealist,"[126] further describing him as "gentler and fiercer by nature than any man I had ever met."[127]

Activists in both Mexico and the U.S. fought to secure the freedom of Flores Magón and Rivera. Anarchist, communist, and other leftist groups in Mexico demanded that their new president, Alvaro Obregón, pressure the U.S. to free the men. People tried to boycott U.S. goods so that its government would liberate Flores Magón and Rivera. Throughout Mexico, various labor unions called strikes to protest their imprisonment. On May Day, 1922, the anarcho-syndicalist Confederación General de Trabajadores demonstrated loudly before the U.S. consulate in Mexico City against the persecution of Flores Magón and Rivera.[128] Workers in the state of Veracruz held an uncanny silent protest before the U.S. consul.[129] On November 8, 1922, workers closed ports along the Atlantic coasts of Veracruz and the Yucatan.

Although Obregón's government gave lip service to the concerns of the Mexican left, he did not push the U.S. to liberate the convicts. His government was courting U.S. political and business support, so he feared alienating the *norteamericanos*. He was also unsure what the radicals Flores Magón and Rivera might do in the nation he now controlled. Unable to secure their liberty, one congressional deputy, Antonio Díaz Soto y Gama, Flores Magón and Rivera's old Liberal Party cohort and a former spokesman for Emiliano Zapata, requested that the Mexican government offer them a pension. The prisoners, however, refused the money, stating that they could not in good conscience accept money stolen from the labor of Mexico's working class. On the other hand, they gladly received contributions from the many humble Mexican and North American workers who freely donated meager yet essential sums.

As in Mexico, radicals in the U.S. Also struggled to liberate Ricardo Flores Magón and Librado Rivera. Members of the immigrant and U.S.-born Mexican community were educated about the legacy of Ricardo Flores Magón and the PLM. White U.S. radicals also continued to publicize his unjust imprisonment. They sent letters to President Wilson asking that Flores Magón and all other political prisoners be freed now that the war had been won. Others petitioned the government to release Flores Magón because of his poor health, or at least to make sure the prison took proper care of this very sick man. As Flores Magón realized, the inhuman, bureaucratic prison machine regarded him as merely a number, #14596, locked away in a cell; and it would allow him to wither away. Even Senator Henry Cabot Lodge and the ACLU petitioned for Flores Magón and Rivera's freedom, but to no avail.

The radical lawyer Harry Weinberger, who had defended the great anarchists Emma Goldman and Alexander Berkman on many occasions, also tried to aid the imprisoned men in numerous ways. He repeatedly pressured the prison to take better care of Flores Magón's physical condition. Emphasizing Flores Magón's fundamental idealism as well as his sickness, Weinberger wrote and even traveled to Washington, DC to solicit a pardon. The Attorney General informed him that a pardon would only be granted if Flores Magón and Rivera accepted the political institutions of the U.S. Naturally, the two convicts refused to accede to this demand, because it would require them to renounce the ideals they so passionately believed in. In any case, the U.S. government, like the Mexican, felt safer having Flores Magón remain behind bars. It feared that his voice would help rebuild the anarchist movement that it had just crushed. It further worried that Flores Magón would radicalize immigrant and U.S.-born Mexicans, whose voices were already alarming authorities in the West and Southwest where they were protesting their exploitation.

THE LAST GASPS OF A PROPHET

Despite protests in Mexico and the U.S., Flores Magón continued to rot away in his jail cell, becoming progressively sicker and losing almost a third of his weight. At five o'clock in the morning on November 21, 1922, Leavenworth Penitentiary pronounced the death of Ricardo Flores Magón. Prison doctors stated that the cause was cardiac arrest. However, the bruises around his neck and his contorted facial features seemed to indicate that he had died in a struggle. Among others, Flores Magón's old comrade, Librado Rivera, believed a guard had strangled him to death. A fellow Leavenworth convict, the socialist leader Eugene V. Debs, later remarked that, in any case, Ricardo was executed through slow torture by the U.S. government. The many Mexican prisoners in Leavenworth deeply resented the death of their hero. One PLM supporter, Jose Martínez, knifed the notoriously brutal guard, A. H. "John Bull" Leonard, who he believed had murdered Flores Magón. In turn, Martínez was killed by seven other guards.[130]

Thanks to the efforts of U.S. And Mexican activists, Ricardo Flores Magón's body would not be condemned to the burial fields of Leavenworth, Kansas, nor would his dream be forgotten in Mexico. The wealthy radical Kate Crane Gartz and other sympathetic contributors funded the transportation of Flores Magón's corpse from Leavenworth to Los Angeles for burial. Hundreds of Mexican, Mexican-American, and white workers and radicals met his body in Los Angeles. His wife María argued that this man who had fought for so long for Mexican liberation should be buried in the country of his birth. However, she refused the Mexican government's offer of assistance to bring back the body of this man who had struggled so long against all governments. Instead, the Mexican Federation of Railroad Unions offered to deliver Flores Magón to Mexico City. The train bearing his coffin stopped at towns along the way. At each site, crowds formed to meet the casket and carry it through the streets.

Since his death, Mexican governments have sought to co-opt the legacy of Ricardo Flores Magón. By the time his body arrived in Mexico, the revolution had ended and new leaders were safely in power. The new corrupt, authoritarian rulers tried to assume the mantle of the revolution to grant themselves legitimacy. Politicians used the death of Ricardo Flores Magón, a man who felt only disgust toward them while alive, to bolster their own careers. They may have been inspired by the example of Ricardo's old Liberal Party comrade, Antonio Díaz Soto y Gama. On hearing of Flores Magón's death, Díaz Soto y Gama delivered a powerful eulogy before the House of Deputies. Although he carefully worded this speech, he may, ironically, have contributed to a cult of personality, or *personalismo*, surrounding Flores Magón by framing him as the true precursor and intellectual author of the Mexican Revolution.[131]

Following Díaz Soto y Gama's example, eager politicians greeted Flores Magón's corpse in their towns with reverential odes. When he finally returned to Mexico City on January 16, 1923, the Mexican government gave him a massive state funeral. Yet the workers and peasants also responded to the death of this man who had loved and fought for them. Supporters garbed in the anarchist colors, red and black, filled the streets singing revolutionary anthems such as the "Marseilles" and the "Internationale."

Years later, a new deeply corrupt, authoritarian, and oftentimes brutal political party, the Partido Revolucionario Institucional, appropriated the mystique of the Mexican Revolution. Even though this political party lorded over the nation for over half a century, it tried to affiliate itself with a man who despised all governments. In 1945, the PRI transferred the body of Ricardo Flores Magón to the Rotunda of Illustrious Men, where it is currently enshrined. Ironically, this tomb is quite close to the place where Ricardo was first arrested during the student protests of 1892.[132]

Despite the Mexican government's manipulations, Ricardo Flores Magón continues to inspire anarchists and other radicals throughout Mexico and the entire world. Shortly after his death, his longtime comrade and avid supporter, Nicolás T. Bernal, formed the Grupo Cultural "Ricardo Flores Magón" that began publishing his collected works. Mexican workers and prominent politicians, including Flores Magón's old associate Antonio Villarreal, offered their assistance to this project. The Grupo Cultural issued the first biography of Flores Magón, *Ricardo Flores Magón, el apóstol de la revolución mexicana* in 1925. The author of this work, Diego Abad de Santillan, later became a prominent member of the Confederación Nacional del Trabajo/Federación Anarquista Ibérica during the Spanish Civil War and Revolution in the 1930s.

And Ricardo Flores Magón's influence lived on in Latin America. By 1926, the Nicaraguan peasant Augusto "César" Sandino had devoured the works of Flores Magón, inspiring him during the 1920s and 1930s to lead a libertarian revolt against the corrupt government of his country.

In Mexico, leftists have always rallied to the revolutionary example of Ricardo Flores Magón. During the student and labor protests of 1968, one spokesman praised the example of Ricardo Flores Magón in contrast to Mexican President Gustavo Díaz Ordaz, a member of the Institutional Revolutionary Party. The orator cried out the question: "¿Fue Flores Magón un vende patria?" ("Was Flores Magón a seller-out of his country?") The quarter-of-a-million protesters proudly responded "No!"[132] In the 1980s, Chantal López and Omar Cortés formed the publishing house Ediciones Antorcha < www.antorcha.net > that has published many works by and about Flores Magón, inspiring a new generation to embrace this revolutionary writer and activist.

More recently, indigenous groups in Flores Magón's home state of Oaxaca have formed the Consejo Indígena Popular de Oaxaca—Ricardo Flores Magón (CIPO-RFM), the Coordinación Oaxaca Magonista Popular Antineoliberal (COMPA), and the Alianza Magonista Zapatista (AMZ) to fight for their political, social, economic, and environmental rights. These groups have been demonstrating against the Mexican federal and the Oaxacan state governments' attacks on their communities. However, their villages are still being attacked. It's a familiar story: massacres of campesinos by paramilitary goons funded by the large land-owners, with the massacres all but ignored by the PRI state government; death threats against and assassinations of indigenous activists by the same paramilitaries; brutal attacks on demonstrators by the police, and the arrests of the brutalized demonstrators on false charges

Eighty years have passed since the death of Ricardo Flores Magón, yet Mexico's government still treats political dissidents with the same disdain as it treated Magón: many members of the CIPO-RFM and COMPA are now withering away in jail cells because they dared to speak up for their human dignity.[133] We urge activists to support our downtrodden sisters and brothers in Oaxaca and to stay informed about their plight by reading the CIPO-RFM web site < http://www.nodo50.org/cipo > and the AMZ web site < http://espora.org/amz >. We further hope that our translations of the poetic words of the great anarchist prophet Ricardo Flores Magón will inspire the English-speaking world to continue his struggle for the liberation of humanity.

NOTES

[1] Michael C Meyers, William L. Sherman, and Susan M Deeds, *The Course of Mexican History*, 6th ed. (New York: Oxford University Press, 1999), p. 276.
[2] For a fascinating discussion of Chávez López, see John M. Hart, *Anarchism and the Mexican Working Class, 1860-1931* (Austin: University of Texas Press, 1978), pp. 32-41.
[3] Ibid, p. 46.
[4] See, Meyers, Sherman, and Deeds, pp. 447-8, for a discussion on how commonly these rapes of peasant women actually occurred. According to lore, before he became a military leader during the Mexican Revolution, Francisco "Pancho" Villa turned to banditry after killing the landowner who had raped his sister.
[5] Meyers, Sherman, and Deeds, pp. 432-433.
[6] Read B. Traven's Jungle Series for a vivid description of this system of exploitation.
[7] Early biographers claim that Teodoro was a full-blooded Indian. For example, see Abad de Santillán, p. 25. However, Gonzálo Beltrán objects, claiming Teodoro did not physically resemble a Oaxacan native: he was too tall and his sons did not possess Zapotec or Mixtec facial features. See his introduction to *Antología* by Ricardo Flores Magón (Mexico: UNAM, 1970), p. vii. It is unclear who is correct: There are many different Indian tribes in Oaxaca with widely varying facial and body types. In addition, because peoples have migrated throughout history, it seems inappropriate to assume that any given individual would reflect the features of only one race.
[8] Samuel Kaplan, *Combatimos la Tirana: Conversaciones con Enrique Flores Magón* (México: Biblioteca del Instituto Nacional de Estudios Históricos de la Revolución Mexicana, 1958), p. 11
[9] Ward S. Albro, *Always a Rebel: Ricardo Flores Magón and the Mexican Revolution* (Fort Worth: Texas University Press, 1992), pp. 5-6.
[10] Kaplan, p. 21.
[11] Ricardo Flores Magón, *Correspondencia* (Compiled, introduced, and annotated by Jacinto Barrera Bassols. México: CONACULTA, 2000), volume I, p 57, footnote 1.
[12] Edith Duffy Turner, *Ricardo Flores Magón y el Partido Liberal Mexicano* (Morelia, Michoacán: Editorial "Erandi" del Gobierno del Estado, 1960), pp. 23-4.
[13] E. D. Turner, *Ricardo Flores Magón*, p. 30.
[14] Ibid, p 32.

[15] Abad de Santillán, p. 28.

[16] Quotation taken from Chantal Lopez and Omar Cortes *El Hombre de la Selva* (Mexico: Ediciones Antorcha, n.d.)

[17] E. D. Turner, *Ricardo Flores Magón*, p. 39.

[18] Ibid, pp. 41-42.

[19] Ibid, p. 52.

[20] The Italian immigrant Bartolomeo Vanzetti can also be numbered among the proud ranks of the anarchist dishwashers. See Bartolomeo Vanzetti, *Story of A Proletarian Life* (Berkeley: Kate Sharpley Library, 2001.)

[21] Contrary to this persistent rumor, Barry Pateman of the Emma Goldman Papers Project contends that no evidence exists that would place her in St. Louis during 1905. Goldman's letter to Peter Kropotkin on May 31, 1907 suggests that she met Flores Magón and the others years later in Los Angeles.

[22] See Albro, *Always a Rebel*, pp. 28-30, 104.

[23] E. D. Turner, *Ricardo Flores Magón*, p. 22.

[24] Francisco I. Madero to Ricardo Flores Magón, January 17, 1905. Cited in Albro, *Always a Rebel*, p. 27

[25] Ellen Howell Meyers, "The Mexican Liberal Party, 1903-1910." (Ph.D. dissertation, University of Virginia, 1971), pp. 41-42.

[26] Meyers, p. 99.

[27] Meyers, pp. 100-101.

[28] Meyers, p. 110.

[29] Meyers p. 97.

[30] See Alfonso Torúa Cienfuegos, *El Magonismo en Sonora (1906-1908): Historia de una persecución*. (Hermosillo: Universidad de Sonora, 2003), pp. 69-102, for a history of Palomarez and the Mayo Indians.

[31] Albro, p. 33

[32] Meyers, p. 49.

[33] Albro, *Always a Rebel*, p. 44.

[34] E. D. Turner, *Ricardo Flores Magón*, pp. 71-72.

[35] Ricardo Flores Magón, *El Sueño Alternativo* (Compiled and introduced by Fernando Zertuche Muñoz. Mexico: Fondo de Cultura Economica, 1995), p. 81. My translation.

[36] Manifesto to the Nation, July 1, 1906, p. *infra*

[37] Ibid, p.

[38] Ibid, p.

[39] Magón, *El Sueño Alternativo*, p. 85. The fact that Ricardo Flores Magón wrote these sentences seems especially distressing when one considers that his own brother, Jesus, had married Clara Hong, whom one would assume was probably Chinese given her surname.

[40] "The Organizing Junta of the Mexican Liberal Party to the Workers of the United States of America, November 7, 1914," *Mother Earth* (April 1915), p. 86.

[41] Patriotism, p. *infra*

[42] Albro, *Always a Rebel*, p. 40.

[43] E. D. Turner, *Ricardo Flores Magón*, pp. 84-5

[44] E. D. Turner, *Ricardo Flores Magón*, p. 86.

[45] Meyers, p. 83.

[46] Albro, *Always a Rebel*, p. 42.

[47] Thompson to Department of State, June 19, 1906, Department of State Record Group 59, NA, Dispatches, Vol. 183. Quoted in Albro, p. 43

[48] Albro, *Always a Rebel*, pp. 54-55.

[49] See Cienfuegos, pp. 103-126 for a vivid history of the PLM, the Yaqui Indians, and Javier Huitemea.

[50] Meyers, pp. 145-146.

[51] Meyers, pp. 147-8

[52] Meyers, p. 148-149

[53] Meyers, pp. 149-150.

[54] Meyers, p. 151.

[55] E. D. Turner, *Ricardo Flores Magón*, pp. 110-113. My translation

[56] E. D. Turner, *Ricardo Flores Magón*, p. 113.

[57] Albro, *Always a Rebel*, pp. 65-66.

[58] Turner, *Ricardo Flores Magón*, pp. 120-123.

[59] Flores Magón to Antonio P. Araujo December 25, 1906. In *Correspondencia* (volume I), pp. 223-224.

[60] Meyers, p. 207

[61] See, in particular, Friedrich Nietzsche's *Genealogy of Morals* (translated by Walter Kaufmann. New York: Viking Press, 1967.) Neither Flores Magón nor any of the secondary literature ever mentions him reading Nietzsche. However, Flores Magón was a voracious reader of world literature, so it would not be surprising if he had consumed Nietzsche's works. In any case, Nietzschean ideas were definitely part of the intellectual culture of the early twentieth century, and prominent anarchists such as Emma Goldman wrote and delivered lectures about him.

[62] Clarion Call of Combat, p. *infra.*

[63] Go Towards Life, p. *infra*

[64] Go Towards Life, p. *infra*

[65] Albro, *Always a Rebel*, p. 90, 97.

[66] See Colin M. MacLachlan's critique of the WFM's legal representation of Flores Magón and his comrades. He asserts, "The WFM used [the trial] … [to] acquire some painless martyrdom at the expense of the PLM's leadership." See Colin Maclachlan, *Anarchism and the Mexican Revolution: The Political Trials of Ricardo Flores Magón in the United States* (Berkeley: University of California Press, 1991), pp. 27-29. See also Albro, p. 97.

[67] Meyers, pp. 249-251.

[68] Letter from L.A. County Jail, June 13, 1908, p. *infra.*

[69] Ibid, p.

[70] Ibid, p.

[71] Colin M. MacLachlan argues that Flores Magon may have found even more supporters if he had clearly proclaimed his anarchism, because many Mexicans had grown quite radical in reaction to Díaz. Thinking that Flores Magon was merely proposing reformist goals, many chose to turn to another revolutionary leader such as Francisco I. Madero. See Maclachlan, p.32.

[72] Meyers, pp. 267-270.

[73] E. D. Turner, *Ricardo Flores Magón*, p. 169.

[74] Read Ward S. Albro, *To Die on Your Feet: The Life, Times, and Writings of Práxedis G. Guerrero* (Fort Worth: Texas Christian University Press, 1996) for information about this fascinating man.

[75] Meyers, p 325

[76] Ricardo Flores Magón to Enrique Flores Magón, June 7, 1908. In *Correspondencia* (volume 1), pp. 454-462.

[77] Ricardo Flores Magón to María Talavera, December 6, 1908. In *Correspondencia* (volume I), pp. 499-501.

[78] Meyers, p. 229

[79] Eric Rauchway's *Murdering McKinley* (New York: Hill and Wang, 203) provides an excellent account on Roosevelt's attack on anarchism. See in particular p. 94. On March 4, 1908, *The New York Times* declared "The United States has declared a war on Anarchists." See Rauchway's article "Are We Repeating the Mistakes of the Last War on Terror" (*Financial Times*, January 21, 2003; online at http://historynewsnetwork.com/articles/1229.html) for an informative comparison of Bush and Roosevelt's repression of civil liberties

[80] MacLachlan, pp. 14-15, 26-27.

[81] MacLachlan, p. 23.

[82] MacLachlan, p. 25

[83] "Manifesto to the American People," *Mother Earth* (February 1908), pp. 546-554.

[84] Meyers, p. 331, footnote 5.

[85] To The Proletarians, p *infra.*

[86] The Revolution, p. *infra.*

[87] Sowing, p. *infra*

[88] Discord, p. *infra.*

[89] The Repercussion of a Lynching, p. *infra*.

[90] Meyers, Sherman, and Deeds, pp. 485-8

[91] MacLachlan, p. 38.

[92] Manifesto to the Workers of the World, p. *infra*.

[93] E. D. Turner and Rey Devis, *Revolution in Baja California,* pp. 44-6.

[94] Francisco I. Madero to Márquez, August 17, 1906. Cited in Albro, *Always a Rebel,* p. 62.

[95] Meyers, p. 346

[96] Albro , *Always a Rebel,* p. 130

[97] MacLachlan, pp. 36-37.

[98] Albro, *Always a Rebel,* p. 132.

[99] *Mother Earth* (July 1911), p. 131.

[100] MacLachlan, p. 33.

[101] MacLachlan, p. 33.

[102] E. D. Turner, *Ricardo Flores Magón,* p. 239.

[103] Albro, *Always a Rebel,* p. 136.

[104] Albro, *Always a Rebel,* p. 135.

[105] *Regeneración,* July 2, 1911. Translated in Ethel Turner and Rey Devis, *Revolution in Baja California,* p. 92-4.

[106] MacLachlan, p. 43.

[107] Manifesto of September 23, 1911, p. *infra*.

[108] Ibid, p.

[109] MacLachlan, pp. 44-45.

[110] Juan Gómez-Quiñones, *Sembradores: Ricardo Flores Magón y el Partido Liberal Mexicano: A Eulogy and Critique* (Los Angeles: University of California Press, 1973), p. 54.

[111] Gómez-Quiñones, p. 57.

[112] "The Organizing Junta of the Mexican Liberal Party to the Workers of the United States of America, November 7, 1914," *Mother Earth* (April 1915), pp. 85-88.

[113] Hart, *Anarchism and the Mexican Working Class,* p. 155

[114] James Sandos, *Rebellion in the Borderlands: Anarchism and the Plan of San Diego* (Norman: University of Okalahoma Press, 1992), p. 84.

[115] See "The Uprisings in Texas", p. *infra*.

[116] MacLachlan, pp. 62-65.

[117] Manifesto to the Anarchists of the Entire World and the Workers in General, p. *infra*.

[118] Manifesto to the Anarchists of the Entire World and the Workers in General, p. *infra*.

[119] Ibid, p.

[120] Regeneracion 1917. p. infra.

[121] MacLachlan, pp. 82-83.

[122] Ricardo Flores Magón to Nicolas Bernal, October 30, 1920, p. *infra*.

[123] Flores Magón to Ellen White, October 26, 1920. In *Correspondencia* (volume II), pp. 51-3

[124] Flores Magón to Ellen White, August 25, 1922. In *Correspondencia* (volume II), pp. 422-5

[125] Gilbert O'Day, "Ricardo Flores Magón." *The Nation* (December 20, 1922), p 689.

[126] Ralph Chaplin, *Wobbly: The Rough and Tumble Story of an American Radical* (Chicago: University of Chicago Press, 1948), p. 255

[127] Ibid, p. 278

[128] Hart, p. 162.

[129] MacLachlan, p. 106

[130] E. D. Turner, *Ricardo Flores Magón,* p. 342.

[131] In addition, the entire notion of "precursors" seems to be a fundamental misunderstanding of the process of history: it judges an event to be a cause in order to promote a certain ideological vision of normative inevitably.

[132] Gómez-Quiñones, p. 69.

[133] John Mason Hart, foreword to MacLachlan, *Anarchism and the Mexican Revolution,* page xiv.

[134] Read http://www.nodo50.org/cipo to learn more about the CIPO-RFM. Thanks to Professor George Salzman for informing of these developments. Thanks to Gabi and Cesar of CIPO-RFM.

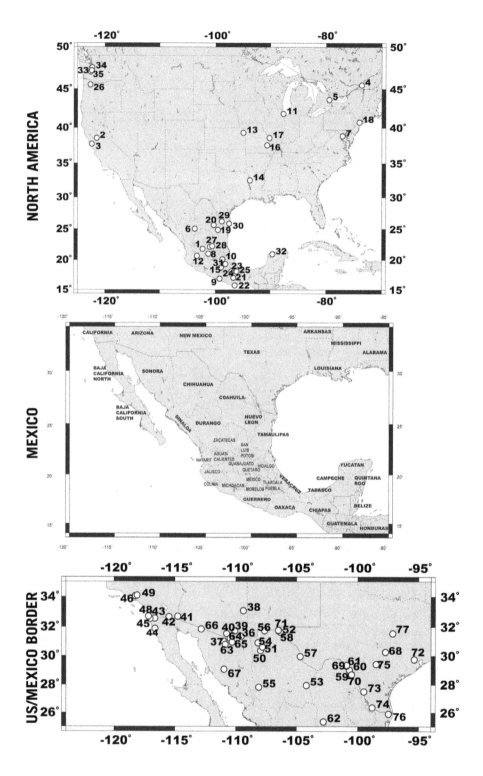

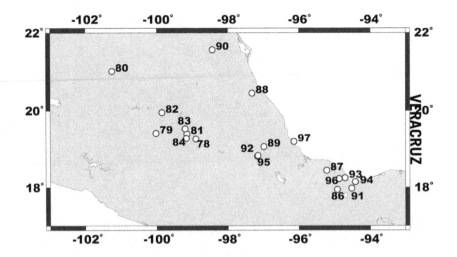

MAP KEY ORGANIZED BY NAME

Aguascalientes, Aguascalientes
Acayucán, Veracruz 86
Algodones, Baja California 41
Austin, Texas 68
Ayala, Morelos 15
Ayutla, Guerrero 9
Brownsville, Texas 76
Camargo, Tamaulipas 29
Cananea, Sonora 65
Casas Grandes, Chihuahua 50
Chalco, Mexico 78
Chicago, Illinois 11
Ciudad Juarez, Chihuahua 52
Ciudad Porfirio Díaz, Coahuila 34
Corralitos, Chihuahua 51
Del Rio, Texas 69
Dolores, Mexico 79
Douglas, Arizona 36
Duranzo, Sonora 64
Eagle Pass, Texas 70
El Paso, Texas 71
Ensenada, Baja Californai 44
Guadalajara, Jalisco 12
Guadalupe, Chihuahua 53
Guanajuato, Guanajuato 8
Guanajuato, Mexico 80
Hermosillo, Sonora 67
Houston, Texas 72
Imuris, Sonora 63
Ironton, Missouri 16
Ixhuatlán, Veracruz 89
Janos, Chihuahua 54

Jimenez, Coahuila 60
Lampazos, Nuevo Leon 19
Laredo, Texas 73
Las Vacas, Coahuila 61
Leavenworth, Kansas 13
Los Angeles, California 46
Matamoros, Tamaulipas 30
Matamoros, Veracruz 90
McNeil Island, Washington 33
Merida, Yucatan 32
Mexicali, Baja California 42
Mexico City, Mexico 81
Minatitlán, Veracruz 91
Monterrey, Nuevo Leon 20
Montreal, Canada 4
Morenci, Arizona 38
Mowry, Arizona 37
New York City, New York 18
Nogales, Veracruz 92
Oaxaca City, Oaxaca 21
Orizaba, Chihuahua 55
Pachuca, Hidalgo 10
Pajapán, Veracruz 93
Palomas, Chihuahua 56
Papantla, Veracruz 88
Patagonia, Arizona 40
Pochutla, Oaxaca 22
Portland, Oregon 26
Puerto México, Veracruz 94
Rio Blanco, Veracruz 95
Rio Grande City, Texas 74
Sacramento, California 2

Saint Louis, Missouri 17
San Andres Tuxtla, Veracruz 87
San Antonio Eloxochitlán, Oaxaca 23
San Antonio, Texas 75
San Bernardino Contla, Tlaxcala 31
San Diego, California 48
San Francisco, California 3
San Gabriel, California 49
San Luis Potosi, San Luis Potosi 27
San Miguel, Mexico 82
San Nicolas Tolentino, San Luis Potosi 28
San Pedro Soteapán, Veracruz 96
Santa Barbara, Chihuahua 57
Seattle, Washington 34
Shreveport, Louisiana 14
Sonotya, Sonora 66
Tacoma, Washington 35
Tecate, Baja California 43
Teotitlán del Camino, Oaxaca 24
Tijuana, Baja California 45
Tlalnepantla, Mexico 83
Tlalpan, Mexico 84
Tombstone, Arizona 39
Toronto, Canada 5
Tuxtepec, Oaxaca 25
Veracruz, Veracruz 97
Verlardena, Durango 6
Viesca, Coahuila 62
Waco, Texas 77
Washington, DC 7
Zaragoza, Chihuahua 58

"Student Riot," by José Guadalupe Posada. This depicts the 1892 anti-reelection student demonstrations in Mexico City, in which the Magón brothers participated.

LETTER TO MARIA
OCTOBER 25, 1908

(Translated by C.B.)

Maria:

I anxiously await Saturdays so that I can see your little letters, my love. All week I've been waiting to see if you show up, from my cell through the window on the alley, which is the third window. Who did I see on Thursday between four and five but my little daughter Lucia [Norman], but she passed by without stopping. When you all pass by the third window on the alley, stop if only for a half minute so that I can see you well. My dear: I feel that you are feeling a bit of pain. Would some of my kisses where you hurt make it well? I would give them so tenderly that you'd feel no discomfort. I know, my life, I understand that you miss me as much as I miss you. But what can be done? More than the tyrants, it is our friends who are keeping us in jail, because their laziness, their indolence, their lack of initiative has them tied up, and they do nothing. I believe that they love us and have us in their hearts; but this isn't enough to rescue us. What's needed is that they work in an effective manner for our liberation, and they're not doing that. Everyone comes forth in manifesting their sympathy for us and deploring our situation. We are devoting ourselves to putting an end to the tyrant in Mexico and nobody will lift an arm to stop the tyrant's henchmen. There is much that could be done in our favor, but little or nothing is being done, and nothing, of course, is being gained. There should be a commission that is constantly after the press so that something could appear favorable to the prisoners, as much in the local press as that outside of California, taking advantage not only of the workers' press but also that of the capitalist press. Another commission could take charge of agitating in every union in the United States in our favor; but all of this would have to be done constantly. Another commission could take charge of organizing meetings in which the only topic would be the prisoners and the infamies which have been committed against us. If this would be done with persistence, we would walk free, and soon. If this would have been done a year ago, we would have been free for some time. I repeat, if nothing practical is done, the sympathy of our friends will do nothing for us. When will something practical be done? Perhaps never. . . . Goodbye my love, look closely and you'll see that it is our friends who are keeping us prisoner through their apathy. Receive my immense love and adoration, you, the only woman who makes my heart beat. What I've told you isn't a reproach for you, my angel. You're doing everything you can, and I thank you

---

from my soul. If you don't win in this struggle against despotism and do not rescue your Ricardo who loves and adores you, it won't have been for lack of effort on your part. With all my soul, your Ricardo kisses you tenderly.

LETTER FROM L.A. COUNTY JAIL
June 13, 1908

(Translated by C.B.)

I'm writing this letter to you on June 13, 1908, dear brothers Práxedis and Enrique, to bring to your attention a matter of which I've already informed our comrade Librado [Rivera], and he's in agreement. Let's get to the point.

You know as well as I do that no revolution has ever managed to prevail after the triumph and make practical the ideals which inflamed the revolution, and this has happened because it was entrusted to the new government to do what the people should have done during the revolution.

It has always happened the same way. In all parts a banner has been raised bearing reforms of more or less importance; the humble unite around it; there is fighting; blood flows more or less abundantly, and if the revolution triumphs, a new congress meets entrusted with transforming into law the ideals that caused the people to take up arms and fight. To the congress come individuals with all types of ideals, some advanced, others retrograde, still others moderate, and in the struggle between these tendencies the aspirations of the revolution wither, become spoiled, and after long months, when not after long years, laws are approved in which one cannot even glimpse the ideals for which the people gave their blood and for which they suffered misfortune. But suppose that by some miracle laws were promulgated in which the ideals of the revolution shone in all their purity, something which has never been seen, certainly, because very few deputies have the same ideals as the people who took up arms. But let's suppose that the miracle became reality and in the special case of our struggle the congress ordered the distribution of the lands, the eight-hour day, and a wage of no less than a peso. Could we hope that the landholders would cross their arms and let escape that which makes them powerful and permits them to live in idleness? The owners of all types of enterprises where workers arms are employed, wouldn't they close their businesses or, at the least, wouldn't they diminish the number of workers they employ in order to force the government to revoke the law under the threat of the hunger of the people, feigning that it's materially impossible to pay more for fewer hours of work?

With their resources exhausted by the revolution, the people would find themselves in a condition more difficult than that under which they found themselves obliged to revolt. The people, without bread, would listen to the words of the bourgeoisie, who would tell them that they had been fooled, and who would lead the charge to overthrow the new government, with which some of them would save themselves from the loss of their lands and others from making concessions to the workers.

The rich would rebel if there would be an attempt to put into practice the Program of the Partido Liberal Mexicano, if, by a true and unique miracle in the history of popular revolutions, the ideals of the revolution would remain intact after the triumph.

As anarchists we know well all of this. We know well what must be expected from even the best government that weighs down on the people, and, as anarchists, we should do everything that is within our reach to make sure that the revolution that is waiting in the wings to break out gives to the people all of the benefits which it is possible to win.

To obtain great benefits for the people, real benefits, it's necessary to work as well-disguised anarchists, even from those who take us as their leaders. Everything boils down to a mere question of tactics. If from the start we would have called ourselves anarchists, no one, not even a few, would have listened. Without calling ourselves anarchists we've been placing in men's minds thoughts of hate against the possessing class and against the governmental caste. No other liberal party in the world has the anti-capitalist tendencies from which a revolution is about to break out in Mexico, and this has been achieved without our saying we are anarchists; and it wouldn't have been accomplished even if we had simply called ourselves socialists, let alone anarchists as we are. Everything, then, is a question of tactics.

We must give the lands to the people in the course of the revolution, because in this manner they won't be swindled. There's not a single government anywhere that can benefit the people contrary to the interests of the bourgeoisie. You know this well as anarchists, and therefore I don't need to demonstrate it to you through reasoning and examples. We must also give the people possession of the factories, mines, etc. In order that the entire nation doesn't turn its back on us, we should continue the same tactic that we've used with so much success: we'll continue calling ourselves liberals in the course of the revolution, but in reality we'll go on propagating anarchy and carrying out anarchist acts. We'll continue expropriating from the bourgeoisie and making restitution to the people with what we seize. I have here the means that has occurred to me, and I submit it to your attention: in virtue of the revolution, the factories, mines, workshops, etc. Are going to close their doors, not because the workers have taken up arms, because not all will take them up, but for other reasons among which could be the paralysis or diminishment of commercial transactions owing to the insecurity affecting commercial interests in times in which respect for authority has diminished, and the order in all places dominated by the revolution will be such that the workers will not be paid less than one peso per the newly established eight-hour day. The consequence of this process, due to the bourgeoisie, will be hunger, because with their stocks exhausted they won't take a step to produce more.

We shouldn't wait for hunger to arrive; therefore as soon as work stops on a hacienda, a factory closes its doors, a mine ceases to extract metal, etc., we'll invoke the public necessity that work not stop, whatever the pretext of the bosses for suspending it, and with the reason that it's necessary to renew work, to impede pauperism, we'll give to the workers the businesses that have been closed by the bourgeoisie, so that they can continue to produce on the footing of equality.

To avoid that the workers who benefit will not try to turn themselves in turn into the bourgeoisie, we'll prescribe that everyone who enters to work in these businesses will have an equal right to participate. The workers themselves will administer these businesses.

If we're dealing with haciendas, it would be unjust to give all of the land to the workers of the same because then many would remain without anything. The workers on the haciendas would be given what they could actually work, with the rest of the lands reserved so that they could be used by the rest of the poor. As the workers on the haciendas would continue to work under this plan, those who wanted lands that are presently lying idle, upon seeing the excellent results of working the land in common practiced by the redeemed peons would, in place of working the lands individually, want also to work them in common, and thus there would be no necessity to divide up the earth into parcels, saving the junta from the odious task of giving to each one who asks it a piece of land.

Even though the businesses would remain in the hands of the workers, their transfer or sale would be prohibited just as the PLM program prescribes for the lands. In this manner, work would begin again in the midst of the revolution and an anarchist work would have been accomplished through invoking the necessity that production could not cease to avoid the hunger of the masses.

It's necessary to take into account that with the workers being unable to count on money being paid them as a daily wage with which to buy the necessities of life, it's essential that they themselves establish a statistics commission which would have a registry of the available resources in each region dominated by the revolution, just as it would register the needs of the laboring masses in each region. Having this register, the workers would mutually exchange their products and would have such an excess of production that they could easily, without sacrifice, support the soldiers of the revolution. In addition, the workers would be counseled to arm themselves to defend what the revolution has given them from the assaults of the soldiers fighting for tyrants, and probably from attacks by the gringos or from other nations.

At first we shouldn't bother ourselves about the foreign bourgeoisie, not until almost the entire people have something material to defend and for which to respect themselves. When the outcasts have something to defend, we'll see that there won't be one who won't pick up a gun.

New problems will present themselves, but I don't believe that they will be difficult to solve, given that the workers themselves will be interested in the matter. There will come, also, many Spanish and Italian anarchists to see what is occurring, and they will provide useful aid. It appears to me that it would be good if one of us would take a trip during the revolution to spur those comrades to give us the valuable aid of coming to agitate the masses and directing them in every matter where direction is needed. I believe that a great many would come, even paying their own way, afterwards leaving a scattering of comrades throughout the entire nation.

Working in the manner I propose, if we don't succeed we'll at least have left the legacy of a great lesson.

I'm already tired. I'm writing in such an awkward position that my chest hurts, and, incidentally, I'm already very ill. I don't stop coughing, my back hurts and I feel bad, very bad. That which sustains me is that I'm not discouraged. The cold which is continually in this jail is aggravating my ill health. I weighed 218 pounds, and today I weigh only 178. The jail is made of iron; I never see a ray of sunshine; the cold wind blows day and night, and as sensitive as my lungs have always been, I feel that I can't stand another winter in this jail in which there is no heating for the prisoners. I have a very bad cold that hasn't left me since they threw me in jail. I'm better for two or three days at a time, but then it attacks me again with more force. At this moment I'm running a fever. The good thing is that I'm not discouraged and so I give myself strength. But back to the matter which motivates this letter.

I believe that it is necessary that many anarchists come to teach the people. Besides, it's good to reprint anarchist books and pamphlets to be distributed by the millions. We can entrust this to our friends and comrades with confidence.

I continue speaking of the same thing today, June 15, dear brothers.

There will be very crafty members of the bourgeoisie who, seeing what's happening to their comrades, will not close their businesses and then there will be no immediate pretext for taking their property. In these cases, which will be more and more frequent, the workers of these businesses will be incited to ask for "impossible" things in such a manner that the owners will be forced to close. Then the workers will take possession of the businesses.

I know that there are two ways to go, both of which would follow the path of expropriation: the junta could decree it, or, better, the workers could carry it out themselves; and in this case, which to me appears the better of the two, because it would disguise very well the anarchist character of the junta, we wouldn't have to approve *faits accompli*. The question is of bringing, once the revolution has commenced and is on foot, a great number of comrades from Europe to foster in Mexico the publication of many anarchist periodicals. As we'll have money, all of this can be done easily. Only the anarchists are going to know that we are anarchists, and we'll advise them not to call us anarchists in order not to frighten some imbecile who in the bottom of his heart harbors ideals like our own, but without knowing that they are anarchist ideals, because he is so accustomed to hearing anarchists talked about in disparaging terms. It's better that the imbeciles remain ignorant. They're not necessarily unjust.

That which is done by the workers themselves will have to be firmer, because it will be the result of conscious effort. So, then, I believe that this will be the best tactic: to agitate the workers, urging them to expropriate. The junta, prior to the carrying out of these acts, will have to approve them. In this manner we'll continue to give the catch phrase of "liberalism" to our beautiful ideals.

It appears to me that there's nothing to add to this. . . .

I also think regarding the publication of *Revolución* that the name after all is of little importance, but due to a natural romanticism it would please me if the name of the periodical would be *Regeneración*.

I now believe that the Old Man [Porfirio Díaz] will not be able to suffocate the revolution and that in the end the people will have justice.

I hope that the blood which will be shed will be fertile in producing benefits for the proletariat, and I believe that it will be if we put ourselves to something better than allying with the bourgeoisie to obtain an easy triumph; we'll obtain real liberties for the people, emancipating it economically, step by step or leap by leap, as can happen in the course of the great revolution in whose shadows we find ourselves.

I dream of great, real conquests during the revolution. We must not hesitate. It's very possible that our revolution will break the European stalemate and that those proletarians will decide to do what we've done. Perhaps if we bring to a head what I propose, the great powers of Europe will pile on us, but this will be the final act of the governmental farce, because I'm sure that our brothers on the other side of the ocean will not let us perish.

If we manage to have success during the revolution, that is, if we manage to expropriate and redistribute, it doesn't matter how many years our movement lasts.

We should strive that the great majority of leaders and revolutionary officials are more or less men of our way of thinking and, to that effect, [Teodoro María] Gaitán, like [Fernando] Palomárez, like others, [Norberto] Loya for example, could be the strength of our side, because there are many, very many, who think only of personal aggrandizement. Having control, the libertarians will achieve great things.

For leaders of the zones in which there are not now groups, we should name libertarians.

A phenomenal amount of libertarian propaganda is necessary. We should undertake to ensure that anarchist periodicals send flyers to be reprinted in Mexico with money yanked from the hands of the bourgeoisie. All this work can be undertaken by trusted friends so that the junta can continue maintaining its apparently "free" role.

Following the tactic that I propose to you in the attached letter, we will never have a better opportunity to work for the ideal than in the midst of the revolution.

I'll say goodbye.

I send a strong embrace to all, and to you, little brother, my great fraternal affection. Librado also sends you his greetings. Greetings to all.

PLM logo. The near-"socialist realist" style of the logo is typical of PLM—
and, indeed, nearly all leftist—graphics of the time.

CHAPTER 2

DOCUMENTS OF THE PLM

REGENERACIÓN

Regeneración, *August 7, 1900*

(Translated by C.B.)

NOTE: This is a fragment of a longer proclamation which is almost unreadable. It was not written by Ricardo Flores Magón and is of purely historical interest (as the founding statement of Regeneracíon*), so we're reproducing only a small fragment of it here. Its first paragraphs, reproduced here, provide a good indication of its flavor.*

This periodical is the product of a painful conviction.

In the speech pronounced in the solemn session of March 9, upon resuming the sessions of the Academia Central Mexicana de Jurisprudencia y Legislación, the attorney, Mr. Luis Mendez, wisely said: "When justice becomes corrupted, when at times decisions are reached more because of external considerations than the law itself, what should those do who exercise the noble profession of advocate or those who watch over interests that have no guarantees for their lives and development than an honest administration of justice? Shouldn't we all, in such a case, form ourselves into firm group, such as a Greek phalanx, to attack obstinate injustices?"

This is what is encountered, with very honorable exceptions, in the administration of justice in the republic; and the Greek phalanx spoken of by the honorable attorney could come crashing down, as have many others protesting against the venality of some functionaries, receiving only unjust persecutions or the obstinate injustice spoken of by Mr. Mendez.

We do not have the pretension of being a phalanx; but our youthful energy and our patriotism induce us to search for a remedy, and to that end, to point out, to denounce all those acts of judicial functionaries not in accord with the precepts of written law in order to publicly shame them into delivering deserved justice. . . .

INDEPENDENT PERIODICAL OF COMBAT

Regeneración, *December 31, 1900*

(Translated by C.B.)

Today, *Regeneración* appears as the "Independent Periodical of Combat."

As we could be dismissed as inconsequential, we'll explain to our illustrious readers the cause which has impelled us to change the overall juridic nature of this periodical.

Justice, badly administered as it has been to date, was the primary thing that induced us to found our periodical, destined to exhibit in all its deformity the arbitrariness and abuses of the abominable functionaries of the judicial branch, local, state, and federal.

Justice has been, here [Mexico City] and in the states, a slave to executives without conscience who have found in it nothing but an easy and truly comfortable means of satisfying their passion, that in a more ordinary setting would have encountered the rude opposition of the correctional judge or the fierce hand of the police.

The judiciary (there are exceptions, though they are, unfortunately, scarce), filled with nonentities from the "cientifico" and many times from the "moral" orders, are resented and continue to be resented for their failure to expedite, and what is worse, in some cases, that elsewhere abound, for lack of honesty.

Our struggle has been hard. It has had all the characteristics of a fight between dwarves and giants; alone in the struggle, finding ourselves facing at every step the livid phantasm of political indifference, we have struggled while isolated, with no other arm than our democratic ideals, and with no shield other than our profound convictions.

What might have pained us the most in our enthusiasm has been that hateful form of political cowardice: indifference, a product of the age, the age of oppression which has made the weak spirits opt for the party of force, because that's what they themselves lack and it's what will protect their cowardice, and that those other spirits, not exactly weak, but not really apt for an open, frank struggle, prefer to find in a retreat from public life a sedative for their political disappointments.

We don't shrink back before political indifference precisely because healthy ideals help us to recover, because firm convictions comfort us and we believe that we possess strong energies.

The day that we lack any of these things we'll have died of that which is called "good citizenship," and we'll hide our ignominy in the hybrid camp of indifference; but while there still blows in us the wind of liberal ideas, while the democratic spirit of our reformers influences us with its healthy, virile life, and while the sacred republican principles inflame our young souls, which are desirous of the public good, we'll struggle without respite, until we attain our ideals, thinking always that these ideals are those of our fathers of 1857, sustained vigorously on the platform, in the book, in the press, and on the battlefields.

Our struggle for justice hasn't been more than a reflection of our principles; but this struggle has been circumscribed to a small radius of action; we couldn't deal with anything more than judicial affairs. Inasmuch as our consciousness takes in the wide view of general administration, the motto of our periodical, "juridical," impeded us from embarking upon other areas of interest more delicate and transcendent, if you will, than the judicial.

But our principles have won out, have pushed beyond the juridical camp, and have entered fully into the camp of general administration.

It has to be so. The administration of justice is no more than a complement, as a power, to the other two: the executive and the legislative. Even though they have distinct attributes, the three powers must exist conjointly. In the manner that, if one of them takes a wrong path and has immense and deplorable omissions, the others will have them equally, because they're part of the same general administration.

These reasons have induced us to change the motto of *Regeneración*.

At the same time, we'll continue to deal with juridical affairs as we've done so far, and we'll continue making critiques, perhaps a little more bitter, but no less just, of the actions of the judicial functionaries.

Let us hope that our efforts are agreeable to the public, which is our judge and whose decision we respectfully await.

BASES FOR THE UNIFICATION OF THE PLM
1905

(Translated by C.B.)

I. The Organizing Junta of the Partido Liberal Mexicano is constituted of the persons who sign the following manifesto. The Junta will exist publicly, and it will reside in exile for reasons of safety, until it is safe to return, due to the attacks of the Mexican government. The Junta will work to organize the Partido Liberal Mexicano and with the aid provided by its coreligionists will struggle with all available means against the dictatorship of Porfirio Díaz. Regeneración will be the official organ of the Junta.

II. Mexican citizens who are in accord with the ideas of the manifesto and who desire the liberty of the country will form in the areas where they reside secret groups that will be in communication with the Junta. We advise our coreligionists in these groups to avoid useless formalities. All that we ask is that the liberal citizens of every area meet from time to time to consider the nation's political affairs and to maintain contact with the Junta, be it to communicate news of political affairs to it, be it to propose projects to it, or simply to maintain established relations. We urge our coreligionists to form groups with as many members as possible; but if in some areas there is only a single citizen who holds our ideas, he shouldn't hesitate to contact us because of his isolation.

III. Those groups or citizens who support the present call should let the Junta know of this, and should record their names with the members of the Party who have reorganized. These groups and citizens will send monthly to the Junta, according to their resources and their individual desires, a contribution which will be invested in the costs required for the fulfillment of the goals of the following manifesto.

IV. The Junta, aside from its own work, will attempt to promote the publication of oppositionist periodicals in Mexico, will distribute funds among the liberal militants who find themselves in poverty, and will sustain those whom the dictatorship has jailed and robbed; if there are cases in which a public functionary loses his position for having complied with his duties, we'll aid him also. We yearn that there be effective solidarity among the liberals, and for that to happen we count on the effective aid of our coreligionists.

V. The Junta will guard in absolute secrecy the names of the initiated. Do not communicate among yourselves, groups or affiliated individuals, until you are convinced that the group or person in question is truly dedicated to our cause. But if some member of the Party does not want to be contacted by the rest, let us know and we'll respect his decision.

Through these means we'll organize ourselves without danger, and when our Party has the strength it will unfurl its banners and undertake the decisive struggle against the odious tyranny.

Mexicans:

Immense are our misfortunes, tremendous our miseries, and many and terrible the outrages which have humiliated us during three long decades of despotism. But you are patriots, you are honorable and noble, and you will not permit that crime will eternally prevail. The Partido Liberal calls for a holy struggle for the redemption of the nation. Respond to the call, unite with our forces and efforts beneath the standards of justice and right, so that the country will surge grandly forward, forever redeemed and free.

Reform, Liberty and Justice.

St. Louis, Missouri, September 28, 1905

MANIFESTO TO THE NATION
THE PLAN OF THE PARTIDO LIBERAL MEXICANO
July 1, 1906
(Translated by C.B.)

Translator's Note: Extremely long single-sentence paragraphs were fairly common in Spanish-language writing of the period in which this was written, and this manifesto provides a good example of this practice. For example, the paragraph beginning with "Public offices ..." is a 700-plus-word single-sentence paragraph in the original Spanish, and I've left it as such here, just as I have left many other very long sentences intact. The primary reason for this is that to alter the structure to put it in line with modern usage would change the "flavor" of this manifesto to an unreasonable degree.

Mexicans:

I have here the program, the banner of the Partido Liberal, under which all of you should unite who have not renounced being free men, all of you who are smothering in this ignominious atmosphere which has enveloped you for thirty years, all of you who are ashamed of the enslavement of the country (which is your own slavery), all of you who hold against your tyrants the rebellion—blessed rebellion—of those restless under the yoke, because that feeling of rebellion is the signal that dignity and patriotism have not died in the heart that shelters them.

Think, Mexicans, of what it would mean for the country if the program of the Partido Liberal Mexicano, today raised like a shining banner, were put into effect—a program calling you to a holy struggle for liberty and justice, to guide your steps along the way of redemption, to show you the luminous goal that you can reach only if you decide to unite your forces in order to stop being slaves. The program, of course, is not perfect—no human work is—but it is benevolent, and under the present circumstances in our country it is our salvation. It is the incarnation of many noble aspirations, the remedy for many evils, the correction for many injustices, the end of many infamies. It's a radical transformation: the end of a world of oppression, of corruption, of crimes that will give way to a freer, more honorable, more just world.

Everything will change in the future.

Public offices won't be for sycophants and schemers, but for those who, by their merits, make themselves worthy of the public trust; public functionaries won't be these depraved, vicious sultans who are today protected by the dictatorship and authorized to dispose of the homes, lives, and honor of the citizens; on the contrary, they will be men elected by the public to watch over the public's interests, and who, if they don't do so, will have to answer before the same people who had favored them; this disgusting venality that today characterizes the tribunals of justice will disappear, because there will be no dictatorship bestowing judicial robes upon its lackeys, but rather the people will designate with their votes those who administer justice, and because the responsibility of functionaries will not be a myth in the democratic future; the Mexican worker will stop being what he is today—an outcast in his own land; instead he'll be master of his own rights, dignified, free to defend himself from this vile exploitation which today is imposed upon him by force; he will not have to work more than eight hours per day; he will not receive less than one peso per day; he will have time to rest, to have a good time, to educate himself, and to enjoy various comforts which he could never afford with his present salary of 50, or even 25, centavos per day; there won't be a dictatorship to counsel the capitalists who rob the worker and to protect the foreign forces who answer with a rain of bullets the peaceful petitions of Mexican workers; in contrast we'll have a government that, elected by the people will serve the people and which will watch over its compatriots, without attack from foreign interests, but also without permitting the excesses and abuses so common at present; the vast holdings that the big landowners hold empty and uncultivated will cease being silent and desolate testimony to the sterile power of a man and, collected by the state, will be distributed among those who want to work them; they will be converted into fertile and happy fields which give sustenance to many noble families; there will be lands for all who want to cultivate them, and the wealth they produce will not be for the enjoyment of a boss who puts in not the least effort in producing it, but it will be for the active worker who after opening a furrow and throwing in the seed with a hand trembling with hope, will bring in the harvest that is his through his sweat and effort; with the throwing from power of the insatiable vampires who today exploit him, and who because of their greed crush him with debts and government loans; taxes will be reduced considerably; now, the fortunes of the government take their leave of the public treasury—when this doesn't happen, there will be a giant savings, and the taxes will have to come down, lowering absolutely, of course, personal taxes and taxes upon moral capital, which today are truly intolerable; there will be no obligatory military service, this pretext under which the current honchos yank men from their homes because they dislike their prideful attitudes or because they're obstacles to the desires of the corrupt little tyrants to their abusing helpless women; education will be widespread, which is the basis of the betterment of all peoples; the clergy, this unrepentant traitor, this subject of Rome, this irreconcilable enemy of native liberties, in place of finding tyrants to serve and from whom to receive protection, will find instead inflexible laws which will put a limit on their excesses and which will confine them to the religious sphere; the expression of ideas will find no unjustifiable restrictions which impede the free judgment of civic men; the inviolability of private life will disappear, which so often has been a shield for corruption and evil, and public peace will stop being a pretext under which governments persecute their enemies; all liberties will be restored to the people and not only will the citizens have won their political rights, but also a great economic improvement; not only will there be a triumph over tyranny, but also a triumph over misery. Liberty, prosperity: here is the synthesis of the program.

Think, fellow citizens, of what it would mean to the country if these redemptory ideas were realized; look at our presently oppressed nation—oppressed, miserable, held in contempt, a prisoner of foreigners whose insolence grows larger with the cowardice of our tyrants; look at how the despots have trampled on the national dignity, inviting foreign forces to invade our territory; imagine to what disasters and to what ignominy these traitors whom we tolerate in power, who counsel that the Mexican worker be robbed and mistreated, who have claimed to recognize the debt contracted by the pirate Maximilian to support his usurpation, who have continually given proofs of the contempt they hold for the nationality of which we compatriots of Juárez and Lerdo de Tejada are proud; imagine to what disasters and what ignominy these traitors can conduct us. Contemplate, Mexicans, that abyss the dictatorship is opening under your feet, and compare this black chasm with the shining summit shown to you by the Partido Liberal so that you'll dispose yourselves to climb it.

Here, slavery, misery, shame; there, liberty, well-being, honor; here, the country in chains, exhausted by so much exploitation, subjected to whatever the foreign powers want to do to it, its dignity trampled upon by its own and by foreigners; there, the country free of yokes, it will prosper, with the prosperity of all its children, great and respected because of the lofty independence of its people; here, despotism with all its horrors; there, freedom in all its glory. Choose!

It is impossible to present to you in simple, benumbing words the picture of the sovereign, luminous nation of tomorrow—redeemed, dignified, full of majesty and grandeur. But don't let this stop you from appreciating this magnificent picture, since you yourselves will bring it forth with your enthusiasm if you are patriots, if you love this soil which your fathers sanctified, irrigating it with their blood, if you haven't denied your race which has known crushing despotisms and monarchs, if you haven't resigned yourselves to death as slaves beneath the triumphal chariot of dominating caesarism. It's useless for us to attempt to lift from your eyes the veil of the future, to show you that which will come into being through you yourselves: you will see what we could show to you. Console yourselves for the sorrow of our current servitude by evoking the picture of the free country of the future; you, the good Mexicans, you who hate the yoke, will illuminate the blackness of current oppression with the radiant vision of tomorrow and the expectation that from one moment to the next your visions of liberty will become real.

From you springs the hope of the country's redemption, from you, the good sons, the ones immune to the cowardice and corruption that the tyrants sow, from you, the loyal, the unbreakable, those who feel yourselves full of faith in the triumph of justice; respond to the call of the country: the Partido Liberal has reserved a place for you beneath its banners, which are raised in defiance of despotism; all of us who fight for liberty have a place open in our ranks; come to our side, contribute to strengthening our party, and so push for the realization of that which we all desire. Let us unite; let us add together our efforts; let us unify our purposes and the program will become a fact.

Utopia! A dream! shout those who, hiding their terror through abject rationalizations, intend to stop the popular reclamations so as not to lose a lucrative post or a less-than-clean business. It's the old refrain of all of those who resist the great advances of the peoples; it's the eternal defense of infamy. They call "utopian" what is redemptory in order that it be attacked or destroyed; all those who have attacked our wise constitution have wanted to excuse themselves by saying that it's unrealizable; today the lackeys of Porfirio Díaz repeat this thing necessary to hiding the crimes of the tyrant, and these miserable persons do not remember that this constitution, which they call so utopian, so inadequate for our people, so impossible to put into practice, was perfectly realizable under noble rulers like Juárez and Lerdo de Tejada. For evildoers, good must be unrealizable; for the cunning, honor must be unrealizable. The mouthpieces of despotism judge that the program of the Partido Liberal is impractical and even absurd; but you, Mexicans who aren't blinded by convenience nor by fear; you, noble men who desire the good of the country, will come to the simple realization of how much rudimentary justice this program contains.

Mexicans:

Upon the proclamation of its program by the Partido Liberal, with the inflexible purpose of putting it into practice, you are invited to take part in this great and redemptory work which must be done in order to have forever a free, respectable, happy country.

The decision is irrevocable. The Partido Liberal will fight without rest to fulfill the solemn promise that it makes today to the people, and there will be no obstacle that it will not overcome, nor any sacrifice that it will not accept to achieve its end. Today we call you to follow its banners, to fill its ranks, to augment its strength, and to make less difficult and less painful the victory. If you listen to the call and come to the post that befits your duty as Mexicans, you'll have a lot to thank the party for, since you'll be working for your own redemption; if you see with indifference the holy struggle to which we invite you, if you refuse to aid those who fight for right and justice, if through egotism or timidness you make yourselves accomplices of those who oppress us, the country owes you nothing other than contempt, and your rebellious conscience will never stop shaming you with the memory of your failure. Those who refuse to support the cause of liberty deserve to be slaves.

Mexicans:

Between that which despotism offers you and that which the program of the Partido Liberal offers you, choose! If you want shackles, misery, humiliation before foreigners, the grey life of the debased outcast, support the dictatorship which gives you all of this; if you prefer liberty, economic improvement, the raising up of the Mexican citizenry, the noble life of the man who is master of himself, come to the Partido Liberal that fraternizes with the noble and the virile, and join your efforts with those of all of us who fight for justice, to hurry the arrival of the radiant day on which tyranny will fall forever and the awaited democracy will surge forth with all the splendor of a star which never ceases shining brilliantly on the clear horizon of our country.

Reform, Liberty, and Justice.

PROCLAMATION

September 1906

(Translated by C.B.)

To The Nation:

Fellow citizens, in legitimate defense of trod-upon liberties, of infringed rights, of the dignity of the country trampled upon by the criminal despotism of the usurper, Porfirio Díaz; in defense of our honor and our lives threatened by a government that considers integrity a crime and smothers in blood the most legal and peaceful attempts at emancipation; in defense of justice, outraged without respite by the handful of brigands that oppress us, we rebel against the dictatorship of Porfirio Díaz, and we will not put down the arms we've taken in hand with complete justification until, united with the Partido Liberal Mexicano (PLM), we've made triumph the program promulgated on July 1 of the current year by the Organizing Junta of the Partido Liberal.

The excesses committed daily by the dictatorship throughout our unfortunate country, the attacks against electoral rights, against the rights of assembly, freedom of the press and freedom of speech, against the freedom to work, the massacres with which the government suffocates demonstrations of good citizenship, the murders and the robberies that the authorities cynically commit in all parts of the nation, the systematic contempt with which the Mexican is treated by the present authorities, the detention of independent citizens, the huge loans with which the dictatorship has saddled the nation, with no more object than the enrichment of a few oppressors, the indignity of our tyrants who have solicited the invasion of our territory by foreign forces, and, in a word, all of this accumulation of iniquities, of oppressions, of thefts and crimes of all types which characterize the Díaz government, must be stopped and punished by the people, who, if during thirty years [of Díaz's rule] have been respectful and humble in the vain hope that their despots would return to proper conduct, today have become convinced of their error and have tired of bearing chains, will know how to be inflexible in the reclamation of their rights.

The crimes of the dictatorship, growing greater each day, and the impossibility of dealing with them via peaceful means (because many times when we've tried to exercise our rights we've been trampled on by the tyrants) impel us to revolution. Those who see an evil in it can't blame the people who during thirty years have been peaceful and suffering to a fault, but rather they should blame the tyranny which through its unbridled and despotic intolerance has made it necessary for us to recur to force of arms to defend our rights and to realize our just and noble aspirations.

There are no personal ambitions behind our movement. We fight for the country, for all of the oppressed, for the betterment of political and social conditions in our country, for the benefit of all. Our flag of struggle is that of the Partido Liberal. The only authority that we recognize while a government elected by the people establishes itself is the Organizing Junta of the Partido Liberal. We're a fraction of this great party which has fought and will fight until the redemption of our country is won, and we work in accord with our coreligionists in the rest of the country who, like ourselves, have risen in arms on this same date against the present corrupt administration which will not be long in being overthrown and which in these moments already trembles before the formidable revolutionary movement which shakes the entire territory of the Mexican republic.

We call upon the officers and soldiers of the national army, rather than serve the vile dictatorship which dishonors and betrays the nation, to join the liberating movement. They are sons of the people like we are; they bear the same yoke that crushes all of us; they are also Mexicans and have the duty to fight for the dignity and the good of the country, and not for the personal good of a thieving, bloodthirsty despot like Porfirio Díaz.

The commanders and officers in the service of the dictatorship who pass over into the liberal files will be granted a promotion of two ranks above what they now have; the plain soldiers will be paid one peso daily with nothing taken out; and the noncommissioned officers will be given equivalent salaries.

We advise the foreigners that we intend to do nothing against them, but we also remind them of the duty they have to be neutral in the political affairs of Mexico, in which they have no right to intervene. We will give to foreign persons and properties all the guarantees possible, because in the interest of our beloved country and our cause we don't want to give rise to international conflicts; but the foreigners who, lacking neutrality, serve the government and fight against us cannot expect any consideration on our part.

Reform, Liberty, and Justice.

1906 PLM PROGRAM

(Translated by C.B.)

Note: The 1906 PLM program was a laundry list of reforms compiled from suggestions sent by hundreds if not thousands of correspondents. The following are the most important suggested reforms in the 1906 program.

CONSTITUTIONAL REFORMS
1. Reduction of the presidential term to four years.

. . .

4. Elimination of obligatory military service and the establishment of a national guard. Those who lend their services to the permanent army will do so freely and voluntarily....

5. To reform and put into effect constitutional articles 6 and 7, eliminating the restrictions that private life and public peace impose upon freedom of speech and freedom of the press ...

6. Abolition of the death penalty, except for treason.

. . .

9. Elimination of military tribunals in time of peace.

THE IMPROVEMENT AND ENCOURAGEMENT OF EDUCATION

10. An increase in the number of primary schools on such a scale that they will more than take the place of those that will be closed because they belong to the clergy.

11. The obligation to provide overall secular teaching in all the schools of the republic, be they those of the government or private, declaring it to be the responsibility of their administrators if they don't comply with this principle.

12. Declaring instruction to be obligatory until 14 years of age, with the responsibility being the government's to provide protection, in whatever form possible, so that poor children, because of their misery, do not lose the benefits of education.

. . .

RESTRICTIONS ON THE ABUSES OF THE CATHOLIC CLERGY

17. The churches will be considered as commercial establishments, remaining therefore obligated to keep books and to pay proportionate taxes.

18. Nationalization, in accord with the laws, of the real estate that the clergy owns in the power of third parties.

. . .

20. Elimination of the schools directed by the clergy.

CAPITAL AND LABOR

21. To establish a maximum of eight hours of work and a minimum wage in the following proportion: one peso overall in the country in areas where the average wage is less than that cited, and more than one peso in those regions in which the cost of living is high and in which this wage [one peso] isn't enough to save the worker from misery.

. . .

24. Absolute prohibition of the employment of children under 14 years of age.

25. To oblige owners of mines, factories, workshops, etc. to maintain their properties in good hygienic conditions and to make hazardous places as safe as possible for those working in them.

...

27. To oblige bosses to pay indemnities for work accidents.

28. To declare null and void the present debts owed by agricultural workers to their bosses.

...

31. To prohibit the bosses, under severe penalties, from paying for work in any other manner than in cash ... And to eliminate company stores.

...

33. To make Sunday an obligatory day of rest.

LANDS

34. The owners of lands are obligated to work productively all that they possess; whatever part of the lands that they leave unproductive will be recovered by the state, which will employ them in conformity with the following articles:

35. Mexicans living in foreign lands who ask for it will be repatriated at government expense and will be given lands to cultivate.

36. The state will give lands to whomever asks for them, with no other conditions than that they dedicate themselves to agricultural production and that they don't sell the lands.

37. So that these benefits are not taken advantage of solely by those few who have the necessary means to work the lands, but also by the poor who lack these means, the state will create or foment the creation of an agricultural bank that will give poor agricultural workers loans at low interest, repayable over time.

TAXES

...

40. To increase the taxes on speculation, luxury goods, and vices, and to lighten the taxes on articles of basic necessity ...

...

47. Measures to eliminate or restrict speculation, pauperism, and lack of articles of basic necessity.

48. Protection of the indigenous race.

...

50. Upon the triumph of the Liberal Party, the goods of those functionaries who were enriched under the present dictatorship will be confiscated, with the proceeds applied to the redistribution of the lands, especially restitution to the Yaqui, Maya, and other tribes, communities, or individuals whose lands were confiscated . . .

51. The first national congress after the fall of the dictatorship will annul all of the changes to our constitution made by the government of Porfirio Díaz; it will reform our Magna Carta in the manner necessary to put into effect this program . . .

SPECIAL CLAUSE

52. It will remain the responsibility of the Organizing Junta of the Partido Liberal Mexicano to address as quickly as possible the foreign governments, making it manifest to them, in the name of the party, that the Mexican people do not want any additional debts placed upon the country and that, therefore, it will not recognize any new debt that under any form or pretext the dictatorship has thrown upon the nation . . .

MANIFESTO TO THE WORKERS OF THE WORLD

Regeneración, *April 3, 1911*

(Translated by C.B.)

Comrades:

It's a little more than four months since the red flag of the proletariat erupted onto the battlefields of Mexico, carried by emancipated workers whose aspirations can be understood from this sublime war cry: Land and Liberty!

The people of Mexico find themselves in these moments in open rebellion against their oppressors, and, taking part in the general insurrection are those who sustain modern ideas: those convinced of the fallacy of political remedies as a means of redeeming the proletariat from economic slavery; those who do not believe in the goodness of paternalistic governments nor in the impartiality of the laws worked out by the bourgeoisie; those who know that the emancipation of the workers must be accomplished by the workers themselves; those convinced of the need for direct action; those who do not recognize the "sacred right of private property;" those who have not taken up arms to elevate any boss, but rather to destroy wage slavery. These revolutionaries are represented by the Organizing Junta of the Partido Liberal Mexicano (519 E. 4th St., Los Angeles, California), whose official organ, *Regeneración*, clearly explains their tendencies.

The Partido Liberal Mexicano does not fight to overthrow the dictator Porfirio Díaz in order to put a new tyrant in his place. The Partido Liberal Mexicano is taking part in the present insurrection with the firm and deliberate purpose of expropriating the land and the means of production to deliver them to the people, that is, to each and every one of the inhabitants of Mexico, without sexual discrimination. We consider this step essential to opening the doors to the effective emancipation of the Mexican people.

Now then, another party also finds itself with arms in hand: the Anti-Re-election Party, whose leader, Francisco I. Madero, is a millionaire who has seen his vast fortune grow through the sweat and tears of the peons on his haciendas. This party fights to make "effective" the right to vote, and to found, in sum, a bourgeois republic such as that in the United States. This party, overall political, is, naturally, the enemy of the Partido Liberal Mexicano, because it sees in the activities of the liberals a danger to the survival of the bourgeois republic which guarantees to the politicians, to the job seekers, to the rich, to all of the ambitious, to those who want to live at the cost of the suffering and the slavery of the proletariat —it sees a danger to the continuation of social inequality, to the sustenance of the capitalist, to the division of the human family into two classes: exploiters and exploited.

The dictatorship of Porfirio Díaz is about to fall. But the revolution will not end because of this sole fact; upon the grave of this infamous dictatorship will remain standing, face to face, with arms in hand, these two social classes: that of the well fed and that of the hungry, the first of these intending the preservation of its class interests, and the second the abolition of these privileges by means of the installation of a system that guarantees to all human beings bread, land, and liberty.

This formidable struggle of the two social classes in Mexico is the first act in the great universal cataclysm which very soon will break upon the scene all over the planet, and whose final act will be the triumph of the magnanimous formula of Liberty, Equality, Fraternity which the bourgeois political revolutions have not been able to translate into physical reality, because these revolutions have not dared to break to pieces the dorsal spine of tyranny: capitalism and authoritarianism.

Comrades of the entire world: the solution of the social problem is in the hands of the disinherited of the entire Earth, because it only requires the practice of a great virtue: solidarity. Your Mexican brothers have had the courage to hold high the red flag; but they haven't made a display of it in puerile demonstrations in the streets and plazas, which almost always end with the arrest and the smashing of the heads of the demonstrators by the cossacks employed by the tyrants. Rather, they've firmly held the red flag on the battlefields in gallant challenge to the old society, as an attempt to plant in solid ground the new just and loving society.

Our efforts, as noble and unself-interested as they might be, will be annihilated by the concerted actions of the bourgeoisie of all the nations of the world. Due to the sole fact of the red flag being raised on the battlefields of Mexico, the American bourgeoisie has forced President Taft to send twenty thousand soldiers to the Mexican border and warships to the Mexican ports. Meanwhile, what are the workers of the world doing? Crossing their arms and contemplating, as if in the seats of a theater, the people and events of this tremendous drama, which ought to move all hearts, which ought to elevate all consciences, which ought to intensely excite the nerves of all of the dispossessed of the Earth. They ought to get up as a single man to stop the squadrons of war and to put a halt to the uniformed slaves of all of the countries.

Agitation! This is the supreme resource of the moment. Individual agitation of conscious workers; collective agitation of workers' and freethought societies; agitation in the street, in the theater, in the streetcar, in the meeting places, in the home, in all places where there are ears to hear, consciences capable of indignation, hearts which haven't been hardened by the injustice and brutality of the environment; agitation by means of letters, manifestoes, flyers, conferences, meetings, by as many means as possible, making understood the necessity of working quickly and with energy in favor of the radical revolutionaries of Mexico who need three things: worldwide protest against the intervention of foreign powers in Mexican affairs; conscious, determined workers to propagate emancipatory social doctrines among the unconscious; and money, money, and more money to foment the Mexican social revolution.

Comrades, reprint this manifesto, translate it into all languages, and make it circulate across all the borders of the Earth. Ask the workers' press to insert it in their columns, read *Regeneración*, and send your bit to the Organizing Junta of the Partido Liberal Mexicano, 519_ E. 4th St., Los Angeles, California, USA.

Our cause is your cause. It's the cause of the taciturn slave working the earth, the outcast of the workshop and factory, the galley slave of the sea, the prisoner working the mine, of all who suffer the iniquity of the capitalist system. Our cause is your cause. If you remain inactive when your brothers go to their deaths clutching the red flag, you'll give, through your inaction, a rude blow to the proletarian cause.

We don't concern ourselves with showing to you that it has been to your indifference, to your lack of solidarity, to your ignoring your duty to join together to bring about the advent of the revolution, that is owed the lamentable delay of the new era, in which will exist the universal country of the free and of brothers. Now you have the social revolution in Mexico in your view. What are you waiting for before you go to work? Are you waiting for this noble movement to be crushed to fill the air with your protests, which will be impotent to return to life your better brothers and to remove from men's breasts the discouragement which would lead to failure, a failure which you yourselves have prepared with your indifference?

Meditate on it, comrades, and get to work immediately, without losing time, before your aid arrives too late.

Understand the danger in which we find ourselves facing the governments of the world, which see in the Mexican movement the apparition of social revolution, which is the only thing the powerful of the Earth fear.

Comrades: Do your duty.

—The Organizing Junta of the Partido Liberal Mexicano in the city of Los Angeles, California, USA, April 3, 1911

MANIFESTO

September 23, 1911

(Translated by C.B.)

Mexicans:

The Organizing Junta of the Partido Liberal Mexicano views with sympathy your efforts to put into practice the lofty ideals of political, economic, and social emancipation, whose reign upon the earth will finally put an end to the long battle of man against man, which has its origin in the inequality of wealth born of the principle of private property.

Abolishing this principle means the annihilation of all political, economic, social, religious, and moral institutions that comprise the ambient within which free initiative and the free association of human beings are smothered—human beings who see themselves obligated, in order to avoid perishing, to undertake a bloody competition from which exit triumphantly not the good, not the self-denying, not the most gifted physically, morally, or intellectually, but rather the most cunning, the most egotistical, the least scrupulous, the hardest of heart, and those who place their personal well-being above any consideration of human solidarity or justice.

Without the principle of private property there would be no reason for government, which is necessary solely for the purpose of keeping the disinherited within bounds in their quarrels or in their rebellions against those who hold the social wealth; neither would there be reason for the church, whose only object is to strangle the innate human rebellion against oppression and exploitation through the preaching of patience, resignation, and humility, and through quieting the call of the most powerful and fertile of instincts through immoral, cruel, and unhealthy penances; and so that the poor will not aspire to enjoying the good things of the earth and thus constitute a danger to the privileges of the rich, the church promises to the humble, to the most resigned, to the most patient, a heaven extending to infinity, beyond the stars one can see . . .

Capital, Authority, Clergy: this is the dark trinity which makes of this beautiful earth a paradise for those who have managed to clutch in their claws, through cunning, violence, and crime, the product of the sweat, blood, tears, and sacrifice of thousands of generations of workers; and these same three things create a hell for those with whose arms and minds work the earth, operate the machinery, build the houses, and transport the products. In this manner humanity is divided into two classes with diametrically opposite interests: the capitalist class and the working class; the class which possesses the lands, the machinery of production, and the means of transporting wealth, and the class which has nothing other than its arms and minds to provide sustenance.

Between these two social classes there cannot exist any ties of friendship or fraternity, because the possessing class is always disposed to perpetuate the economic, political, and social system that guarantees it the tranquil enjoyment of its plunders, while the working class makes efforts to destroy this iniquitous system in order to install one in which the lands, the houses, the machinery of production, and the means of transport are for everyone's use.

Mexicans: The Partido Liberal Mexicano recognizes that every human being, by the simple fact of coming to life, has the right to enjoy each and every one of the advantages that modern civilization offers, because these advantages are the product of the effort and sacrifice of the working class in all ages.

The Partido Liberal Mexicano recognizes that work is necessary to subsistence, and therefore all, with the exception of the old, the physically impaired, and children, must dedicate themselves to producing something useful in order to provide necessities.

The Partido Liberal Mexicano recognizes that the so-called right of individual property is an iniquitous right, because it subjects the larger number of human beings to work and to suffer to satisfy and keep in idleness a small number of capitalists.

The Partido Liberal Mexicano recognizes that Authority and the Clergy are the support for the iniquity of Capital, and therefore the Organizing Junta of the Partido Liberal Mexicano has declared solemn war upon Authority, Capital, and the Clergy.

Against Capital, Authority, and Clergy the Partido Liberal Mexicano has raised the red banner on the fields of action in Mexico, where our brothers battle like lions, contesting victory from the followers of the bourgeoisie, be they followers of Madero, Reyes, Vazquez, or be they "científicos" or any others whose only purpose is to elevate some man to the head of state or to conduct some shadowy business without consideration of the entire Mexican population; and they all recognize as sacred, every one of them, the right of individual property.

In these moments of confusion, so propitious for attacking oppression and exploitation; in these moments in which Authority, broken, reeling, vacillating, harassed on all sides by the forces of unleashed passions, by the tempest of appetites revived by the hope of a coming feast; in these moments of sinking feelings, of anxiousness, or terror for all the privileged, the compact masses of the disinherited invade the lands, burn the property titles, place their creative hands upon the fertile earth, and shake their fists at everything that was respectable yesterday: Authority, Capital, and Clergy; they open the furrow, spread the seed, and wait, emotionally, for the first fruits of free labor.

These are, Mexicans, the first practical results of the propaganda and the actions of the soldiers of the proletariat, of the noble holders of our egalitarian principles, of our brothers who defy all impositions and all exploitation with the cry of death to those above and life and hope for those below: Long live Land and Liberty!

The storm grows fiercer day by day: partisans of Madero, Vazquez, Reyes, De la Barra, and the "científicos" call to you, Mexicans, to fly to defend their faded flags, to protect the privileges of the capitalist class. Don't listen to the sweet songs from these sirens who want to take advantage of your sacrifices in order to establish a government, that is, a new dog to protect the interests of the rich. On your feet everyone!—but in order to bring about the expropriation of the goods kept for themselves by the rich!

Expropriation must be carried out through blood and fire during the course of this great movement, as is being done by our brothers, the inhabitants of Morelos, Southern Puebla, Michoacán, Guerrero, Veracruz, Northern Tamaulipas, Durango, Sonora, Sinaloa, Jalisco, Chihuahua, Oaxaca, Yucatán, Quintana Roo and regions of other states, as even the Mexican bourgeois press has to confess, in which the proletarians have taken possession of the lands without waiting for some paternal government to decree that they're worthy of happiness, conscious that they cannot expect anything good from governments and that "the emancipation of the workers must be the task of the workers themselves."

These first acts of expropriation have been crowned by the smile of success; but it's not necessary to limit oneself to taking possession of the lands and agricultural implements; it's necessary that the workers themselves determinedly take possession of all the industries, ensuring in this manner that the lands, mines, factories, workshops, foundries, cars, railways, ships, warehouses of all kinds, and the houses remain in the power of each and every one of the inhabitants of Mexico, without sexual discrimination.

The inhabitants of each region in which such an act of supreme justice is carried out have nothing else to do but to come to an accord that all the things found in the stores, warehouses, granaries, etc. be taken to a place easily accessible to all, where men and women of good will will take a careful inventory of everything that's been gathered in order to calculate how long these things will last, taking into account the needs and the number of inhabitants who need to make use of these things, from the moment of expropriation until the first harvest is taken from the fields and the other industries produce the first articles.

With the inventory taken, the workers in the different industries will come to a fraternal understanding among themselves on the management of production. In this manner, during the course of this movement, no one will lack anything, and the only ones who die of hunger will be those who don't want to work, with the exceptions of the old, the handicapped, and the children, who will have the right to the use of everything.

All that is produced will be sent to central community warehouses from which everyone will have the right to take everything that they need, according to their needs, with no other requirement than that they show proof that they work in one or another industry.

The aspiration of the human being is to have the maximum amount of enjoyment with the minimal amount of effort, and the best way to ensure this result is to work the land and the other industries in common. If the land is divided and each family has a plot, besides the grave danger of falling again into the capitalist system—because there will be no lack of cunning men or of those in the habit of saving who will manage to amass more than others and eventually will be able to exploit their brothers—there is also the fact that if a family works a plot of land, it will have to work more or less like it does today under the system of private property in order to obtain the same mean result. While if the land is held and worked in common, the workers will labor less and produce more. Of course there will be no lack of land for everyone to have their own house, as well as a good plot to put to use however they want. The same can be said of working the factories, workshops, etc., as of working the land. But each person, according to his temperament, desires, and abilities will have to choose the type of work he wants to do, and with this enough will be produced to cover his necessities, and to ensure that he won't be a burden on the community.

Working in the manner indicated, that is, following immediately after the expropriation of production, free of bosses and based upon the needs of the inhabitants of every region, no one will lack anything despite the armed movement, until, with the end of this movement and with the end of the last member of the bourgeoisie and the last representative of authority, with the law sustaining privilege broken into pieces and with everything in the hands of those who work, all of us will stretch our arms in a fraternal embrace and celebrate with cries of jubilation the installation of a system which guarantees every human being bread and liberty.

Mexicans: This is what the Partido Liberal Mexicano fights for. This is what the pleiades of heroes shed their blood for. This is what is fought for under the renowned cry, "Land and Liberty!"

The liberals haven't put down their arms despite the treaties between the traitor Madero and the tyrant Díaz, and despite, also, the urgings of the bourgeoisie who have tried to fill the liberals' pockets with gold. This is because the liberals are men who are convinced that political liberty will not be taken advantage of by the poor, but rather by the seekers after offices, and our object is not to obtain offices or honors, but rather to snatch everything from the hands of the bourgeoisie so that everything will be in the hands of the workers.

The activity of the various political bands in these moments is in dispute of supremacy, that is, following the triumph, who will do exactly the same thing as Porfirio Díaz, because no man, no matter how well intentioned he might be, can do anything in favor of the poor once in power. But this political activity has produced the chaos of which the disinherited can take advantage, that is, taking advantage of the special circumstances in which the country finds itself in order to put into practice on the march, without wasting time, the sublime ideals of the Partido Liberal Mexicano, without waiting for peace to carry out expropriation. Because if we wait, by then the provisions in the stores, granaries, warehouses, and other places will have been exhausted, and at the same time, because of the state of war in which the country finds itself, production will have been suspended and hunger will result; but if we carry out expropriation and organize work in a free manner during the revolutionary movement, no one will lack what he needs during the movement or thereafter.

Mexicans: if you want to be free, do not fight for any cause other than that of the Partido Liberal Mexicano. Everyone offers you political liberty after the triumph: the liberals invite you to take the lands, the machinery, the means of transport, and the houses immediately, without waiting for anyone to give you all this, without waiting for some law to decree these things, because the laws are not made by the poor, but rather by the frock-coated bosses who guard well against making laws to the disadvantage of their own caste.

It's the duty of all the poor to work and to struggle to break the chains that enslave us. To leave the solution of our problems to the educated and rich classes is to voluntarily put ourselves in the grasp of their claws. We are the plebeians; the ragged; the hungry; those who don't have a clod of dirt on which to lay our heads; those who live tormented by the uncertainty of having bread for our women and children; those who, when we become old, are fired ignominiously because we can no longer work. We must look to our own powerful efforts, our thousand sacrifices to destroy to its foundation the edifice of the old society which has been until now a caring mother for the rich and a wicked and evil stepmother to those who work and are good.

All of the evils that afflict the human being originate in the present system, which obliges the majority of humanity to work and to sacrifice itself so that a privileged minority has all of its needs, and even its caprices, filled, while living in idleness and vice. And it wouldn't be so bad if all the poor were assured of work; but production is not arranged to satisfy the needs of the workers, but rather to provide profits to the bourgeoisie, who take pains not to produce more than they can afford; and from this results the periodic work stoppages in industry or restrictions on the number of workers, which also comes from the improvements in machinery which supplant the arms of the proletariat.

To put an end to all this it's necessary that the workers have in their hands the lands and the machinery of production, and that it be themselves who organize the production of the wealth while paying attention to their own needs.

Robbery, prostitution, murder, arson, and swindles are all products of the system which places men and women in conditions under which, if they don't want to die of hunger, they are obligated to seize what they can or to prostitute themselves, since in the majority of cases, even if they have a great desire to work they can't find it, or the pay is so low that their wages don't cover even the most urgent necessities of the individual and the family; and the hours of labor under the capitalist system and the conditions under which it is carried out destroy the health of the worker in little time, if they don't kill him outright in an industrial accident which has no other origin than the contempt with which the capitalist class views those who sacrifice themselves for the benefit of the capitalists.

The poor man, angered by the injustice of which he's the object; choleric before the insulting luxury which those who do nothing flash before him; beaten in the streets by the police for the crime of being poor; obligated to rent his body to work at jobs he dislikes; badly paid; despised by all those who know more than he does or by those who believe themselves superior because of their money; contemplating a sad old age and the death of an animal dispatched from the stable for being unfit to serve; nervous about the possibility of being without work from one day to the next; obliged to see as enemies the members of his class, because he doesn't know if they will be the ones who rent themselves to the capitalists for less than he does—it's natural that under these circumstances antisocial instincts develop in the human being, instincts which are unleashed in crime, prostitution, and betrayal: the fruits of the old, hateful system which we want to eradicate down to its deepest roots in order to create a new system of love, equality, justice, fraternity, and liberty.

Let everyone arise as a single man! In the reach of all are tranquility, well-being, liberty, the satisfaction of all healthy appetites—but not if we allow ourselves to be guided by rulers. Let everyone be the master of himself. Let everything be arranged by mutual consent between free individuals. Death to slavery! Death to hunger! Long live Land and Liberty!

Mexicans: With our hands placed on our hearts and our consciences tranquil, we're making a formal and solemn call for you—everyone, men and women —to adopt the lofty ideals of the Partido Liberal Mexicano. While there are poor and rich, rulers and ruled, there will be no peace, nor is peace to be desired, because such peace would be founded in the political, economic, and social inequality of millions of human beings who suffer hunger, outrages, prison, and death, while a tiny minority enjoys all types of pleasures and freedom for doing nothing.

To the struggle! Expropriate with the ideal of benefitting all, and not just a few, so that this war will not be a war of bandits, but of men and women who desire that all be brothers and, as such, enjoy all the good things provided by nature and by the arms and minds of the men who create them, with the only condition being that everyone dedicates himself to truly useful work.

Liberty and well-being are within the reach of our hands. The cost is the same in effort and sacrifice to elevate a ruler, that is, a tyrant, as it is to expropriate the wealth held by the rich. Choose, then: either a new ruler, that is, a new yoke, or redemptive expropriation and the abolition of all religious, political, indeed all types of impositions.

Land and Liberty!

Written in the city of Los Angeles, state of California, United States of America, on the 23rd day of the month September 1911.

—Ricardo Flores Magón, Librado Rivera, Aneslmo L. Figueroa, Enrique Flores Magón

MANIFESTO TO THE ANARCHISTS OF THE ENTIRE WORLD AND TO THE WORKERS IN GENERAL

Regeneración, *March 16, 1918*

(Translated by C.B.)

The clock of history is close to marking, with its inexorable hand, the instant that this society going through its death throes expires.

The death of the old society is close, it won't be long in coming, and the only ones who can deny this fact are those who want it to live, those who draw advantage from the injustice on which it is based, those who view with horror the social revolution, because they know that on the day after it comes they will have to work elbow to elbow with their slaves of the evening before.

Everything strongly indicates that the death of bourgeois society won't be long in coming. The citizen looks grimly upon the policeman, who yesterday he considered his protector and a source of aid; the assiduous reader of the bourgeois press shrugs his shoulders and contemptuously throws down the prostituted sheets in which appear the declarations of the heads of state; the worker goes on strike without it mattering to him that his attitude harms "the national interest," conscious now that the nation isn't his property, but the property of the rich; in the streets one sees faces that clearly betray inner discontent, and there are arms that appear to be itching to construct barricades. There are whispers in the bars; whispers in the theater; whispers on the streetcars; and in every home, especially in our homes, in the homes of those on the bottom, there are laments about a son sent off to war; and the hearts grow heavy and the eyes fill with tears thinking that tomorrow, and perhaps even today, the big boy who is the life of the hovel, the youth who with his impudence and grace wraps in the colors of the rainbow the sad existence of his parents who are in their declining years, will be yanked from the loving breast of the family to go to confront, gun in hand, another youth who is, like him, the light of his home, and whom he doesn't hate and can't hate, because he doesn't even know him.

The flames of discontent are blown by the winds of tyranny, constantly growing stronger and crueler throughout the country, and here, there, and yonder, everywhere, fists are clinching, minds are getting wrought up, hearts are beating violently, and there isn't murmuring, there is shouting, a yearning for the moment in which the callused hands hardened by a hundred centuries of labor have to put down the useful tool in order to raise the rifle that awaits, impatiently, the caress of the hero.

Comrades: the moment is solemn; this moment is the precursor of the greatest political and social cataclysm recorded in history: the insurrection of all the peoples against existing conditions.

It will be, surely, a blind impulse of the suffering masses; it will be, undoubtedly, a chaotic explosion of anger, menaced hardly at all by the revolver of the thug and the noose of the hangman; it will be an overflow of indignation and bitterness, and it will produce chaos, chaos favorable to the prosperity of all of the fishermen in the river of revolt, chaos from which can surge new oppressions and new tyrannies, because in this chaos, regularly, the leader is a charlatan.

Let us then, those who are conscious, prepare the popular mentality for when the moment arrives, because if we don't prepare for the insurrection it will give rise anew to tyranny.

Let us prepare the people not only so that they will tranquilly await the great events which we glimpse, but so that they will be capable of refusing to allow themselves to be dragged along the primrose path by those who would lead them to an identical state of slavery or a tyranny similar to that which we now suffer.

In order to ensure that unconscious rebellion doesn't form with its own arms the new chain that will again enslave the people, it's necessary that we, those who do not believe in government, those who are convinced that government, whatever its form and wherever it shows its face, is tyranny, because it is not an institution created to protect the weak, but rather to protect the strong, place ourselves at the forefront of circumstances and fearlessly proclaim our holy anarchist ideal, the only human, just, and true ideal.

Not to do so is to knowingly betray the slumbering aspirations of the people for liberty without limits other than the natural ones, that is, a liberty which does not endanger the preservation of the species.

Not to do so is to leave the sacrifice of the humble in the hands of those who would want to take advantage of it for purely personal ends.

Not to do so is to affirm what our opponents say, that the time when our ideal can take root is still distant.

Activity, activity, and still more activity, that is what the moment demands.

Let every man and every woman who loves the anarchist ideal proclaim it with tenacity, with stubbornness, taking no notice of taunts, without fearing dangers, without regard to the consequences.

Shoulders to the wheel, comrades, and the future will be the unfolding of our ideal.

Land and Liberty.

"Attack on Puebla (1911)," by José Guadalupe Posada.

CHAPTER 3

THE REVOLUTION

CLARION CALL TO ARMS

Revolución, *June 1, 1907*

(Translated by C.B.)

It's a lie that virtue resides in the suffering, pious, and obedient spirits!

It's a lie that meekness is a sign of goodness. It's a lie that to love our fellow men, that to yearn to alleviate their pains and to sacrifice onself for their well-being is a quality only of the peaceful, tender, eternally kneeling, eternally submissive souls!

What is a duty to suffer without losing all hope, to feel upon oneself the whiplash of inclemency, without repelling the aggression, without even a glance of defiance?

What a poor morality that encloses virtue in the circle of obedience and resignation!

What an ignoble doctrine that repudiates the right to resist and insists on denying the virtue of the combative spirits who do not tolerate outrages and who refuse to surrender their free wills!

It is not true that submission reveals lofty sentiments; on the contrary, submission is the lowest form of egoism: it is fear.

The submissive are those who lack sufficient moral development to subordinate their self-preservation to the demands of human dignity; those who flee sacrifice and danger, yet sink themselves in opprobrium; those incorrigible cowards who in all times have been a grave obstacle to the triumph of liberating ideas.

The submissive are traitors to progress, the contemptible stragglers who retard the march of humanity.

Never has altruism budded in these morbid, terrified temperaments; altruism is the patrimony of strong characters, of those abnegating individuals who love others too much to forget about themselves.

It's a lie that submission is an act worthy of praise; it's a lie that submission is proof of spiritual health! Those who submit, those who renounce the exercise of their rights, are not only weak, they are also detestable. To offer one's neck to the yoke without protest, without anger, is to castrate the most precious potencies of a man, to make a work of degradation, of one's own debasement; it's to make oneself infamous and to merit the contempt which bites and the hatred which tortures.

There's no virtue in being servile. In this bitter epoch of injustice and oppression, it's necessary to raise one's gaze to the shining heights, to the free minds, to the combative souls.

The serene apostles who preach that peace and good have conquered death; those who offer themselves up for sacrifice; those who believe that to sacrifice themselves marching defenseless to martyrdom; those embodying Christian virtues are not sprouting up nor are they necessary in our day: this caste of strugglers has self-extinguished, has disappeared forever, enveloped in a shroud of their mystic errors. Through their example they leave us a living proof that meekness is death. They preached and they suffered. They were insulted, spit upon, trod upon, and they never raised an indignant glance. The development of their ideas was slow and very hard; their triumph impossible. They lacked the violence to demolish the castles of reaction, the war-like vigor to knock down the enemy and to raise with fierce fist the liberating banner. Their sheep-like example doesn't seduce the new ranks of reformers, elevated by their devotion to the ideal, but perfectly educated in the school of resistance and of attack.

To fight for a redemptory idea is to practice the noblest of the virtues: that of fertile and disinterested sacrifice. But to fight is not to deliver oneself to martyrdom or to look for death. To fight is to fight to win. Fighting is life, bristling, roaring life which abominates suicide and knows how to wound and how to triumph.

Let us fight for liberty; let them come to our ranks—the modern evangelists, strong and beneficent, those who preach and act, the libertarians with clear consciousness who know how to sacrifice everything for principle, for the love of humanity. Let those come who are disposed to disdain danger and to tread on the sands of combat where there will be scenes of fatally necessary barbarism, and where valor is acclaimed and where heroism has its seductive apotheosis.

Let join the cultivators of the ideal, those emancipated from fear, which is black egoism! Join! There is no time to lose!

To conceive an idea is to commence to make it real. To remain quiescent, not to execute the deep-felt ideal, is not to drive it forward; to put it in practice, to make it real on all occasions and in every moment of life is to work in accord with what one says and preaches. To think and to act in harmony should be the work of the thinkers; to dare always and to work on all occasions should be the labor of the soldiers of liberty.

Abnegation pushes one to combat: let us hasten to fight for more than ourselves, for our children, for the generations to come, who will call at our crypts to scoff at us if we remain petrified, if we don't destroy this regime of abjection in which we live, but who will salute us with affection if we agitate, if we are loyal to the glorious shield behind which humanity advances.

Let us work for the future, to save our posterity from pain. It is force which will destroy this slave pit of shame and misery; it is force which will prepare the advent of a new, egalitarian, happy society.

It doesn't matter if we perish in the hazardous battle if we have gained the noblest satisfaction in life: the satisfaction that in our name history will speak to the man of tomorrow, emancipated through our efforts.

"We've shed our blood and tears for you. You will inherit our legacy.

"Son of the dispossessed, you will be a free man."

PREACHING PEACE IS A CRIME

Regeneracíon, *September 17, 1910*

(Translated by C.B.)

Pale and shaking, eyes darting from side to side, lips trembling, a man, dragging his feet as if they were made of lead, stumbles his way through the crowd to the podium: Fear is going to speak. He preaches the philosophy of four-footed beasts. "Peace is good, he says; peace is a great good. Life is sweet and agreeable," he continues, "let us care well, then, for life."

Moments before, the loftiest orators had shaken that multitude, and heroism, fearlessness, and revolutionary audacity had resonated in the souls of the crowd, in the souls of workers, in the souls of crushed spirits who, at the cry of rebellion, had felt rise within the most hidden corners of their beings the eagerness of heroes, the courage of the valiant. One more cry and these slaves would have angrily thrown off the burden which keeps them in subjection more effectively than the prison and the scaffold: respect for those above them. But Fear becomes manifest and speaks; its words pass over their heads like the winds of winter; and their enthusiasm dims; their burning eagerness becomes numbed; and those human beings who had arrived at the gates of heroism and had already crossed its threshold open their eyes in fright and retreat, to fall once again humiliated and submissive at the feet of their bosses, repeating these damnable words: "Peace is good; peace is a great good."

This is the history of all human efforts toward attaining freedom and happiness. Put your life and well-being at risk says the apostle. The slaves stand straighter and listen. The living words of the apostle fall upon their saddened souls like a healing salve. It's consoling to know that everyone, simply by the fact of being born, has the right to live and to be happy. We aren't happy? It's because someone has put obstacles in the way of being happy. And the apostle speaks then of the boss, of the priest, of the soldier, of the ruler. These have weighed down the worker since the appearance of the first thief who said, "This piece of earth is mine;" and since then they have capriciously weighed down human intelligence, frightening some with the specter of hell and terrorizing others with the fear of jail and death. From this derives the devout respect for the powerful; respect for the priest who treats workers like brutes; respect for the soldier who kills; respect for the ruler who oppresses; respect for the boss who lives off the labor of the dispossessed. And this respect, prescribed by the law, is so admirably arranged that it benefits only those on top and works against only those on the bottom. It oppresses humankind, makes it a race of slaves; it corrupts because it takes away the right of free inquiry; it snatches away the prerogative of enjoying all the good that nature gives us; it mars civilization and makes a man incapable of looking up and staring his oppressors in the eye.

The apostle speaks against this respect, and his words are injections of healthy sanity that invigorate the multitudes. The desire to be free takes them over, and the immortal spirit of justice seizes them so that in the end they decide to uproot this respect from the hearts of men. But then Fear speaks, and terrorizes their hearts; the firmest arms let fall in discouragement the weapons of liberation, and the debased lips spout one after another the hateful words: "Life is sweet and agreeable; let us care well, then, for life."

And so to preach peace is a crime. To preach peace when the tyrant imposes his will and humiliates us; when the rich extort us to the extent of turning us into slaves; when the government, big business, and the church kill all aspiration and all hope; to preach peace under such circumstances is cowardly, vile, criminal. Peace in chains is an affront that should be refused. There is peace in the dungeon; there is peace in the cemetery; there is peace in the convent. But this peace is not life; this peace does not elevate; this is the peace of Porfirio Díaz, the peace in which the eunuch thrives and the citizenry prostitutes itself. It's the peace of the pharaohs, the peace of the tsars, the peace of the Caesars, the peace of oriental satraps. Let such a peace be damned!

Everyone who walks on two legs should rebel against such a peace. Death in the midst of revolution is sweeter than life in the midst of oppression. "Liberty or death" ought to be our cry, and upon hearing it we should rise first to crush the cowards who preach peace, and then the tyrants.

First the cowards, because they are the most certain support for all despotisms and the most dangerous enemies of all progress. "Blasphemy!" cry the cowards. Yes, blessed blasphemy replies the revolutionary; creative blasphemy; farseeing blasphemy; wise blasphemy; just blasphemy. This blasphemy puts its hands on all the altars and thrones of the earth and smashes them into pieces. This blasphemy elevates itself to heaven where another court, the celestial, rules, and breaks it into pieces through reason and leaves in its place bodily souls whose chemical composition is known; this blasphemy removes the brake of ignorance which made the Earth a fixed point in space and allows it to assume its glorious ellipse around the sun; and this blasphemy seizes the lightning of Jove and reduces it to electricity in Leyden's jars. And this tireless and audacious blasphemy, after reaching into the heavens and dethroning gods; after unchaining the blind forces of nature; after having exposed the fraud of "divine right" of the kings of Earth; after having searched the seas to find the original protoplasm, or the tiniest root of the zoological tree whose most attractive fruit is the human being, rises calmly, with the august serenity of science, to ask of Capital this simple question: "Why do you rule?"

Revolutionary workers: Cultivate disrespect.

THE REVOLUTION

Regeneración, *November 19, 1910*

(Translated by C.B.)

The well ripened fruit of internal revolt is about to fall. It's a bitter fruit for all those who were pampered in a situation that produced honors, riches, and distinction for some based upon the pain and suffering of the rest of humanity. But it's a sweet fruit for those who for whatever reason have felt their dignity trampled upon for thirty-four years by the hooves of those who have robbed, raped, killed, swindled, and betrayed, and who have hidden their crimes beneath the mantle of the law, avoiding punishment through their official standing.

Who fears the revolution? The same people who have provoked it—those who through their oppression or exploitation of the masses have made desperation overtake the victims of their infamies, those who through their injustice and greed have incited those with consciences to revolt and have made the honorable men of the earth turn pale with indignation.

The revolution is going to break out at any moment. Those of us who have followed all of the events in the social and political life of the Mexican people cannot deceive ourselves about this. The symptoms of this formidable cataclysm leave no doubt that something will surge forth and something will come tumbling down, that something will rise and something will fall. Finally, after thirty-four years of shame, the Mexican people will raise their heads, and, finally, after this long night, the black edifice, the nightmare which has smothered us will be smashed into ruins.

It's proper, now, to say once again what we've said so many times before: it's necessary to make sure that this movement, caused by desperation, is not simply a blind movement aimed at ridding ourselves of the burden weighing us down, that it not be a movement in which instinct almost completely dominates reason. We libertarians ought to strive that the orientation of this movement be that indicated by science. If we don't do this, the revolution which is coming will serve no other purpose than to replace one president with another, or that which is the same, one boss with another. We ought to keep in mind that what is needed is that the people have bread, shelter, and land to cultivate; we ought to keep in mind that no government, no matter how good its intents, can declare the abolition of misery. It's the people itself, the hungry, the dispossessed who must abolish misery, taking, in the first place, possession of the earth which, by natural right, cannot be monopolized by a few, but is the property of every human being. It's not possible to predict where the work of reclamation will take the coming revolution; but if we who struggle in its ranks carry in good faith the purpose of advancing as far along this road as is possible; if upon taking up the Winchester we go forth decided, not upon the enthronement of another boss, but upon the reclamation of the rights of the people; if we carry to the field of battle the pledge of conquering economic liberty, which is the basis of all liberties, which is the condition without which there is no liberty whatsoever; if we carry this purpose we will channel the coming popular movement upon a course worthy of this epoch. But if because of the desire for an easy triumph; if because we want to abbreviate the conflict we moderate our radical tendencies, which are incompatible with the tendencies of the bourgeois and conservative parties, then we will have done the work of bandits and murderers, because the blood which has been shed will serve no more purpose than to give greater power to the bourgeoisie, that is, to the class which possesses wealth and which will, after the triumph, once again put the chains on the proletarians whose blood, sacrifice and martyrdom brought it to power.

It is necessary, then, proletarians, it is necessary, then, you dispossessed, that you not be confused. The conservative and bourgeois parties speak to you of liberty, of justice, of law, of honest government, and they tell you that if the people exchange the men currently in power for others, that you will have liberty, justice, law, honest government. Don't allow yourselves to be swindled. What you need is that which will ensure the well-being of your families and your daily bread; and no government can provide the well-being of families. It is you yourselves who must conquer these things, taking immediately the possession of the earth, which is the primordial wellspring of riches; and no government can give you the land. Understand this well! The law defends the "right" of those who hold the wealth. You have to take it yourselves despite the law, despite the supposed right of private property; you have to take it yourselves in the name of natural justice, in the name of the right of every human being to live and develop his body and mind.

When you are in possession of the land, you will have liberty, you will have justice, because liberty and justice cannot be decreed: they are the result of economic independence, that is, the ability of an individual to live without depending on a boss, the ability of an individual to receive the full product of his labors.

So then, take the lands. The law says that you can't take them, that they're private property; but that law was written by those who hold you in slavery and as such does not represent a social necessity that requires the force of arms to uphold it. If the law were the result of the consent of all, it wouldn't need the support of the police, the jailer, the judge, the hangman, the soldier, and the apparatchik. The law is imposed on you; and against these arbitrary impositions, upheld by force, we honorable men should respond by rebelling.

Now: to the struggle! The revolution, uncontainable, inevitable, will not be long in arriving. If you want to be truly free, gather together beneath the banners of the Partido Liberal; but if you only want the strange pleasure of shedding blood and playing at soldiers, gather together under other banners: those of the anti-re-electionists for example, who after you play at soldiers will bestow on you once again the yoke of your bosses and the yoke of government—that is, in the end, you will have had the pleasure of kicking out the old president, who still annoys us, with a bright, shiny new one.

Comrades: the question is grave. I understand that you are disposed to fight; but fight for the good of the poor. Until now the upper classes have taken advantage of all revolutions because you didn't have a clear idea of your rights and interests which, as you know, are completely opposite those of the rich and the intelligentsia. The interest of the rich is that the poor be poor eternally, because the poverty of the masses is the guarantee of their riches. If there weren't men who must work for others, the rich would find themselves obligated to do something useful, to produce something of value in the struggle for life; then they wouldn't have slaves to exploit.

I repeat, it's not possible to predict where the revolutionary reclamations of the people will take us; but it's necessary to procure the most that is possible. It would be a great step forward if the lands were the property of all. And if there wouldn't be sufficient force or sufficient consciousness among the revolutionaries to obtain more advantages than this, it would at least be the basis for further, future reclamations taken by the people by force.

Forward comrades! Soon you will hear the first shots; soon the oppressed will cry out in rebellion. Let there be no one who fails to rally to this movement launched with all of the force of this grand cry: Land and Liberty!

THE RIGHT TO REBEL
Regeneración, *September 10, 1910*

(Translated by C.B.)

From high on his rock the Old Buzzard [Porfirio Díaz] watches. An unsettling clarity begins to dissipate the shadows on the horizon surrounding the Crime, and in the washed-out countryside he begins to see the silhouette of an advancing giant. It's the Insurrection.

The Old Buzzard sinks down into the abyss of his own consciousness, stirring up the mud at its absolute bottom. But he finds nothing in those dark depths that explains the rebellion. He resorts then to his memories: men, things, dates, circumstances pass through his mind like a line of dancers. The martyrs of

Veracruz pass, showing the wounds on their bodies that they received one night by the light of a lantern in the courtyard of a barracks from drunken soldiers commanded by an officer who was also drunk on wine and fear. The workers of "The Republican" pass, pale, their clothes and bodies cut into shreds by the sabers and bayonets of their bosses. The families of Papaatla pass by, old men, women, and children riddled by bullets. The miners of Cananea pass by, sublime in their sacrifice, gushing blood. The workers of Rio Blanco pass, magnificent, showing the accusing wounds of the official crime. The martyrs of Juchitan pass. Of Velardeña, of Monterrey, of Acayucan, of Topochic. Ordoñez passes, Olmos y Contreras, Rivero Echegaray, Martínez, Valadés, Martínez Carreón, Ramirez Terrón, García de la Cadena, Ramón Corona, Ramirez Bonilla, Albertos, Kankum, Leyva, Lugo. Legions of specters pass, legions of widows, legions of orphans, legions of prisoners, and the entire people pass, naked, gaunt, weak from ignorance and hunger.

The Old Buzzard zealously preens the feathers disturbed by the whirlwind of his memories, without encountering in them the reason for the revolution. His conscience as a bird of prey justifies death. Are there cadavers? Life is thus assured.

So live the dominating classes: on the suffering and death of the dominated classes; and poor and rich, the oppressed and despots, in virtue of customs and inherited prejudices consider this absurd state of affairs natural.

But one day a slave picks up a newspaper and reads it; it's a libertarian newspaper. In it he sees how the rich abuse the poor with no more right to do so than force and shrewdness; in it he sees how the government abuses the people with no right other than force. The slave thinks then, and ends by concluding that, today as yesterday, force is sovereign. Force is not dominated by reason; the way to dominate force is with more force.

The right to rebel penetrates into consciousness, the discontent grows, the dissatisfaction become insupportable, and protest breaks out in the end and the environment bursts into flames. One breathes an atmosphere heavy with the saturating odor of rebellion, and the horizon begins to clear.

From his high perch on the rock the Old Buzzard watches. From the plains rumors and complaints do not rise, nor do whispers, nor cries; a roar is what's heard. He lowers his gaze and shivers: he doesn't see a single back; the people are on their feet.

It's a blessed moment when the people rise. Now it's no longer a flock whose backs are toasted by the sun; now it's no longer a sordid crowd of the resigned and submissive; rather it's an army of rebels who have launched themselves into the conquest of the earth, and who are ennobled because they do it so that in the end men will walk on it.

The right to rebel is sacred because its exercise is indispensable to sweeping away the obstacles blocking the right to live. Rebellion! cries the butterfly when breaking the chrysalis that imprisons it. Rebellion! cries the chick when breaking through the shell that closes it in. Rebellion! cries the seedling in the furrow when it breaks through the earth to receive the rays of the sun. Rebellion! cries the human infant when it leaves its mother's womb. Rebellion! cry the people when they rise up to crush tyrants and exploiters.

Rebellion is life. Submission is death. Are there rebels among the people? Then life is assured, as are art, science, and industry. From Prometheus to Kropotkin, rebels have advanced humanity.

The supreme right of the supreme moments is rebellion. Without it, humanity wandered around lost even in the faint dawn of history called the stone age. Without it, human intelligence would have long ago run aground on the mud flats of dogma. Without it, the peoples would still live on their knees before princes and their divine right. Without it, this beautiful America would continue sleeping protected by the vast ocean. Without it, men would still see profiled the harsh outlines of the affront to humanity called the Bastille.

And the Old Buzzard watches from his perch high on the rocks, fixing his bloody eye on the giant that advances without even yet understanding the reason for the insurrection, because tyrants simply do not understand the right to rebel.

TO THE PROLETARIANS
Regeneración, *September 3, 1910*

(Translated by C.B.)

Listen workers: very soon the infamous peace which we Mexicans have suffered for more than thirty years will be broken. The calm of the moment hides the power of tomorrow's insurrection. Revolution is the logical consequence of the thousand facets that have constituted the [Díaz] dictatorship, now in its death agony. It must come inevitably, like clockwork, with the punctuality of the rising sun that dispels the darkness of night. And it is going to be you, the workers, who are the force of this revolution. It will be your arms which take up the weapons of redemption. It will be your blood, like fiery red flowers, which will tint the soil of our nation. If some eyes will weep in mourning, in widowhood, they will be those of your mothers, wives, and daughters. You, then, will be the heroes. You will be the backbone of this thousand-headed giant called insurrection. You will be the strong right arm of the national will become manifest.

The revolution must effect itself mercilessly, and what is better yet, it must triumph. That is, it must arrive with blood and fire even at the final feast in the lair of the jackals who have devoured you for the past thirty-four years. But is this all there is to it? Doesn't it seem absurd to come to the point of self-sacrifice simply for the trifle of changing bosses?

Workers, my friends, listen: it's necessary, it's urgent that you carry the revolution to the point where it reflects the consciousness of the epoch; it's necessary, it's urgent that it incarnates the great spiritual battle of the century. If on the contrary, the revolution which we look on lovingly while it takes shape is no different than the already forgotten revolts fomented by the bourgeoisie and directed by the military, your role will not be that of heroic, conscious liberators, but simply that of cannon fodder.

Realize it well once more: to shed blood in order to raise to power another bandit that oppresses the people is a crime, and this is what will happen if you take up arms with no objective beyond overthrowing Díaz and replacing him with another ruler.

The long oppression that the Mexican people have suffered and the hopelessness that has taken hold of everyone as a result of this oppression have fed a single ambition in the saddened soul of the people: a change of the men in government. Already those in power feel no support; the people, in the restricted way that they could, have hated them for so long that the fixed idea of changing only rulers has taken hold, and has diminished their ideals; the first saviors have remained subordinate to the sole desire to change the public administration. A sad example of this truth can be found in the crazy enthusiasm, the absurd joyousness greeting the candidacy of one of the most depraved functionaries, one of the cruelest thugs in the Mexican nation: the candidacy of Bernardo Reyes.

When his candidacy was launched, the people of Mexico didn't reflect on the personality of the candidate. The people's interest in him was simply that he represented change. The general hopelessness seems to have crystalized in these words: "anybody but Díaz," and as Díaz is at the point of rolling into an abyss, the people have tied themselves to the Reyes candidacy like a hot nail [driven through a horseshoe]. Fortunately, even if Reyes is ambitious, at the same time he's afraid to openly face Díaz and struggle against him. This cowardice has saved the Mexican people from suffering a crueler tyranny, a more savage oppression—if that were possible—than they are presently suffering.

To avoid such lamentable dead ends, it's necessary to reflect. The revolution is imminent: neither the government nor the opposition can delay it. A body falls of its own weight, obeying the laws of gravity; a society in a state of revolution obeys unalterable sociological rules. Attempting to oppose the outbreak of the revolution is a form of insanity adopted only by those who have an interest in seeing that the revolution does not succeed. And because the revolution must break out, and nothing and no one can contain it, it is good, workers, that you seize all of the advantages that this great movement carries within itself. If you are not conscious of your rights as the class that produces social wealth, you will be, in this great contest, simply machines that kill and destroy for the benefit of the bourgeoisie. This will happen if you don't carry in your minds a clear, precise concept of your own emancipation and social improvement.

Take into account, laborers, that you are the only producers of wealth. Houses, palaces, railways, factories, cultivated fields—everything, absolutely everything is made by your creative hands, and nonetheless you lack everything. You weave the cloth, but you walk around almost naked; you harvest the grain, and you hardly have a miserable crumb to take home to your families; you build houses and palaces, and you inhabit huts and attics; the metals which you drag out of the earth only serve to make your bosses more powerful and your chains stronger and heavier. The more you produce the poorer and less free you become, for the simple reason that you make your bosses richer and freer, because only the rich can take advantage of political liberty. So then, if you revolt with the purpose of overthrowing the despotism of Porfirio Díaz, something which you will undoubtedly achieve, as that triumph is certain; if things go well for you after that victory you'll get a government that will put in effect the Constitution of 1857; and with that you'll have obtained, at least in writing, your political liberty. But in practice you'll be slaves every bit as much as you are today, and like today you'll have only one right: that of being worked to death.

Political liberty requires another, concurrent liberty to be effective: economic liberty. The rich enjoy this economic liberty and it's for this reason that they alone benefit from political liberty.

When the Organizing Junta of the Partido Liberal Mexicano formulated the program set forth in St. Louis, Missouri on July 1, 1906, it had the conviction—

which it still has—the very firm conviction that it guards with care, that political liberty must be accompanied by economic liberty if it is to be effective. For this reason it outlined in its program the steps that the Mexican proletariat must take to conquer its economic independence.

If you don't carry to the approaching struggle the conviction that you are the producers of social wealth, and because of this sole fact that you have the right not only to live, but to enjoy all of the material goods and all of the moral and intellectual benefits now enjoyed exclusively by your bosses, you will not be doing revolutionary work like your brothers in the more developed countries. If you aren't conscious of your rights as the productive class, the bourgeoisie will take advantage of your sacrifice, of your blood and pain, in the same manner that today they take advantage of your labor, of your health, of your future, in the factories, fields, shops, and mines.

So then, workers, it's necessary that you understand that you have more rights than those delivered to you in the Constitution of 1857 and, above all, it's necessary that you're convinced that by the sole fact of being part of humanity you have the inalienable right to happiness. Happiness is not the sole patrimony of the bosses and owners; it's also yours, and with better right, because you produce everything that makes life pleasant and comfortable.

All I have left to tell you is not to lose heart. I see in you the firm purpose of launching yourselves into the revolution in order to overthrow the most shameful, most hateful despotism that has ever weighed down the Mexican race: that of Porfirio Díaz. Your attitude merits the applause of every honorable man. But I repeat: carry into combat the realization that the revolution is made by yourselves, that the movement is sustained through your blood, and that the fruits of this struggle will be yours and your families'—if you hold firmly to the conviction that you have the right to enjoy all the benefits of civilization.

Proletarians: realize that you are going to be the nerve center of the revolution. Go to it not like cattle going to slaughter, but like men conscious of their rights. Go to the struggle; strike firmly on the doors of the epoch. Glory awaits, impatient that you haven't already broken your chains into pieces over the heads of those who oppress you.

TO THE STRIKERS AND TO THE WORKERS IN GENERAL

Regeneración, *August 5, 1911*

(Translated by C.B.)

The special circumstances in which our country finds itself are exceptionally propitious. The working class can take advantage of them and conquer once and for all its economic liberty.

Capitalism and authority are crumbling in the vast expanses of our national territory under the liberating blows of the Partido Liberal Mexicano. Commerce is suspended; the factories, the workshops, the mines have closed their doors; in the haciendas the instruments of agriculture lie idle; railway traffic has fallen considerably; the panic caused by the activities of the liberals who fight for land and liberty have caused the export of millions of head of cattle from the haciendas of Madero, Treviño, Terrazas, and other brigands; the possible disobedience of the soldiers of Madero who don't surrender their arms; the division of the capitalist class into a multitude of parties; the rupture of the friendly relations between Madero and De la Barra; the monarchism brewing in the barracks; the clerics showing their heads and audaciously waving the banner of reaction; the bosses flagellating communities to the point where they feel pushed to the point of taking extreme actions; the intellectual elite, filing the dagger which has already passed through the heart of Reyes and prods the cadaver of Madero to make it plunge more quickly to the depths where his dastardly ambitions have already sunk; the smoldering coals of hatred between the partisans of Madero and the federales being blown back to life by the opportunism of the bosses of both bands; the eagerness for power and glory of the political bosses of all types incitement of the passions of the masses over the illusory benefits of the electoral ballot; the legislatures and municipal assemblies dissolved by force when they didn't lend themselves to serving a boss who offered these flocks of "representatives of the people" less than the previous boss; the frequent armed fights between Madero's followers over questions of control; the general strike unleashed equally against the bosses and political tyrants; the army of unemployed filing through the streets and plazas of our cities; the multitudes of the hungry and malnourished beginning to launch hateful looks at the frightened bourgeoisie; the looting of stores by women, children, and old people; the peons avenging grievances by burning crops and killing their bosses: all of this equals chaos, the boiling up of all tendencies, both good and bad, of all ambitions, of all appetites. Crime and virtue, good and bad, the great and the small, all contributing to fanning the flames which will result in either the disappearance of the race, if it's incapable of regenerating itself by means of struggle and submits itself in cowardly fashion to its rulers, or the luminous regeneration of the race if it courageously pursues the struggle to its end: the political, social, and economic emancipation of the Mexican people.

Mexican comrades: in these solemn moments of the history of the struggle of humanity for progress and perfection, millions of intelligent eyes contemplate you from across the oceans, from other continents, from other lands, with the same emotion that awaits a life or death decision, because, know it well Mexican workers, because your triumph will be the dawn of a new day for all of the oppressed of the Earth, just as your defeat will result in the tightening of the chains on every worker on Earth.

Hundreds of strikes of a more or less revolutionary character are going on all over the country. Until now, the best strikes have been those of the laborers in the fields of Yucatán, because those comrade workers have not assumed the inoffensive tactic of simply walking away from their tools and crossing their arms expecting better wages and a shorter work week. The peons of the Yucatán haciendas have taken possession of many of them and are operating them themselves, resolutely refusing the right of the rich to keep the workers as wage earners. Other notable acts of reclamation of the rights of the producers have been the taking of the land by the inhabitants of Morelos, to work it without bosses, as they've repudiated the "right" of private property; the taking of the lands by our Yaqui comrades and their heroic fight against the forces of Madero, which are trying to dislodge them; the taking of lands by revolutionaries in various communities along the coast of Veracruz; the taking of the lands by some indigenous communities in Jalisco. The same thing is happening with other noble peoples in other states who have lost faith in government and who are bringing about justice with their own hands.

The revolutionary strikes have been characterized by the blowing up of factories with dynamite, the uprooting of plants, the caving in of mines; but it's necessary to think about this. If the machinery is destroyed, little will be gained. It's necessary to resolutely take possession of the factories, workshops, mines, foundries, etc. In place of putting down tools and crossing one's arms, in place of destroying the common inheritance, comrades, revolutionary brothers, continue working, but under this condition: do not work for the bosses, but for yourselves and for your families.

Let the factory stay standing, don't cave in the mine, don't pull up the plants; take advantage of everything. While your liberal brothers do battle with the hired assassins of capital and authority, continue your labors and arm yourselves, also, to defend you and yours. Don't think that the rich have the right to exploit you. This "right" is criminal, because everything that the rich have has been made by your hands or is a part of nature and should belong to all—the lands, the forests, the rivers. Work so that you don't lack anything during this tremendous struggle against all oppression. The workers of the countryside will supply food and raw materials to the workers of the factories and workshops, and, reciprocally, the workers of the factories and workshops will supply their brothers in the countryside with tools, clothing, etc. The same will happen between the mine workers, foundry workers, construction workers, bringing about an interchange of products, the distribution of which will have to freely use the railways and other means of transportation of raw materials or finished goods.

Comrades: the occasion is propitious for the workers to conquer their economic liberty. Authority at this moment is a feather at the mercy of the winds. Capitalism is a throne eaten by termites to its base. Nothing else is needed to triumph but to repudiate the right of individual property and to give the coup de grace to authority.

Hands to the work, comrades! Take immediate possession of everything that nature and the hands and minds of men have created.

A strike is not redemptory. A strike is an old weapon that has lost its edge striking against bourgeois solidarity and the iron law of supply and demand. A strike is not redemptory because it recognizes the right of private property and accepts the right of the owner to a part of what labor produces. A strike is won, but the price of products goes up and the gain for the producer is perfectly illusory. That which before the strike cost, for example, one cent, after the strike has been won will cost two; and thus capital never loses and the striker never wins.

The abolition of misery will be attained when the worker resolves not to recognize private property.

Mexicans: this is the opportune moment. Take possession of everything that exists. Don't pay taxes to the government; don't pay rent for the houses you occupy; take the haciendas and work them in common, making use of the excellent machinery of the bourgeoisie; remain in and take the factories, workshops, mines, etc. That's the way you'll end misery; that's the way you'll achieve dignity in the intelligent eyes which in these solemn moments turn toward Mexico.

Don't fear death: have fear of the humiliation of being slaves, of being beaten, of being viewed with contempt by the fat bosses who exploit you. Spit in the faces of those who tell you that everything can be won by peaceful means. Spit in the faces of those who promise to redeem you when they're in power. To these: hang them!

And so, comrades, expropriate!

TO THE SOLDIERS OF CARRANZA
Regeneración, *November 6, 1915* ·

(Translated by C.B.)

Soldier of Carranza, listen: very soon your commander in chief will almost be the master of the situation; and I say "almost" because there are rebels who will not submit to the authority of Venustiano Carranza, but will prefer to continue on, gun in hand, pursuing a valuable way of life for the cause of humanity—a way of life that shows that surrendering arms to this government, like any other government on Earth, would be nothing other than to provide the support that capitalism counts on in exploiting to its heart's desire the working class, that is, to hold the poor perpetually under the domination of the rich.

These rebels who continue to stand are your brothers; they're poor like you and, like you, before taking up the gun their sweat watered the furrows of a piece of land they didn't own. They, like you, bravely submerged themselves in the darkness of the mine, wringing from the rock the precious metals that would fill other pockets than their own. They, like you, defied anemia and tuberculosis in the factories at the side of those workers of iron called machines, producing cloth which wouldn't cover their nakedness, shoes which would never shield their feet, furniture which they would never use in their shacks. They, like you, built the houses that provide shelter from inclement weather; they laid the rails for the rail line; they herded the cattle, so that they could feed on grass and stubble; they cut the firewood to provide heat against the cold.

These rebels are your brothers. They also have those who await them in their shacks, shooting anxious looks down the dusty road—the melancholy mother, the sad wife, the beloved sister, the adored daughter, the ancient father, the tenderly loved children, the beloved beings who make existence magic, the family, in a word, without which we appear incomplete, as if something was lacking.

These rebels are your brothers, only they're more intelligent than you are; they don't sacrifice themselves and they don't sacrifice their families to elevate to the presidency someone who will deliver happiness to the humble, because experience, observation, and the teachings of history have shown that never in the history of humanity has this rare phenomenon existed: that a government concern itself with the well-being of the poor people. Totally the contrary. It has always been the case that the government supports the rich against the poor. You don't know why this is, Carranza's soldier, but I'll explain it to you in a few lines.

At first, human beings didn't have a government; then everything belonged to everybody; then the earth was free to be cultivated by anybody who wanted to do it; then the forest supplied wood and meat to anyone who wanted to go to the bother of going in search of these things so necessary to life; then the springs didn't have an owner; then everyone had equal right to take from the river, the lake, or from the sea the fish they needed. In that happy time there was no government, because there was no private property to protect, and the people understood this so well that the major part of their labors were done in common, and the products of their labors were divided fraternally, with everyone taking what they needed. But then came the tribal wars, and the vanquished were reduced to slavery, having to work for their dominators, who, naturally, declared themselves owners of everything that existed. Then was born authority, since there were already privileges to protect: those of the victors from the vanquished.

Here we have how the principle of authority was born—not, as is generally supposed, in the need of the weak to defend themselves against the aggressions of the strong, but in the need of the strong to safeguard their riches against possible reclamations from the weak, from the dispossessed.

If you, soldier of Carranza, don't have material goods to lose, it's a bad thing to sacrifice yourself and to sacrifice your family to elevate to the presidency a man who, as governor, will be your whip and your exploiter, since he will do nothing to your benefit, because his mission is not to protect you from the aggressions of the strong, but to keep you subjugated by means of the laws made by the strong for their own protection—not yours.

The strong own the lands, the machinery of production, the houses, the means of transportation and distribution of the raw materials and manufactured products, and also the transport of persons. All this is what is called social wealth, and the possession of this wealth gives power to those who own it, the power to play at their whim with those who don't have it. Because of this, we, the anarchists who form the Partido Liberal Mexicano, don't fight for increases in wages, nor to diminish the hours of work, nor for compensation for accidents, nor for pensions for the old—not for any of this, but rather for the abolition of the "right" of private property which makes possible the cornering of the social wealth in a few hands. We desire that the social wealth be the common patrimony of all of the inhabitants of Mexico, men and women alike, without discrimination based on race or color.

All wages, high or low, compensations, pensions, and the rest, can be easily obtained because they don't threaten the "right" of private property, that is, the right to exploit the people and to hold them in slavery. While the "right" of individual or private property remains, there will also remain the same evil that obliged you to take up arms: misery, because it will serve you nothing to increase your wages and to "benefit" from other reforms, such as the lowering of the hours of labor and all the rest, if you have to buy at a higher price that which you need to sustain life, to pay higher rent to the owner of the house; and that doesn't even count the taxes which if the government doesn't take them from you it'll take from your bosses, who'll then reimburse themselves by periodically raising the price of everything. In reality, you'll pay the taxes, not the rich.

See then, brother who follows Carranza, that the problem that the rebels are trying to resolve with arms in hand will remain when Carranza is president, and it's that same problem that you have to resolve, because it affects you in the same manner that it affects them. Your duty is to aid them, and in order to do that do not give up your arms when you're ordered to do so when Carranza's troops are discharged. What you ought to do in that moment, or sooner if possible, is to rebel, turning your gun upon your leaders and their officials, without trembling as you shoot your weapon, because they are your enemies, because they have an interest in the persistence of the institutions that enable them to live a life of privilege. A good heart, a steady pulse, and an accurate eye are all you really need, then, to put an end to your immediate exploiters.

If you surrender your arm, you'll return to your home in misery, disposed to sell the force of your body to whatever bourgeois for whatever he feels like paying you. You'll have gained nothing, while your leaders and their officials will enjoy all types of pleasures in the city, savoring distinctions and ostentatiously displaying crosses and medals on their chests. If you remain in the army permanently, soldier of Carranza, you'll be a thug and an exploiter of your class brothers, because you'll be serving to maintain the rich.

Honor shows you the way you should take: rebellion against all government until the triumph of the principles contained in the manifesto of September 23, 1911, issued by the organizing junta of the Partido Liberal Mexicano—principles which call for the death of capitalism, authority, and the clergy of all religions.

Decide to follow this path. Don't be fooled by know-it-alls spouting inanities about needing this or that before starting such a struggle. These are the tricks of politicians; these are sophisms formulated and propagated by your enemies, even when they present themselves as being your friends. This was the argument of those who opposed the great French Revolution, to impede the people from giving themselves political liberty; this was the argument of Porfirio Díaz, to impede you from giving yourselves liberties; this is the argument of the politicians of Carranza, to impede you from obtaining economic liberty, the basis of all liberties; and that is no other thing than the ability to make a living through working, without having to depend on anybody, an ability that can be obtained only—understand this well—by making the lands, the houses, the machinery, the means of transportation and the warehoused goods, by means of expropriation, the common property of all, men and women, without discrimination based on race or color. To those who tell you the contrary, spit in their faces and then kill them, because it is necessary, absolutely necessary, to initiate a severe process of revolutionary cleansing. We must suppress those who stand in our way, who stand in the way of us, the dispossessed, by any means necessary, be it good or bad! We must suppress them like one eliminates a tiger or a rattlesnake, as one crushes a tarantula. Those who tell you that you're not prepared for any conquest that benefits you, they are those who have an interest in delaying your emancipation in order that they might live at your expense.

Now, soldier of Carranza, work as a man convinced that the rich and poor have nothing in common but the hatred they mutually profess, a hatred which it's not necessary to mitigate, but rather to deepen, to exacerbate, to increase as much as possible. Stir up its coals so that it doesn't die, because the existence of this hatred between the two social classes, the exploiters and the exploited, is the guarantee of struggle and the hope for emancipation of those who today find themselves on the lowest rung of the social ladder.

Long live Land and Liberty!

THE CARRANZA REFORMS

Regeneración, *November 25, 1915*

(Translated by C.B.)

Venustiano Carranza has managed to have his partisans make good on their promises of distribution of the land and of the endowment of communities with lands to be worked in common.

Seeing that the people have no faith in promises to be fulfilled "following the triumph," he's making effective these promises, putting into practice the reforms that he added to his program when he realized that the people fight to acquire material goods which give them economic independence, without which liberty of the individual is impossible.

In Veracruz, Yucatán, and other states controlled by Carranza, distribution of the lands to campesinos and the endowment of common lands to communities are coming to a head. But will the realization of these promises give to the dispossessed the liberty and well-being they have a right to as human beings? We don't believe they will, because such reforms do not bring death to private or individual property. This iniquitous "right," the fount of all of the evils which afflict humanity, remains standing, as likewise do its two powerful supports: the church and state, that is, the priest and authority, without which capital cannot exist.

It wouldn't be so bad if these distributions of land were made with the title gratis, that is, that there be no compensation from the beneficiaries. But that's not the way it is; the campesino who receives a piece of land has to pay the value of that land to the rich man, by means of the government. He also has to pay taxes so that president of the republic, the ministers of the cabinet, the representatives, the senators, the judges, the employees of all kinds, the soldiers, the cops, the jailers, can live and can enjoy themselves . . . And that's not even counting the diplomatic and consular representatives, who must be given enormous amounts of money because they represent the country, the thousand and one salaries and sinecures which are divvied up among the favorites of the government, and the immense quantities of money flowing through the hands of the functionaries, large and small, in addition to their legal wages.

All of this must be paid, apart from the fabulous sums of money which are invested in the materials of war, to produce public buildings and a thousand other things, all of which are very costly because everyone wants to draw advantage from them, and apart, additionally, from the national debt, which climbs to amounts the mind cannot conceive.

The campesino, inside this system of private or individual property, has to pay for the water to irrigate his parcel; he has to pay for the firewood from the forest or from the warehouse of the bourgeois; he has to construct his hut, which costs money, and he has to buy the tools and beasts necessary to his labors; he has to lay in provisions in order not to die of hunger awaiting his first harvest; he has to have funds to buy the seeds necessary to planting. In sum, he needs money for everything, and even for that which he doesn't need, but which weighs upon him, brutalizes him, bloodies him, and exploits him: authority and the church.

And if it's a bad year? What grief! The government demands its taxes as if the harvests had been good; the usurer demands what he's lent to the campesino, with no ifs ands or buts. The campesino will then have to sell or pawn his horse or ox, or ask for the loan of more money which will go forth and fill other stomachs, the stomachs of our exploiters, while our children and old people languish in our view, victims of our stubbornness in continuing to want government, suffering the consequences of our lack of courage to say to the revolutionary chiefs: "We don't want reforms! We want the abolition of the 'right' of private or individual property! We want that everything should be the property of everyone!" And breaking into a thousand pieces the personal banners of the political bosses, agitate on high for the Manifesto of September 23, 1911, the principles of which are the only ones that guarantee to all human beings well-being and liberty, because they want no more private property, nor authority, nor church.

The poor man, the veritable pariah, the dispossessed who can't count on a clod of dirt to lie his head on, he will gain nothing from the reforms of Carranza, because he needs money to work a piece of land. But suppose that he has the money for provisions, the tools of work, and everything else that is indispensable before the first harvest. And suppose still more: that the first harvest is good enough. Then, the market being controlled by the capitalists, the campesino will have to subject himself to selling his products at very low prices to the monopolists, and he'll have worked more than any day laborer for a miserable pittance, and misery and sadness will continue to reign in his home, while abundance and happiness reign in the homes of the bourgeoisie in the same manner as before the revolution.

The reforms of Carranza are the bloodiest joke that the proletariat has ever been the butt of. Carranza's agrarian reform is a slap in the face, delivered directly to the dispossessed.

Enough of reforms! That which the hungry need is complete liberty based on economic independence. Down with the so-called right of private property! And while this iniquitous "right," remains standing, so will the proletarians with arms in hand. Enough hoaxes! Proletarians: to he who speaks to you of Carranza and his reforms, spit in his face and smash his snout.

Long live Land and Liberty!

AT THE EDGE OF THE ABYSS

Regeneración, *March 16, 1918*

(Translated by C.B.)

The bourgeoisie finds itself at the edge of an abyss, of an abyss dug deep by its rapacious claws, of an abyss deepened even more by its biting like an enraged boar.

The bourgeoisie finds itself at the edge of an abyss, of a black, profound abyss opened by centuries and centuries of oppression and crime.

And the bourgeoisie slides toward that abyss on soil saturated with blood and tears, blood and tears that its cruelty have caused to be shed.

There is nothing in sight to anchor it; there is not sprig of a bush to which it can cling; it doesn't even have a hot branding iron to clutch to.

The plunge is fatal: a gush of air that is like the angry breath of all suffering humanity pushes it into the darkness of the abyss, of the black, profound abyss opened by centuries and centuries of oppression and crime.

It is the inexorable breeze from the proletarian masses who are tired of the yoke, filled with bitterness, overflowing with hate.

It is a formidable breeze from the phalanxes of misery, the sirocco of the dispossessed who resolve to raise their rags as a banner of redemption and retaliation, of justice and vengeance.

The bourgeoisie trembles beneath a sky in which all of the suns which bring them heat, which give them life are extinguishing; Díaz has disappeared; Nicholas has vanished in the darkness; Huerta has been eclipsed; Kerensky is an errant star that doesn't shine; Menocal [Mario García Menocal, the Cuban dictator] is sinking in the mud while flinging it about; Alfonso loses his equilibrium and to sustain himself even for an instant makes the stupid mistake of supporting himself on the proletariat's neck; Yrigoyen sinks; Guillermo, condemned by the conscience of humanity, flaps his wings furiously in the muck, like a wounded vulture.

The suns are going out! The suns are dying!

In the overcast night, Poincaré flickers like the light of a cheap lantern, and Edward hardly shines with the yellow light of a candle.

This great tragedy could well have for its title "The death of the gods" or "The twilight of the idols."

And what death and what a twilight, without glory and without luster!

Already at the edge of the abyss, the bourgeoisie wants to play its final card: it won't resign itself to die; it can't renounce its pleasures and privileges, drawn from the sweat and the tears of the poor, without inflicting its final gnashes and its final blows with its paws, claws extended.

And the gnashing, the clawing are directed today against Russia, the spring from which pours intrepid currents of fertile rebellion; and tomorrow they'll direct them against Mexico, the fertile land of proletarian redemption.

The heat from this fire will enliven the timid and the strong will fill their lungs with an atmosphere saturated with rebellion; it will signal to the fearful masses that the radiance of Russia extends to the entire globe.

The ground is ready for the new harvest: the emancipation of the proletariat.

The reign of the bourgeoisie is coming to an end.

No one has killed it; it has committed suicide!

A merciful kick, and it will disappear into the darkness of its own creation.

"Calavera Zapatista" is modeled on the work of Posada. It mimics Posada's famous "calavera" (skull) figures and depicts either Zapata or one of his followers.

THE MEXICAN PEOPLE ARE SUITED TO COMMUNISM

Regeneración, *September 2, 1911*

(Translated by C.B.)

The inhabitants of the state of Morelos, like those of Puebla, Michoacán, Durango, Jalisco, Yucatán and other states, in which vast areas have been invaded by proletarians who have immediately dedicated themselves to cultivating the lands, have shown the entire world, with their acts, that one doesn't need a society of savants to solve the problem of hunger.

To arrive at this result they took possession of the earth and the instruments of production in Mexico. They didn't need "leaders," nor "friends of the working class," nor "paternal decrees," nor "wise laws"—they didn't need any of this. Their actions did it all and continue doing it all. Mexico is marching toward communism more quickly than the most extreme revolutionaries had hoped for, and the government and the bourgeoisie now find themselves not knowing what to do in the presence of acts they believed were very far from being carried out.

It wasn't even three months ago that Juan Sarabia, in a long, sickening open letter directed to me, which was published in the bourgeois press in Mexico, told me that the working class didn't understand what we are advocating and that the people were satisfied with the fruits of Madero's revolt: the electoral ballot. But facts have shown that we members of the PLM are not under illusions, and that we fight convinced that our actions and propaganda respond to the necessities and to the manner of thinking of Mexico's poor.

The Mexican people hate, by instinct, authority and the bourgeoisie. Everyone who has lived in Mexico can assure us that there is no one more cordially hated than the policeman, that the word "government" fills the simple people with uneasiness, that the soldier, admired and applauded in all other places, is seen with antipathy and contempt, and that anyone who doesn't make his living with his hands is hated.

This in itself is enough for a social revolution which is economic in nature and anti-authoritarian, but there is more. Four million Indians live in Mexico who, until twenty or twenty-five years ago, lived in communities possessing the lands, the waters, and the forests in common. Mutual aid was the rule in these communities, in which authority was felt only when the tax collector appeared periodically or when "recruiters" showed up in search of men to force into the army. In these communities there were no judges, mayors, jailers, in fact no bothersome people at all of this type. Everyone had the right to the land, to the water to irrigate it, to the forests for firewood, and to the wood from the forests for the construction of small houses. The plows passed from hand to hand, as did yokes of oxen. Each family worked as much land as they thought was sufficient to produce what was necessary, and the work of weeding and harvesting was done in common by the entire community—today, Pedro's harvest, tomorrow Juan's, and so on. Everyone in the community put their hands to the work when a house was to be raised.

These simple customs lasted until authority grew strong enough to pacify the country, until it was strong enough to guarantee the bourgeoisie the success of its businesses. The generals of the political revolts received large grants of land; the *hacendados* [plantation owners] increased the size of their fiefdoms; the most vile politicians received vast tracts of "barren" lands; and foreign adventurers obtained concessions of lands, forests, rivers, of, in sum, everything, leaving our Indian brothers without a clod of dirt, without the right to take from the forests even the smallest branch of a tree; they were left in the most abject misery, dispossessed of everything that had been theirs.

As regards the mestizo population [of mixed Indian and Spanish heritage], which is the majority of the people of Mexico—with the exception of those who inhabited the great cities and large towns—they held the forests, lands, and bodies of water in common, just as the indigenous peoples did. Mutual aid was also the rule; they built their houses together; money was almost unnecessary, because they bartered what they made or grew. But with the coming of peace authority grew, and the political and financial bandits shamelessly stole the lands, forests, and bodies of water; they stole everything. Not even twenty years ago one could see in opposition newspapers that the North American X, the German Y, or the Spaniard Z had enveloped an entire population within the limits of "his" property, with the aid of the Mexican authorities.

We see, then, that the Mexican people are suited for communism, because they've practiced it, at least in part, for many centuries; and this explains why, even when the majority are illiterate, they comprehend that rather than take part in electoral farces that elect thugs, it's better to take possession of the lands—and this taking is what scandalizes the thieving bourgeoisie.

All that's left to be done is that the workers take possession of the factory, the workshop, the mine, the foundry, the railroad, the ship, in a word, everything—that they recognize no bosses of any type. And this will be the culmination of the present movement.

Forward comrades!

EXPROPRIATE!

Regeneración, *February 10, 1912*

(Translated by C.B.)

We know that agents of Emilio Vázquez Gómez, the new pretender to the presidential seat, are putting into play the same swindles used by Francisco I. Madero to attract our partisans to his files. The agents of Vázquez Gómez assure our partisans, in private, naturally, that we are in accord with their "chief" in overthrowing Madero. This is a lie. We work independently of Vázquez Gómez because our object is not the achievement of power. We don't want to get rid of one bandit to elevate another—and everyone who comes to power necessarily becomes a bandit.

Emilio Vázquez Gómez is a lawyer, that is, he belongs to the bourgeoisie, and as one of them he must serve the bourgeoisie. He does not approve of the expropriation of the lands by means of violence. Vázquez wants Madero to fall, to assume his seat in the presidential palace, and then he will dictate laws which resolve the social problem. Madero said the same thing. Don't forget it!

That which the proletarians can obtain in the midst of revolutionary ferment cannot be obtained later. When peace comes, authority will become strong, and as it necessarily must fulfill its mission, which is none other than to defend the interests of the capitalist class, the Mexican proletariat will remain in the same or worse conditions as before.

More than thirty thousand Mexicans have lost their lives in the course of this revolutionary movement, and the blood spilled and the blood that will be spilled in what follows cannot serve—we cannot permit it to serve—to elevate a few bandits to power. To arms!—but to snatch the earth and the means of production from the hands of the bourgeoisie, leaving everything in the power of the workers!

Our manifesto of September 23, 1911 clearly expressed the goals of the Partido Liberal Mexicano. Convinced by experience and the lessons of history that political liberties do not guarantee the right to life, we invite all Mexicans to back our goals of conquering this primary right, without which humanity will never be free. What good to a human being is the right to vote, to think, to write about whatever matter, to meet, to go from one place to another, etc., if to eat he needs to rent his arms to the rich for a miserable wage, and then is fortunate to find someone to exploit him?

War against the wage system, Mexicans! To end this system there's only one way: to make the lands and the machinery of production for common use; and this can be achieved only through means of force, since if one waits for the government to decree expropriation, millions and millions of years will pass without this phenomenon ever coming into being.

So then workers, expropriate! Whatever the banner you militate under: expropriate and everything will become the property of all. And if those who direct the operations of war oppose this work of supreme social justice, kill them!

Whoever it may be, with arms in hand, that tells you that you'll obtain this or that improvement after the triumph is a swindler: execute him! You would have saved yourselves so much fatigue, so much blood, so many tears, so much despair, if you would only have listened to our words when we told you to turn your guns on your leaders and officials last year! Well then, let this painful experience benefit you this time. Don't serve as cannon fodder so that your chiefs and officials can adorn themselves with gold and feathers. Don't elevate anyone to the presidency of the republic, because the pay you'll receive for your sacrifices will be, once you've elevated new exploiters, that you'll be commanded to return to your homes, to begin again that same life of privations and humiliations, because nothing will be changed then; the capitalist system will continue to oppress you, and with more cruelty, because the rich will be anxious to recoup the losses suffered during the revolution, and you'll be the ones paying for all the broken glass.

Miserable, unfortunate brothers: Now or never! Expropriate!

"Calavera of a Revolutionary Zapatista," by José Guadalupe Posada.

CHAPTER 5

CLASS WAR

THE CHAINS OF "THE FREE"

Regeneración, *October 22, 1910*

(Translated by C.B.)

Upon reading the constitutions of the advanced countries of the world, the philosopher can't do anything other than smile. The citizen, according to these constitutions, is an almost all-powerful being, free, sovereign, the boss and owner of presidents and kings, of ministers and generals, of judges, magistrates, representatives, senators, mayors, and a swarm of great and small functionaries. And the citizen, with an innocence that experience hasn't destroyed, believes himself free . . . because the law says so.

"Within our national territory everyone is born free," says our constitution. Free! And with the eyes of our imagination we see the peon bent over the furrow; he leaves his bed before the sun comes up; he returns to it late after night has fallen. Free! And in the black, loathsome, deafening factory, swarms a multitude of sweaty, panting, prematurely aged men who should be in their full vigor. Free! And everywhere we see men and women, old and young, work without rest in order to lift to their mouths a piece of bread—a piece of bread which is nothing more than is strictly necessary for the worker to continue his labors. Was it perhaps totally different when slavery was maintained under the law? Does the man of today, the "citizen," work less, even, than when he was a slave?

The slave was happier than the free worker today. As the slave cost the owner money, the owner was careful with the slave; he had him work in moderation, he fed him well, he sheltered him when it was cold, and if he fell ill, he entrusted him to the care of doctors. Today the great bosses don't give a damn about their workers. It doesn't cost them money to acquire them and they have their workers undertake exhausting tasks which in a few years cost them their health. They don't care that the workers' families will lack food and other necessities, because the slaves and their families do not belong to them.

The worker of today is as much a slave as the chattel slave was yesterday, with the only difference being that the worker can choose his boss. But he pays highly for this privilege in that he doesn't enjoy the conveniences, attention, and care of which the slave of old and his family were objects. But if one must lament the situation of the modern worker, that's no reason to sigh longingly for the days when slavery was legal. We should instead search for the most appropriate means of destroying the present system, because experience shows us that the worker of today, who carries the pompous title "citizen," is a true slave upon whom weighs the authority of the boss. The worker also has to support upon his weak back all of the social and political weight, the burden of which has been cleverly shifted from the rich and illustrious to fall with crushing weight exclusively upon the backs of the proletariat.

Capital, according to political economics, is accumulated work. The machinery, buildings, docks, railways are accumulated labor, that is, the work of intellectual and manual laborers in all of the ages up to the present day, and, therefore, there's no reason that this work should belong to a few individuals. Capital, in effect, is simply the laborious work of generations who contributed their science, art, or simply their manual labor to form it. Modern machinery is no more than the perfection brought to a head by generations of inventors, workers, artisans, each one of whom played his part in producing the complicated mechanisms that we admire today, and that should be the property of all, because they are the result of a collective work; but they belong—so declares the law, the law made by the rich—to only a few individuals.

If capital is the work of generations of laboring human beings, as is indisputable, it can't belong to a small number of individuals, but rather it belongs to everyone who is disposed to follow the path of members of previous generations who exerted themselves in increasing the amount of capital with their individual work. This is what logic and justice counsels; but the law, to which logic and justice are bothersome obstacles, orders the contrary. It's because of this that the proletariat must put itself at the orders of a boss to be able to live, permitting that the product of its labors pass almost entirely into the pockets of those who hold the social wealth.

All rights are guaranteed, except the right to live. The right to live is the basis of all rights, and consists of the right that all human beings have to take full advantage, simply by the fact of being alive, of all that exists, with no other obligation than that of allowing all other human beings to do the same, with all dedicated to the conservation and increase of the social wealth.

Understand, proletarians, that you have the right to something more than the handout that you are given for your labor under the name of "wages." You have the right to receive the full product of your labor, because capital belongs to all, men and women, old and young. A wage, therefore, is an outrage: it's the chain of the "free"—the chain that it's necessary to break in order that the word "citizen" ceases to be an affront, that it ceases to describe slaves. If this is done, we'll have achieved economic liberty.

The task, however, is not easy. Not only are the law and its upholders—the priest, the soldier, the cop, the judge, and all the machinery of government—opposed to this beautiful ideal, but also the passivity of the multitudes, the inaction of the masses accustomed to servitude and outrages to the point of finding them absolutely natural, a normal order: that the poor be a beast of burden for the rich and that the government be an abusive stepfather empowered by god to punish the people. It's necessary that the masses think differently, that they comprehend their rights so that they are inclined to reclaim them; and the principal right is the right to live.

This requires an arduous amount of education, and going to the public schools isn't adequate to attain it. The public schools educate the people in the sense of making every man a supporter of the present system. If the people learned in the public schools not to recognize the "right" of the capitalists to appropriate the product of the work of the proletariat, the United States, for example, would already have taken a pace on the road to economic liberty, since almost all North Americans know how to read and write. But in the schools they teach totally the contrary: they teach the child to admire the dexterity with which some men take advantage of the sweat and the exhausting work of others, in order to make themselves into kings of steel, oil, and other things. In the school the child is taught that saving and hard work are the origin of these modern Midases who leave the imbeciles gaping, when experience shows that only evil deeds, violence, and crime can bring wealth to a man.

The people then need education, but not the education of the public schools, whose programs have been suggested or dictated by those with an interest in perpetuating the slavery of the poor for the benefit of the evil and brazen. The education of the masses, in order to be truly in their interests and in line with the advancements in human understanding, must be in the charge of the workers, that is, those who pay the costs should suggest the educational program. This will ensure that young proletarians will enter fully into life, well armed with the modern ideas which will blow upon humanity the healthy breath of social justice.

At the side of proletarian education there should also be a workers' union; and so, with the joining of the union of the exploited and education, we will manage to break forever the evil chain which make slaves of the poor and bosses of the rich: the wage system. When we break it, all of humanity will freely and intelligently enjoy all that has been accumulated by the previous generations and that at present is under the control of a small number of slaveholders.

But before the Mexican proletariat can unite and educate itself, it is necessary that there be at least some material well-being. The long hours of labor, the insufficient food, the hard conditions in the places of labor and habitation, make it so that the Mexican laborer cannot progress. Tired from long hours of work, he hardly has enough time to rest before he must return to his prisoner-like task. And of course this doesn't allow time to meet with his comrades from work and discuss and think over the common problems of the proletariat, nor does this allow him time to open a book or read a workers' newspaper. The laborer, thus, is absolutely at the mercy of voracious capitalism. Therefore it's necessary to reduce the hours of work and to increase wages at the same time as land is delivered to the poor. In this way we can create an environment propitious for the education and the unity of the working class.

But in order to do this we must resort to violence. Opposed to the interests of the dispossessed are the interests of the rich and the interests of the bandits who are in power. Those who possess wealth are not going to allow the people a respite to catch their breaths and enter fully into the great struggle against those who oppose the emancipation of humanity. There remains no other recourse for the disinherited than to resort to force of arms to form, through our own efforts, a better environment in which we can educate ourselves and unite firmly for the great conquests that are to come.

Education and solidarity, having as their base the alleviation of present conditions, will be the immediate fruit of the coming revolution. A step beyond this and we'll have arrived in the shadows of the ideal.

Welcome the revolution. Welcome this sign of life, this sign of vigor in a people who are at the edge of the grave.

EVERYONE WITH HIS OWN CLASS
Regeneración, *April 22, 1911*

(Translated by C.B.)

Proletarian: your condition pains you. Your anemic, weak, filthy children demand your attention. Your woman suffers, almost always in silence. These are the consequences of your docility toward those who scourge you.

You are to blame that your children are hungry; upon your conscience hangs the pain and misfortune of your family.

Yes, you are culpable because you have contempt for your own class and admire, follow, applaud, and cheer the rich, those who shine with the gold that you have amassed with your sweat. It's in this manner that you yourself forge the chains that make you a slave.

Rebel, proletarian; but rebel with those of your own class, with those who, like you, have their hands callused and their backs curved by hard labor. Moreover, don't rebel in any manner whatsoever. Don't be a blind force, but a conscious force; that is, attack, burn, overthrow, destroy, spread death; but carry in your mind the idea that you fight for your class, that you're going to emancipate your class, that you're going to destroy the right of private property so that the riches of the earth cannot continue to be the exclusive patrimony of the rich and the intellectuals, that is, of knowledgeable men.

Join the files of the Partido Liberal Mexicano. Refuse indignantly those who try to tell you to follow Madero, because, hear this well: Madero is your exploiter; he is the exploiter of your class. Madero is rich and doesn't think of anything other than increasing his wealth. Yesterday he made millions exploiting your brothers on his haciendas. Now he wants to make more millions with the blood of the humble.

Awake proletarian: call your shame to your aid. You don't feel humiliated before the haughtiness of the rich? They rob you of the product of your labor and scoff at your dirtiness and rags. For the rich you aren't the creator of the wealth and luxury that they enjoy, but simply a bum. You make their palaces, and if you dare to go to those palaces they call a cop to take you to jail. You raise the crops, but be careful about taking them from the warehouses because you could die of a gun shot or end up in jail. You make the rich fabric and the comfortable furniture and carpets that aren't for your woman or for your children. You make everything that makes life agreeable, you keep the parks well tended, you construct and maintain the streets and highways, you tend the rails, you make the houses that you have to pay to live in. In sum, you make everything; everything flows from your creative hands. And nonetheless you don't get anything for it beyond that which is strictly necessary for you to continue to create more riches, riches, riches—and for that you get the contempt of those who exploit you, since to them you're nothing but a bum, an inferior being belonging to the lesser people, to the rabble.

Rebel indignantly, brother. Go and take up arms, but not with your oppressors, not with Madero, but with your brothers, the members of the Partido Liberal Mexicano. Madero wants you to continue working as you have, since his "revolution" only benefits the members of the upper classes.

Rebel with the unbreakable resolution to take possession of the earth and of the means of production for the benefit of all. Remember that the earth came to be in the power of a few only by means of conquest, that is, violence, and through other more or less evil means such as robbery, fraud, cunning, and speculation. Those who didn't obtain it through any of these means bought it or inherited it. And if they bought it, they bought it with the money that was created through the sweat of the working class.

The members of the Partido Liberal are not going to commit a robbery, but rather an act of justice, the most beautiful act of justice that has been contemplated in centuries, the most sublime witnessed throughout the ages.

Women: push your men to work for the happiness of your family. It's shameful that in this century there are poor and rich. Science has shown that we are all equal, that all, inherently, have a right to live. To conquer this right we must take possession of the earth and the machinery, and labor no more for the bosses.

CLASS STRUGGLE

Regeneración, *March 4, 1911*

(Translated by C.B.)

Humanity is divided into two classes: the capitalist class and the working class. The capitalist class possesses the lands, the machinery, the factories, the workshops, the tools of labor, the mines, the houses, the railways, the ships, and other means of transportation, and as the keeper of all of these, it can count on the government in any of its forms: absolute monarchy, constitutional monarchy, and republic, be it in centralized or federated form. The working class possesses no more than its arms, its brains, and the essential energy invested in performing any kind of labor—while it can remain on its feet.

The capitalist class, under whatever form of government, can live idly, because it is in a materially advantageous situation in respect to those who have nothing, that is, the workers; and the capitalist class enjoys by the same measure a great deal of independence and a great deal of liberty, since not only can it satisfy its needs without being beholden to anyone, but in addition it is supported by the governmental apparatus upon which it depends, with its laws, judges, police, soldiers, and prisons. In short, the capitalist class has all the means necessary to guarantee its free enjoyment of its riches.

The poor class, in virtue of finding material wealth monopolized by the rich, is forced to depend on the rich. If the poor man wants to work the earth, he has to rent himself for a price ("wages") which represents a small part of what he produces with his arms. If the worker wants to work in a factory, in a mine, on a ship, on a railway, in construction building a house, or any other kind of work, he equally has to rent his arms in order to receive a wage which represents, always, a small part of what he produces. It has been calculated that the bosses pay only a tenth the value of what is produced by the worker's labor, and in Mexico it's even worse, because as is well known wages in our country amount to little more than alms. Nine-tenths of what a worker produces passes into the pockets of the boss as profit, despite his having worked nowhere near as hard as the worker. This profit, naturally, is protected by the law which, as I've said many times, is a product, as are all laws, of the capitalist class; this class, of course, has to make laws that benefit itself, laws that protect the exploitation of workers by their bosses. These laws prevail in all parts of the world, in all of the so-called civilized countries, from those ruled by absolute monarchs to those governed by constitutional presidents, as in the United States and Switzerland, both renowned as "free" countries, as "model" republics.

The worker, then, is a slave everywhere. A slave in Russia, a slave in the United States, a slave in Mexico, a slave in Turkey, a slave in France—a slave literally everywhere. The famous political liberties which Maderismo [the movement to put Francisco Madero in power] wants to conquer, such as the rights to vote, to meet publicly, to think freely, and many others, are in truth nothing but swindles which divert the proletariat from its sacred mission: economic liberty. Without economic liberty, it's not possible to enjoy political liberty.

There are countries, such as Russia, for example, where there are no political liberties and, nonetheless, the worker is no more unfortunate than he is in the United States, the country which trumpets its "freedom." In the streets of Saint Petersburg, Moscow, or Odessa you'll see the same rags, the same pallid faces as in the streets of New York or Chicago. This is to say that in Russia, that barbarous and oppressive country, there exists the same problem, the same social question as exists in the United States, the country that boasts of being free and civilized.

In Canada, despite there being no law guaranteeing everyone the right to vote, that is, in that land where there is nothing called "universal suffrage," where only those with property can vote, the worker lives with more ease than in the United States where universal suffrage exists, that is, where every man of a certain age can elect his rulers.

This proves that it is not the vote, not the right to think freely, not the right to meet freely, nor any of the other political rights conferred by law which gives the worker food to survive. The right to vote is a joke. Here, in the United States, we have proof of this. The people of this nation have always had the right to vote and, nonetheless, the miserable ghettos of New York, Chicago, St. Louis, Philadelphia, and of all of the other great American cities are eloquent witnesses to the inefficiency of the vote in bringing about the happiness of the people. In these ghettos, hundreds of thousands of persons rot, both physically and morally, in squalid tenements, and in the entire nation, every morning four million human beings leave these palaces of filth and hunger to search for work so that they can return to these palaces with a crumb of bread for their wives and children; but as they often don't find work, they return with empty hands, their stomachs pinched, and they go out again the next day on their perilous, wandering journey in search of bosses to whom to rent their arms. And when election time rolls around, these hungry wretches clamor to fill out ballots to elevate another ruler who will continue to weigh down upon their necks.

If we have this example before us, why would we attempt to gain the illusory power of the right to vote? Wouldn't it be better to dedicate ourselves to the conquest of the lands, the lands which are the fount of all riches and which, in the hands of the people, would assure to all the means of life, and by the same measure economic liberty—and as a consequence of this true liberty?

Material well-being is what the people need to be free. That the people take possession of the earth and of the instruments of production is what the Partido Liberal wants. When the people themselves are the lords of the earth, everything else will fall into their hands through the force of this circumstance. Is this crazy? That's what the cowards, the ignorant, and all those who have an interest in the continuation of the present system of exploitation of the working class say. All of those who desire to occupy great or small public offices, all of those who want to live at the expense of others, desire that Madero will triumph. But those conscious workers who possess no more capital than their callused hands—callused by the hard work to which they've been subjected by the bourgeoisie—those workers who have understood what *Regeneración* has taught, these will not follow Madero; they can't follow those who make politics their means of living. Rather, they are disposed to continue the class struggle, the struggle against capitalism, until it crumbles to dust.

There are two social classes: that which exploits and that which is exploited. That which exploits has as its interest that Madero rises to power, so that it can continue to exploit. The exploited class, for its part, has as its interest that the lands be shared by all, that there be no bosses—and that there be no more misery.

Comrades, follow the banner of the Partido Liberal which carries this motto: Land and Liberty. -1P6

LIBERTY, EQUALITY, FRATERNITY
Regeneración, *October 8, 1910*

(Translated by C.B.)

How far is the ideal, how far! A mirage in the desert, a phantasm of the steppes, the twinkling image of a star reflected in a lake. First was the bottomless abyss separating humanity from the promised land. How to fill this abyss? How to plug it? How to reach the inviting beach that we divine is on the far shore? The thirsty Arab suddenly sees the waving of palm fronds in the distance and whips his camel toward them. It's in vain: he advances toward the oasis and the oasis appears to recede in the distance. The distance is always the same between him and it, always the same.

Defending the abyss are prejudices, traditions, religious fanaticism, the law. In order to be able to cross this abyss, one must vanquish its defenders until the abyss is filled with blood and then sail over this new Red Sea.

And the most noble men have dedicated themselves throughout the ages to filling this abyss with the blood of the wicked—and with their own blood as well. But the abyss isn't filled. One could empty into it all of the blood of humanity without filling it. What is necessary is for humanity to smother in blood all of the prejudices, traditions, religious fanaticism, and laws that oppress it.

The great revolutions have had as their goal these three things: Liberty, Equality, Fraternity. These words have been inscribed on a hundred banners and hundreds of thousands of men have had them on their lips as they died on the fields of battle; and, nonetheless, the abyss doesn't fill; the blood level doesn't rise. Why?

No revolution has seriously concerned itself with Equality, which is the basis for Liberty and Fraternity. Equality before the law, which was won in the French Revolution, is a lie which is rejected by modern consciousness. Revolutions up till now have been superficial wildfires. They could burn the trees in the woods, but the roots remained intact. Thus the revolutions so far have been superficial because they haven't gotten to the root of social evil; they haven't scraped away the putrefied flesh to get to the bottom of the wound; and for this their so-called leaders are to blame.

The leaders have always been less radical than the men they pretend to lead, and there is a reason for this: power makes a man conservative, and in addition he falls in love with ruling others. In order not to lose their positions, leaders moderate their radicalism; they compromise it; they disfigure it; they avoid clashes with opposing interests. And if in the nature of things a clash is inevitable and armed struggle is necessary, leaders always arrange things so that their positions are not in danger and they conciliate, as much as they can, with the interests of the ruling class, managing thus to diminish the intensity of the clash and the duration of the struggle; they content themselves with obtaining a more or less easy, superficial victory. The ideal ... the ideal remains very distant after these struggles of dwarves. With such struggles one scratches the surface and not much more.

Because of this, and despite the blood spilled throughout the ages; despite the sacrifice of so many noble men; despite the beautiful words Liberty, Equality, Fraternity having glowed on a hundred banners, the chains still exist. Society is still divided into classes and the war of all against all is still what is normal, what is legal, what is honored, what the "serious" call "order," what the tyrants call "progress," and what the slaves, blinded by their ignorance and made timid by centuries of oppression and injustice, venerate and sustain through their submission.

It's necessary to go deeper, to get to the bottom of things. The leaders are cowards; they don't go deep and they don't get to the bottom of things. The revolutionary impulse always stumbles over the moderation of the so-called leaders, who are deft politicians, if you will, but who lack revolutionary vigor. Above all, if you want to do something revolutionary rather than the vulgar work of politicians, it is necessary to place one's hands upon "private" lands. While the earth continues to be the property of a few; while there are millions of human beings who have no more than the tiny space needed to lay out their cadaver when they die; while the poor continue to work the land for their bosses, any "revolution" will have no other outcome than a change of bosses—and at times the new ones will be worse than the ones thrown out.

The revolution is imminent. At any moment the telegraph cable will announce to all of the nations of the Earth that the Mexican people are rebelling. The assaults of the tyranny are growing in brutality, and every time it is done more cynically. Porfirio Díaz is crazy: he's no longer content with snatching the lives of men, but he's also murdering women whose corpses lay unattended to be eaten by dogs. The Old Beast is precipitating the revolution, and the ambitious will take advantage of it if the people do not take possession of the land.

Liberty, Equality, Fraternity: three beautiful words which it is necessary to make into three beautiful acts. Let the revolutionaries place their hands upon this god called "the right of private property" and make the land belong to everyone.

If there is going to be bloodshed, let it be for the good of the people. To shed blood to elevate a candidate to the presidency of the republic is a crime, because the ills which afflict the Mexican people won't be cured by kicking out Díaz and putting another in his place. Let's suppose that the most honorable of citizens, the best man in Mexico, triumphed by way of arms and came to occupy the spot now possessed by the most perverse and criminal of Mexicans: Porfirio Díaz. That which this good man would do would be to put in force the Constitution of 1857. The people, therefore, would have the right to vote; they would have the right to freely express their ideas; the press wouldn't be gagged; there would be a division of powers in the federation; the states would recover their sovereignty; there would be no perpetual re-election of the same man. In sum, the Mexican people would obtain what is called political liberty. But would this make the people happy? The right to vote, the right to meet, the right to write about any matter, the doing away with "re-election," the division of powers—would this provide bread, shelter, and clothing to the people?

It's necessary to say it one more time: political liberty doesn't give the people anything to eat; it is necessary to achieve economic liberty, which is the basis of all the liberties; and without it political liberty is a bloody irony which converts "the people as king" into the king of jokes, because if in theory the people are free, in reality they are slaves. So it is necessary to take possession of the land, to yank it from the claws that hold it now, and deliver it to the people. Then the poor will have bread; then the people will come to be free; then, with a little more effort, we'll come close to the ideal that we see from afar because the leaders of the revolutions haven't had the guts to throw down idols, to slay prejudices, to break into pieces the law which protects this crime called private property.

One must, however, speak honestly. The people's taking possession of the land will be a great step toward the ideal of Liberty, Equality, Fraternity. But only a great step. However, thanks to it, the people will have the opportunity to obtain the education they need in order to construct, in the more or less near future, the just and wise society that today is only a pretty illusion.

And while there is no effective advance along the road of economic liberation, no healthy work will be done. Liberty cannot exist while one part of society makes the laws that the rest must obey. Since it's easy to comprehend that nobody will make a law contrary to their own interests, and as the class that possesses the riches makes the laws or, at least, orders that they be made, this must result, in toto, in laws favorable to the capitalists and unfavorable to the poor. That's the reason that the law doesn't extend its reach to punish the rich and doesn't bother them at all for any reason. All of the social and political costs fall upon the poor. Taxes must be paid exclusively by the poor. Gratuitous services, such as night watchman rounds, unpaid extra hours of work, and others, weigh exclusively upon the backs of the poor; the army recruits exclusively among the proletariat; and in brothels the daughters of the rich are not degraded, solely the daughters of the poor. This is inevitable: it's absurd to think that the rich would make laws contrary to their own interests.

Under such conditions, can equality exist? Socially, equality is a chimera under present conditions. How can the rich and poor be equals? Neither in appearance, nor in dress, nor in living style are the dominators and the dominated similar. The work of the poor is hard and tiring; their lives are a series of privations and worries, caused by their misery; their distractions are scarce: alcohol and sex; they can't partake in the enjoyments of the rich because those cost a lot of money and, besides, they don't have the clothes to mingle with elegant people; the manner in which they've lived hasn't been the best preparation for acquiring cultivated manners; the opera and drama, apart from being costly, require a certain artistic or literary preparation that the poor cannot have, having been pushed since children to earn the bread they need to survive.

So, equality before the law is one of the greatest idiocies those who wish to govern offer the masses. If social equality is impossible while there are social classes, the same holds true politically. The judges rule in favor of the rich and against the poor when they hand down their decisions; the exercise of the right to vote is always directed, organized, and carried to a head by the dominant classes, because they have the time for it, leaving to the poor only the "right" to carry their ballots to the ballot boxes with the name marked of someone chosen by those who have organized and directed the election. This results in the workers electing whomever the ruling class wants them to elect. The right of free expression cannot be exercised by the poor, because they haven't been able to acquire the necessary facility in writing or public speaking, so this right is taken advantage of, almost exclusively, by the dominant classes. And if one would compile a list of all political rights, one would eventually arrive at the conclusion that the poor cannot exercise these rights because their slave jobs leave them only the time absolutely necessary to rest themselves in their short hours of sleep. They don't have the social presence provided by education; they don't have economic independence; they don't even dress well; and they lack the polish to compete well with the smoke-blowing bourgeois intellectuals.

Fraternity! What fraternity can exist between the wolf and the lamb? Social inequality makes natural enemies of the different social classes. The possessors cannot harbor friendly sentiments toward the dispossessed, in whom they see a constant threat to their enjoyment of their riches; and likewise the poor cannot harbor fraternal feelings toward those who oppress them and who enjoy the fruits of their labors. From this grows a constant antagonism, an interminable dispute, a hidden struggle—and at times an open and decisive struggle—between the two social classes, a struggle which gives life and force to hateful sentiments, to desires for revenge that are not appropriate to the creation of fraternal ties and real friendship, things which are impossible between a thug and his victim. But that's not all. There's even more today that impedes human beings from becoming closer, opening their hearts to their brothers. The struggle for life, even though it's shameful to admit it, reveals in the human species the same brutal and wild characteristics as in the lower animals. As long as the human species isn't steeped in solidarity and mutual aid, everyone will go in search of bread in competition with others in the same manner that snarling dogs will fight each other over the opportunity to chew up a rancid bone. This is the truth in all social classes. The rich man, envious of the wealth of another rich man, will make war on him in order to augment his own treasure with the plundered wealth of the other. This is called, with the hypocrisy of the epoch, "competition." The poor man, for his part, is the enemy of his equally poor brothers. The poor man sees an enemy in those he comes near to, perhaps because they might rent themselves to the rich for a lower price than he would. If there's a strike, there's no lack of the hungry dispossessed who will betray their class brothers, taking the places of the strikers. In this way of things, fraternity is a dream, and in its place we find only the hatred of one class for another; the hatred of the individuals in one class for each other; the frightening war of all against all that dishonors the human race and delays the coming of the day of love and justice of which noble men dream throughout the world.

The revolution will break out. Everyone, those who choose to struggle in it and those who don't, will be dragged along by the great movement. No one will be able to remain indifferent to the great clash. It is necessary, then, to choose a banner. If one desires simply a change of bosses, there are parties other than the Partido Liberal that will struggle solely to install new presidents and vice-presidents. But those who desire a genuine revolution, a deep, great revolution that will benefit the poor, will come to our files and gather together under the equalitarian banner of the Partido Liberal Mexicano; and, united, we will yank the land from the few hands that now grasp it and deliver it to the people; and we will come closer to the ideal of Liberty, Equality, Fraternity via the well-being of all.

"Calavera Huertista" depicts the brutal, reactionary General Victoriano Huerta, a vicious foe of the PLM and the Mexican Revolution. This image mimics the work of Posada, but was probably produced by another artist.

THE REPERCUSSIONS OF A LYNCHING

Regeneración, *November 12, 1910*

(Translated by C.B.)

The daily papers in this city have occupied themselves over these last few days telling their readers about the outrages inflicted upon U.S. citizens by rebellious mobs in Mexico City. The stories told by the press are really hair-raising; but we believe that they are greatly exaggerated.

One can't deny that there is a reaction against U.S. imperialism in all of the Latin American countries; the reason for this is that imperialism is a grave threat to the lives of the Latin countries as autonomous nations. There is a sentiment of hostility in our countries, one that is more marked every day, against the engulf-and-devour politics of the U.S. government.

The reason is not the North American people, but rather the greed of the great U.S. millionaires—the thirst for gold of the plutocracy of this country has been the origin of this hostile sentiment which makes slow and hard the achievement of fraternal relations among the human beings who populate this continent, because while those of us who have liberated ourselves of racial prejudice work toward creating fraternal ties among all human beings, the millionaires, the big businessmen, the financial bandits, manage through their acts to divide the peoples, to open abysses between the diverse races and nationalities, and in this manner to ensure their empire. "Divide and conquer," says Machiavelli.

The attacks suffered by the peoples of Latin America have been motivated by the ambitions of the great millionaires, who use patriotism as a vehicle to commit outrages upon peoples who have committed no crime other than to live upon rich lands which have tempted the greed of Wall Street. Who doesn't recall the attack on its sovereignty suffered by Colombia? [This refers to Teddy Roosevelt's fomenting a "revolution" to split Panama off from Columbia so as to be able to build the Panama Canal.] Who has forgotten the intrigues of the great millionaires of this country against the independence of Venezuela? For whom is it a mystery that the politics of the White House toward Latin America is a politics of absorption, and a politics which tends, moreover, to support the most unbridled tyrannies, such as that of Porfirio Díaz in Mexico? And who doubts now that wherever there appears a government that doesn't submit to the shameful tutelage of the U.S. plutocracy, sooner or later it will see itself subjected to revolts shaped, directed, and fomented by rich North Americans? Who now doubts that interventionist expeditions depart from the ports of the United States to overthrow, to make "revolution" against, those Latin American governments that refuse to submit to the demands of U.S. capitalism? Isn't it public knowledge that the revolution against President Zelaya of Nicaragua was the work of North American adventurers paid with the gold of Wall Street? And if this isn't enough, don't the Mexican people remember that they shed their blood combating the U.S. plutocracy due to the ambitions of the rich toward the lands of Mexico? [in the Mexican-American War of 1846–1847, in which the U.S. seized half of Mexico's national territory]

These are facts which speak eloquently. These are facts which are in the memories of all, facts whose origins lie in the insatiable thirst for riches of the great U.S. millionaires, and facts which have come to raise a great wall between the two peoples of this beautiful hemisphere: a wall which would continue to stand erect, insurmountable, and which would end up turning into bitter enemies two important factions of humanity if the propaganda of the libertarians hadn't fired the sentiments of love and fraternity in the hearts of all races, sentiments that when they flare up will bring down this barrier raised by the crimes of capitalism, making of all the interests of one: beautiful, grand solidarity.

In Mexico, especially—there's no use in denying it—there exists a very marked hostility toward the absorptionist tendency of the U.S. government, a sentiment which day by day deepens because of the individual or collective actions of the North Americans against the Mexicans who reside in this nation. Everyone knows the contempt with which Mexicans in general are treated; everyone knows that in Texas Mexicans are treated worse than blacks. Mexicans are not admitted to hotels, restaurants, and other public establishments in Texas. The public schools close their doors to children of our race. North American semi-savages take target practice on Mexicans. How many men of our race have died because a white-skinned savage decided to prove his ability with firearms by shooting at us?—and without having any dispute with us! In the so-called courts of justice, Mexicans are judged, generally without bothering with legal formalities, and are sentenced to hang or to suffer other horrendous penalties without there being proof, or even the suspicion, that they actually committed the crimes for which they are sentenced. All of this is added to the arrogance shown by the U.S. rich who consider our unfortunate country a conquered country, because the cowardly and traitorous tyrant who oppresses us gives them everything that they want; he concedes everything on their demand, puts them in possession of cultivated lands that were possessed by humble laborers—because it's always the poor who suffer; he gives them ample authority to cut down our forests, in order that they exploit for their own sole benefit the riches of the Mexican lands and seas, and in order that they function as authorities, in almost every case more brutal than native authorities. All of this has come to raise even higher the barrier that capitalism has put between the two races; all of this has made more difficult the task undertaken by the libertarians of the world, through our acts and our propaganda, of building fraternity and love among all the races of the world.

That's the way things are. And when the Mexican people see in the North American plutocracy the worst enemy of their liberty; when they realize that all of the persecutions and tortures we've been subjected to in this country are the result of the desires of the great U.S. millionaires that the conditions of tyranny and barbarism continue in Mexico, conditions that make possible the rapid enrichment of the very worst of men; when they see the way things are, we say, it won't take more than a single event to set off a storm of protest—and the event that produced an explosion of indignation, as reported in the daily papers of this city, took place upon the savage plains of Texas, and its perpetrators were a mob of white savages who viciously targeted a humble Mexican. This Mexican, Antonio Rodríguez—accused of murdering a white woman, but who was never tried for it—was tied to a post by a horde of white North Americans and burned alive. This horrifying crime took place in Rock Springs, Texas on the third day of this month [November 1910].

Students in Mexico City organized a protest against this lynching, and it took place on the night of Tuesday the 8th. A great multitude gathered; there were fiery speeches denouncing this outrage. A large group of demonstrators went to the offices of the U.S. periodical, *The Mexican Herald*, which as is well known is supported by Díaz and which is one of the principal adulators that the despot counts on. The demonstrators smashed the building's windows into pieces with rocks.

On the following day, Wednesday, the students, followed by an immense multitude, roamed through the main streets of the city crying out against the murders of which Mexicans are victims in Texas. Various businesses ended up with their windows broken. A U.S. flag was seized by the multitude and torn to pieces amidst cries of indignation against the crimes committed against Mexicans in this country.

The papers also report that a North American was lynched and a North American child beheaded, but there is no proof of this, and it all boils down to the desire of these papers to attract readers through sensationalism.

Similarly, these papers report that dynamite bombs were thrown toward the residence of the U.S. Ambassador to Mexico. Again, these reports are unfounded.

On Wednesday the multitude invaded the building where the lowest, most abject paper published in Mexico—*El Imparcial*—is edited, and undertook the task of destroying the shop. The mounted police arrived, and with machete blows dispersed the demonstrators, with one of them succumbing to a saber slash from one of the cossacks.

On Wednesday, more notable things happened: troops fired upon demonstrators, resulting in men being killed. When they were dispersed in one place, though, the demonstrators reunited in another. This happened repeatedly. There were many encounters between the thugs and the people.

The protest of the residents of Mexico City resonated in Guadalajara, where students also organized a protest demonstration. For several hours the multitudes were the rulers of the city. Many U.S. businesses were stoned. The entire garrison was put under arms, and after several clashes between troops and demonstrators the crowds were dispersed.

The government of Díaz, with its customary barbarity, had more than a hundred students arrested in Mexico City; it also gave definitive orders to the police and soldiery to ferociously repress any cry of protest, and reacting to the protests from the White House, has given forth explanations, promises of satisfaction, and promises to suppress all of the papers that, in virtue of having published articles protesting the lynching of Rodríguez, excited the public to demonstrate its disgust.

This is all that is known as *Regeneración* goes to press. The Catholic periodical *El País* ["The Country"] recommends a boycott of U.S. products as a protest. Other periodicals are publishing articles energetically denouncing the crimes of which Mexicans are the object in this country; but none of them dare to speak the truth; none of them will open their lips to say that it is capitalism—the voracious octopus that sucks the life of the people—that is the cause of all of these disturbances, of all of these crimes, because capitalism foments racial hatred so that the peoples never come to understand each other, and so it reigns over them.

THE UPRISINGS IN TEXAS

Regeneración, *October 2, 1915*

(Translated by C.B.)

Several weeks ago the bourgeois press was reporting on the clashes between Mexicans and the forces of the United States in the territories that comprise the Texas counties of Hidalgo, Cameron, Starr, and others neighboring them.

As is natural, the cause of this contest is hidden. Some wish to spread the belief that the uprisings of Mexicans in that portion of the United States was due to an agreement among Mexicans to bring to a head the Plan of San Diego, which advocates for the independence of the vast territory that the United States snatched from Mexico in the middle of the last century. But time passes and the true cause of this movement is appearing.

It's not the desire to put under the control of Mexico the U.S. territory that comprises the states of Texas, New Mexico, Arizona, Colorado, California, and parts of some others, which has impelled the Mexican residents of Texas to rise in arms against the authorities of the United States, but something very different: the desire to defend themselves against the attacks of which members of our race are so often victims in this country.

I have here the explanation of the origin of the uprisings from the bourgeois paper, *El Presente*, of San Antonio, Texas: "The origin of the revolt can be found in the following events. A Mexican was dancing in a little town near Brownsville, and an American wanted to snatch his woman away from him. The Mexican refused, and upon going out to the street was treacherously shot by the American. The Mexicans immediately avenged the death of their countryman, and then returned to the town, already armed and disposed to defend themselves from lynching or hanging. The precarious [economic] situation of several men made them see in this an opportunity for an armed uprising, and they took it, in order to take what they needed to live in this violent form."

How different this is from the lies propagated in the rest of the bourgeois press!

As can be seen, the movement in Texas commenced with the rebellion of a handful of men who didn't want to be the victims of the rampant injustice which afflicts our race in that state, and this handful was joined by all those tired of offering their arms to the bourgeoisie to be exploited, and then not even getting the work they wanted. They found in the attitude of the rebels a good opportunity to snatch from the hands of the capitalists that which the capitalists deny to the poor: a piece of bread for themselves and their families.

Naturally, these rebels were the victims of a ferocious persecution, because the grand dame Authority is intransigent and ferocious to such an extent that rather than procuring peace among men, her criminal acts incite them to war. Instead of approaching these men and politely attempting to calm them by guaranteeing their being left in peace and freedom, her representatives, these barbarians called "rangers," a type of rural police in the border region with Mexico, opened fire on the rebels as soon as they had them in view. The rebels shot back, and this was the commencement of the state of war in which that portion of the United States found itself.

Nonetheless, the struggle still could have been confined to the fight between the rangers and the original rebels. But authority is not a shield nor a shelter for the poor, but rather a scourge, and therefore rather than protecting the poor inhabitants of the region in which authority was persecuting the rebels, it commenced to antagonize them in a thousand ways, pretending to find a rebel in every male Mexican the thugs stumbled upon; and then commenced an infamous hunt of Mexicans by the rangers. The rangers, reinforced by civilians, groups of cops, and inhuman types of all descriptions, entered en masse into the humble houses of the Mexicans (but not into the houses of the bourgeoisie, for which authority is the guard dog) and there delivered themselves into a veritable cannibalistic saturnalia, shooting old men, women, and children, attempting to avenge themselves upon the innocent for the casualties inflicted upon them in open battle by the rebels.

One of many such invaded houses belonged to the comrade Aniceto Pizaña, an honorable man who resided in his dwelling on the de los Tullvos ranch in the jurisdiction of Brownsville. The house was assaulted by a mob of savages representing authority on August 3, with the invaders discharging their weapons upon the inhabitants without respect of sex or age. Aniceto is not a man who will allow others to trample him, and with three other comrades who at the time were in his house returned the fire of the rangers, who numbered thirty-five. A vicious fight followed. Our four comrades made prodigious, valorous efforts, and the assaulters found themselves pinned down, and despite the thugs' great advantage, our heroic comrades held them at bay for over half an hour, shooting some dead and wounding some. Unfortunately, one of Aniceto's children was wounded in the leg by one of the bandits, and there was no remedy other than amputating the leg. Since then, Aniceto has found himself under arms and, according to the bourgeois press, his revolutionary activity is intense.

The case of Aniceto is not an isolated instance. The same occurred in other places in the Brownsville region. These reckless acts were carried out by the representatives of authority upon persons who perhaps had never even thought of rebelling, but who were impelled by circumstances to take up arms to defend themselves against the invasive savages in order to save their own lives and those of their families, or even to have the satisfaction of exchanging a laborious and honorable life for the criminal life of a ranger, a cop, or a vigilante of the savage state of Texas.

We have here the manner in which the spark of rebellion was blown into flames, and that which commenced as the vulgar persecution of a handful of individuals has been transformed through the stupidity of authority into a true revolution. There is no "Plan of San Diego" nor any other such hoax; what we have is a legitimate movement of self-defense of the oppressed against the oppressor.

Those who have taken up arms are not bandits, as they are labeled by the bourgeois press, but rather men who having found no protection in authority reach for the rifle. These are men who prefer to sell their lives dearly rather than allow themselves to be killed like lambs by bandits with neither conscience nor honor.

The crimes committed by the rangers in these last two months, and particularly in these last weeks, would rub the nerves raw of the most phlegmatic man.

Hundreds of innocent Mexicans have been killed by these savages, with the victims including men, old people, women, and children. The houses of Mexicans have been burned, their fields destroyed, and these attacks have contributed to the spreading of the revolutionary movement. *The Los Angeles Tribune* says, in its edition of September 8, referring to the zone enveloped by the revolution in Texas, "... A territory as large as the state of Illinois is seized by fear of midnight assaults, the burning of ranches, and death."

In another part of the same edition, it says: "More than five hundred Mexicans have been killed in the Rio Grande area over the past three weeks according to information given by the 'rangers' this day—September 7—to police officials in the counties affected by the revolution."

This is what the rangers confess; but knowing the criminal instinct of the vicious beasts that inhabit the police bodies in the state of Texas, one can presume that their information is incomplete, and that the number of the victims of authority is higher.

I have here how *El Presente* refers to the victims of the rangers: "Nobody knows who killed the men who show up hung from the trees or riddled with shots; but the entire world points at the rangers."

And it adds: "Men have been killed hiding under their beds, and they have been killed inside their houses, in spite of having asked for a moment of peace to explain themselves. They have been taken to the jail to be hung, and even more have been shot in the back after giving up their arms and surrendering."

Shot in the back after they've surrendered! What better proof of a felony can be demanded against a ranger?

This, in grand strokes, is what has occurred in Texas. It's not a movement of bandits, as the bourgeois press tries to make it appear, but rather a natural movement of men who see their existence threatened and who defend themselves as best they can.

Justice, not gunshots, is what should be given to the revolutionaries in Texas. And, of course, everyone should demand that these persecutions of innocent Mexicans should cease and, in regard to the revolutionaries, we should also demand that they not be shot.

Those who should be shot are the rangers and the mob of bandits who accompany them on their depredations.

THE UPRISINGS IN TEXAS (2)
Regeneración, *October 9, 1915*

(Translated by C.B.)

The uprisings of Mexicans in the state of Texas, uprisings which according to the news in the bourgeois press the militia has not been able to suppress, are giving an opportunity to our enemies to attribute to us participation in them. The papers that support Carranza openly accuse us of being the intellectual directors of the revolt, with the perverse goal of throwing us to the dogs of authority.

It appears that the infamous labors of the Carranzistas are having some effect, as can be seen in the lines which we'll quote in a second from the paper in San Antonio, Texas, *La Prensa* ["The Press"]. The Los Angeles correspondent for that paper says in an article dated September 30: "The agents of Carranza in this city, acting under orders received directly from Veracruz, have for the last few days been undertaking a secret assignment, and have ended up making an accusation against the well known Mexican socialist Flores Magón, who has taken root here form some time; these agents say that 'he is the intellectual author of the disturbances which have been occurring along the Texas border for the past two months.'"

What is true in this will be seen later. Carranza simply wants that we be hung, this being the penalty of the prostituted law that applies to those who rebel against the state.

We are tranquil. We know that our activity, our dedication, our rebellion disgust those who tyrannize and exploit, and that they will not lack a pretext to throw us to the bottom of a dungeon or onto the steps of a gallows. We fear nothing, however. Before suffering humanity, we have promised to be loyal to the cause of the oppressed of the Earth. And we'll continue to be loyal until we exhale our final breath. All this we have resisted in our hazardous lives as unshakable rebels, and we'll continue resisting it: misery, exhaustion, prison, and death. Onward!

We give this notice, so that our brothers in chains will not be alarmed when they see us in the claws of authority; we give this notice so that no one will be discouraged, so that all will continue onward. If we are persecuted, we do not want discouragement to spread, but rather that with doubled vigor all proceed with the great work undertaken until the goal is achieved: the death of the capitalist system.

THE UPRISINGS IN TEXAS (3)

Regeneración, *October 30, 1915*

(Translated by C.B.)

The truth makes the world progress; the lie is a log placed in the path of the cart of progress. The truth, like liberty, like justice, cannot exist in part: there is entire truth or there isn't, as white is white or it isn't. The truth doesn't threaten anyone other than those with an interest in hiding it, and this interest cannot be honorable, because honor is the twin sister of truth; they are inseparable: where there is truth, there is honor; where there is honor there must be truth.

The bourgeois press has the habit of hiding the truth; the truth is light, and there are certain businesses that can only prosper in the darkness. That inveterate camouflager of crime, the bourgeois press, has to hide the truth. That is its business!

The bourgeois press along the border, from the *Los Angeles Times* to the insipid bourgeois Mexican periodicals that abound in the southwest of the United States, when referring to the uprisings that for three months have shaken the southern part of Texas, has not had more than a single preoccupation: hiding the truth, distorting the facts, calling us the authors—at least the intellectual authors—of the Mexican proletarian revolt in Texas. This can be seen in their writings, in the speed with which they denounced us as being, with no justification whatsoever, responsible for what occurred in Texas. In the revolution in Texas there are anarchists, comrades of ours, but they don't obey any leadership, because if they did so they'd cease to be anarchists.

We are likewise accused of having printed several proclamations that those revolutionaries have circulated, apparently in profusion, urging the Mexican workers to rise up in arms; and corresponding to the excitement in the bourgeois press, the authorities sent their agents marauding through the humble shacks in which we have our offices to see if they could discover anything. For the past month, thugs of all descriptions have come to poke their snouts into this corner of the city, which was formerly very peaceful. On any pretext they've come near to our place of work to see what we were doing.

In respect to the revolution in Texas, the bourgeois press continues to insist upon treating it as a racial clash, whose principal objective is to kill whites and to carry the war forward until the vast territory that Mexico lost in 1847 will return once again to Mexican sovereignty.

The origin of the revolutionary movement, as we mentioned in the October 2 issue of *Regeneración*, was a common quarrel in a place near Brownsville between an American and a Mexican. The Mexican was treacherously killed by the American, and then several Mexicans avenged the victim by killing the American. The authorities persecuted the avengers, who took up guns rather than be taken with their arms folded. Others, being in misery and seeing an opportunity to win bread through violence, rallied to these men. Then occurred the first clashes between the pursuers and the pursued, in which some of the American thugs died, and then the representatives of authority commenced a veritable orgy of blood-shed. The Mexicans who fell into the grasp of the thugs were killed without any proof that they had taken part in the uprising. Hundreds of innocent persons of the Mexican race died—men, women, old people, children. Mexicans were killed wherever they were found. Such actions of authority provoked many Mexicans to rise in arms, some in order not to die without taking someone with them, some pushed by indignation over the injustice. Comrade Aniceto Pizaña, who appears up till now to be the most notable figure in the movement, found himself surprised in his house by a gang of thugs who assaulted him for the sole fact of being Mexican. Pizaña, as an anarchist, didn't appreciate this outrage, and in union with three comrades from the vicinity resisted the brutal attack, in which Aniceto's only son, who is only eleven years old, lost a leg. In the struggle several thugs lost their lives, and Aniceto and his three comrades found themselves in the dilemma of either delivering themselves to the fury of bourgeois law or of declaring themselves in open rebellion. They preferred the second alternative, and they joined to the revolutionary movement that which carries great force: the anarchist idea.

This occurred on the third of August. Since then to date, the revolutionary movement has attained great size judging from troop movements in this part of the country, movements which are not carried out as a mere pastime, but which have to be motivated by the presence of armed bands of Mexicans from various parts of the district affected by the revolution; and this belief is fortified by seeing in the bourgeois dailies the news of encounters between revolutionaries and soldiers from the U.S. Army in various places.

The movement in Texas is a true economic and social movement. Born in a common incident, a transcendent movement has been developing for the last three months. This movement is now considered so important that General Funston has had to ask for considerable reinforcements in order to suffocate it.

The bourgeois periodicals call the proletarians in arms bandits, but the facts demonstrate that they are not bandits. There are still no accounts of these men committing attacks on defenseless people. No. They are not bandits; they are men; they are revolutionaries; and we have the proof of this in the following leaflet which we received by mail from Texas. The following document—which we publish to demolish the lies of the bourgeois press, and to allow the public to know what is really going on in that state—says this:

"To arms, Mexicans!

Declaration of principles. What we want and why we fight:

"Brothers and sisters, read this and reflect.

"We the people, we who work the lands, are those who produce everything and possess nothing, not even what is indispensable for the sustenance of our beloved families, which is bread.

"Because of this, we are convinced that it is cowardice to live in this world of misery and pain, misery and pain caused by the thieves who steal our labor, that is the rich. In order to end this, today we launch ourselves into an armed struggle, waving the red flag which is the symbol of the disinherited, of those who suffer in the fields, workshops, and mines.

"We take this step, which is to go toward a life in pursuit of progress, a life in which every man with a good heart should desire to live in a society in which everyone works according to their abilities and receives according to their needs, and to make this a fact. It's necessary to destroy capitalist society, which is based on crime and theft, and once it's destroyed build the new society upon its ruins, with the entire working class forming a single family, the universal family, in which peace and justice reign.

"But this cannot be obtained by begging on one's knees, but rather by going with arms in hand and putting the flaming torch to everything which is based upon the exploitation of man by man.

"Mexicans! Don't pamper these damned bourgeois gringos who have contempt for us, who mistreat our families, and lynch us as if we didn't even have the right to live.

"Rebel to the cry: Down with the exploiters and thieves who steal our labor!

"Yes, take the lands that a few have in their power and put them in the hands of those who work them, that is the campesino who day after day waters the furrow for a little bad food to eat.

"Mexican, awaken, put down the plow and take up the gun so that you don't merit the contempt of your brothers who have nobly taken this decision that honors the race that today is so despised by those who live off our labor, the American capitalists.

"Yes, we fight for no political party but rather for our liberty and that of our children.

"Be men, Mexicans! Take the gun in hand and don't allow that our families die in the most frightening misery, caused by the landowners who steal the product of our labors.

"Rise up to the cry of 'Death to the bourgeois gringos and long live libertarian communism!'

"Bread and land for all.

"We fight for the economic and social emancipation of the universal proletariat.

—The group in arms in Texas, USA, October 1915

"Note: We will not put down our arms until the following four goals are attained:

1. Abolition of all government of man by man.
2. Elimination of the capitalist.
3. Extermination of clericalism.
4. That the land become the common property of the producers of social wealth.

"Mexicans: Live to be free, or die for allowing yourselves to be slaves!"

Bandits don't express themselves in such a manner. They don't express themselves in the manner of those who sent us the flyer we've just reproduced. Bandits do not harbor in their hearts desires for human redemption, as do those who wrote this flyer, in which is advocated the creation of a single human family composed of the working class and, to use their words, "the universal family in which reigns peace and justice."

It can be seen that the revolutionaries of Texas are not animated by race hatred. On the contrary, they want "the universal family."

Nor do bandits dream of working, while these men don't desire anything other than to work, as can be seen in the paragraph in which they say: "take the lands that a few have in their power and put them in the hands of those who work them, that is the campesino who day after day waters the furrow for a little bad food to eat."

These are not, then, bandits, these workers rising up in arms in Texas, but rather revolutionaries who, as they themselves say, "fight for the economic and social emancipation of the universal proletariat."

Let the bourgeois press, then, stop its lying. The truth is not to be feared; what is to be feared is the lie.

Ricardo and Enrique Flores Magón in the Los Angeles County Jail, 1907.

CHAPTER 7

POLITICAL REPRESSION

THE INTERVENTION AND THE PRISONERS OF TEXAS

Speech, May 31, 1914

(Translated by C.B.)

Let my words resound as a condemnation of the powerful of the Earth; let my words rise angrily and fearlessly to announce to the exploiters of the people that there is a will greater than that of the tyrants, that there is a force more powerful than the fist of the despot, and that this will and this force reside in us, those on the bottom, among those contemptuously dismissed by those who exploit us, among those who with our arms and intelligence construct the buildings and with our sweat and blood cultivate the fields, maintain the railways, drill the tunnels, draw the useful minerals from the bosom of the Earth, and who, when hopelessness fills our breasts, with the same hands that create the wealth, will raise the barricade and fire the gun.

The necessities of the moment are truth and valor. It is necessary to speak the truth, whatever the cost. If U.S. forces have planted the stars and stripes on the coast of Mexico, it hasn't been to satisfy a worthy desire for benevolence and justice. This banner has been planted in Veracruz like a dagger in the breast of justice; this banner did not appear on those beaches as a luminous symbol of civilization and culture, but as the black rag that covers the face of crime while it empties the pockets of its victim. This banner is the mask of all the great bandits of industry, commerce, and finance of all countries whose interest it is that the Mexican worker remain a slave. This banner is the knife and the whip, the chain and the noose. It doesn't shine as an insignia of redemption and progress; rather, it floats in the breeze like a shroud blown in the night by the winds of death.

What noble impulse impelled this rag to land on the beaches of Mexico? What friendly breeze dragged it toward these lands? What noble idea is represented by it, flying above a city taken by surprise? Fear and greed: this is what is at the bottom of this farce which will end in tragedy—the fear that all the oppressors and all the exploiters of humanity feel before the unmistakable awakening of the enslaved masses who struggle to break their chains. If the Mexican Revolution were a movement which had as its object the unseating of a president in order to put another in his place, the exploiters of the people would laugh, because such a movement wouldn't threaten them, because the social system that allows them to become rich and powerful at the expense of the suffering of the workers would remain intact. But this is not what is occurring in Mexico. Before the frightened eyes of the international bourgeoisie and the governments of the world, one of the most stirring and sublime dramas in the history of the peoples of the world is unfolding in that beautiful country. There is being disputed, with guns in hand, the right of all human beings to live; there the workers tear to shreds the property titles of the rich, and showing to the astonished world, with their hands, what tradition and the law call sacrilege, they emit this heroic cry: "No more titles sanctioned by the law! From today forward, in order to live and enjoy the wealth, there will be no other titles to property than the calluses on the hands."

The international bourgeoisie and all governments fear that the spark which glows in Mexico will be the beginning of a formidable conflagration which, sooner or later, will turn the world into a single flame which will reduce the capitalist system to ashes when the worker puts down his tools, which serve only to enrich the owner, and takes up the banner of Land and Liberty. Because example is contagious, the hungry in the United States, the French outcast, the Russian slave, the British serf, the disinherited of all countries could take a lesson from their brother, the Mexican worker and, undertaking on their own count that task of winning their liberty and well-being, could apply the torch and dynamite to political and monetary power, which is the only means left to the poor man to rid himself of his exploiters.

Fear and greed were the trembling hands which brought the stars and stripes to Mexico. The fear of the oppressors and exploiters of the entire world is that their respective flocks will imitate the Mexican worker and will wave, in every land, the red banner of Land and Liberty. The fear is that the Mexican worker, having taken possession of the land, and free by that sole act, will refuse to rent his arms to enrich the parasites. The U.S. forces did not come to Mexico in the name of civilization and benevolence; these forces came to murder Mexicans to benefit the bandits of finance and the principle of authority. These forces have been pushed by capitalism to kill the workers who don't want bosses, who want to be free, who no longer supplicate, who do not ask anymore, and who, resolved, noble, and virile, pluck from the chest of the rich the black heart that never contracted when faced with the pain of the humble.

Such is the motive for the intervention, and on this black page of international politics, like the serpent that slithers noiselessly through the weeds to strike the heel of his victim, two reptiles drag themselves, two reptiles who it will eventually be necessary to crush: Villa and Carranza, two sons of Judas. The plan forged in the shadows is simple: with the aid of the U.S. forces, Villa and Carranza will be able to arrive in Mexico City, seat themselves in power, and deliver the Mexican worker, tied hand and foot, to capitalist exploitation. The threat from the

U.S. forces in Veracruz to Mexico City is no other thing than a move in a military game that has for its entertaining object the tying up of the Mexican forces which oppose the invasion, while Carranza and Villa can advance with no real obstacles toward the heart of the country. Santa-Anna died, but he has been reincarnated in these two bandits: Carranza and Villa. These are the men who invite U.S. capitalism to invade Mexico; these are the vultures who hope that American arms give the coup de grace to Mexican liberties, so that they can seat themselves and then devour the cadaver.

Without the consent of Villa and Carranza, U.S. capitalism wouldn't have dared to invade Mexican territory, and this lesson, like so many others, should serve to show the workers that they should entrust to no one the resolution of their affairs, because while the proletarians, deaf to the voice of reason, blind to the light of experience, entrust to one or a number of individuals the mission of giving them their liberty and of making them happy, the chains of slavery will continue to be their prize for their good faith and their trust. The proletarians who follow Carranza and Villa do not follow them, certainly, for the pleasure of changing bosses, nor to permit themselves the luxury of exchanging yokes, but in their simplicity they believe even yet that somebody can give them liberty and well-being, when, hear it well proletarians, liberty is not a thing to be given, but a conquest taken by the oppressed for themselves, and liberty, understand it well, cannot exist side by side with misery, but rather is a direct, logical, natural product of one thing: the satisfaction of all human needs, without depending on anyone to deliver them.

A man is free, truly free, when he doesn't need to rent out his arms to anyone in order to lift a piece of bread to his mouth, and this liberty is obtained solely in one manner: taking resolutely, without fear, the lands, the machinery, and the means of transport so that they will be the property of all, men and women alike.

This will not be gained by elevating anyone to the presidency of the republic, because the government, whatever its form—republican or monarchical—can never be on the side of the people. The government's mission is to guard the interests of the rich. In thousands of years, there has not been a single case in which a government has put its hands upon the property of the rich to deliver it to the poor. On the contrary, wherever government has been seen and wherever it is seen, the government makes use of force to repress any attempt of the poor to better their situation. Remember Rio Blanco, remember Cananea, where the bullets from the government soldiers smothered in blood, in the throats of the proletarians, the voices that asked for bread; remember Papantla, remember Juchitán, remember the Yaqui, where the machine guns and rifles of the government decimated the energetic inhabitants who refused to deliver to the rich the lands which gave them subsistence.

These experiences should serve to show you never to entrust to anyone the task of delivering your liberty and well-being. Learn from the noble proletarians of the south of Mexico. They do not aspire to elevate a new tyrant so that their hunger will be mitigated. Valiant and noble, they don't ask; they take. Before the women and children who ask for bread, they don't wait for a Carranza or a Villa to rise to the presidency and to give them what they need; rather, valiantly and nobly, with gun in hand, in the thunder of combat and the flashes of the incendiary, they yank from the haughty capitalist his life and riches.

They do not wait for a caudillo to rise up who will give them something to eat. Intelligent and dignified, they destroyed the titles to property, tore down the fences, and put their productive hands upon the earth. To ask is for cowards; to take is the work of men. On our knees we can arrive at death, not life. Let us rise.

Let us rise, and with the shovel that now serves to pile up gold for our masters, let us split their skulls in two, and with the sickle that weakly cuts off ears of corn, let us cut off the heads of the bourgeoisie and the tyrants. And above the smoldering embers of this damned system, let us plant our banner, the banner of the poor, to the cry of Land and Liberty!

Let us no longer elevate anyone; let us all rise! Let us no longer hang medals or crosses on the chests of our leaders; if they want to be decorated, let us decorate them with our fists. Whoever is an inch above us is a tyrant; let us topple him! The hour of justice has arrived, and in place of the ancient cry, the terror of the rich, "Your money or your life!" let us substitute this cry: "Your money and your life!" Because if we leave a single member of the bourgeoisie alive, he will know how to arrange things so that sooner or later he'll have his foot on our necks.

To put into practice the ideals of supreme justice, the ideals of the Partido Liberal Mexicano, a group of workers began a march one day in the month of September last year in the state of Texas. These men had a grand mission. The revolutionary movement of northern Mexico having been corrupted by the heads of the movement, they went overflowing with noble ideas to inject new energy into the spirit of rebellion that had quickly degenerated in this region into the spirit of discipline and subordination to leaders. These men went to establish a tie between the revolutionary elements in southern and central Mexico and the elements that had remained pure in the north. You know well what the fortunes were of these workers: Juan Rincón and Silvestre Lomas fell dead after being shot by thugs employed by the state of Texas before reaching Mexico, and the rest, Rangel, Alzalde, Cisneros and eleven more find themselves prisoners in that state, some of them sentenced to long prison terms, others to life imprisonment, while Rangel, Alzalde, Cisneros and others are going to fall victim to the death penalty. All of these honest workers are innocent of the crime imputed to them. It happened that one night during their journey to Mexico a Texas sheriff named Candelario Ortiz died, and they dumped the responsibility onto the fourteen revolutionaries. Who witnessed the act? No one! Our comrades were found at a great distance from where the thug's body was found. Nonetheless, they tried to throw the responsibility for the death of this dog of the capitalists upon them, for the simple reason that our prisoner brothers in Texas are poor and are rebels. It was enough that they were members of the working class and that they had the intention of crossing the border to fight for the interests of their class, for North American capitalism to pile on top of them trying to avenge the loss of its businesses in Mexico. If our comrades had been partisans of Villa or Carranza, if they had had the intention of going to Mexico to put a Villa or Carranza in the presidential seat, so that these men could direct business to the North Americans, nothing would have been done to them; on the contrary, the U.S. Authorities would have protected them. But as they are noble men who want to see the Mexican worker completely free, the U.S. bourgeoisie discharged its anger upon them and asked for the death penalty as a compensation for the losses to its businesses it's suffering in the proletarian revolution.

In contrast, the murderers of Rincón and Lomas are free. The same U.S. bourgeoisie which asks for the death of Rangel and his comrades heaps honors and distinctions upon the felons who took the life of two honorable men. We have here, proletarians, bourgeois justice. The worker can die like a dog, but don't touch the thug who did it! Here and everywhere the worker is of no value. Those who are valued are those who do nothing! The bees kill the drones that eat in the hive, but who don't produce anything. The humans, less intelligent than the bees, kill the workers—who produce everything—so that the rich, the rulers, the cops, and the soldiers, who are the drones in the social hive, can live comfortably without producing anything useful.

This is bourgeois justice. This is the accursed "justice" that we revolutionaries must destroy, let it pain whomever it pains, and let fall whomever will fall.

Mexicans: the moment is solemn. The time to count ourselves has arrived: we are millions and the exploiters are only a few. Let us claim our brothers who are prisoners in Texas from the hands of bourgeois justice. We cannot permit that the hands of the hangman put the rope of the noose around those noble necks. Contribute money toward the defense of these martyrs; agitate to shift opinion in their favor.

Enough with the crimes committed against persons of our race! The ashes of Antonio Rodríguez haven't even been spread by the wind yet; on the plains of Texas the blood of the Mexicans murdered by the white savages is still drying. Let us raise our arms to impede the new crime that the North American bourgeoisie is preparing against Rangel and his comrades.

Mexicans: if you have blood in your veins, unite to save our prisoner brothers in Texas. By saving them you'll save not only Rangel, Alzalde, Cisneros and the other workers, you'll save yourselves, because your actions will earn you respect. Who of you hasn't been the victim of an outrage in this country for the sole reason of being Mexican? Who of you hasn't heard daily of crimes committed against our race? Don't you know that in the south of this country that Mexicans are not permitted to sit by the side with North Americans in restaurants? Haven't you entered a barbershop where you've been told, while they look you up and down, "We don't serve Mexicans here"? Don't you know that the prisons in the United States are full of Mexicans? And haven't you even counted the number of Mexicans who have been lynched or burned alive by brutal mobs of whites?

If you know all this, help in saving our racial brothers who are prisoners in Texas. Contribute with your money and with your minds to saving them. Let us agitate for them. Let us declare ourselves on strike for a day as a demonstration of protest against the persecution of those martyrs, and if protests and legal defenses don't serve, if agitation and strikes don't produce the desired effect of putting the fourteen prisoners at complete liberty, then rise up, rise up in arms against injustice with the barricade and dynamite. Let us count ourselves—we are millions.

Long live Land and Liberty!

ONCE AGAIN AT OUR POST

Regeneración, *January 13, 1914*
(Translated by C.B.)

After a forced absence we once again find ourselves free. We entered jail with our heads held high and we leave it with our heads held high, saying to all, friends and enemies: "Here we are! Here we are!" If the enemy believes that he has crushed us, it's necessary to confess that the enemy has failed. Shackles tortured our flesh, but our will is whole and today we are the same men as always, tenacious rebels, enemies of injustice.

Upon renewing our labors we send our cordial greetings to the oppressed of the entire world and our defiance to the powerful of the world. For the oppressed we bring our love and our sympathy; for the powerful we bring damnation and a whip.

Through means of these lines we wish to make know the affection we have for all of the comrades, both male and female, who with their monetary contributions or through their personal labors aided our comrades Teodoro M. Gaytán, Blas Lara, and P. Araujo in sustaining this periodical.

Now we hope that all will continue their aid in the best manner possible to help ensure that the periodical of the oppressed will continue its propaganda work. The circumstances in which we've found the paper are truly terrible. The deficit has continued to grow week by week, though thanks to the heroic efforts of our comrades Gaytán, Lara, Araujo, Owen, Téllez and a few others we've found that our beloved periodical still has life. But we believe that it will be very difficult to prolong this life unless each and every one of our friends and sympathizers, men and women, make some sacrifices and undertake not only to save the life of *Regeneración*, but also to help the periodical reach a press run of at least 50,000 copies weekly.

Those who truly have a commitment to making the periodical live, those who understand the necessity of its publication, should make powerful efforts to sustain it. We are ready to suffer jail or assassination; we've sacrificed everything for the cause of the workers and hope that all of the poor, men and women alike, will make the sacrifice of dedicating a few centavos or pesos every time they can to sustain the paper.

Now, to work with the same enthusiasm as before until victory or death.

Long live Land and Liberty!

WINDS OF THE TEMPEST

Regeneración, *November 13, 1915*

(Translated by C.B.)

Regeneración has always had the privilege of attracting a tempest, in the same manner as a summit attracts lightning. This is because *Regeneración* is great, because *Regeneración* is the summit, because *Regeneración* is an eminence from whose heights the truth is spoken.

And this is what causes pain: that the truth is spoken. The beautiful, grand, sweet truth for those who suffer; the same truth is horrible, is bitter for those who exploit and swindle. This is why the poor love truth and the tyrant hates and fears it.

Regeneración has always spoken the truth. For that truth, it has been crushed on more than one occasion by tyranny, its editors thrown into prison, its presses confiscated, its offices invaded, its archives seized.

Once again the tempest announces itself. Something hatched itself in the shadows against the beloved periodical in which we're growing old, for which we have sacrifice the pleasures that flourish in youth, for which we have offered the only wealth which the poor can possess: our health.

The honest periodical, the enlightening periodical, the periodical that leads the way is going to be snatched from our hands and thrown into the mud without life, dead—the periodical that injects strength into the hearts of the sad; the periodical that puts a touch of roses into the minds darkened by misfortune; the periodical that as an arm holding aloft a torch in the darkness signals to the people the path that they should take.

With its death, *Regeneración* will carry away part of our lives, because in its columns we have emptied unmeasurable amounts of blood from our arteries, illumination from our minds, and in its cramped lines we have deposited huge amounts of energy, will, sincerity, and determination.

Regeneración is a periodical that, by its very nature, is always in danger of its life, not because it offends virtue and loves crime, but rather quite the contrary: because it educates, instructs, awakens enthusiasms that endanger the existence of a social, political and economic system that permits a few to do nothing useful and still enjoy all the good things in life, and that condemns the rest of humanity to fatigue, pain, slavery, and death.

Naturally, those who have an interest in maintaining the present iniquitous system, because they could never obtain advantages under a system based on liberty, equality, and fraternity, are the most bitter enemies of *Regeneración*.

Regeneración, despite everything that is said to the contrary, is a periodical that exercises great influence within the Mexican revolutionary movement. This is why Díaz pursued it to the death in Mexico as in the United States, spending around a million dollars to ensure that we were stopped by three years in prison, after being arrested in August 1907 until we were freed in August 1910.

Later, Madero, spending a similar amount, managed to have us returned to prison from June 1912 to January 1914.

Now that Carranza is the persecutor, another torrent of gold will be necessary to put us in prison under new charges. Of course, he has already begun to channel this gold which does not come from his own pockets, but rather from the sweat of the poor people who inhabit the part of Mexico dominated by his soldiers. These people, who yearn for their liberty, will be obligated to contribute to the buying of their own chains, or, what is the same thing, to the putting in prison of those who truly fight for their liberty.

The influence that *Regeneración* exercises in Mexican affairs has been confessed by the most prominent politicians and businessmen in Mexico, and by the U.S. Senator Falls, based on the information he gathered during three years on the foreign aid received by the Mexican Revolution; he concluded that the Partido Liberal Mexicano and its organ, *Regeneración*, were responsible for the constant state of agitation in which the Mexican people have found themselves.

Those interests which want to confuse the people deny that the astonishing progress of the Mexican Revolution over the past five years is due to the Partido Liberal Mexicano; and they deny that if principles of communist anarchism triumph in Mexico it will be due to the Partido Liberal Mexicano and its organ, *Regeneración*.

For several weeks we've noted an increase in the vigilance with which the authorities have watched us here, to the point where it's not only the occasional isolated dog who spies on us, but the entire pack that watches us. If one adds to this the insistence with which the Carranzist periodicals have been accusing us of being the intellectual authors of the revolutionary movement of Mexicans in Texas, there is good reason to believe that a plot is being hatched against us, the purpose of which on the part of the United States is to aid Carranza in ridding himself of anyone who could stand in the way of his plans for consolidating his government.

One final circumstance has furthered the belief that someone is preparing an accusation against *Regeneración*. Various comrades have received a circular sent out by the postal inspector, W.M. Cookson, of the post office in this city, asking that they serve as witnesses against *Regeneración*. Some of the comrades have sent us these circulars. I have here a translation of said circular:

Los Angeles, Cal.
November 4, 1915

Dear Sir:

I am informed that you are a subscriber to *Regeneración*, a periodical published in Los Angeles. I would like to obtain from you two or three issues of this periodical, which have been sent to you by post during the month of October 1915 or September 1915.

Examples of this periodical are needed in the investigation of a matter being studied by the Post Office, and therefore I would appreciate it if you would send to me, in the enclosed return envelope, which does not need postage, the issues of *Regeneración* which you have received by post in the United States during the month of October 1915, issues which will be carefully preserved in order to be returned to you after they have been utilized for what is needed.

In this matter, I would appreciate it if you would put your initials on every issue to identify it, as well as to certify that the periodical was received by you via regular post.

Attached is a return envelope for the mailing of the issues, and I would appreciate it if you would act on my request as soon as you are able.

From your attentive, faithful servant,
Inspector W.M. Cookson

As can be seen from this circular, the matter is serious. They are trying to bring charges against *Regeneración*, and for charges against a periodical to be admitted in court, it's necessary to demonstrate that it's circulated via the mails. The testimony that *Regeneración* is circulated via the mails is what the postal authorities want to obtain from our comrades.

The charge against *Regeneración* must be founded in some writing that has appeared in the October issues, as can be deduced from Cookson's circular. They're trying, therefore, to violate one of our constitutional rights: that of writing about any matter, a liberty fully conceded to all writers: to the socialist, to the free-thinker, to the Republican, to the Democrat, to the religious, to the prohibitionist, to everyone except the anarchist, which demonstrates that the famous political liberties, in the United States as in every other country on Earth, are a farce when one attempts to use the truth to show that the present system under which we humans suffer is evil, and that it's necessary to overthrow it in order to build from the ground up a new one more in accord with liberty and justice.

Comrades: the purpose of doing away with *Regeneración* can be clearly seen, the purpose of suppressing the periodical and throwing us in prison. It's necessary to defend against this brutal assault on freedom of thought. It's necessary that in these trying moments that we unite as a single man around the periodical. Two things are needed immediately, on the march, without delay: to protest and to collect funds to defend against the persecution.

On the third page you'll find a protest in both Spanish and English. Everyone who values the life of the periodical should sign it and send it to Woodrow Wilson in Washington, DC.

To confront the persecution which draws near, send funds without wasting time, since we lack them. Remember that we've sacrificed everything in this long contest we've been sustaining and that we can't count on anything other than the solidarity of honorable workers.

Venustiano Carranza wants to cement his rule with the aid of the United States. This is why we're being persecuted. Don't permit such a government to become strong, because if this succeeds all will be lost that has been won through so much sacrifice.

Help us!

SARCASM

Regeneración, *April 21, 1917*

(Translated by C.B.)

While all the partisans of war deceive themselves by saying that the United States fights for liberty, the judiciary committee of the senate is considering a law against espionage. This law, which will shortly be approved by congress, prohibits the criticism of what's going on now, and only allows criticisms of past events.

No one will be able to give his opinion of what's occurring now. If the acts of the government are rash, those of a headless man, well, they'll remain reckless, the acts of a headless man, because after they approve this law it'll be a treasonous crime to think with your own head.

This law also gives the postal general wide power to impede the circulation through the mails of anarchist periodicals.

One couldn't ask for greater freedom nor a greater spirit of justice.

If an anarchist periodical denounces the war as a crime, as there can't be a greater crime than the killing of human beings to maintain exploitation and tyranny, then this periodical will be denied all mailing privileges, its editors will be arrested, and if the government wishes they'll be shot.

In contrast, if a bourgeois periodical stirs up a war of proletarians against proletarians, to the benefit of privilege and tyranny, well then, this bourgeois periodical, this fomenter of hatred between peoples, will be given full mailing privileges and its editors will be overwhelmed with honors and distinctions.

There is liberty, but only for lies and crime.

"Calavera of Revolutionary Woman," by José Guadalupe Posada. Women took an active role in the military operations of many rebel bands during the 1910 Revolution.

MARGARITA ORTEGA

Regeneración, *June 13, 1914*

(Translated by C.B.)

It's difficult to follow pace by pace the actions of the comrades in Mexico who are working to channel the revolutionary movement toward communist anarchism. One can't count on easy means of communication; the railroad lines are destroyed; the bridges have been blown up; the mountain passes are watched by the soldiers of Huerta, those of Carranza, the libertarians, the zapatistas, or by armed members of other factions. Apart from all this, the contingencies of the struggle oblige the different combative forces to change positions, to cut the telegraph lines, or to take refuge in the heart of the mountains and forests.

For all of these reasons, the news arrives very late when it does arrive, since frequently the messengers are shot before they get to their destination, or are stopped in some other manner. There's no reason to think it strange, therefore, that it's taken us so long to confirm the death of the great anarchist who in life was known as Margarita Ortega.

This extraordinary woman was a member of the Partido Liberal Mexicano, whose anarcho-communist ideals she propagated through word and action. In 1911, Margarita was the link between the combat forces of the Partido Liberal Mexicano in Baja California. An able horsewoman and an expert in the use of firearms, Margarita crossed the enemy lines and smuggled arms, munitions, dynamite, whatever was needed, to the comrades on the field of action. More than once her boldness and coolness saved her from falling into the clutches of the forces of tyranny. Margarita Ortega had a great heart: from her horse, or from behind a rock, she could shoot down a government soldier, and a little later one could see her caring for the wounded, feeding the convalescents, or providing words of consolation to the widows and orphans. Apostle, warrior, nurse—this exceptional woman was all of these simultaneously. She could never stand to see anyone suffer in her presence, and many will testify how she took a piece of bread from her own mouth in order to give it to the hungry.

A woman of exquisite sentiments, she loved her family deeply; but her family was composed of unconscious people, of bourgeois persons and proletarians who aspired to be bourgeois, and they could never understand how a woman endowed with such extraordinary talent and such inexhaustible energy, and who possessed a substantial fortune, could make common cause with the disinherited. And for this reason they hated her; they hated her as those with vulgar hearts hate the noble and pure who stand in the way of their mean ambitions.

Margarita had enough of a fortune that she could have lived an easy, lazy life; but she couldn't enjoy that life while she knew that there were millions of human beings who struggled painfully to gain subsistence. With the energy that one finds only among persons with convictions, Margarita said in 1911 to her unconscious partner: "I love you, but I also love those who suffer; and I fight and risk my life for them. I don't want to see any more men and women giving their energy, their health, their minds, their future to enrich the bourgeoisie. I don't want men to command men any longer. I'm resolved to continue fighting for the cause of the Partido Liberal Mexicano, and if you're a man, come with me to the battle. If that's not the case, forget me; I don't want to be the partner of a coward." The persons who witnessed this scene affirm that the coward didn't want to follow her. Then she turned to her daughter, Rosaura Gortari, speaking to her in these terms: "And you, my daughter?" This heroine responded to the other: "And separate myself from you, mama? Never! Let's saddle the horses and launch ourselves into the battle for the redemption of the working class!"

When Madero rose to power, Margarita and Rosaura were expelled from Mexicali on orders of Rodolfo Gallegos. In order to make the situation of the martyrs more painful, Gallegos ordered that they march through the desert and its immense sand dunes under the scorching sun without water, without food, and on foot with the notice that if they returned to the town they'd be put in front of a firing squad. For several days the poor victims of the capitalist system dragged themselves through the sand dunes. Thirst devoured them; hunger made them weak. Not one traveler lent them aid; not one arroyo slaked their thirst. Rosaura weakened visibly, making Margarita's situation even sadder. In the end, in spite of her extraordinary energy, Rosaura fainted, fell to the earth, and closed her eyes. Margarita believing that the daughter she loved with all her heart had died and, crazy with pain, tried to commit suicide. But when she put the gun to her head she saw that her daughter was looking at her and, overcome with emotion, ran in search of water to give to the stricken one. Fortunately, this time she found it.

They arrived in Yuma, and there they were arrested by the immigration authorities. A woman like Margarita, an honor to humanity, a splendid example of the human race, couldn't reside in this land of vulgarity and stupidity. For a person to be able to enter the United States, it's necessary that they believe in law and authority. The libertarian Margarita, in accord with the imbecile laws of the U.S., couldn't be admitted and was to be deported to Mexico. Thanks to the services of some excellent comrades, Margarita escaped the claws of the immigration inspectors and with Rosaura went to seek refuge in Phoenix, where she adopted the name María Valdés to throw off the thugs. Rosaura adopted the name Josefina.

Rosaura remained ill as a consequence of the hardships suffered in the desert, and her only desire was to return to Mexico, but with arms in hand, fighting for Land and Liberty. She didn't want to die in bed, but rather on the battlefield, exchanging life for life. When her illness grew so grave that she couldn't even get out of bed, she said to Margarita: "Mama, I don't want to die here. Carry me out to the street, where the Mexican workers gather. I want to die in their midst, with my brothers, speaking to them of their rights as the producers of social wealth." A little later the sweet child died without repenting that she had abandoned the comforts of a bourgeois life for the turbulent life full of the dangers and miseries of a true revolutionary.

Margarita remained alone. Her daughter and comrade in struggle could no longer share the hardships, the worries, the miseries that are the reward of the sincere fighters. But this didn't cause the noble sower of ideals to slacken in her work. With the comrade Natividad Cortés, she undertook to organize the revolutionary movement in the northern part of Sonora, having as a base of operations the little town of Sonoyta in that state. This occurred in October of last year. Both comrades worked with ardor, coming to an agreement with the comrades who resided on Mexican territory, when Rodolfo Gallegos, who this time was a partisan of Carranza and who was given the charge by his boss of watching the border, tripped over them by accident. Comrade Natividad Cortés was shot on the spot, and Margarita carried off as a prisoner to Baja California, where Gallegos ordered that she be left in a spot where she would certainly be seen and captured by the forces of Huerta, in this manner leaving to them the task of murdering her.

Margarita was arrested on November 20 of the past year by the forces of Huerta, and put in jail with a guard standing watch. The felons who boast of being authorities went to pains to martyr her. She didn't fear confessing that she was a member of the Partido Liberal Mexicano, and as such she fought the hydra with three heads: authority, capitalism, and the clergy. But she didn't denounce any of the comrades who were in accord with her about launching the cry of Land and Liberty! in the northern part of the state of Sonora. Then they tortured her, as in the dark times of the Inquisition. Her cowardly torturers wanted to make her disclose the names of the comrades who were pledged to rebel. But all of their efforts shattered against the will of steel of that admirable woman. "Cowards!" she cried. "Tear my flesh to pieces, break my bones, drink my blood. But I will never denounce my comrades!"

Then the paid assassins of tyranny condemned her to stand day and night in the middle of the cell, without permitting her to sit or support herself against the wall. Exhausted by fatigue, at times she wobbled and had to support herself on the guard who watched her; and then a push and a kick put her back in the middle of the cell. Other times she fell to the floor, weak and exhausted from so much suffering; she would be kicked until she managed once again to get to her feet.

She endured this torture for four days and nights, until the authorities in Mexicali took her from her cell on November 24 to shoot her. They formed the firing squad in a deserted place in the night so that no one would be aware of the murder. Margarita smiled. The executioners trembled. The stars twinkled as if they were trying to descend to crown the head of the martyr.

A volley caused the noble woman to fall to the earth without life, a noble woman whose exemplary existence should serve as a stimulus to the disinherited to redouble our efforts against exploitation and tyranny.

REVOLUTIONARY PROGRESS
Regeneración, *February 12, 1916*

(Translated by C.B.)

As a note that demonstrates the great revolutionary progress achieved in the five years and some months of the revolution, we reproduce the following notice, which we've copied from the "cientifico" periodical, *La Prensa*, which is published in San Antonio, Texas:

"El Paso, Texas, February 1.

"The Congress of Women, meeting in the city of Merida, at the behest of General Salvador Alvarado, governor of the State of Yucatán, has ended its series of scheduled sessions. The final resolution of the Congress, according to information received in the constitutionalist consulate of this city, is that the woman is exactly equal to the man in intelligence and that, therefore, she should have the same rights as he does to fill public posts.

"The Congress of Yucatán Women intends, with this declaration, to authorize a campaign which will soon be initiated to make the campaigns of women in the upcoming Yucatán elections triumph."

This, so far, is the notice.

The resolution that "the woman is exactly equal to the man in intelligence" is magnificent and honors the ideals of the revolution, which sees in the woman not an inferior, contemptible being, but rather the comrade, the sister of the man, with whom he ought to struggle side by side for human emancipation, because if humanity is enslaved, she is also enslaved, and if it is free, she is also free.

We anarchists consider the woman entirely equal to the man and entitled to the same rights, and we observe with pleasure the important resolution of the Congress of Yucatán Women that declares "the woman is exactly equal to the man in intelligence." The only thing that disgusts us is that the woman aspires to occupy public posts, and this does disgust us—not because we're dealing with women, but because we're dealing with the preservation of the system that oppresses us equally as women and men.

How much better it would be if the beautiful and intelligent Yucatán women, upon realizing that the woman is exactly equal to the man in intelligence, would fight for an anarchist society inside which the woman would be entirely equal and would obtain the maximum amount of liberty and well-being to which every human being is entitled.

Within the system of private property, no matter how much the woman exerts and sacrifices herself to conquer her liberty and well-being, she will never attain it, just as the man will never attain it. The capitalist, authoritarian system is not evil because men rule it, but rather because, in itself, it is a system that enslaves the human being from the moment that the greater number are condemned to servitude so that a handful of parasites can enjoy all of the delights and enjoy all of the liberties.

The proletarian woman, whether men or women govern, will be as much a slave as the proletarian man.

The evil is, then, the capitalist, authoritarian system, and it is in working against this odious system that we should demonstrate ourselves, men and women, to be equals.

The participation of women in public affairs connected to the capitalist system is, certainly, progress, because it's based upon a consideration of social justice: that of giving the woman the same rights as the man. But it constitutes, at the same time, a step backward due to the hidden consequences of this feminine participation in political affairs, because if until now lack of feminine participation was a disgrace which distracted the proletariat in the economic and social struggle, which should be sustained so that it can achieve its total emancipation, elections and other democratic farces will equally distract women in this fertile struggle, which has so lacked their determined cooperation; this must, naturally retard the triumph of anarchy.

The politicians are astute. They clearly see that the revolution marches toward an anarchist society, and they go to meet it with reforms that put obstacles in its path, that make its march slower. This is because all reforms, even when at first glance they appear to be a forward step, when you get below the surface you'll find that they are obstacles placed in the path of progress.

Reform is not a medicine which produces health, but rather a sedative that delays it. The politicians are like quack doctors. Rather than use a medicine that will quickly return the patient to health, they apply sedatives in order to exploit for the longest time possible the ill health of the patient.

How much better would the pretty and talented Yucatán women make humanity if, in a moment of healthy aspiration, they would set to one side democracy and adopt in its place the anarchist principles set forth in the manifesto of September 23, 1911!

How much that would please the cause of progress!

TO WOMEN
Regeneración, September 24, 1910

(translated by M.V.)

Women comrades, the cataclysm is afoot, her eyes furious, her red hair blowing in the breeze, her nervous hands ready to knock upon all the doors in the country. Wait for her calmly. Although she carries death in her bosom, she is the announcement of life; she is the herald of hope. She will destroy and create at the same time; she will tear down and construct. Her fists are the formidable fists of the people in rebellion. She does not bring roses or kisses; she carries an axe and a torch.

Interrupting the millennial feast of the complacent, sedition raises its head and Balthasar's phrase changes with the times into a shaking fist, suspended above the head of the so-called managing class.

The cataclysm is afoot. Its torch will light the blaze that will consume privilege and injustice. Women comrades, do not fear this cataclysm. You constitute half of the human species, and whatever affects it affects you as an integral part of humanity. If men are slaves, you will be, too. Shackles do not recognize gender; the infamy that shames man disgraces you as well. You cannot separate yourselves from the degradation of oppression. The same claw that strangles men's necks strangles yours as well.

It is therefore necessary to be in solidarity in the great contest for freedom and happiness. Are you mothers? Are you wives? Are you sisters? Are you daughters? Your duty is to aid man: be with him when he vacillates—inspire him; fly to his side when he suffers to soothe his pain; and laugh and sing with him when triumph smiles. What if you do not understand politics? It is not a question of politics: it is a question of life and death. The chains of men are your own. Ay! Yours are perhaps heavier and blacker and more degrading. Are you a worker? Just because you are a woman, you are paid less than a man, and you are made to work more; you have to suffer the insolence of the foreman and the boss. If you are pretty as well, the bosses will assault your virtue, they will surround you, they will embrace you until you surrender your heart to them, and if you give up, they will steal it from you with the same cowardice that they steal the products of your labor from you.

Under the empire of social injustice where humanity rots, a woman's existence oscillates within the restricted field of her destiny, whose frontiers are lost in the blackness of fatigue or hunger and the shadows of matrimony or prostitution.

It is necessary to study, it is essential to see, it is indispensable to scrutinize page by page this somber book called life, this bitter briar patch that tears the flesh of the human heart, in order to realize exactly how woman participates in this universal suffering.

The misfortune of woman is so ancient that its origin is lost in the shadow of legend. In the infancy of humanity, the birth of a girl was considered to be a misfortune by the tribe. The woman worked the earth, fetched firewood from the forest and water from the stream, tended the herd, milked the cows and the goats, built the cottage, made fabric into clothing, cooked the food, and cared for the sick and the children. The dirtiest jobs were performed by the woman. If an ox died of fatigue, the woman took its place hauling the plough. When a war flared up between two enemy tribes, the woman's owner changed, but she continued, under the lash of her new master, to perform the tasks of a beast of burden.

Later, under the influence of Greek civilization, woman ascended a few steps in the regard of men. She was no longer the primitive clan's beast of burden, nor did she live a cloistered life as in Oriental societies. At that time, if she belonged to a free family, her role was that of producer of citizens for her country, or of slaves, if she had the rank of a helot.

Christianity arrived after this, worsening the situation of woman with its contempt for the flesh. The Great Fathers of the Church focused their hatred against feminine graces. Saint Augustine, Saint Thomas, and other saints before whose images poor women kneel, called woman the daughter of the devil, a vessel of impurity, and condemned her to suffer the tortures of hell.

The condition of woman in this century varies according to her social class, but, despite the softening of customs, despite the progress of philosophy, woman continues to be subordinate to man by tradition and by law. Eternally treated as a minor, the law places her under the tutelage of her husband. She cannot vote or be elected, and she would have to be extremely fortunate to enter into civil contracts.

Throughout the ages, woman has been considered to be an inferior being to man, not just by the law, but also by custom, and this erroneous and unjust conception is responsible for the hardship she has suffered ever since humanity barely lifted itself above primitive fauna through its use of fire and the flint axe.

Humiliated, scorned, tied by the strong bonds of tradition to the pillory of an irrational inferiority, familiarized by a priest with the affairs of heaven, but totally ignorant of the problems of Earth, woman finds herself suddenly swept up by the whirlwind of industrial activity that needs workers, cheap workers above all, that takes advantage of the fact that she is not educated like men are for the industrial struggle, that she is not organized with those of her class to fight with her brother workers against the rapacity of capital.

To this we owe the fact that women, who work more than men but earn less, are abused and abased and held in contempt today like they were yesterday —that these are the bitter fruits she harvests for a life of sacrifice. A woman's salary is so paltry that frequently she must prostitute herself to be able to support her family when she cannot find a man who will marry her in the matrimonial market, which is another kind of prostitution sanctioned by the law and authorized by a public functionary. And marriage is nothing other than prostitution when a woman weds without love, but solely with the intent of finding a man to support her, that is, as she does in the majority of marriages, she sells her body for food, just like a fallen woman.

And what can be said about the immense army of women who do not find a spouse? The growing shortage of primary goods, the disturbing decrease in wages for human labor resulting from the perfection of machinery, together will all of the more and more pressing demands the modern world creates, are incapacitating man economically from taking upon himself the burden of maintaining a family. Obligatory military service, which seizes a great number of strong young males from the bosom of society, further diminishes the masculine supply in the matrimonial marketplace. The emigration of workers, provoked by various economic and political reasons, reduces the number of men capable of entering into matrimony even further. Alcoholism, gambling, and other vices and illnesses reduce even more the quantity of marriage candidates. All this results in an extreme reduction in the number of men suitable for marriage and, as a consequence, the number of single women is alarming. As single women's financial situation is very stressful, prostitution increasingly expands its ranks and the human race degenerates further through the debasement of the flesh and the spirit.

Women comrades: this is the dreadful scene that modern societies offer. In this scene, you see that men and women suffer equally from the tyranny of a political and social environment that is in complete disaccord with the development of civilization and the advances of philosophy. In your moments of worry, stop raising your beautiful eyes to heaven: that is where are those who have contributed most to making you eternal slaves. The remedy is here on Earth, and it is rebellion.

Make your husbands, your brothers, your fathers, your sons, and your male friends take up a rifle. Whoever refuses to raise a firearm against his oppressors, spit in his face.

The cataclysm is afoot. Jimenez and Acayucan, Palomas, Viesca, Las Vacas, and Valladollid are the first gusts of this formidable storm. It's a tragic paradox: freedom, which is life, can only be conquered by meting out death.

Práxedis Guerrero, one of the PLM's most gifted writers and military leaders, was killed in the early days of the Revolution while leading an uprising in Chihuahua.

CHAPTER 9

THE FIGURE OF THE REVOLUTIONARY

THE UTOPIANS

Regeneración, *November 12, 1910*

(translated by M.V.)

"Dreamers, utopians!" this is the least said about us, and this has been the conservatives' cry at all times against those who try to place a foot outside the corral that imprisons the human herd.

"Dreamers, utopians!" they yell at us, and when they know that our reclamation begins with taking possession of the land so that we can hand it over to the people, their cries become sharper and their insults stronger: "thieves, wicked murders, traitors," they call us.

Nevertheless, in all eras, the progress of humanity has been due to the dreamers and the utopians. This thing called civilization, what is it if not the result of efforts by utopians? The visionaries, the poets, the dreamers, the utopians, so disdained by "serious" people, so persecuted by the paternalism of governments; lynched here, shot down there, burnt to death, tortured, imprisoned, torn to pieces in all epochs and all countries, these people nevertheless, have been the engines of all progressive movements; they have been the prophets who have pointed the blind masses towards luminous paths leading to glorious summits.

One would abandon all progress or, better, one would abandon all hope for justice and human betterment if in the span of even one century the human family could no longer count dreamers, utopians, and visionaries among its members. Which persons are on the list of the dead who these "serious" people admire so much? What were they if not visionaries? Why are they so admired if not because they were dreamers? What covers them in glory if not their utopian character?

From this scorned group of human beings sprang forth Socrates, disdained by the "serious" and "sensible" people of his epoch and who is now admired by the same kind of people who made him swallow hemlock. Christ? If the "sensible" and "serious" people of today had lived in that epoch, they would have judged him, sentenced him, and even nailed the great utopian to the defiling cross—and now they cross themselves and kneel before his image.

There has never been a revolutionary, in the social sense of the word, there has never been a reformer who the authorities of his epoch have not attacked as a utopian, visionary, and dreamer.

Utopia, dream, vision! So much poetry, so much progress, so much beauty, yet how much they disdain you!

Surrounded by an environment of banality, the utopian dreams of a more just, more healthy, more beautiful, more wise, more happy humanity, and while he expresses his dreams, the envious grow pale, daggers search for his back, government lackeys spy on him, the jailer rattles his keys, and the tyrant signs the death warrant. In this way, humanity has mutilated its best members in all epochs.

Onwards! Insults, imprisonment, and even the menace of death cannot impede the utopian dream.

OUTLAWS

Regeneración, *September 3, 1910*

(Translated by M.V.)

The true revolutionary is an outlaw par excellence. The man who adjusts his actions to conform to the law, can be, at best, a good domestic animal, but not a revolutionary.

The law conserves; the revolution renews. For the same reason, if one must renew, one must begin by breaking the Law.

Claiming that the revolution can be made within the law is lunacy, is a contradiction. The law is a yoke, and he who wants to free himself from the yoke must break it.

He who preaches to the workers that they may secure emancipation through the law is a charlatan, because the law ordains that we cannot snatch from the hands of the rich the wealth they have robbed from us; and the expropriation of the wealth for the benefit of all is the condition without which human emancipation cannot triumph.

The law is a brake, and with the brakes on we'll never arrive at liberty. The law castrates, and the castrated can not aspire to be men.

Throughout history, the liberties conquered by the human species have been the work of outlaws who took the law into their own hands and tore it to pieces.

The tyrant dies from stab wounds, not from articles of the legal code.

Expropriation is achieved through trampling over the law, not by lifting it to the heavens.

For this reason, revolutionaries must necessarily be outlaws. We must abandon the well-worn road of conventionality and open up with our whiplashes upon the old flesh new paths out of the conventional ruts.

Here we are, with the torch of the revolution in one hand and the program of the Partido Liberal in the other, announcing war. We are not whining messengers of peace: we are revolutionaries. Our electoral ballots will be the bullets our guns fire. From today onwards, the swords wielded by the mercenaries of Caesar will encounter not the defenseless breast of the citizen who exercises his civic functions, but the bayonets of the rebels ready to repay blow with blow.

It would be senseless to respond through the law to someone who does not respect the law; it would be absurd to open statute books to defend ourselves from an attack with a bayonet or from being shot down as a fugitive. Do they take revenge? We take revenge! Do they want to subdue us with their gunshots? We will subdue them with our gunshots as well!

Now, let's get to work. We must separate out the cowards: we do not want them; only the valiant enlist in the revolution.

Here we are, as always, at our combat station. Martyrdom has made us stronger and more resolved. We are ready for the greatest sacrifices. We are coming to the Mexican people to tell them that their day of liberation is drawing near. On the new horizon, the splendid aurora of the new day is shining; to our ears comes the sound of the storm of salvation of a humanity about to unshackle itself: it is the ferment of the revolutionary spirit; it is that the entire country is a volcano on the verge of angrily spitting out the fire buried in its core. "No more peace!" is the shout of the valiant; better death than a shameful peace. The flowing hair of the future heroes floats on the air blown by the first gusts of the coming cataclysm.

A sharp, strong, and healthy spirit of war emboldens the effeminate atmosphere. The apostle will proclaim from one ear to the next how and when the cataclysm will begin, and rifles are impatiently awaiting the moment when they may emerge from the hiding places where they lie, in order to shine proudly under the sun of combat.

Mexicans: to war!

BANDITS!

Regeneración, *December 9, 1911*

(Translated by M.V.)

This is the name that the people in charge have given us. Why? Because, as well as teaching our miserable brothers that all that exists should be for all people, we also invite them to take possession of all of it.

Who made the earth? The frock-coated, gloved gentlemen who say it belongs to them; did they make it? No; the land is a natural good, common to all living creatures. Who made the houses, the clothing, everything that makes life comfortable? Was it the gentlemen living in rich palaces and lodging in luxurious hotels? No; all of this emerged from the hands of poor people who live in hovels, who are rotting in prisons, who are withering in the bordellos, who are dying all over the world, in hospitals, in the middle of the road, on the gallows...
Bandits! We who want to put an end to banditry!

No, bourgeois gentlemen: the bandits are all of you who, without any right, have usurped the natural goods which you have not created, and which are the products of men who labor so that you would not have to spill a drop of sweat.

You are all bandits, you bourgeois gentlemen who have, through the law that pimps for your rapacity, illegally taken most of what the workers have produced without your risking being caged in a jail cell. Ah! Between bandit and bandit, I prefer the one who, dagger in hand and with a resolute spirit, jumps out from some thicket by the road shouting "Your money or your life!" I prefer this one, I insist, to the bandit who, sitting down at his desk, coldly, quietly, calmly drinks the blood of his workers.

As for the first bandit, the one who attacks and faces danger in his daring adventure, there is prison or the firing squad; for the white-gloved bandit, there is respect, honor, contentment.

This is how things pass under the present system of supreme social injustice. For the honored people in charge, robbery is not a crime if one robs a great deal; but it is if the robber is a mere "hoodlum." A banker, a businessman can make deals which bring sadness to hundreds of thousands of homes: this is considered to be a skillful financial operation. A ravenous man takes a piece of bread from a shop: this man is a thief.

Authority, an even bigger pimp than Law, as well as its executioner, sustains all of this. Death to Authority!

SOWING

Regeneración, *November 5, 1910*

(Translated by M.V.)

I can imagine the satisfactions and the worries of the sower of seeds. What emotions the man who plants the grain in the earth must feel! Behold a wasteland; yet the sower of seeds comes and turns over the earth, slices it up, breaks up the rough clods of earth, combs it over, sows the grain, and irrigates it. After this, he waits! However, this waiting does not consist of just crossing his arms: he must struggle; he must struggle against the birds who descend to eat the kernels, against the animals who feed upon the tender shoots, against the cold, against the streams that threaten to overflow, against the weeds which spread to cover the seed. With what emotion he awaits the new day anticipating whether he will see the green tips of the plants breaking forth from the black earth! Finally, they appear, and then he lifts his worried gaze to the skies; he knows how to read the coming weather in the clouds; likewise, the direction that the wind blows has great importance. Looking at the clouds, surveying the winds, his face will grow pale or will glow, depending on whether he deduces the coming of fair, good, or poor weather.

However, these tortures are not at all comparable to those suffered by the sower of ideals. The earth welcomes tenderly. The mind of the human masses refuses to welcome the ideals that the sower places into it. The weeds, the undergrowth represented by old ideals, by preoccupations, by traditions, by prejudices have established themselves so much, have sunk their roots so deeply, and have cross-pollinated to such an extent that it is not easy to exterminate them without resistance, without making the patient suffer. The sower of ideals casts the seed, but the weeds are thick and cast such dense shadows that most of the time nothing germinates; and if, despite this resistance, the seed of ideals is endowed with such vitality, with such vigorous potency, that it succeeds in making a sprout emerge, it grows feeble, sickly, because the old weeds feed off of its essence, and this is why it takes so much effort for the new ideals to successfully take root.

The fear of the of the unknown contributes strongly to the resistance of the mind of the masses against the new ideals. The cowardice of the herd is perfectly expressed in the phrase that issues from the mouths of all the swindlers: "The devil you know is better than the one you don't." The fruits of old ideals are bitter: nevertheless, the imbecility and the cowardice of the masses prefers them to the cultivation of new, healthy ideals.

The sower of ideals must struggle against the masses, who are conservative, against institutions, which are likewise conservative; and alone, surrounded by the comings and goings of a herd that does not understand him, he walks through the world not hoping for any reward more than fools slapping him in the face, tyrants throwing him in jail and, at any moment, the scaffold. Yet nevertheless, as long as he can sow, sow, sow, the sower of seeds will continue sowing, sowing, sowing...

Librado Rivera was a member of the PLM's Organizing Junta. He was a close comrade of Ricardo Flores Magón for decades, and was imprisoned with Magón in Leavenworth. After his release in 1923, he continued to be active in the Mexican anarchist movement until his death in 1932.

THE LEADERS

Regeneración, *June 15, 1912*

(Translated by C.B.)

It's not necessary to be part of the masses; it's not necessary to have the biases, the prejudgments, the mistaken beliefs, the habits of the unconscious multitudes. The masses have the firm belief that it's necessary to have a leader or a man on a white horse at their head, that he'll conduct them toward their destiny, that he'll carry them to tyranny or liberty; the question is whether he'll lead them with kindness or by spitting on them toward the good or the bad.

This customary belief, so deep rooted in human beings, is the fount of innumerable evils for the cause of those working to redeem the human species. Life, honor, well-being, the future, liberty—all are put in the hands of the man who the masses make the leader. It's the leader who has to think for all; it's the leader who is entrusted with watching over the common well-being and liberties of the masses in general and of the individual in particular, which results in the millions of minds that constitute the masses not thinking, because the leader is entrusted to think for all. This gives rise to the passivity of the masses, that they don't undertake any initiative themselves, and that they carry on a sheep-like existence, being flattered by politicians and aspirants to public office in times of elections, but who later turn on them. In times of revolutionary action, they're swindled by the ambitious, who reward them with a kick in the ass after the victory.

It's not necessary to be part of the masses; it's necessary to be united as a group of thinking individuals, united in order to obtain common ends; it's necessary that every one, man or woman, think with their own head, that every one make the effort of having an opinion about what is necessary to obtain our goals, which are nothing other than the liberty of all founded in the liberty of every one, the well-being of all founded in the well-being of every one. And for us to arrive at this, it is necessary to destroy that which opposes it: inequality. It is necessary that the lands, the tools, the machines, the provisions, the houses, everything thing that exists, be it a natural product or a product of industry, pass from the hands of the few who presently have it all to the hands of everyone, men and women alike, so that we can produce in common, everyone producing according to his abilities and everyone consuming according to his needs.

To achieve this we don't need leaders; on the contrary, they impede this, because the leader wants to dominate, wants to be obeyed, wants to be above the rest. And a leader will never look favorably upon the intention of the poor to install a social system based on the economic, political, and social equality of human beings. The reason for this is that such a system doesn't guarantee leaders the easy, lazy life they want to lead, full of honors and glory, at the cost of the sacrifice of the humble.

So then, Mexican brothers, learn to work under your own initiative to bring into practice those noble principles set forth in our manifesto of September 23, 1911.

We don't consider ourselves your leaders, and it would sadden us if you'd see in us chiefs to follow, and without whom you wouldn't dare to do anything to further the cause. We're on the verge of going to prison, not because we're criminals, but because we won't sell out—neither to the rich nor to the authorities; we don't want to tyrannize over you by accepting public posts or bundles of bank notes, converting ourselves into the bourgeoisie who exploit your labor. We don't consider ourselves your leaders, but rather your brothers, and we'll go contentedly to prison if you don't let it interfere with your confrontations with capital and authority.

Don't be part of the masses, Mexicans; don't be part of the multitude dragged along by the politician or the rich man or the military chieftain. Think with your own heads and do what your own consciences dictate.

Don't become discouraged when you see us separated from you by the black gate of the prison. Then you'll lack our friendly words and nothing more; but selfless comrades will continue publishing *Regeneración*. Lend them your support, because they're going to continue this propaganda effort which must become even more widespread and more radical.

Don't do what you did last year when we were arrested; then your enthusiasm cooled, and your resolve to further by any means necessary the destruction of the capitalist, authoritarian system weakened, with very few of you holding firm. Be firm now; don't become fixated on our personalities, and with renewed enthusiasm lend your moral, material, and individual support to the revolution of the poor against the rich and against authority.

Let each one of you be your own leader; there's no other necessity than that you push yourselves to continue the struggle. Don't call yourselves leaders; simply take possession of the lands and all else that exists, and apply yourselves to being free of your bosses and authority. In this way peace will come of its own accord, as a natural result of the well-being and freedom of all; but if you allow the accursed bourgeois education you received to influence you, and you lift up another ruler upon your powerful shoulders, then the war will continue because the same evils will remain that caused you to take up arms: misery and tyranny.

Read, all of you, our manifesto of September 23, 1911 and cry: "Death to Capital! Death to Authority! Long live Land and Liberty!"

DEATH TO AUTHORITY!
Regeneración, *March 23, 1912*

(Translated by C.B.)

I tell you the rich scream to high heaven when they hear the redemptory cry: "Death to Authority!" They have good reason, because if authority disappears the privileges of capital will fall into the same grave, never to rise again. Authority is necessary to social inequality; it guarantees that the rich will live in idleness while it condemns the poor to hard labor and abject misery. The bourgeoisie then, need authority, because without it they would have to take up the plow, the wood plane, or the hammer to gain subsistence for themselves and their families.

But the poor man, why does he need authority? Authority has never been to his benefit. For the poor, authority has always been the abusive, foul-tempered stepmother, the castrator of wills. And I know of no land on Earth where authority has been the shield or guardian angel of the poor, and this is because it can't serve two bosses at the same time: the rich and the poor. Authority was instituted to guard the material goods of the rich class, which sees itself menaced by the hungry.

Those of us who don't have a clump of dirt on which to lie our heads don't need authority. On the contrary, we detest it because it snatches from our files the most vigorous of our brothers, stockpiling them in the barracks and making them take up arms for the bourgeoisie; and in the second place we detest it because it extorts money from us to maintain these soldiers and the whole gang of great and small functionaries called government.

We ourselves, the dispossessed, those who have nothing they can steal, are those who are obliged to pay the costs of maintaining authority, when what is just is that these costs would be paid by those who benefit from it, the bourgeoisie.

The soldier with gun in hand, the policeman with the hangman's noose in hand, the rural cop with his saber drawn—have they ever served to protect the weak? Has there ever been a case in which the soldier, the policeman, the rural cop have interposed themselves between the boss and the worker in order to stop the first from sucking the blood of the second? When the poor man hasn't been able to pay the rent on his land or house, have the soldier, the policeman, the rural cop ever flown to his aid to prevent his being tossed into the street or tossed off the land which he's watered with his sweat? And if we rebel, outraged by the social injustice which obliges us to put our muscles and brains at the service of the rich, will authority take our part, that is, the part of the weak, of the victims of voracious capitalism? Won't we see, instead, that the soldiers, policemen, and rural cops will bring death to the poor who want to bring about a more equitable distribution of bread?

I say that the rich scream to high heaven when they hear the redemptory cry: "Death to Authority!" But I don't say that the poor, the shabbily dressed, the workers become angry and sputter in rage when we give them this friendly advice: "Don't elect authorities; govern yourselves."

[Octave] Mirbeau spoke a great truth when he exclaimed: "Of all animals, man is the stupidest, because at least the animals don't elect the butcher who slits their throats."

And men, while we kill ourselves for the benefit of those who draw the knife across our throats when they're in power, yes, we are stupid!

We'll give our liberty, our tranquility, our blood, not to elect exploiters, but to put an end to them, to put an end to the bourgeoisie, to found the free society of all for one and one for all.

Let's elevate to power neither Vazquez Gomez nor anyone else. Let's at least be as dignified as the animals who don't elect a butcher to cut their throats. Let us take the earth, the machinery of production, the means of transportation, the houses, the provisions; let us fraternally organize ourselves for production and consumption in common, and raise our heads, Mexicans, proud of having known how to resolve the social problem.

DOWN WITH THE FRAUDS!

Regeneración, *March 9, 1912*

(Translated by C.B.)

The revolution gains ground with every passing moment. The "holy" right of private property, in contrast, loses ground with every instant, to say nothing of authority, which, sliding into the abyss, with no respect, clutches in vain at the law—that poor weed which doesn't have the power to stop its fall—or at arbitrariness, that sword which wounds the aggressor as much as the aggressed upon.

Events have unfolded with such rapidity that the fall of Madero will not dispirit those impatient to occupy his post and the posts of his favorites, but the revolution continues its triumphant march; it will not be detained by the mere occupancy of the presidential seat by a Vázquez Gómez or an Orozco. In the mountains, on the plains, wherever there is a man with heart, the struggle will continue against capital, authority, and the church.

The people are no longer satisfied with promises. From 1821 [the year Mexico achieved independence from Spain] to date, all of the ambitious ones have made promises, all of those who have had their eyes on coming to power have presented the people with shining programs which must be carried out after the revolution; and in every case, without a single exception, the dispossessed have been fooled. Those who aspired to be rulers as well as the simple hunters of jobs have told the people: rise up and I'll make you happy. And the people have risen up, shed their blood, have sacrificed themselves so that, come the day of the triumph, the leaders will take possession of great offices, while the soldiers, deprived of their arms so that they won't constitute a danger, have been dispatched back to their homes, where their families anxiously awaited them, afflicted by hunger, bitten by the cold, but with the hope of "a change" in their sad conditions of life. No change ever came: the humble hero of a hundred battles turned again to taking up the hammer or other instruments of labor for his bosses, exactly the same as before; daughters of the people continued to be sweet meats for the bosses; conscription didn't disappear with the rise of the new government; hunger continued to gnaw at the flesh of the proletarians; the children of the workers wallowed in the same mud and grew up in the same ignorance, exactly the same as the children of the previous generation.

That's how it was, because the proletarians had confidence in their leaders and believed that their leaders could deliver the miracle of a good government; and they put in the hands of the ruling classes of society, precisely in the hands of the classes that are the natural enemies of the working class, the resolution of their problems. Ninety years of swindles on the part of the economic and intellectual ruling elites have opened the eyes of, if not all, at least of a good number of workers, who have understood in the end that the lands and the machinery of production cannot fall into the hands of the proletarians if they participate in elections that name another exploiter, but only through the manly actions of workers armed with guns and dynamite.

Proletarians who work militantly in the files of Vázquez or Orosco: wherever you are, open warehouses and granaries so that the poor will be able to eat, and put the lands and the industries in the hands of the workers. Only in this manner will the purposes of this great revolution avoid disappointment. If your leaders and officials oppose this, shoot them without compassion! Neighbors of the towns and cities that are in the hands of the rebels: don't pay rents for the houses you occupy, and if the forces of Vázquez or Orosco want to make you pay, blow them up with dynamite, because the revolution should be for the benefit of the poor and not the bourgeoisie.

WE DON'T WANT HANDOUTS
Regeneración, *April 1, 1911*

(Translated by C.B.)

It's always the same. When the bourgeoisie feels that it needs the support of the masses to assure its domination, when it feels the emptiness around it, it decides to descend a little, to lower itself to where the proletariat vegetates, and to smile at it, to pass a hand over its back, and to tell it: "I'm your friend, your hardships bother me, and I want to alleviate your pain." And, regularly, the proletariat curls up and gets sleepy listening to the political siren song, and it forgets the humiliation it's been subjected to for thousands of years by its haughty bosses.

All politicians have a good feel for the popular pulse. He who wants to live above the people has to do no more than adulate it, applaud its passions, celebrate its vices, play to its preoccupations. This, naturally, is done when the politician needs the support of the people, in those abnormal moments when the passive masses commence to stir, bitten by rebellion; but in normal times, the masses are back to being kicked around and whipped.

Porfirio Díaz and Francisco I. Madero feel in these moments the need to unite, in their own turn, with the popular masses. The first of these has been a savage beast who has sustained his dominion by cutting the throats of the Mexican race; the second has been an evil hacendado [large rancher] who has accumulated millions and millions [of pesos] exploiting the peons on his haciendas in the state of Coahuila. Well then, these two types of oppressors—the political oppressor and the economic oppressor—try to drag the masses behind them, offering to alleviate their sad condition. But it's necessary to remain conscious of who is doing this at the precise moment that the workers are commencing to wake up and realize the iniquities they suffer: political despotism and economic tyranny. While the workers were dreaming of the panacea of "real suffrage," while they had faith in the good will of the legislators and paternalistic governments, both Díaz and Madero had no interest in studying methods of alleviating the suffering of the poor. But the Partido Liberal has spoken loudly; the Partido Liberal has opened the eyes of the workers; it has clearly explained that no congress can work in favor of the proletariat, because it isn't proletarians who sit in congresses, but rather the bourgeoisie, and the bourgeoisie has an interest in keeping the proletariat permanently enslaved. The Partido Liberal has shown, through history, that movements headed by the ruling classes in society, that is, by the intellectuals and the rich, will carry the people to the slaughterhouse, but never to liberty, precisely because the interests of the rich and the intellectuals are diametrically opposed to the interests of the workers. The most that revolutionary movements have achieved, in all lands throughout history, is the attainment of the already discredited "human rights," which guarantee everything except that which is essential: the means of subsistence. Take a look at the Constitution of 1857, and in no part of it will you encounter a single line that guarantees the right to live, and this is because the bourgeoisie has guaranteed everything it needs to take advantage of the constitution; but it doesn't guarantee that which the working class needs, since everything that the working class truly needs for its emancipation and dignity has been forgotten by the legislators; and since the politicians have forgotten the people, it's time that the working people, on their own count, produce a movement which pushes directly toward the establishment of social equality, the right to live, a right which can only exist when the lands are under the control of each and every one of the inhabitants of Mexico.

The propagation of such health ideals has been the result of the rapid growth in influence of the Partido Liberal Mexicano. In little over six months of propaganda headed by *Regeneración*, we've seen the more than satisfactory results of this propaganda. Hundreds are joining the party every month. Membership forms are signed every day by compañeros and compañeras convinced of the necessity of employing direct action to take possession of the earth, ignoring the "sacred right of private property."

The movements of Díaz and Madero, upon seeing the growing power of the Partido Liberal Mexicano, have remembered the people and have bowed down toward it saying, "We're also your friends; we're going to give you the lands."

Díaz has said that he'll spend 80 million pesos buying lands from the rich to give to the poor. Madero offers the same thing; but now is not the time to be fooled, comrades. Before the resolute attitude of the Partido Liberal, Díaz has pulled in his claws and the bourgeois Madero has done the same thing.

Neither Díaz nor Madero can deliver on their promise of lands for the people. In order to do so, they would have to ignore the "right" of private property, because to pretend to buy the lands is the dream of a crazy man. There isn't enough capital in the world to buy the lands of Mexico. How then are Díaz or Madero going to buy it with the humble resources of the national treasury? The budget, in terms of income and expenses, in normal times, is always out of balance. Income is always less than expenses, and this is what happens in normal times. What condition will the budget be in when this country emerges from this war? With business paralyzed, and misery and hunger everywhere? From what are Madero and Díaz going to draw the resources to buy the land from the rich and give it to the poor?

If in normal times there aren't enough taxes gathered in the country to pay for the costs of the public administration, and if it's necessary to resort to loans to sustain this spending, it'll be much harder to pay these costs after the current insurrection. There will hardly be enough for Díaz or Madero to reimburse themselves for their own expenses. It is, then, economically impossible to buy the land from the rich, and when the partisans of Madero and Díaz speak of this they are shamefully deceiving the workers because they're offering something they can't deliver.

What ought to be done is not to buy the land, but to seize it from the hands of the rich; and we shouldn't wait for a merciful government to do it, but rather we should take it ourselves, refusing to recognize the "right" of the rich to keep for themselves the earth that belongs to all.

Both the Madero and Díaz partisans come to the people, as do all frauds when they need the force of the people. This has always happened, and it will continue to happen until the people open their eyes and send their eternal swindlers to hell. "The emancipation of the workers must be the task of the workers themselves." We can't wait for the rich to give to us; we must take! We can't extend our hands to receive alms. We must resolve to do everything under our own power!

The fact that Madero or Díaz would give some land to some people doesn't resolve the problem of hunger. The lands should be for all, and should not be sold as Díaz and Madero claim, with the people paying over time. This would recognize the so-called right of private property. The bourgeois respect this right; the poor can't recognize it because it's hideously unfair. The lands shouldn't be for just a few, but for all.

Comrades: this is the moment in which we should be intransigent in our demands. Already the bourgeoisie and the government tremble at the possibility of seeing themselves dethroned. Let's not stop; let's not vacillate. While Diaz and Madero respect the "right" of private property, while this "right" subsists, don't expect your liberation. It is necessary to recognize this for what it is: we can't pull back because the bourgeoisie and its lackeys call us bandits. They are the bandits, they who have lived at the cost of the blood, sweat, tears, pain, and desperation of a thousand generations of workers. They are the bandits, they who have never had anything for the workers except maltreatment, contempt, judges, cops, jailers, gallows. Don't forget these wrongs! The bourgeoisie are our enemies! Throw them down! Blood is running in torrents. Let it be for the redemption of the proletariat and not to elevate another bandit.

We must be firm in our purpose to convert this political movement into a social revolution. Don't ask for the earth. Take it!

The revolution of the Partido Liberal is gaining ground. We have confidence that within a year the red flag will wave sovereign over all of Mexico. But I don't want to say with this that the revolution is going to last a year. That's a very short time for a true revolution. Díaz will fall in less than a year, but the revolution will continue because the people will not gain their liberty with the fall of this tyrant. What is needed is the fall of the present social, political, and economic system. Let those leave our ranks who are cowards and those who expect to prosper after an easy triumph; let march out of the ranks of the Partido Liberal Mexicano those who want to be governors, deputies, or simply mayors. Let those remain who want the establishment of an environment that guarantees bread, land, and liberty to all.

Onward!

THE POLITICAL SOCIALISTS
Regeneración, *March 2, 1912*

(Translated by C.B.)

The swindlers speak to you of the "necessity" of the workers having representation in the legislative chambers, and they speak to you precisely in these moments of pressing action, when the campesinos, arms in hand, are taking possession of the lands; when the laborers, disillusioned with strikes, are uniting with rebel forces to conquer their economic liberty; when we ourselves put the provisions stored in the great haciendas of the Rio Grande district in the state of Coahuila into the hands of the poor; and when we invite the inhabitants of this vast region to take possession of the lands and instruments of production, or equally to invade the inherited lands of the hacendados of Durango and the great plantations of the slavers in the lakes region; when in the entire area of Mexican soil, from sea to sea, and from border to border, one hears the formidable cries: "Down with hunger!" and "Expropriate!"

What a wonderfully opportune time the swindlers of the proletariat have picked to preach about political action! Two small periodicals from Mexico City have arrived at our editing desk; they have appeared with the pretension of representing the interests of the working class, which is a very strange thing given that neither of them breathes a word about the class war which is raging in the Mexican republic. On the contrary, they feign to ignore it due to the orientation of their editors, who view with terror the path that the Mexican proletariat has chosen—violence—to yank from the grasping claws of the bourgeoisie the social riches to which it clings; rather, the editors of these little periodicals are trying to put to sleep the powerful revolutionary energies which are giving good proof while being put to the test, and to convert the revolutionaries into an electoral flock.

One of these little magazines says: "In these moments our bourgeoisie laughs and makes jokes about our party (the so-called Partido Socialista de Mexico). Likewise the German bourgeoisie laughed a few years ago and today they've seen how four million citizen socialists have sent 110 representatives to parliament, including one from the district in which the emperor lives. Now they don't laugh, but rather look from one to the other anxiously. What will happen in the next election? Perhaps the social revolution."

As can be seen, the little periodical to which I'll continue to refer considers the German Social Democratic Party as a party which can accomplish nothing less than the social revolution, when in reality this party is recognized in the entire intelligent world as a conservative party like any other bourgeois party, and so inoffensive to the capitalist class that many of the rich participate in it.

One couldn't ask for greater submission or greater degradation! And all of this is said when the proletarians have taken up the red flag and fight like heroes on the battlefields! It's bad enough when such things are said in times of peace; but not even then would we allow such a cynical attempt to annihilate one of the major virtues of the Mexican people: its spirit of rebellion.

Workers: you don't need to appoint idlers to represent you in the legislative chambers, and much less do you need to resort to the authorities to patronize and represent you in your struggles against capital. To those who ask you to vote for them to represent you in the legislative chambers, spit in their faces; to those who counsel you to put your fates in the hands of authority, slap them in the face. In the German parliament, say those who would swindle you, there are 110 socialist deputies. And what benefit has the working class in the German empire received from this great number of leeches? Misery is greater every day in the entire empire; people are literally dying of hunger; and the poor sections of the great cities are literally filled with rags and miserable flesh rotting in its own filth. And while this happens the socialist deputies tranquilly receive large salaries, taken in the form of taxes from all this misery, filth, and pain of the proletariat; and [August] Bebel, the Pontifice Maximo of German socialism, lives the grand life devouring his income in the presence of the nakedness and hunger of millions and millions who wait, hoping that a socialist government will put in their hands the lands and the means of production. And these poor people will continue to wait until desperation pushes them to pick up a gun to secure their economic, political, and social emancipation via the logical means: violence!

While the worker rejects the bullet for the ballot box, he can't wonder at being a wage slave. No more! Enough of your farces, you swindlers! All around

---

you the proletarian crowds battle, bizarrely in your view, to conquer land and liberty. And it's a stupidity when you're in the presence of such an expenditure of energy, such valor, such boldness, such manliness to counsel pacifism, to counsel the electoral ballot, and that the dispossessed put their fate in the hands of their exploiters.

WITHOUT RULERS
Regeneración, *March 21, 1914*

(Translated by C.B.)

To want rulers and at the same time to want to be free is to want the impossible. One must choose definitively one or the other: to be free, entirely free, refusing all authority, or to be slaves, perpetuating man's command over man.

A ruler or governor is necessary only under a system of economic inequality. If I have more than Pedro, I fear, naturally, that Pedro may seize me by the throat and take from me what he needs. In this case, a governor or ruler is needed to protect me against the possible attacks of Pedro; but if Pedro and I are economically equals, if the two of us have the same opportunity to take advantage of the natural riches, such as the earth, the water, the forests, as well as the riches created by the hands of man, such as the machinery, the houses, the railroads, and the thousand and one manufactured objects, reason indicates that it would be impossible that Pedro and I would grab each other by the hair fighting over things we both enjoy equally; and in this case, there would be no need to have a ruler.

To speak of a ruler among equals is a contradiction, unless one is speaking of equals in servitude, of brothers in chains, as we workers currently are.

There are many who say that it is impossible to live without a ruler or a government; when it is the bourgeoisie who say such things, we admit they are right, because they fear that the poor will seize them by the throat and take back from them the riches they amassed by making workers sweat. But why do the poor need a ruler or government?

In Mexico, we have had and we still have hundreds of proofs that humanity does not need a ruler or a government except when economic inequality exists. In the villages or rural communities, the inhabitants have not felt the need for a government. The lands, the forests, the waters, and the fields have been, until recently, the common property of the inhabitants of the regions. When one speaks about government to these simple people, they begin trembling with fear, because the government, for them, has been the same as a tormenter: it means the same as a tyrant. They lived happily in their freedom, without, in many cases, even knowing the name of the president of the republic, and they only knew that a government existed when the military chiefs passed through their territory searching for males to draft as soldiers, or when the government's tax collectors made visits to collect levies. The government has been, then, for a great portion of the Mexican population, the tyrant that uprooted the hard-working Mexican men from their homes to make them soldiers, or it has been the brutal profiteer who snatched taxes from them in the name of the state treasury.

Could these villages have felt that it was necessary to have a government? They had no need for it, and thus they were able to live for hundreds of years, until their natural wealth was stolen from them by the hacendados (great landowners). They did not devour each other, as those who have only known the capitalist system fear might happen, because under capitalism, every human being must compete with every other to be able to lift a crust of bread to his mouth. In these villages the strong did not tyrannize the weak, as they do in capitalist civilization, in which the most knavish, the most greedy, and the most clever dominate the good and the noble. All were brothers in these communities; everyone helped everyone else, and with all feeling equal, as they truly are, they did not need any authority to watch over the interests of owners, who dread possible assault by those who have nothing.

Right now, is government needed by the free communities of the Yaqui, in Durango, in southern Mexico, and in the many other communities throughout the country where the people have taken possession of the earth? From the moment that they considered each other as equals, with the same right to Mother Earth, they have not needed a ruler to protect privileges against those who do not have privileges, because everyone was privileged.

Disabuse yourselves of illusions, proletarians: government must only exist when there is economic inequality. Therefore, adopt as your moral guide the manifesto of September 23, 1911.

PATRIOTISM

Regeneración, *February 24, 1917*

(Translated by C.B.)

We poor people are incited in a thousand ways to be patriots. From the time we're born until we exhale our last breath, these words buzz in our ears: "Love your country, love your country, love your country."

It could be said that we suck in patriotism with the first drops of milk from the breasts of our mothers. The mother lulls us to sleep with songs that glorify the nation. Later, we're taught to love the flag, whose colors appear more brilliant to us than those of any other flag. As children, we're overwhelmed with playthings that make us play at being soldiers: drums, wooden swords, flags, clay or lead soldiers, and, stuffed full of the legends which extol the exploits of the nation's heroes, we pretend in our games to be on battlefields where we would make all those who had committed the crime of being born outside the nation's boundaries bite the dust, because every good patriot is the enemy of those who aren't born inside his country's borders.

Patriotic education doesn't end with childhood games: it continues in grammar school. There, the good teacher makes us intone choruses in which we exalt the country; in our reading book we spell out compositions in prose and verse in honor of the country, and our eyes fill with wonder before the illustrations representing acts of war, with each one of us wanting to be the happy flag-bearer who has the great honor of holding aloft his country's banner in the midst of the butchery. We hear the national anthem, and our blood stirs faster in our veins.

The priest, in his sermons, exhorts us to love the nation; the politician, in his speeches, speaks to us about the greatness of the country; the bourgeois periodical stimulates our patriotic sentiments; wherever we turn our gaze we find a statue of a patriot or a drawing with a patriotic theme; patriotic holidays, besides being numerous, have an air of great solemnity. Everything, in the end, is carefully calculated to light, and to keep lit, the patriotic fire in our breasts.

Prepared in this manner, and even when we don't own a clod of earth to recline our heads on; even when we don't possess a square inch of the country we've been taught to love; despite all the indignities, humiliations, abuses, and misfortunes we've been subjected to in our place on the lowest rungs of the social ladder; despite everything we find ourselves disposed to commit the worst excesses, to kill and allow ourselves to be killed for the nation, for this thing which for its part provides us no benefit and in exchange demands of us the greatest sacrifices.

It's necessary to confess that all of the demands implied in patriotism fall exclusively on the shoulders of the poor. The poor man knows only that he has a country because he has to serve in the army, and the benefits he receives from the country are the clubbing by the cop, the taxes to pay the government's costs, his unpaid nightly rounds, the "fatiga" [provision of unpaid services], and the law which subjects him to eternal servitude beneath the claws of the owners of the lands and machinery.

To the poor man, the country provides no benefit because it's not his. The country is the property of the few who are the owners of the lands, the mines, the houses, the factories, the railroads—of everything that exists; but the poor man is indoctrinated from childhood to love the country so that he'll pick up a gun in defense of interests that aren't his when his bosses realize that their interests are in danger and send out a patriotic call to the masses. It's so certain that material interests are at the heart of the country that the bourgeoisie will not oppose a foreign invasion when its aim is not to despoil them of their properties, and they'll even welcome it when the foreign bayonets can lend some support to the principle of private property and this principle is in danger of falling to pieces under the furious assaults of popular justice.

The two invasions that Mexico has suffered during the course of the revolution have had no other object than to suffocate the revolutionary movement that threatens the stability of the principle of private property. The two U.S. invasions were carried out to place Venustiano Carranza in the presidential seat and to consolidate a strong government capable of making the law respected, that is, capable of being the shield of the strong, their defense against the possible attacks of those who possess nothing.

The Mexican bourgeoisie haven't protested these two invasions, because they were intended to save their properties which were threatened by the virile attitude of Mexicans eager to gain their economic liberty. If it hadn't been that the American workers protested against this invasion and refused to join the army to go put Carranza in the presidential seat, there would have been long months in which this acting president would have had the shelter of strong contingents of U.S. soldiers.

Patriotism is a dish seasoned exclusively for the consumption of the poor. We're informed that the invasion is an affront and that we ought to resist it. Did Carranza resist it? He didn't resist it because it benefitted the social class which every government must support: the capitalist class.

Now, deprived of the hope that American bayonets will keep him in power, Carranza is throwing himself into the arms of Germany. In a note which he's sent to the neutral nations, Carranza invites these nations to suspend commerce with the belligerent nations, arguing that in this manner they will be left isolated and will see themselves forced, in the end, to agree to peace in view of not being able to count on provisions from the outside.

The Central Powers will be the beneficiaries if this project of Carranza is put into practice, because England will receive a mortal blow impeding it from obtaining from the petroleum-producing area of Tampico the oil it needs to keep its fleet in motion, and England will have to adopt extreme measures to keep its supply lines open. What will happen? England will send soldiers to occupy the Tampico region.

It's patently obvious that patriotism isn't practiced by those who inculcate it into others. It's a sentiment that's infused in us so that we'll put ourselves at the disposition of our exploiters. When we take the gun in hand to defend the nation, that which we're defending is the property of our bosses. Let us open our eyes.

FRANCISCO FERRER
Speech, October 13, 1911

(Translated by C.B.)

Capital, Authority, Clergy: This is the hydra which guards the gates of this prison called Earth. The human being, so prideful, so boastful, so self-satisfied about his supposed liberties—what else is he other than a galley slave, a shackled and numbered prisoner since he came into the world, subject to a shameful rule called Law, punished or rewarded according to his ability to violate the law and get away with it, to his own interest and against the interests of the rest.

That martyr of the proletariat, whose exemplary life of abnegation and sacrifice has awoken in so many noble proletarian hearts the desire to follow in his footsteps, often said to me: "To be alive is to be a prisoner." I refer to the young martyr of Janos, Praxedis G. Guerrero, the first Mexican libertarian who had the audacity to emit for the first time in Mexico the sublime cry: Land and Liberty!

The world is a prison, a much larger one than those with which we're familiar, but a prison nonetheless. The prison guards are the police and soldiers; the wardens are the presidents, kings, and emperors; the watchdogs are the legislators; and in this sense we can exactly equate the armies of prison functionaries and their acts with the armies of government functionaries and their acts. The downtrodden, the plebeians, the disinherited masses are the prisoners, obliged to work to support the army of functionaries and the lazy, thieving rich.

To free humanity from everything that contributes to making this beautiful Earth a vale of tears is a task for heroes, and this was what motivated Francisco Ferrer Guardia. As his means, he chose the education of young children, and he founded the Modern School, from which would come beings emancipated from prejudices of all types, men and women suited for reasoning and for understanding nature, life, and social relations. In the Modern School, the child was stimulated to have the habits of investigation and reasoning, so that he wouldn't blindly accept religious, political, social, and moral dogmas with which children's heads are stuffed in the official schools. It was the aim that the child arrive at understanding, through his own efforts, the natural history of the Earth and universe, the appearance and evolution of life, natural history as a whole, and the formation and development of human societies throughout the ages, up to our days.

The Spanish clergy viewed with disgust this type of education which would counteract their efforts to perpetuate prejudices, traditions, and atavisms; the Spanish clergy today is the same clergy as in the time of Loyola and the Inquisition. For these clerics, fomenters of fanaticism which makes possible resignation in the face of capitalist tyranny and exploitation, the work of Ferrer was an affront and, making the sign of the cross, they decreed in the shadows, like the cowards they are, the death of Ferrer's work and its author.

Their opportunity didn't delay in presenting itself. One pretty day a flashy procession passed through the streets of Madrid in celebration of the marriage of Alfonso XIII with Enna de Batenberg. All was silks, perfumes, colors, the shine of gold, luxury—an extravagance of riches in that brilliant procession. The aristocracy of money and parchment used that day to ostentatiously show their power, influence, insulting opulence, and the haughty disdain with which those on top see those below, while in the barrios, thousands and thousands of human beings smothered in the infernal heat of their garrets for the simple crime of working and sweating so that the good-for-nothings in the procession could make a wasteful show of their gold and silks.

Military bands filled the air with heroic harmonies; the fortunate members of the bourgeoisie laughed; the soldiers, with blows, made the crowd retreat; the streets shone with patriotic adornments. The king and the queen formed part of that parade of the greatest leaches in Spain. Flowers rained down from the roofs and balconies. From the hands of one man, from a roof, came a pretty wreath, whose flowers smiled in the sun. This wreath exploded. It was a bomb adorned with flowers! The man who had thrown it was a friend of Ferrer, Mateo Moral. The monster of clericalism shivered with satisfaction. "Now we have him!" cried the clergy. And while Mateo watered the earth with his blood, the earth that he dreamed of seeing peopled by a free humanity, in Barcelona the hands of the police grabbed the noble founder of the Modern School.

The trial was long. They resorted to every device they had to convict that innocent man, until, after he spent a year and a half in prison, the government put him at liberty. The clerical beast returned to its scheming, spying on the movement of that extraordinary man, until a new opportunity presented itself.

Spain was at war with the Moors in mid-1909. The conscious workers were opposed, naturally, to this stupid shedding of proletarian blood to defend the interests of a few mine owners in North Africa. The government, defender of capital, sent soldiers and more soldiers to the battlefield. Demonstrations against this criminal war spread throughout Spain. In Barcelona, a general strike was called against the sending of more soldiers to fight for the interests of their oppressors. Clashes between the police and the strikers commenced, and there was a general insurrection in the city. Groups of revolutionaries set fire to the churches and convents, and battled like lions in the streets of the great city until, due to the arrival of troops in great numbers, they had to hide their arms awaiting a better opportunity.

Then the persecutions commenced, having Ferrer as the target, even though Ferrer, as was well demonstrated, had taken no part in the insurrection. Arrested, he was tried by judges who had orders to sentence him to death, and despite having clearly shown his innocence, he was shot on October 13, 1909 in the Montjuich fort.

The Modern Schools, then numbering 120, were closed by the authorities, and thousands and thousands of children were left without bread or the healthy education that, according to the noble dreams of its author, would inevitably make humanity better, freer, happier.

I have here demonstrated, comrades, the impossibility of resolving the social problem through peaceful means. Capital, Authority, and the Clergy, with all the influence they have, with all the forces at their disposal, are determined to defend their interests and to drown in blood even the most peaceful activities involving what we love and what we're forced to do to bring about the advent of liberty, equality, and fraternity.

The work of Ferrer was being conducted in a perfectly legal manner; it didn't go a step beyond the guarantees in the political constitutions which have cost the people so much blood; he didn't advocate violence as a means of reaching the desired communist system, and nonetheless the bloodied cadaver of the teacher proclaims to the world that political liberty is a vile lie, that by taking the peaceful way one will surely arrive at martyrdom, but not victory, which is what the disinherited need.

The Mexican people do not deny the excellence of a rationalist education. But we understand, through the lessons of history, that to struggle against force with no other arm than reason is to retard the arrival of the free society for thousands and thousands of years, during which exploitation and tyranny will have ended up converting the proletariat into a separate species, incapable through heredity of rebelling and crushing the bourgeoisie, tyrants, and monks with their fists.

The privileged classes will never permit that the proletariat open its eyes, because this would signify the thundering downfall of their empire, which is sustained as much through force of arms as it is through the ignorance of the dispossessed.

Comrades: Let the death of the teacher serve to convince the pacifists that in order to put an end to social inequality, to kill off privilege, to make every human being a free person, it's necessary to use force and to rip, through its use, the riches from the bourgeoisie who interpose themselves between the human being and liberty.

The revolution that the Partido Liberal Mexicano is fomenting is based on the realization that reason without force is a weak reed at the mercy of the repressions unleashed by the forces of infuriated reaction, and that because of this the Mexican libertarians will not surrender; because of this they struggle without respite; because of this, audacious and gallant, they stand waving the red banner of proletarian redemption, while the idol worshipers wait for the despots to throw them a crumb, without thinking—idiots!—that they have the right to take everything.

ALL RULERS ARE THE SAME

Regeneración, *July 25, 1914*

(Translated by C.B.)

A man can have good intentions prior to being a ruler, but it's very difficult for him to conserve those intentions upon reaching power, and it's impossible that he'll still have them when he's a ruler.

To reach power it's necessary that the candidate enter into compromises with the enemies of his party so as to assure his election, offering those enemies benefits that can only be delivered through sacrificing his ideals. He arrives then in power, without anything left of his desires favoring the people, and disposed simply to do everything he can to assure his remaining in the coveted position.

If, by mere chance, the man has been able to elevate himself without entering into compromises with his enemies, and, therefore, conserves intact the intentions he had when promising to pursue the good of the people, these intentions will die in his breast one by one before he begins to put them into practice. As soon as he's in power he'll see himself surrounded by individuals who are powerful by virtue of their wealth, their influence, their talent, their knowledge, and by astute politicians who know how to contrive to be in the good graces of the government, men who get up with the rising sun disposed to change their stripes with each day if it's necessary to the pursuit of their selfish ends.

In such an environment, the man who previously rubbed elbows with the common people will forget them. Sickened by the incense of adulators, regaled by distinguished men and women of high rank, in continuous contact with diplomats and other gilded insects of international politics, he'll come to believe that he is better than other men, and he'll feel himself superior or make himself into a tyrant like any other ruler.

The projects that he had in his head about freeing the people from tyranny will make him laugh; he'll consider them unrealizable, criminal attacks on acquired rights, monstrous crimes. It's simply that a new manner of looking at things will unfold within him. Before, he saw things from the bottom looking up; now he sees things from the top looking down. His psychology is different: before, he thought and felt as a part of the great mass that comprises the nation; now, he feels detached from this great mass, he sees himself about this mass, he believes himself better than the mass, he imagines himself superior to the mass.

As he's no longer in contact with the people, he doesn't see in it anything other than a flock that it's necessary to whip, a herd that it's necessary to force to march along the beaten path, something which he formerly combated with all his strength and energy. His new friends will appear better, given that they supply to him many more pleasures and refinements which make life comfortable and sweet.

History does not register in its pages the name of a single ruler who was seriously concerned with saving the people from misery and tyranny, and the history of humanity already goes back thousands of years. Through it, we know that the ruler, the rich man, and the priest of whatever religion have been inseparable allies, conniving together throughout the ages to keep the people in slavery.

Let us not fall under the illusion, Mexicans, that a grizzled, bearded man is better suited to govern us than a fresh-faced youth. Neither is good! The best thing is not to have anyone on our shoulders; the best thing is to be our own guides; the best thing is to think and to resolve our own affairs with our own heads.

If you trust that Carranza will make you free and happy, I don't know what to think of you, proletarians, because this would indicate that experience and the lessons of history have not been able to destroy the vice injected into you by your oppressors, and that vice consists of believing that a man can only live beneath the yoke of another. Understand, brothers in chains, that the principle of authority lives in the minds of the humble; those who have indoctrinated you in this error have been your oppressors.

The deciding moment is at hand. Huerta is high tailing it toward other countries and a new ambitious one prepares to take his place. If you want to have more governments, submit yourselves; and with your submission the true revolution—that which wants to clear from the table all tyrants and exploiters—will die, crushed by your indifference. But if, on the contrary, you labor like true workers, like men who know that the social wealth has been made by yourselves and, therefore, only you yourselves have the right to enjoy it, then rise up to support your brothers who continue with arms in hand; then you'll merit the applause of all of the intelligent men of the world and you'll be able to say with pride: "In Mexico the institution called authority is a thing of the past, because there you'll find men."

"Clerical Calavera," by José Guadalupe Posada.

DISCORD

Regeneración *October 29, 1910*

(translated by M.V.)

   Imagine the earth without mountains, the ocean without waves, the heavens without stars, the flower without colors. Imagine all the birds adorned in the same plumage, all the insects displaying the same form and color. Imagine the plains without any rises, without any unevenness; sand and pebbles here, sand and pebbles there, sand and pebbles everywhere; not a tree, not a shrub; nothing to break the monotony of the landscape, nothing to interrupt the uniformity of the scene; neither a brook that murmurs, nor a canary that sings, nor a breeze to remind that there is movement, that there is action. Imagine, finally, a humanity, without passions, all having the same tastes, all thinking in the same way, and decide whether it would not be preferable to die at once than to suffer the prolonged death agony of having no choice but to live under these conditions.

   Order, uniformity, symmetry appear to be better than death. Life is disorder, is struggle, is critique, is disagreement, is a tumult of passions. From this chaos emerges beauty, from this confusion emerges science; from criticism, from conflict, from discord, from the tumult of passions, beams of light shine like embers, yet are enormous like suns: truth and liberty. Discord: here you have the great creative agent that works in nature. The actions and the reactions in inorganic and organic material, generators of movement, of heat, of light, of beauty: what are they if not the work of discord? Breaking the monotony of the simple substances, discord brings them closer to each other, mixes them, combines them, crushes them to bits and transports them from one place to another: the iron that sleeps in the entrails of the earth is the same that blazes across the terrestrial atmosphere as a meteorite, that reddens the lips of a woman, and that gleams in the blade of a dagger; the carbon that appears black in the ashes of a fire is the same that appears green and handsome in the leaves of plants, clear like a droplet of dew in a diamond, warm and endearing in the breath of a beloved woman. All is transformed by discord: it dissolves and creates, destroys and creates.

   In human societies, discord plays the most important role. An innovator, it breaks the old molds and creates new ones; it destroys traditions that are cherished, but which are pernicious to progress, and it puts new longings, new fires into the soul of the people, after it has extinguished the embers that still warm the cold, senile old ideals. An aesthete, it pushes art from its beaten path and makes it take new routes, where there are sources the literary herd has not yet discovered, new colors, new harmonies, unexpected turns of phrase that have never existed on any palette, that have never vibrated in any string, which have never sprung like jets of light from any pen. Always revolutionary, discord makes disgust ferment in proletarian breasts until, their nerves stressed until they are ready to snap, desperation makes hands search for rocks, bombs, daggers, revolvers, rifles, and men cast themselves against injustice, each one disposed to be a hero.

While the poor acquiesce to being poor, while the oppressed acquiesce to being slaves there will be no liberty, there will be no progress. But when discord tempts the hearts of the humble, when it comes and tells them that while they suffer their masters rejoice, and that we all have the right to rejoice and to live, the passions then blaze and they destroy and create at the same time, ravage and cultivate, demolish and build. Blessed be discord!

DEATH TO ORDER!

Regeneración, *May 13, 1911*

(Translated by M.V.)

"Order, order!" This is the whine of those who advocate what today is called "order." Order, for these poor people, can only exist by subjecting humanity to the clubs of the policeman, the soldier, the judge, the jailer, the executioner, and the governor.

But this is not order. I understand order to be harmony; and harmony neither can nor should exist while upon this planet's surface there are human beings who gorge themselves and others who do not even have a crust of bread to lift to their mouths

If things were well arranged, if every member of the human species had enough to eat, had a place to shelter himself from harsh weather without having to pay rent, in a word, if everyone, from just doing a bit of work in healthy conditions each day, had everything he needed to live decently, without worrying about the future, then there would be no one who would dare say: I am greater than you, obey me!

Then there would be order because there would be harmony. No one would have to quarrel with anyone else; no one would have to envy anyone else. All would be brothers, and the policeman, the soldier, the judge, the jailer, the executioner, and the governor would be gone because they'd be useless. They would be useless because, once harmony between human beings was won through the triumph of economic freedom, the parasitism of public officials would no longer have any reason to exist.

Public functionaries are not, as is commonly believed, the guardians of order. Order, which is harmony, does not need guardians, precisely because it is order. What does need guardians is disorder, and what reigns in the political and social life of humanity is a scandalous, shameful and humiliating disorder for those of us who were not born to be slaves.

Disorder consists of one social class holding down another social class, for there should exist only one class: that of the producers, that is, that of the workers. Humanity will be converted into the working class when the land and the machinery belong to everyone, for then everyone will have to work in order to eat.

Maintaining disorder, that is, maintaining political and social inequality, maintaining the privileges of the upper class and the submission of the lower class—those are the things that require rulers, laws, cops, soldiers, jailers, judges, hangmen, and the whole throng of great and small functionaries who suck the life from the peoples of the Earth. These officials do not exist to protect humanity, but rather to keep it in submission, to enslave it for the benefit of those who have contrived to the present moment to monopolize the land and the machinery

"Order! Order!" This is the whine of those who advocate disorder, that is, those who advocate social and political inequality among the human species.

No. Order is not the enslavement of one part of humanity by another, but rather liberty for the entire human species. To bourgeois "order," we Mexicans answer with our rebellion. Against this "order," we shout: "death to order!" because this is the "order" that binds the hands of a human being's free initiative, because it is the order of the barracks or the penitentiary. Death to order!

THE RIGHT TO PROPERTY

Regeneración, *March 18, 1911*

(Translated by M.V.)

Among all the absurdities that humanity venerates, this is one of the greatest as well as one of the most venerated.

The right to property is archaic, as ancient as the stupidity and blindness of men; but the antiquity alone of a right can not give it the right to survive. If it is an absurd right, it must be aborted, no matter how it was born when humanity covered its nakedness with animal hides.

The right to property is an absurd right because it originates in crime, fraud, and the abuse of force. In the beginning, the right of a single individual to territorial property did not exist. The lands were worked in common, the forests provided firewood for the homes of everyone, and the harvests were distributed to members of the community according to their needs. Examples of this natural condition can be seen even now in some primitive tribes; in Mexico this practice still flourished among indigenous communities during the epoch of Spanish domination, and it still survived until a few years ago. The despotic attempt to seize lands from indigenous tribes, lands that they cultivated in common for centuries, was the cause of war with the Yaqui in Sonora and the Maya in the Yucatan.

The right of a single person to territorial property was born in the attack of the first ambitious person who brought war against a neighboring tribe in order to subdue them into servitude, putting the land which this tribe cultivated in common under the control of the conqueror and his captains. Thus, it was through violence, through the abuse of force, that private territorial property was born. Financial speculation, fraud, more or less legal robbery, but in all ways robbery—these were the other origins of private property. Afterwards, once the first thieves turned the earth over to themselves, they made laws to defend what they called and still call in this century a "right," that is, the ability that they give themselves to use lands which have been stolen and to enjoy the produce of the lands without being molested. One must notice well that it was not the despoiled who gave the right of ownership of the lands to those thieves; it was not the people of any country who gave them the license to appropriate the good of nature, to which all human beings have a right. It was the thieves themselves who did it by force, writing the laws that would protect their crimes and keep the despoiled away from recovering what was rightfully theirs.

This so-called right of property has descended, transmitted from fathers to sons through inheritance, making all these goods, which should be possessed in common, remain at the disposition of one social caste, to the flagrant disadvantage of the rest of humanity, whose members began their lives well after the land had already been allotted to a handful of idlers.

The origin of territorial property has been violence, and by violence it is still sustained: thus, if any man wants to use a scrap of earth without the consent of it's so-called owner, he must go to jail, which is guarded closely by cops who are sustained not by the owner of the lands, but by the working people. Even though the taxes apparently emerge from the coffers of the rich, they have contrived to reimburse themselves by paying starvation wages to the workers and by selling them primary necessities at a high price. Therefore, the people, with their work, sustain the cops who prevent them from taking back what belongs to them.

And if this is the origin of territorial property, if the right to property is nothing but the legal consecration of crime, why do they raise their arms in prayer to heaven when one knows that the Mexican Liberal Party is working to expropriate the land monopolized by the rich—that is, by the descendants of the thieves who appropriated it through crime—in order to hand it over to its natural master, the people, that is, all the inhabitants of Mexico?

Some of Madero's followers sympathize with the idea of delivering the land to the people; but, conservative to the end, they want to decree the action in a solemn legal setting; that is, they want the congress to decree the expropriation. I have written much about the matter, and I wonder that there are those who apparently cannot understand what I've said, because I have the presumption to believe that I've spoken very clearly. "No congress," I have said, "would dare to decree the expropriation of the land, because the benches of congress are not filled with the workers, but with their bosses; they are not filled with the ignorant and the poor, but with the intellectuals and the rich." That is to say, you'll find in congress representatives of the so-called directing classes: the rich, the educated, the men of science, the professionals—but no worker of the pick and the shovel, no peasant, no worker would be allowed to squeeze through; and if, by some veritable miracle a worker would manage to cross the threshold of the legislative chamber, how could he fight against men accustomed to such verbal battles? How could he make his ideas prevail if he lacked the scientific knowledge that the bourgeoisie possesses in abundance? But, let us suppose that the working people did send competent representatives to the congress. Throughout the world, these so-called workers' representatives in parliaments are held in contempt. They are as bourgeois as every other representative. What have the labor representatives of the English people done in the House of Commons? What are the achievements of the workers' representatives in the French Parliament? In the German parliament, there are a great many workers' representatives, and what have they done on behalf of the economic liberty of the workers? The Austro-Hungarian parliament is notable for the growing number of workers' representatives who sit on its benches, but nevertheless the problem of hunger remains unresolved in Austro-Hungary, as in every country where there are no labor representatives in the congress.

It is necessary, therefore, to give up these illusions. The expropriation of the earth from the hands of the rich must be accomplished during the present insurrection. We liberals will not be committing a crime by handing the land over to the working people, because it is theirs, the people's: it is the land which their most distant ancestors lived upon and irrigated with their sweat; the land which the Spanish invaders stole by force from our Indian forefathers; the land that these invaders handed down through their estates to their descendants, who currently possess it. This land belongs to all Mexicans by natural right. Some people have purchased it; but from where was the money for making this purchase extracted if not from the labor of the Mexican peasants and laborers? Others took this land by claiming it as wasteland; but even if it were just wasteland, it belongs to the people, and no one has the right to give it to someone who offers a few pesos for it. Others have acquired the land by taking advantage of their friendship with men of government, obtaining it without it costing them a single penny, as if it were wasteland. If the land belongs to one of the dictator's enemies or to some person without influence or money, others have gotten it through judicial corruption. Still others have acquired the land through making loans to subsidize small ranchers, which, in the end, wound up obligating these ranchers, powerless to pay their debts, to relinquish their fields to the hands of the moneylender.

Comrades, all who believe that the course pursued by the Partido Liberal is humanitarian should try to persuade those who still adore capital and venerate the so-called right to property that the Partido Liberal is in the right, that its work will be a work of justice, and that the Mexican people will be truly great when they can enjoy, without obstacles, land and liberty.

SOLIDARITY

Regeneración, *October 29, 1910*

(translated by M.V.)

Before the spectacle of the bestial struggle of all against all that began with the appearance of the first lord over the earth, and which has been prolonged until our days, producing as a logical result the division of humanity into two classes, of oppressors and oppressed, of masters and slaves, before the spectacle of this struggle which has completely alienated man from man, and which makes the men of one nation seem to be the natural enemies of other nations, before this apparently eternal spectacle of war, one must ask: has man progressed?

The material progress achieved by humanity is enormous: it is gigantic if compared to the moral progress; for while we all admire the phonograph, the camera, the wireless telegraph, and aerial navigation, the more noble conceptions of philosophy—those which, when put in practice, would open ample horizons to the free enjoyment of the blessings of life—are being asphyxiated between the bindings of rarely opened, and, even worse, rarely understood books.

It isn't strange then that, today like yesterday, the struggle for life retains the same character of ferocity, of reciprocal hostility that makes man, as Hobbes says, a wolf to man: "homo hominis lupus." No, it is not strange that the man of today who knows how to use electricity and who has discovered how to fly has, regarding other men, the same sentiment of animosity that made the caveman's blood boil when, returning from the hunt, he found in his rocky home a bear or a hyena prepared to fight him for housing and for food. Humanity progresses, but in one direction only.

For this reason, when one speaks of solidarity, those who understand are very few. Solidarity is the consciousness of the common interest, and the actions that follow from this consciousness. Despite its simplicity, solidarity is an unknown concept to almost everyone. An increasingly greater egoism dominates men's relations between themselves. Isolated protests against this state of affairs perish as quickly as they are formulated, silenced by the racket of the struggle; noble spirits who dare to raise themselves up among the combatants to preach brotherhood fall to pieces like flowers trampled underfoot by a stampede of beasts, for each redeemer, there is a Cavalry or a Montjuich.

And in this implacable struggle, the victorious are always the same: the clever and the wicked. The only difference is that yesterday they justified their triumph as a result of divine will, and today, embarrassed, they justify their depredations with science. Darwin's theory of natural selection, which explains how individuals better endowed for the struggle of life are the ones who triumph, is the rationalization that the rich and the despotic brandish against those who question their appropriation of the right to exploit and to oppress, even though they are forgetting to say, because this benefits them, that animals of the same species do not destroy each other, nor do some declare themselves the masters of the others. The struggle of species is directed against other species, but a single species works together in its process of adapting to the environment. Only the human species displays the repugnant spectacle of some individuals devouring the others, producing through this an obvious retardation of progress, when, by acting in solidarity thousands of years ago it would have been able to control nature and obtain across-the-board progress.

Ignorance of humanity's common interest, that is, ignorance of solidarity, makes each man see in the other man a competitor who must be vanquished so that he can live. The rich man lives off the poor; but in turn he fears that other rich people might ruin him in order to enrich themselves further. The poor man, for his part, sees in each newborn one more mouth that will reduce the portion of bread that the rich permit him to eat, and in each poor person an enemy who could be hired for cheaper wages, leaving him and his family without bread.

This implacable struggle, which originates in the lack of solidarity among all human beings, kills in man, or at least weakens in him, the instinct of sociality which is characteristic of the superior animal species, thereby making him a liar, a fraud, a coward, and an egotist. In this way, the wicked, the insincere, the greedy, and the brutal triumph, and for this reason, even though material progress is great, the still more beautiful philosophical concepts live only in the pages of books consumed by moths on library shelves.

However, seeing how the rich and distinguished classes do not understand this solidarity or pretend not to understand it, or, at most practice it only when it concerns the narrow interests of their class, without understanding or practicing the solidarity that should unite the human species into a single intelligent and active force and place nature at man's service; seeing the aggressions of these dominating classes, the proletarian class should unite; it should tighten its ranks in order to be able to unleash a decisive battle in which it would have to be victorious for it contains the greater number of individuals.

Instead of seeing in each poor person a bothersome competitor, one more mouth against whom we must compete for the crumbs the rich contemptuously give us as wages, we should think of him as our brother; we should make him understand that our interests are his, and that we should join together in the struggle against the dominating class. Is there a strike? It is in the interest of all to help out those who are on strike. To take a job replacing a striker is an act of treason to the common interest of the poor, because this only helps the oppressing classes and delivers nothing to the oppressed classes. To take a job for less pay than the other worker earns is equally an act of treason, because it is making the rich receive more and is worsening the condition of the working class through the reduction of salaries. One must consider an injury to one an injury to all.

In the revolution that is coming, the Mexican worker must show his solidarity. By uniting forcefully with other workers he could turn the revolution toward his desires, toward the course that agrees with his interests. Taking possession of the land, increasing wages, and decreasing working hours, along with improving education, will be the first preparatory advances toward the great final battle that will snatch from the hands of the few the things necessary to the production and distribution of wealth. But one must understand well: this can only be accomplished if the revolution is conducted with this aim in mind. However, if the proletarians deviate, starting a revolution only to indulge in the luxury of having a new president, or what amounts to the same thing, a new master, they should understand they will not alleviate their misery in this manner, nor shall they approach the ideal of Liberty, Equality, and Fraternity that should live in the hearts of all men and all women.

SPEECH IN EL MONTE, CA
1917

(Translated by C.B.)

I want to say a few words to you about a bad habit which is common in human beings. I refer to indifference, the bad habit of not paying attention to matters that affect the interest of humanity in general.

Everyone has interest in his own matters and those of the persons near to him, and nothing more; everyone looks after his own well-being and that of his family, and nothing more, without realizing that the well-being of the individual depends on the well-being of everyone else, and that the well-being of a collectivity, of a people, of humanity, is the product of conditions which make it possible, is the result of favorable circumstances, is the natural, logical consequence of a measure of liberty and justice.

Well then, the well-being of everyone depends on the well-being of the rest—well-being that can only be possible through a measure of liberty and justice, because if tyranny rules, if inequality is the norm, the only ones who can enjoy well-being are the oppressors, those who are above the rest, those whose privileges are founded in inequality.

Therefore, the duty of all is to concern themselves with the general interest of humanity through pursuing creation of an environment favorable to the well-being of all. Only in this manner will the individual enjoy true well-being.

But we see that in current life the exact opposite is the case. Each one struggles and sacrifices for his personal well-being, and he doesn't obtain it, because his struggle is not directed against the conditions which are an obstacle to the well-being of all. The human being struggles, he strives, he sacrifices himself to win his bread each day; but this struggle, this striving, this sacrifice doesn't yield the desired result, that is, it doesn't produce the well-being of the individual because he doesn't direct his efforts to change the general conditions of life; creating circumstances favorable to all individuals doesn't enter into the calculations of the individual that struggles, strives, sacrifices himself—only the mean interest in the satisfying of individual necessities, without appreciation of the needs of the rest, and often even with disregard of the needs of others. No one is interested in the fortunes of the rest. He who is working only thinks of not losing his job and is happy when he's not among the number who get laid off, while at the same time he who doesn't have a job longs for the moment in which the rich man discharges some worker so that he can see himself, in this manner, obtain the vacant post; and there are even some so vile, so abject, that they don't hesitate in offering their arms for lower pay, and others who during strikes rush to fill the jobs temporarily abandoned by the strikers.

In sum, the workers fight over bread; they snatch mouthfuls away from each other; one is the enemy of the other, because every individual only seeks his own well-being without concern for the well-being of the rest; and this antagonism between members of the same class, this deaf struggle for mere crumbs, makes our slavery permanent, it perpetuates misery, it creates our misfortune, because we don't understand that our interest is that of our neighbor, because we sacrifice ourselves for poorly understood individual interest, seeking in vain the well-being that can only be the result of our interest in the matters that concern humanity as a whole—an interest that, if intensified and generalized, would yield as its product the transformation of the present conditions of life, which are not suited to procuring the well-being of all because they are founded in the antagonism of individual interests, in contrast to those based on the harmony of interests, in fraternity and justice.

Therefore, understand comrades that in order to achieve well-being it is necessary, it is indispensable, to pay attention to the general interest of humanity, setting aside indifference, because indifference makes our slavery eternal. We all feel unfortunate; but we don't try to find one of the principal causes of our misfortune, which is our indifference, our apathy toward the general interest.

Indifference is our chain, and we ourselves are our own tyrants because we make no effort to destroy it. Indifferent and apathetic, we see ourselves file by earthly affairs with the same impassivity as if they were taking place on another planet; and as everyone is interested only in his own person, without concern for the general interest, for the common interests of all people, no one feels the need to unite with others to be strong in the struggle for the general interest. This results in there being no solidarity among the oppressed, that there are no limits on the abuses by government, and that the bosses of all types make prisoners of us, enslave us, exploit us, oppress us, and humiliate us.

When we reflect that all who suffer the same evils have the same interest, an interest common to all of the oppressed, and we decide to be in solidarity with each other, then we'll be capable of transforming the circumstances that produce our misfortunes into those that are favorable to our liberty and well-being.

Let us leave behind the clasping of hands and anxiously asking ourselves what will be effective in resisting the assaults of governmental tyranny and capitalist exploitation. The remedy is in our hands: that all who suffer the same evils unite, certain that before our solidarity the abuses of those who base their strength in our separation and indifference will crumble.

The tyrants have no more force than we give them with our indifference. The tyrants are not the ones to blame for our misfortunes; we ourselves are. It's necessary to confess it: if the bourgeois strain us with hard labor and demand the last drop of our sweat, who do we owe this evil to but ourselves, who haven't known how to oppose this bourgeois exploitation through protest and rebellion? How can the government not oppress us when it knows that any of its orders, no matter how unjust and no matter how much it wounds our dignity as men, is observed by us, with our eyes cast down, without even a murmur, without even a gesture than shows our discontent and anger? And aren't we ourselves, the disinherited, the oppressed, the poor, those who lend ourselves to receiving from the hands of our oppressors the guns destined to exterminate our working class brothers, in those rare moments in which the herd and its habitual indifference are replaced by an explosion of dignified, honorable actions? Don't the policeman and the majordomo, the jailer and the hangman come from our ranks, from the great proletarian mass?

It is we ourselves, the poor, who weld our own chains, who are the cause of our own misfortune and that of our loved ones. The old man who extends a trembling hand asking for a crumb, the child who cries from cold and hunger, the woman who offers her body for a few coins, they are of our making, to us they owe their misfortune, because we don't know enough to make of our chests a shield; and our hands, accustomed to begging, are incapable of sinking in, like pincers, into the throats of our exploiters.

THE CASSOCK STIRS
Regeneración, *September 16, 1911*

(Translated by C.B.)

Will someone please tell me when the little priests of San Gabriel, California became so enamored of the initiator of Mexican political independence, Miguel Hidalgo y Costilla?

Don't these little priests remember that it was the monks, the clerics of all stripes who were the fiercest enemies of that noble elder? Don't these little priests in San Gabriel remember that the clergy in Mexico excommunicated Hidalgo? Don't these little priests remember that the Inquisition degraded, insulted, and committed outrages against the martyr of Chihuahua, Miguel Hidalgo y Costilla?

The clergy has always been the worst enemy of human liberty. So why do the clergy now take the name of Hidalgo and bless it, extol it, and even raise altars to Hidalgo and call on the simple people to venerate him?

Because the clergy are always hypocrites. If a new idea is broached, there you'll find excommunications and anathemas fulminating. But when the idea triumphs, you'll see them patronizing it and bragging about being the most disinterested defenders of what they were combating yesterday with all the cunning at their disposal. The priests condemned Christ, but the doctrines of the martyr of Calvary triumphed, and they now have to adore him. But they safeguard themselves very well from following his doctrines; they guard themselves well from being humble, frugal, and virtuous. They thunder against lust from the pulpit, without jeopardizing their keeping of several women; they threaten drunks with hellfire, but they wake up every morning with hangovers; they counsel others not to rob, but they sell junk in their churches at exorbitant prices. And so on.

Today, the little priests in San Gabriel are celebrating the 16th of September [marking the initiation, by Hidalgo, of Mexico's war of independence against Spain]; and from what I hear it's simply to increase business. Don't attend this celebration, Mexicans. Remember that the monks were the persecutors of Hidalgo; remember that the clergy gave full honors to the American invaders in 1847; remember that the priests went to Europe to bring to Mexico that poor fool called Ferdinand Maximilian Hapsburg. Turn your back on the clergy and join with the Partido Liberal Mexicano that wants neither priests, nor authorities, nor the rich.

EARTH

Regeneración, *October 1, 1910*

(Translated by C.B.)

At this moment, millions of human beings turn their sad gaze toward the heavens, in the hope of finding something beyond the visible stars. This something is everything, because it constitutes the purpose, it forms the object of this painful effort, of this arduous battle of the human species since its first hesitating steps put it in advance of the unreasoning species: this thing called happiness.

Happiness! "Happiness is not of this world," say the religious: "Happiness is in the heavens, it's beyond the grave." And the human herd raises its eyes, and ignorant of the science of the heavens, thinks that this must be very far away when its own feet support themselves upon this heavenly body, which with its fellows constitutes the glory and the greatness of the firmament.

The Earth forms part of the heavens. Humanity, therefore, is in the heavens. It's not necessary to gaze upwards in the hope of finding happiness beyond those stars that beautify the night: happiness is here, on our own heavenly Earth, and it won't be won through prayers; it won't be won through orations; it won't be won through begging; nor through humiliations; nor through laments. It's necessary to fight for it standing and through force, because the gods of the Earth aren't the same as those of the religions, softened by prayers and begging; the gods of the Earth have soldiers, they have cops, they have judges, they have hangmen, they have prisons, they have nooses, they have laws—everything that constitutes what are called institutions, daunting mountains which impede humanity from extending its arms and taking possession of the Earth, making it humanity's own, turning it to humanity's service, making happiness the inheritance of all and not the exclusive privilege of the few who today enjoy it.

The Earth is for all. When it formed millions and millions of years ago, when it had not separated from the chaos that whirled around forming new suns, and later, when this cloud cooled producing new planets, some more some less suitable to life, the Earth did not have a master. Neither did it have a master when humanity made of every tree trunk in the woods or of each cave in the mountains a living space, a refuge from bad weather and wild beasts. Neither did the Earth have a master much later when humanity's painful path arrived in the pastoral period: the tribe, which possessed cattle in common, would station itself wherever there were pastures. The first master appeared with the first man who took slaves to work the fields; and to make himself master of the fields and of the slaves he had to use arms in war against an enemy tribe. Violence, then, was the origin of landed property, and through violence this property has been maintained to the present day.

Invasions, wars of conquest, political revolutions, wars to dominate markets, the pillage carried out by rulers or their proteges are the source of the titles of private property. These titles are sealed with the blood and with the slavery of humanity. And the monstrous origin of this absurd "right," which is based in crime, is no obstacle to those who write the laws—in fact, they call it "sacred"—because those who write the laws are the same as those who possess the lands.

Landed property is based in crime, and as such is an immoral institution. This institution is the fount of all of the ills which afflict humanity. Vice, crime, prostitution, despotism are born of it. In order to protect it, these are necessary:

the army, the judiciary, the parliament, the police, the prison, the scaffold, the church, the government, and the whole swarm of employed drones, with all of them being maintained precisely by those who don't have a clod of dirt upon which to recline their heads, by those who were born when the Earth was already partitioned up by a few bandits who had appropriated it by force, or when it was owned by the descendants of these bandits, who have been possessing it under the so-called right of inheritance.

The earth is the principle element in the extraction or production of everything that is necessary to life. The useful minerals, metals, and materials are extracted from it: coal, stone, sand, lime, salts. When it's cultivated, it produces every type of nutritious and rare fruit. Its prairies provide food for the cattle, while its forests supply their wood, and its springs their beautiful, life-giving waters. And all this belongs to a few; it makes happy a few; it gives power to a few, when nature made it for all.

From this tremendous injustice are born all of the evils which afflict the human species, the evils that produce misery. Misery debases, misery prostitutes, misery incites crime, misery bestializes the human face, body, and mind.

Degraded and, what is worse, unaware of their degradation, generations pass their lives in the midst of abundance and wealth without tasting the happiness monopolized by a few. With the Earth belonging to a few, those who don't possess it have to rent themselves to those who possess it in order to keep skin and bones together. The humiliation of wages or hunger: this is the dilemma that private property presents to every human who comes to life. It's an iron dilemma which impels humanity, if it doesn't want to perish of hunger, to put itself in the chains of slavery or turn to crime or prostitution.

Ask yourselves now why the government oppresses, why men rob or kill, why women prostitute themselves. Behind all of the bars of those charnel houses called prisons, where flesh and spirit rot, thousands of unfortunates pay the consequences—the torture of their bodies and the anguish of their spirits—of this crime elevated by law as a sacred right: the right of private property. In the debasement of bordellos, thousands of young women prostitute their bodies and maim their dignity—suffering equally the consequences of private property. In the asylums, in the poorhouses, in the orphanages, in all of these dark places where misery finds refuge, helplessness, hopelessness, and pain are the consequences of private property for men and women, old and young. And the prisoners, beggars, prostitutes, orphans, and the sick raise their eyes to the heavens in the hope of finding something beyond the visible stars: the happiness which was stolen from them by the lords of the Earth.

And the human flock, unconscious of its right to life, bends its back working for others the earth which nature delivered to it, perpetuating with its submission the dominion of injustice.

But from the enslaved, muddied masses surge rebels; from a sea of bent backs emerge the heads of the first revolutionaries. The flock trembles, fearing punishment; tyranny trembles, fearing attack; and, breaking the silence, a cry, which sounds like thunder, rolls above the bent backs and arrives at last to the thrones: Land!

"Land!" cry the Roman land reformers. "Land!" cry Munzer's Anabaptists. "Land!" Cries Babeuf! "Land!" Cries Bakunin. "Land!" cries Francisco Ferrer. "Land!" cries the Mexican revolution. And this cry, smothered a hundred times in blood in the course of the ages; this cry, which corresponds to an ideal held lovingly through all times by all rebels on the planet; this sacred cry will transport the human herd to the heavens dreamed of by the mystics in this vale of tears when the herd stops looking toward the skies and fixes its gaze here, on this piece of rock which is shamed before its celestial brothers by leprous humanity.

Melancholy slaves of the Earth, resigned peons of the fields, throw down the plow. The trumpet blasts of Acayucan y Jiménez, of Palomas and Las Vacas, of Viesca and Valladolid, call you to war to take possession of the Earth, to which you give your sweat, but whose fruits are denied to you, because you have consented through your submission to the idle hands which have taken possession of that which belongs to you, of that which belongs to humanity as a whole, of that which cannot belong to a few men, but rather to all men and all women who, by the fact of being alive, have the right to its common enjoyment, through means of work—through your submission you have consented to the possession by the idle of all the riches which the Earth is capable of producing.

Slaves, take up the rifle! Work the earth only when you've taken possession of it. To work the earth now is to reinforce your chains, because you'll produce more wealth for your bosses, and wealth is power, riches are force, physical and moral, and the strong will always hold you in subjugation. Be strong yourselves; let all be strong and become the masters of the Earth. But for this the gun is needed. Buy it, ask someone to lend one to you as a last resort, and launch yourselves into the struggle crying with all your heart: Land and Liberty!

"Continuation of the Anti-Reelection Demonstrations (of 1892)," by José Guadalupe Posada.

CANNON FODDER

Regeneración, *October 15, 1910*

(Translation by C.B.)

It's the hour to reflect. For centuries and centuries the task of thinking, of studying, of reflecting, has been the task of the so-called ruling classes of society: the rich and the intellectuals. The masses haven't thought, and, naturally enough, those who have done it for them have been well paid for this "service," done contrary to the interests of the multitude. But the moment to reflect has arrived. The moment has arrived to decide whether the poor will continue under the self-interested direction of the rich or if we'll bravely take charge of the study of our problems and entrust in ourselves the defense of our interests. Now is the time to do it. Let us choose: let us be either an easily led flock or a phalanx of conscious beings: shame or glory.

Dragged along by the interests of the ruling classes, the proletarian masses have shed their blood throughout the ages. There has always been discontent among the poor, discontent occasioned by misery and injustice, by hunger and oppression. At the same time, the proletariat has always been disposed to rebel in the hope of attaining an improvement in its conditions. But being proletarians they haven't thought with their heads; rather, it's the ruling classes that have thought for them; it's the ruling classes who have channeled the tendencies in insurrectionary movements. And they have been the only ones who have taken advantage of the sacrifices of the working class.

Look then, workers, how important it is that you undertake on your own count the conquest of your own well-being. Every time that the ruling classes need the force of numbers to ensure a victory beneficial to themselves, they go to the proletariat, to the masses always disposed toward rebellion; they are certain of finding heroes in the mob that they cordially despise, but who at the time of need they adulate. They will praise the passions and even applaud and stimulate the vices of their dupes, as if passing the hand over the back of a beast in order to tame it with kindness when it's not necessary to employ the whip.

In this manner the proletarian masses have been hurled into war, have been pushed into committing acts contrary to their own interests. Wars of conquest, wars of commerce, wars of colonialism, political insurrections—all have been waged with the blood of proletarians, who are wildly applauded while they live their lives as heroes, and who are scorned and spit upon after the victory when it's necessary that someone sows grain, takes care of the cattle, makes clothing, builds houses. Then the heroes are kicked off the pedestal erected for them by the ruling classes and forced to return to their work in the fields, the workshops, the factories, the mines, the railways, each of them carrying, as if a prize, a paper, an official declaration of their valor, and a copper medal that shines upon their rags on holidays—plus some physical scars as well as the bad habits they picked up from their days in the barracks. Meanwhile, the rich and the intellectuals split up the lands of the conquered country. And in the nation whose government won via the sacrifice of the common people, they'll squander the copious booty seized from the vanquished by the plebeian army.

And this has been repeated since time immemorial; those below are always swindled, made the butt of a joke, and those above always win, without the experience opening the eyes of the flock—without the great swindle, constantly repeated, making the masses revolt, without even making them think. The present crowd is the same crowd that, inflamed and innocent, carried the great captains of antiquity on its shoulders: the crowd of Alexander, the rabble of Cyrus, the plebeians of Cambises, the flock of Scipio, the multitudes of Hannibal, the barbarians of Attila, all of them thought the same as the Napoleonic mobs, the conquering rabble of the Transvaal, the American plebes of Santiago and Cavite, and the triumphant yellow legions in Manchuria. The psychology of the contemporary masses is the same as that of the French masses in 1789, of the masses of Hidalgo in 1810, of the republican masses of Portugal today. It's always the same: the sacrifice of well-intentioned proletarians to the benefit of the ruling classes; the suffering and pain of the humble to the benefit of the intellectuals and the rich.

This has all been because the proletarians have not had the purpose of channeling popular movements toward the goal of their own best interests, but rather have obeyed the orders of the dominating minority that, as is natural, has always worked in the interests of itself. So, for example, in wars of conquest, in commercial and colonial wars, wars that the government of one nation has carried out against the people of another in order to extend its territorial domain or to conquer markets that will consume the industrial or agricultural products of the aggressing nation, the proletariat has done nothing other than give its blood to obtain, in exchange, no material benefit. The great industrialists, the great financiers, the great bankers and the men in government are those who benefit from these wars. To the proletariat nothing remains but the glory, if it's possible that murder on a grand scale committed against foreign peoples, to satisfy the absurd greed of the kings of industry, banks, and commerce, provides glory. Are the British workers happier today after the triumph of British arms in the Transvaal? Are the American workers happier as a result of the triumph of the U.S. Army over the Spanish army? Do the Japanese today enjoy more comforts than before Japan's triumph over Russia? No, not a bit of it. The British, Americans, and the Japanese continue being confronted with the same social problems as before, aggravated even more by the increase in the power of the ruling class provided by the acquisition of new markets.

And in regard to revolutions, one can observe the same result. Acts performed solely to obtain political liberty, triumphs obtained with the blood of the proletarian masses, have left the workers enslaved just as they were before they shed their blood. Our own history provides sufficient examples to prove this great truth, which could appear as blasphemy to those who don't probe deeply enough to get to the bottom of things, to those conservators of political institutions already fallen in deep disgrace. The insurrection of 1810, which gave us political independence, didn't have the power to give, to a people hungry for bread and education, that which was necessary for their elevation, and this was because the proletariat didn't decide to undertake its own redemption, to channel the movement led by the martyr Miguel Hidalgo toward an end that would benefit the working class. The insurrection against Santa Anna, initiated in Ayutla, and which had as its result the promulgation of the Constitution of 1857, likewise didn't have the power to deliver bread and education to the people. As is well known, it provided political liberties, but these were only taken advantage of by those who occupied prominent places in the political and social life of the country, but not by the proletarians who, because of their lack of money, education, and even social status, found themselves totally subordinated to the will of the ruling classes. Again, the proletariat derived no benefit from the movement initiated in Ayutla because it didn't make the decision to channel the rebellion toward a practical end, that of benefitting itself. The insurrection of Tuxtepec, which dragged the people behind the banner of "Real Suffrage and No Re-election," reconquered for the masses the choosing of alternatives via popular election, and had as its result the despotism that today we suffer in the political terrain and in the increased misery and misfortune of the working people, because the working class didn't take charge of the revolutionary movement of Porfirio Díaz and instead entrusted its future to the ruling classes of society.

Now, a new revolution is brewing. The excesses of Díaz's tyranny have injured all, both proletarians and non-proletarians, both men and women, both old and young. Political power has been monopolized and held in very few hands, and many members of the ruling classes have seen themselves obligated to allow the power they held under former governments to remain in the few hands [of the Díaz clique]; these individuals, naturally, have undertaken to work toward recapturing their former power. As always, these members of the ruling classes go down to the proletariat now that they need the force of numbers, and they caress it, extol it, they put in play the traditional scam of applauding it to the point of numbness; in the end, they pass their hand over the back of the monster in order to entice it with sweetness, without in any way hindering their ability to make the slavery harder in the haciendas, more arduous and less remunerative in the factories, workshops, and mines the day after the victory achieved through the blood, sacrifice, and heroism of the proletarian masses.

Proletarians: this is the hour to reflect. The revolutionary movement cannot be detained; it must, naturally, explode because of the forces producing it. But there's no reason to fear this movement. It's best to desire it and even to bring it about. It's better to die for honor, better to die defending the future of our families, than to continue suffering, in the midst of peace, the affront of slavery, the shame of misery and ignorance. But, comrades, don't let the so-called directing classes do your thinking for you and don't let them organize the revolution in such a way as to favor their interests. Take an active part in the great movement which is going to break out, and make sure that it takes the direction necessary so that this time if benefits the working class. Go over the pages of history, and in them you will find that in armed struggles in which the ruling classes have taken part, your role has always been that of cannon fodder, for the simple reason that you didn't want to go to the pain of thinking with your own heads and of undertaking the task of your own redemption. Remember that the emancipation of the working class must be the task of the workers themselves, and that this emancipation will begin with taking possession of the earth. Get ready, then, for the great revolution; but carry with you the purpose of taking the earth, of yanking it from the claws of those who now hold it for themselves. Only by doing so will you not be cannon fodder, but rather heroes who will know how to respect yourselves, in the midst of revolution and after the triumph, because you will have, through only the acquisition of the land, the power necessary to achieve, with little more effort, your total liberation.

Bear in mind, once again, that a simple change of rulers is not a fount of liberty, and that any revolutionary program that doesn't contain a clause concerning the taking of the lands by the people is a program of the ruling classes, who will never struggle against their own interests, as history has shown, and who only go to the masses, the plebeians, the rabble, when they need heroes to defend them and to sacrifice themselves for them—heroes who a few hours after the triumph will see themselves with their flanks bloodied by the spurs of the bosses who ride them.

Proletarians: take in hand the gun and gather behind the banner of the Partido Liberal, which is the only one which invites you to take possession of the earth for yourselves.

TO THE SOLDIERS
Regeneración, *April 18, 1914*

(Translated by C.B.)

To be a soldier is to be a machine, and to be a machine is degrading to a human being; to command is bad; to obey is worse.

Soldier of Huerta or soldier of Carranza, these are two machines that really are the same, because the two do the same thing: kill to keep some bandit in power who defends the interests of the capitalist class.

The first duty of a soldier is to obey his superiors. His superiors! An honorable man should prefer to be dead rather than to renounce his dignity by considering another man his superior.

Superior! And why is this doll dressed in a manner that would shame a sensible man superior? Superior! How can a marionette be superior simply because he drags around a sword and adorns himself with shiny ribbons like a circus clown?

No. These presumptuous fools can't be superior. These little officials, these little chieftains aren't superior to the common soldiers. These, the so-called superiors, eat, sleep, etc., like any other mortal. They're flesh and blood like the soldier; they're born, they grow up, and they die, like the soldier. Where does the "superiority" of these ridiculous men come from? Perhaps they know better than the soldier the undignified art of killing; but the soldier, proletarian that he is, knows how to plow the field, sow the grain, gather the harvest, tend the rails for the trains, go to the bottom of the mine for precious metals, weave the cloth, make the clothing, build the houses. In a word, he knows how to do everything, and everything that exists has come from his creative proletarian hands; and that which makes life agreeable or at least less hard is owed to him, to the proletarian, the true master of the Earth.

The soldier shouldn't consider any man his superior. All men are equal, and it's shameful to subordinate oneself to the will of another. The duty of a soldier is to kill—as if dealing with poisonous vermin—all those who consider themselves superior to him.

And so, death to all "superiors"!

THE WORLD WAR

Regeneración, *November 14, 1914*

(Translated by C.B.)

The size of *Regeneración* is so small that, sadly, we cannot give a detailed account of the tremendous conflict in which the principal world powers are involved .

We can only say that the war will continue on its course of destruction, mourning, blood, flames, tears, and that every day there are more expectations that other nations will become dragged into this struggle for industrial and commercial supremacy by their respective bourgeois classes.

How many have died in the present conflict? If one said that a million workers have died, that would be a low estimate of the number of lives lost. But let's suppose that the number lost in this evil war is a million; this would signify that a million families find themselves without protection because their men were so stupid that they preferred to march to the slaughterhouse to defend the interests of their exploiters rather than to go to war in defense of the interests of their class.

That such lambs die is a good thing. There's no lack of men who are obstacles to the desire for liberty of the other individuals of their class. When our own die, we should cry. When imbeciles die fighting for the glory of their own exploiters, we should laugh: that means we'll encounter fewer obstacles in our struggle for the destruction of the present system.

The men who are dying on the battlefields of the world's bourgeoisie won't be missed by humanity. They are an obstacle to the development of the world's peoples; they are the ballast that must be painfully carried by the revolutionaries; they are the ones who laugh to themselves when we tell them it's necessary to do away with all tyrannies; they are the ones who insult us when we tell them that all human beings are equal; they are the ones who believe in social superiority. Let them die! Blessed be the war that saves us the labor of cutting such throats!

To cry because such men die is stupid; to lament that thousands and thousands of families are without protection because their kinsmen have perished in this clash of bandits is a weakness. Humanity needs this type of bloodletting, this discarding of the bad so that the healthy part can prosper.

Let us hope that governments and the bourgeoisie will be weakened by this stupid war, and that this will facilitate our triumph. The good should flee this war and prepare themselves for the one to come: the class war. This will be the holy war.

Upon seeing weepy articles in various periodicals about this war, one feels as if one's nerves were rubbed raw. These aren't our brothers who are perishing by the thousands on the battlefields of Europe, Asia, Africa, and Oceania. They are our enemies; they are those who want this system which holds us in contempt to survive; they are the lackeys of capital, the church, and authority.

What we revolutionaries should do is wait and be ready for the opportune moment to unleash our fists against our oppressors. We'll continue to follow the course of this war with interest. We have our hand over the heart of the bourgeois system, and when we feel its pulsations weaken we won't vacillate. We'll finish it off!

A better opportunity will not be presented to the true revolutionaries of the entire world than this crazy, suicidal war; it offers the opportunity for us to unite our forces and to coordinate our plans. We can't lose such a great opportunity; we can't permit the governments weakened by this conflict to revive.

Don't cry. The sheep who suffer on the battlefields of the bourgeoisie are a threat to our liberty while they are alive. Dead, they're a guarantee of victory for the interests of our class.

Long live Land and Liberty!

THE WAR

Regeneración, *April 21, 1917*

(Translated by C.B.)

The U.S. government has declared war on Germany and has placed the American people at the center of the great world catastrophe.

The principle that the government has invoked to drag the people into the abyss couldn't be more attractive: liberty.

Liberty. What evil cause hasn't covered itself with that mantle to seduce the public? The tyrant oppresses in its name; invoking it, the executioner chops off the head of his victim; the law crushes in its behalf; and as a guarantee of its benefits the military barracks are raised and the prison constructed.

In the name of liberty the bourgeoisie has been permitted to suck the blood of the people; in the name of liberty the priest stupefies the masses; the system of private property lives in the name of liberty.

In what manner does the great European conflict threaten the liberties of the American people? Whether the allies triumph or whether the central powers triumph, to whichever side would come the victory, the American people would have continued being the unarmed and humiliated victims of the rich, the priest, and the ruler, but with the advantage of not having lost a drop of blood in that stupid conflict. Whereas once dragged to war it won't matter to which side comes victory, because the people will continue to suffer the same evils, aggravated to infinity by the natural consequences of all struggles undertaken in pursuit of narrow interests.

The European conflict doesn't threaten the liberty of the American people, but rather the liberty to steal granted to the bourgeoisie. The vigorous German submarine warfare campaign is a formidable obstacle to the free exercise of robbery on a grand scale practiced by the American bourgeoisie under the name of commerce. The German submarine campaign hasn't threatened the American people, but rather the manufacturers of arms and munitions and the food exporters. The American people would have benefitted from a resurgence of the submarine campaign, because the foodstuffs exported to Europe would have remained here, lowering the price of food.

A government that concerned itself with the well-being of the people would have given its blessing to the resurgence of the submarine campaign that impeded the export of foodstuffs. But when has there been the miracle of a government that concerns itself with the well-being of the masses? All governments have as their first duty the protection of the interests of the bourgeoisie, and the American government, faithful to this duty, declared war on Germany in the name of liberty . . . the liberty to rob.

It can be seen clearly enough that this declaration of war hasn't been made to benefit the American people, but rather to benefit their exploiters: the rich. And to benefit their exploiters, these poor people will have to shed their blood in the trenches, be smothered with enormous taxes to offset the costs of the war, will suffer the most extreme misery, and will lose, under the iron rule of militarist legislation, the last crumbs of liberty permitted them by their bosses so that they can dream of themselves being free and sovereign.

The date on which Woodrow Wilson signed the declaration of war opened a black period for the inhabitants of this country. Persecutions are becoming more frequent; all foreigners are viewed with suspicion; every German is seen as a spy; sentries open fire upon the first suspicious person who approaches an arsenal, a bridge, a munitions factory, a tunnel, or a fort; the jails are overflowing with spies or suspected spies; the muzzle upon the press has been made stronger; and in the offices of the great men methods are studied of how to recruit an army of two million men, that is, of two million proletarians ripped from the arms of their families in order to defend the interests of the rich.

Forward! The American people will have to convince themselves that all government is bad and that there will only be peace in the world when the so-called right of private property has disappeared.

The peoples are accustomed to walking with their eyes closed, and it's not a bad thing that they stumble now and then so that they'll open their eyes.

THE BOURGEOIS COUNTRY AND THE UNIVERSAL COUNTRY

Speech, September 19, 1915

(Translated by C.B.)

Humanity finds itself in one of the most solemn moments in its history. Nothing in the universe is stable, everything changes. We find ourselves in the moment in which a change is occurring in ... the manner in which human beings affiliate themselves to the conjunction of economic, political, social, moral and religious institutions that is called the capitalist system, or the system of private or individual property.

The capitalist system is dying of self-inflicted wounds, and humanity, astonished, is witnessing the impressive suicide. It's not the workers who have dragged the nations into falling upon one another; it's the bourgeoisie itself which has provoked the conflict in its zeal to dominate all of the markets. The German bourgeoisie has made colossal strides in industry and commerce, and the English bourgeoisie felt jealous of its rival. This is what's at the bottom of this conflict that's called the European War: the jealousy of peddlers, the enemy status of traffickers, the quarrels of adventurers. On the battlefields of Europe, the honor of a people, a race, or a country is not at issue; rather, what's in dispute, in this struggle of wild beasts, is everyone's pocketbook: they are hungry wolves trying to snatch away a prize. We're not dealing with wounded national honor nor with an insult to the flag, but with a struggle for position by the monied interests, monied interests which first made the people sweat in the fields, factories, mines, in all of the places of exploitation, and that now want these same exploited people to guard with their lives the pockets of those who rob them.

What sarcasm! What bloody irony! First the people are made to work for a crumb while the bosses retain the profits, and then the people are made to destroy each other in order that these profits aren't yanked from the claws of their exploiters. For we the poor to protect ourselves is good; this is our duty, it's an obligation imposed on us by solidarity. For us to protect one another, to aid each other, to defend ourselves mutually, is a necessity which we must satisfy if we don't want to be annihilated by our bosses. But to arm ourselves and fall upon each other to defend the pocketbooks of our bosses is a crime of the first order; it's a felony which we should indignantly refuse to commit. Taking up arms is good—but against the enemies of our class, against the bourgeoisie; and if our arms have to cave in some heads, let them be those of the rich; if our daggers have to pierce some hearts, let them be those of the bourgeoisie. But we the poor should not destroy one another.

On the battlefields of Europe, the poor destroy one another to the benefit of the rich, who have made the poor believe that they are fighting for the benefit of their country. Well then, what country does the poor man have? He can't count on more than his arms to make a living, a living which he'll lack if the accursed boss doesn't want to exploit him. What country does he have? The country ought to be like a good mother who shelters equally all of her children. What shelter do the poor have in their respective countries? None! The poor man is a slave in all nations; he's a wretch in all of them; he's a martyr under all governments. The nations don't give bread to the hungry; they don't console the sad; they don't wipe the sweat from the face of the worker done in by fatigue; they don't interpose themselves between the weak and the strong to protect the weak from abuse. But when the interests of the rich are in danger, then they'll call on the poor to give up their lives for their country, the country of the rich, for a country that isn't theirs, but that belongs to their exploiters.

Open your eyes brothers in chains and exploitation; open your eyes to the light of reason. The nation is for those who possess it, and the poor possess nothing. The nation is the doting mother of the rich and the neglectful stepmother of the poor. The nation is the cop armed with a club who kicks us, hurling us to the floor of a jail or who puts a rope around our necks when we don't want to obey the laws written by the rich for the benefit of the rich. The nation is not our mother; it's our scourge!

And to defend this scourge, our proletarian brothers of Europe have snuffed each other out of existence, one by the other. Imagine the space occupied by over 6,000,000 bodies—a mountain of cadavers, rivers of blood and tears; this is what the European war has produced to this moment. And these dead are our class brothers, the flesh of our flesh and the blood of our blood. They are workers who from childhood were taught to love the bourgeois country, in order that come the day they would allow themselves to be killed for it. What do these heroes own in their countries? Nothing! They possess nothing more than a pair of strong arms with which to make a living for themselves and their families. Now the widows, those grieving these workers, will have to die of hunger. The women will prostitute themselves in order to lift a piece of bread to their mouths; the children will steal in order to bring something to eat to their old parents; the sick will go to the hospital and to the tomb. Whorehouse, prison, hospital, miserable death: we have here the prize which the heirs of the heroes who died for their country will receive. Meanwhile the rich and the rulers will carouse, squandering the gold they've made the people sweat for in the factories, workshops, and in the mines. What a contrast! Sacrifice, pain, tears for all those who produce, for the self-denying creators of wealth. Pleasures and good fortune for the lazy who ride on our shoulders. We must shake ourselves, we must agitate ourselves, we must work so that the parasites who are putting an end to our existence fall to our feet. Let's resolutely place our hands around the neck of the enemy. We're stronger than he is. A revolutionary speaks this great truth: "The great appear great only because we are on our knees. Let us rise!" [Max Stirner, *The Ego and His Own*]

Well then, as horrible as the senseless butchery is that converts the old world into a slaughterhouse, it has to produce immense benefits for humanity, and in place of delivering ourselves to sad reflections thinking only of the pain, the tears, and the blood, we should recognize that such a great slaughter had to take place. The people, degraded by bourgeois civilization, haven't realized that they have rights, which has made such a great shakeup indispensable to waking them up to the reality of things. There are many who need pain to open their minds to reason. Mistreatment makes vile the humble and timid, but in the chest of a man, sentiments of dignity and noble pride are awakened by being shamed, and these feelings make him rebel. Hunger brings the coward to his knees and he delivers himself kneeling to the rich; but at the same time it's a spur to the people to rise up. Suffering can lead to patience and resignation, but it can also put the dagger, bomb, and revolver in the hands of the valiant. And this will be what will happen when this vile war ends, or it is what will make it end. The great battles in the trenches will end on the barricade and with the mutinies of the rebelling people, and the national flags will fall, giving place to the red banner of all the disinherited of the world.

Then the revolution which was born in Mexico, and which lives still as a whip and punishment for those who exploit, those who swindle, and those who oppress humanity, will extend its cleansing flames throughout the entire Earth, and in place of proletarian heads the heads of the rich, rulers, and priests will roll, and a single cry will escape from the breasts of millions and millions of human beings: Long live Land and Liberty!

And for the first time the sun will not be ashamed of sending its glorious rays to this melancholy Earth, now glorified by a new humanity, more just, more wise; all of the lands on Earth will become a single large, beautiful, good country:

the country of human beings, the country of the man and the woman, with a single flag: that of universal fraternity.

We salute, comrades of hardships and ideals, the Mexican Revolution. We salute this sublime epoch of the peon becoming a free man through rebellion, and we put everything we have, our money, our talents, our energy, our good will, and if necessary we'll sacrifice our well-being, our liberty, and even our lives in order that the revolution does not terminate in the elevation of any man to power, but rather, continuing its redemptive path, terminates with the abolition of the right of private property and the death of the principle of authority, because while there are men who possess and men who have nothing, well-being and liberty will be a dream; they will continue only as a pretty, never realized illusion.

The revolution should not be the means by which the wicked elevate themselves, but rather a movement for justice which gives the death blow to misery and tyranny, things which will not end through the election of rulers, but that will end with the abolition of the so-called right of private property. This "right" is the cause of all of the evils that humanity suffers. There's no reason to search for the origin of our ills in any other place; because of the "right" of private property there are governments and there are priests. The government is entrusted to see that the rich are not dispossessed by the poor, and the priests have no other mission than to infuse in the hearts of proletarians patience, resignation, and the fear of God, so that they never think of rebelling against their tyrants and exploiters.

The Partido Liberal Mexicano—a revolutionary union of workers—understands that liberty and well-being are impossible while capitalism, authority, and the clergy exist, and to the death of these three monsters, or this monster with three heads, the PLM directs all of its efforts; and to the propaganda and to the actions of the members of this party we owe the fact that there is no stable government in Mexico, that is, that a new tyranny has not consolidated itself. We don't want the rich, nor rulers, nor priests; we don't want idlers who exploit the efforts of laborers; we don't want bandits who sustain these idlers via the law; nor do we want evildoers who, in the name of whatever religion, make the poor into sheep who, without resistance or complaint, allow themselves to be devoured by wolves.

Those of you who want to investigate to the bottom what the Partido Liberal Mexicano fights for need do nothing other than read the manifesto of September 23, 1911, issued by the organizing junta of the party.

As the European war is a necessary evil, the Mexican Revolution is a blessing. That there is blood, that there are tears, that there are sacrifices is certain; but what great conquest has ever been obtained amid parties and pleasures? Liberty is the greatest conquest which a dignified breast can hope for, and liberty can only be obtained by facing death, misery, and prison.

To think that there is any other way of winning liberty is to sadly fool oneself.

Our liberty is in the hands of our oppressors; and we can't get it from them without sacrifice.

Forward! If in Europe they're still fighting for "their country," that is, for the rich, in Mexico the fight is for Land and Liberty! Forward! The moment is solemn. In Mexico the capitalist system is crumbling under the blows of the noble plebeian, and the outcry of the rich and the clergy arrives in Washington, upsetting the mind of that poor puppet of the bourgeoisie called Woodrow Wilson, the dwarf president, the functionary in a farce who, through the irony of fate, has been touched to be an actor in a tragedy in which the only ones who should take part are men of iron.

Forward! The remedy is within our grasp. To put an end to the capitalist system we don't need to do anything other than put our hands upon the goods held by the claws of the rich and declare them the property of all, men and women alike. A man risks his life to elevate someone to be a ruler, and however much a friend of the poor that ruler is said to be, he'll never be more of a friend to the poor than he is to the rich, because his job is to see that the law is respected, and the law orders that the right of private or individual property be respected. Why should one kill oneself to have a government? Why not, rather, sacrifice oneself not to have one? There's better reason to do so, because, with the same effort required to kick one ruler out and put another in his place, one could snatch the wealth from the hands of the rich.

Expropriation: this is the remedy—but it must be expropriation for the benefit of all and not the benefit of only a few. Expropriation is the golden key which will open the gates of liberty, because the possession of wealth gives economic independence. He who doesn't need to rent his arms in order to live is free.

Forward! It is not possible to sit and be simple spectators to this formidable drama. Let everyone unite with those of his class: the poor with the poor, the rich with the rich, so that everyone finds himself with his own and in his proper place for the final battle: that of the poor against the rich, that of the oppressed against the oppressors, that of the hungry against the well fed; and when the smoke of the final gunshot has dissipated, and the bourgeois edifice no longer has stone resting on stone, the sun will shine on our ennobled faces and the Earth will feel the pride of being trodden on by men and not by flocks.

We must learn something from our revolutionary, expropriating brothers in Mexico. They haven't waited for someone to elevate himself to the presidency of the republic to initiate the era of justice. As men, they have destroyed everything that was in the way of redemptory action. Real revolutionaries, they have smashed the law to pieces—the law, the underhanded support of injustice; the law, the pimp for the strong. With strong hands they have broken to pieces the jail bars, and with the heavy bars they've sunk in the craniums of the judges and pen pushers. They've caressed the necks of the bourgeoisie with the rope of the noose and, with a heroic face not seen for centuries, they have put their hands upon the earth, which has palpitated emotionally upon feeling itself possessed by free men.

Forward! Let everyone in this solemn moment do his duty.

Long live anarchy! Long live the Partido Liberal Mexicano! Long live Land and Liberty!

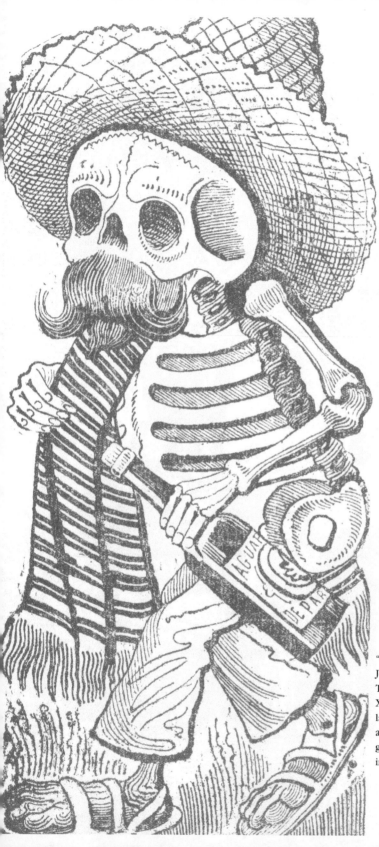

"Calavera of Madero," by José Guadalupe Posada. This depicts Francisco X. Madero, a wealthy landowner, who took advantage of the groundwork of the PLM in seizing the Mexican presidency in 1910.

PEDRO'S DREAM

Regeneración, *May 4, 1912*

(Translated by M.V.)

Sitting on the threshold of the doorway to his humble abode, Pedro, the robust and spirited day laborer thinks, thinks, thinks. He has just read *Regeneración*, which a thin, nervous, intelligent-looking worker had given him yesterday as he was returning home. He has never read this newspaper, though he has heard people talk of it, sometimes with scorn or anger, other times with enthusiasm.

Sitting on the threshold of his doorway, Pedro thinks, thinks, thinks, and within his skull revolves, until it fills his body with physical malaise, this simple question: how will it be possible to live without government? Pedro accepts everything, everything, except that one could live without government, and, feeling his head burn, he stands up and begins to wander aimlessly, while the question repeats torturously within his skull: How will it be possible to live without government?

It is eight in the morning on the final day of April. The roses open their petals, allowing the sun to kiss them. The hens keep busy, scratching the earth in search of worms while the gallant roosters sweep their wings around them, looking for love. Pedro walks and walks, the fronds of the palm trees sway beneath the luminous sky, the swallows haul mud for building their nests; Pedro finds himself surrounded by fields; the cattle pace tranquilly, without needing a policeman to beat them; the rabbits frolic without need of legislators to pass laws that will make them happy, the hummingbirds enjoy the blessing of life, without having among them one that says: "I am in charge; obey me!"

Pedro feels as if he has been freed from a massive weight and exclaims, "Yes, it is possible to live without government!" The spectacle of animal life has given him the answer, and the question has ceased bouncing around inside his skull. The herds he sees before him do not need a government to be able to live. Without private property, there is no need for anyone to guard this property from the attacks of those who possess nothing. They possess, in common, the beautiful prairie and the crystalline water, and, when the sun furiously casts down its rays, they share, in common, the shadows projected by the trees. Without government, those dignified animals do not smash each other to bits, nor do they need judges, nor jailers, nor hangmen, nor policemen. Without private property, there is not this dreadful rivalry, this cruel war of one class against the other, of one individual against the other, that weakens the feeling of solidarity, which is so powerful among animals of the same species.

Pedro fills his lungs with a deep breath; a vast horizon is opening before him, as his intelligence perceives crumbling down before it the black scaffolding of prejudices, biases, and primitive myths that bourgeois society has so carefully fomented in order to perpetuate its existence. Pedro had been taught that it is essential that there be masters and servants, rich and poor, governors and governed. Now he understands it all: those who are interested in the continued existence of the present political, economic, and social system are those who are determined to teach that political, economic, and social inequality must exist between human beings.

Pedro thinks, thinks, thinks. The coyotes, the wolves, the ducks, the wild horses, the buffalo, the elephants, the ants, the sparrows, the swallows, the doves, and almost all other animals live socially, and their societies are based on a solidarity practiced on a level that the poor human species still has not reached, despite the discoveries made by science. This has caused humanity to be absolutely done in by the existence of private property rights, which permit the strongest, the smartest, and the wickedest to hoard, for their exclusive benefit, natural resources and the products of human labor, denying the others their rightful social inheritance and subjecting them to working for a crust when they have the right to take the whole loaf.

The midday sun rains down like lead, and Pedro takes refuge under a tree and falls asleep. The insects flit around and around his head, like jewels escaping from a jewelry store, eager to glitter in the sun.

Pedro sleeps and dreams. He dreams of an open field where thousands of his fellow men work the land, while from their throats spring the triumphal notes of a hymn to Work and Freedom. Never before has anyone conceived of such a melody. Never before has anyone felt so free and so fortunate to be alive! Pedro works and sings with the others, and, at the end of several hours, which pass like seconds, the joyful workers embark on the journey back to their village, where pretty little homes, surrounded by gardens, lacking nothing needed to make life pleasant and beautiful, welcome them. All of the homes have hot and cold water, electrical outlets, electric stoves, bathrooms, washrooms, comfortable furniture, curtains, carpets, pianos, and pantries jam-packed with supplies. Pedro, like everyone else, has a house and lives happily with his partner and their children. Nobody works for wages anymore. Everyone owns everything. Those who are inclined to do agricultural work join together to work in the fields, those who are inclined to do factory work join together with their brothers, and ultimately everyone from all industries join together, reaching agreements about how to produce according to the needs of the community, putting the products of all the industries into a vast common warehouse from which all the working population can draw freely. Each takes what he needs, for there is an abundance of everything. There is neither a beggar nor a prostitute to be seen on the streets because the needs of all people are satisfied. Among the workers an elderly person cannot be seen, because they worked when they were capable, and they now live tranquilly from the work of younger strong men, awaiting a tranquil death surrounded by those who love them; the disabled enjoy the same privilege as the elderly.

To achieve this, the inhabitants of this region began by refusing to recognize all authority, while declaring the land and the means of production to be common property. The workers of each industry gathered together to discuss the way to proceed with production, having at hand statistics detailing the stockpiles in the warehouses of the bourgeoisie, and which are now located in a vast warehouse available to all.

Many unnecessary industries have been eliminated now that no one is interested in financial speculation, and the arms that once did this work, along with the arms of former policemen, soldiers, bureaucrats, and office workers, lighten the load that previously weighed solely upon the manual laborers. There are no longer parasites of any type, because all of the inhabitants are simultaneously workers and bosses, simultaneously producers and owners. Why would a government be necessary? Why would one have to destroy someone else when everyone feels himself to be an owner? Here, no one can rise above the others. Each produces according to his strength or intelligence, and each consumes to fill his needs. Why would one have to hoard? It would be idiotic to do so.

Pedro feels blessed, smiling in his sleep. Butterflies flutter around him, as if they were part of his dream.

Suddenly, Pedro feels a sharp pain in his head, and he awakens with a shock. It is a policeman, a representative of Her Majesty Authority, which timid people believe they could not live without. The officer just kicked the robust and spirited day laborer in the head to wake him up, brusquely ordering him to go sleep in his house or else he'll haul him off to jail for vagrancy. Vagrancy! When only yesterday the boss told Pedro that he would have no work for the next two days.

Pedro trembles with indignation; he turns his back to the officer, and marches away. He approaches his house, kisses his children, emotionally says

---

goodbye to his beloved partner, and proceeds towards the battlefield where the valiant are fighting to the cry, "Long Live Land and Liberty!"

BAH! A DRUNK!

Regeneración, *April 29, 1911*

(Translated by M.V.)

That joyous morning was perhaps the saddest for the poor consumptive. The sun shone intensely, enriching the beautiful city of Los Angeles with its golden radiance.

A few weeks ago, Santiago had been fired from work. The disease had infected his bronchial passages and the "good" bourgeois who exploited him for many long years decided it was best to throw him out on the streets as soon as he understood that the weakened arms of his slave could no longer give him the rich profits of the previous year.

When he was a young boy, Santiago worked earnestly. The poor boy dreamed, as many other poor people dream, that he would some day earn a "good" wage that would allow him to save some pennies with which to pass the final days of his life.

Santiago saved. He tightened his belt, and, in this manner, successfully accumulated some money; but each coin he saved signified a privation, so that, if he were ever able to stuff his money box with coins, the arteries of his body would find themselves passing less and less blood.

"I will not save anymore," Santiago said valorously one day when he understood that his health was declining. In fact, he did not save anymore, and, in this way, he could prolong his agony. His wages went up; there is no doubt of that. The strikes conducted by his union had resulted in an increase in wages. However—there was always a "however"—even though the wages were better than before, the cost of primary necessities had reached a level which turned the gains of the strike into an illusion, an illusion which had required the sacrifices of hunger, homes without heat, beatings from police, and even jail and death in clashes with the miserable strikebreakers.

Years passed and his salary rose, and the cost of primary necessities rose and rose, while poor Santiago's family increased in size. The number of working hours had been reduced to eight, thanks again to the strikes. However—again the "however"—the job that he had to perform in eight hours was the same, exactly the same, which he performed before in ten or twelve hours, so that he had to mobilize all his abilities, all his force, all the experience acquired in his working life in order to come out intact. The cold "lunch" gulped down quickly in a few midday minutes; the nervous tension which his body suffered so that he would not miss a movement of the machine; the filthiness and poor ventilation of the factory; the maddening racket of the machinery; the poor nourishment he could obtain, given the high cost of food; the poor residence where his large family slept, without any light, without comfortable shelter; the worry that crushed his spirit whenever he considered his family's future; everything, everything conspired against his health. He wanted to save some more, thinking that he must leave something to his family when he died. But what could he save? He limited his family's expenses to the bone, observing more and more that his poor children were losing the healthy rose color from their cheeks and that he himself was feeling weak.

Santiago, because he was made of flesh and blood rather than iron, didn't know what to do. He found himself on the horns of a dilemma: whether he should scrimp on the cost of his family's health in order to leave them some money when he died, money that should be invested in medicine to combat his offspring's anemia, or whether he should not save anything so that he could feed his family better, leaving them penniless when he passed away. And then he thought about his family's helplessness, about the possible prostitution of his daughter, about the probable "crimes" that his beloved sons would have to commit to obtain a loaf of bread, about the bitter sorrow of his noble partner.

Meanwhile, tuberculosis had progressed throughout his shaking body. His friends fled from him, afraid of contracting the illness. The bourgeois still retained him in the factory because he could still work: the boss could still extract good sums of money from his unfortunate slave.

The moment came, however, when Santiago was no longer useful to either God or the devil, and this bourgeois, who had slapped him on the back when, exhausted with fatigue, he had left the factory late at night, after having made his boss richer and his own health poorer, this bourgeois now expelled him from the factory because there was no longer any reason to have him there: he produced very little.

Santiago arrived at his house with tears in his eyes one afternoon when the natural world and everything else seemed to be laughing. The children were playing in the streets; the little birds were pecking here and there on the pavement; the dogs, with their intelligent and sympathetic eyes, contemplated the march of passers-by, incapable of understanding the pain or joy that dwelled in each human heart. The horses swatted their tails at the stubborn flies assaulting their lustrous flanks; the young boys selling newspapers brightened the scene with their cries and their mischief; the sun prepared to recline on its purple bed. So much beauty outside! So much sadness in Santiago's home!

Between coughing fits, between deep sighs, between desolate tears, Santiago communicated the sad news to his loyal partner: "Tomorrow, we will no longer have bread..."

Oh, kingdom of social equality, how much longer will you delay your arrival?

Everything that could be pawned would be given to the pawnshop—they are called pawnshops, these dens of thieves protected by the law. To the pawnshop they would give, one by one, the modest jewelry which they had possessed, transmitted from parents to children in this humble class; to the pawnshop they would give the shawl which had illuminated the visage of Santiago's mother-in-law during her youth and which they guarded like a beloved relic; to the pawnshop they would give their exquisite painting, the only luxury in their shabby living room, which was simultaneously the kitchen, the dining room, the room for receiving visitors, and ... the bedroom; to the pawnshop, they would send even their most humble clothing.

Meanwhile, the sickness didn't waste time: it worked and worked without rest, burrowing into Santiago's lungs. Masses of black spittle shot from the sick man's mouth with each coughing fit. The poor nourishment, the sadness, and the lack of medical assistance had pushed the sick man to the brink of the grave, as is commonly said. His only recourse would be to enter the prison of the loathsome official charities, to which the bourgeoisie condemned the human beings who had spent their lives producing so many beautiful things, so many rich things, so many fine things, for the pittance they could earn from their miserable salary.

To the hospital, the unfortunate Santiago, all skin and bones, would go, while his noble partner went from workshop to workshop, from factory to factory, pleading for a tormentor to exploit her arms. How long, disinherited brothers, will it take you to decide to smash the iniquity of the current capitalist system with your rebellion?

He remained in the hospital a few days ... the doctors said it was hopeless, his condition had no remedy, and he was confined to the ward for the terminally ill. No medicine, poor food, no attention: this was what charity did for our sick man, while the bourgeois who exploited him his entire life squandered, on enormous feasts, the money gained at the expense of this miserable man's health.

Santiago asked to leave the hospital. He doubted whether there was any point in remaining in that prison. On that pretty morning that was, perhaps, the saddest morning for the poor consumptive, a policeman arrested him for "vagrancy" in a public park, thus transporting him from one prison to another.

The beautiful California sun shone intensely. The handsome avenue blossomed with well-dressed, cheerful people, little dogs, happier than millions of human beings, rested in the arms of pretty, elegant bourgeois women, who strolled around shopping, while Santiago, in the police car, occasionally heard this exclamation: "Bah! A drunk!"

THE BEGGAR AND THE THIEF
Regeneración, *December 11, 1915*

(Translated by C.B.)

Pedestrians—men and women, perfumed, elegant, arrogant—come and go along the pleasant avenue. The beggar sticks to the wall, his insistent hand in front of him, a servile supplication trembling on his lips.

"Alms for the poor, for the love of God!"

Occasionally a coin falls into the beggar's hand, and he hurriedly stuffs it into his pocket, while lavishing degrading praise and thanks. The thief passes by, and he scowls contemptuously at the beggar. The panhandler becomes indignant, because even the undignified can take offense, and he growls with irritation:

"Why don't you blush with embarrassment, scoundrel, upon looking upon an honorable man like me? I respect the law; I don't commit the crime of putting my hand in someone else's pocket. My footsteps are firm, like those of all good citizens who don't go slinking around at night around other peoples' houses. I can show my face everywhere; I don't have to evade the policeman's gaze; the rich see me with benevolence and, when they throw a coin in my hat, they slap me on the back saying, 'good man!'"

The thief pulled the brim of his hat down to his nose, in a gesture of disgust, and gave a scrutinizing glance in his own turn. He replied to the beggar:

"Don't expect me to blush before you, vile beggar! You, honorable?! Honor does not live upon its knees waiting for someone to throw it a bone to gnaw on. Honor is pride par excellence. I don't know if I'm honorable or not; but I know that I don't have the courage to ask the rich to give me a crumb, for the love of God, from what they've taken from me. Do I violate the law? Certainly. But the law is very different from justice. I violate the laws written by the rich, and this violation is itself an act of justice, because the law authorizes the robbery of the poor by the rich, that is, it authorizes an injustice; and when I snatch from the rich part of what they've stolen from the poor, I commit an act of justice. The rich pat you on the back because of your servility, your abject lowliness, that you guarantee their peaceful enjoyment of what they've stolen from you, me, and all the poor people of the entire world. The ideal state for the rich is that all of the poor have the soul of a beggar. If you were a man, you'd bite the hand of the rich man who throws you a crumb. I despise you!"

The thief spat and lost himself in the crowd. The beggar raised his eyes to the heavens and whined:

"Alms for the poor, for the love of God!"

HARVESTING

Regeneración, *December 23, 1911*

(Translated by M.V.)

On the side of the road, I met a man with tearful eyes and black unruly hair contemplating some thistles lying at his feet. "Why are you crying?" I asked him, and he responded, "I am crying because I did all the possible good for my fellow man, I worked my plot of land as well as I could, as all self-respecting men should do; but those to whom I did good made me suffer. My plots of land, lacking the water the rich people had taken from me, only produced these thistles you see at my feet."

"It's a bad harvest," I tell myself, "that good people reap," and I resumed my march.

A bit further down, I stumbled upon an old man, who kept falling down and then getting back up, with bent back and sadness in his wandering gaze. "Why are you sad," I asked him, and he said: "I am sad because I have labored since I was seven years old. I was always a hard worker; however, this morning, the boss told me, 'You are much too old, Juan; there's no longer any work you can do, and he slammed the door in my face.'"

"Such is the harvest of years and years of honorable labor!" I told myself, and I continued walking.

A much younger man, who was missing a leg, came out to meet me, hat in hand, begging for "alms for the poor, for the love of god." Following this, he uttered something that sounded like a howl. "Why are you howling?" I asked him, and he told me, "Madero told us that we were going to be free and happy, provided that we helped elevate him to the presidency of the republic. All my brothers, and my father as well, died in the war; I lost my leg and my health, forcing all our families to beg for bread."

"This is the harvest of those who fight to elevate tyrants and to sustain the capitalist system," I told myself, and continued onwards.

Walking a bit more, I met a group of men, walking sluggishly, with sullen gazes, shoulders slumped, with dejection, anguish, and even rage in their faces. "What motivates your disgust?" I asked them. "We are leaving the factory," they said, "after working twelve hours, with barely enough for a miserable supper of beans."

"Their bosses are the ones who harvest the wealth, not them," I told myself, and I continued along my path.

Finally, it was nighttime. The crickets sang their love songs in the cracks of the earth. My ear, attentive, perceived the murmur of a party in the distance. I went toward the place where the sound originated, and I found myself before a sumptuous palace. "Who lives here," I asked a servant. "It is the owner of the lands you see all around you, as well as the owner of the water that irrigates the lands."

I understood that I was at the foot of the residence of the bandit who made that poor man's field produce only thistles, and, shaking my fist at the handsome structure, I thought, "Your next harvest, bourgeois thief, you will have to reap with your own hands, because, know this: the slaves are awakening..."

And I continued my march thinking, thinking, dreaming, dreaming. I thought of the heroic resolution of the disinherited people who have the courage to take revenge and reappropriate the lands that, according to the law, belong to the rich, yet, according to justice and reason, belong to all human beings. I dreamt of the happiness of the humble homes after the expropriation; the men and the women feeling truly human; the children playing, laughing, enjoying life, their stomachs filled with plenty of healthy food.

Rebellion will give us the best harvests: Bread, Land, and Liberty.

WORK, BRAIN, WORK

Regeneración, *number 23, February 4, 1911*

(Translated by M.V.)

"Work, brain, work: shed all the light that you can, and even if you are feeling tired, work, work. The revolution is a maelstrom: it is nourished by brains and brave hearts. Evil people do not go to revolution, only good ones; idiots don't go, only thinkers.

"Work, brain, work: shed light. Work until fatigue annihilates you. Afterwards, other brains will come, and after this, more and more. The revolution is nourished by brains and noble hearts."

This is what the revolutionary was thinking one day when the intensity of his intellectual work had undone his nerves. From his tiny room he could see people walking in different directions: men and women who seemed occupied, anxious, as if dominated by an idea. Everyone bustled about in pursuit of bread. In some faces, the disappointment was evident; without a doubt, these people had gone out to look for work and were returning to their houses empty handed.

Night was approaching, and people circulated in the sad glow of twilight. The workers returned to their houses with drooping arms, black with sweat and dirt. The plump, complacent bourgeoisie, casting scornful looks at the noble commoners who sacrifice themselves for them and their mistresses, headed towards the grand theaters or the luxurious palaces that those very same slaves had constructed, but where they were not permitted to enter.

The revolutionary's heart was weighed down by sadness. All these dispossessed people were sacrificing themselves pointlessly in the workshops, in the factories, in the mines, giving up their health, their futures, and the futures of their poor families to profit the arrogant bosses, who, whenever they passed close to a worker, avoided contacting him in order to protect their fine clothing from the his grease and grime. Yes. These poor people sacrificed themselves working like mules in order to make their exploiters more powerful, because this is how things are arranged: the more the worker sacrifices himself, the richer his bosses become and the stronger the worker's chains become.

The revolutionary continued thinking of the dispossessed crowd and also of the complacent: the former were care worn, the bourgeoisie had faces radiant with joy. With this disinherited stream of people he had to sweep away the dominators; but these people were a tranquil, tame river, very tame, far too tame. It would be another thing if they understood their force and their rights.

The revolutionary thought and thought: he was the only rebel in that flock; he was the only one who had discovered the way they must resolve the grave problem of the proletariat's economic emancipation. And it was essential that the herd know it. "The way is revolution, but not political revolt, whose superficial work comes down solely to substituting the personnel of one government with that of another which will follow in the steps of the previous one. The way is revolution; but a revolution that finally guarantees sustenance to all human beings. What use could a revolution be that did not guarantee sustenance to all?

This is what the revolutionary was thinking while the monotonous procession of the unconscious continued in the street—those who still believe that it is natural and just that their bosses profit from their labor. This is what the revolutionary was thinking, witnessing the comings and goings of the herd—those who did not know how to leave on this Earth any other sign of their passage than their skeletons in the common grave, misery for their families, and abundance and luxury for their political and economic overlords.

"Work, brain, work: shed light. Work until you are annihilated with fatigue. Within the skulls of the multitudes, there are many shadows: illuminate this darkness with the blaze of your rebellion!"

WHAT GOOD DOES AUTHORITY SERVE?

Regeneración, *July 11, 1914*

(Translated by M.V.)

One day Juanito and Luisita, the children of Rosa, could not leave their beds: fever was devouring them. Rosa wrung her arms in desperation before the pain of her own flesh and blood. It had been three weeks since she had been laid off from the factory: there were too many workers in the labor market. In vain she scratched to the bottom of the drawers, but she pulled out only playthings and utensils: not a penny in the first ones, nothing of value in the last. And there was not a piece of bread nor a cup of coffee on the table, and the children, reddened by the fever, shook their tiny arms out from under their sheets asking for food. The door opened suddenly, and some individuals dressed in black, with paper ledgers beneath their arms, penetrated the dwelling without ceremony of any sort. It was a notary and his clerks and some assistants who were going to fulfill the mandates of the Law. Rosa had not paid her landlord rent for the slum because she had no money, and the representatives of Authority had come to throw her in the middle of the street.... How would Rosa respond, if she were asked if Authority is good for the poor?

* * *

Amidst the comings and goings and the confusion of the business district, a rich man suddenly waves his arms: "Thief! Thief!" From the buttonhole of his vest dangles a chain without a watch. The crowd whirls around him; the representatives of Authority, clubs in the hand, open a passage among the throng; but where is the thief? Everyone who is surrounding the rich man is dressed elegantly. Pedro, after searching uselessly for work the entire morning, happens to pass by the crime scene. He approaches the multitude trying to inquire about the reason for such excitement, and he was pursuing this diligently when he feels a vigorous hand grab him by the collar and an arrogant voice shout at him "Come with me, thief!" It is a policeman. Could Pedro say that Authority is good for the poor?

* * *

José is feeling tired. He has been running around the city all day in search of work. Exhausted, he sits down on a park bench. As soon as he relaxes, he falls asleep. A violent jolt wakes him: It is a representative of Authority, who is reprimanding him for the "crime" of falling asleep. José presents his excuses the best he can, but the police officer orders him to leave the park. José walks and walks until, exhausted, he sits down on the edge of a bench on a by-road, falls asleep yet again, and is jolted for the second time, a welcome from a representative of Authority, who orders him to get on his feet and beat it. José explains his situation to the policeman: it has been three months since he has worked because there is an abundance of slaves, and it has been necessary for him to walk from place to place in search of a rich man who will exploit him. The representative of Authority tells him that only bums do not find work: the policeman handcuffs him and brings him to jail, where he is put to work for the benefit of Authority. Meanwhile, the old parents of José, and his family, languish in hunger in the village he left. Could José say that Authority is good for the poor?

* * *

A streetcar cuts off both of Simon's legs when he is setting out to his work place. Simon hires a lawyer whom he will pay as soon as the lawyer succeeds in making the company indemnify him for damages suffered. The restitution that Simon should receive has grown large, but the company's lawyer arranges a deal with Simon's lawyer and the policemen who witnessed the incident, dividing the money among themselves and leaving the victim without a share. Simon and Simon's family must live by mendicancy and from prostitution under the pain of perishing. Could Simon think that Authority is good for the poor?

* * *

Life on the plantation is unbearable for Lucas and his family. The master wants to steal his partner's affection from him; the master's son wants to rape Lucas's daughter; the majordomos are quite insolent; the wages that he earns are starvation wages. Lucas decides to depart with his family; however, they must keep it a secret from the master, who, as is known, is the lord of lives and lands. The escape is carried out; but so that the talons of Authority will fall upon the runaways, the master notifies it of the flight of his slaves. The women are returned to the plantation, where they are placed at the mercy of the master and his son, while Lucas is sent to jail as a man with a "wretched history," according to the master's declaration. Could Lucas say that Authority is good for the poor?

* * *

The streets have decomposed from the torrential rains. The bourgeoisie need the streets to be replaced as quickly as possible so that their carriages and their automobiles can take their short cuts with ease. Authority, then, puts its hands upon all of the territory's working class males and makes them work on the reparation of bridges, on the construction of ditches, on the erection of dams, without paying them at all, so that the bourgeoisie can continue doing business, while the proletarian families gnaw the bones of hunger. Could these proletarians say that Authority is good for the poor?

* * *

For what do we poor people need Authority? It casts us into the garrison and drafts us as soldiers so that we defend, rifle in hand, the interests of the rich, as is happening right now in Cananea, where the soldiers are protecting company property so that the strikers do not reduce it to rubble; they make us pay taxes to sustain presidents, governors, deputies, senators, all manner of policemen, all manner of little civil "servants," judges, magistrates, soldiers, jailers, hangmen, diplomatic representatives, and the whole flock of idlers who only serve to oppress us for the benefit of the capitalist class. The poor do not need anything from this bunch of leeches, and we must lighten our shoulders of the burden of the capitalist system and send it crashing to earth. We must take possession of the land, of the houses, of the machinery, of the means of transport, and of the provisions and other warehoused articles, and declare that all of this belongs to everyone, men and women, in the manner expounded in the Manifesto of September 23, 1911.

Down with Authority, disinherited brothers!

THE TWO TRAVELERS
Regeneración, *December 25, 1915*

(Translated by M. V.)

Two travelers stopped to rest at the same point on the road, dripping with sweat, burdened by the weight of their bundles.

"What are you carrying?" one asked the other.

"Hopes," he replied. "And you, what are you carrying?"

"Disappointments."

And the two travelers regarded each other steadily, the hopeful one smiling, the disappointed one sighing.

The disappointed one said, "Once, I also carried hopes, but one by one they succumbed, like flowers transplanted during a frost, and now I carry corpses. What is a disappointment but the carcass of a hope?"

The disappointed one sighed, and his eyes, embellished by sorrow, let loose liquid pearls, the sublime condensation of human bitterness. After a brief pause, he continued:

"With my pack chock full of hopes, I cast myself into the world searching for a strong man who would rescue the people from misery and tyranny. The redeemers abounded like cobblestones, each one possessing a plan about how to wipe out all the evils that afflict humanity, each one of them urging his fellow citizens to vote for him so he could make the people happy. The people elected one or the other of these redeemers, and I did the same as them. Everything was in vain. When this or that redeemer reached a position of power, he became a tyrant. Man is a liberator when he is down low, an oppressor when he is up high. Down with the rest of humanity, a hero considers himself an equal to others and feels himself a brother to those who suffer; on the heights, he believes himself to be greater than the rest. If you want to corrupt a good man, the only thing you have to do is to transform him into a leader."

The disappointed one lowered his head, like those who are sunk in profound meditation, and continued in this manner:

"This is how, one by one, my hopes died. Humanity is condemned to everlasting shackles, because it cannot find a man who can save it."

And he sighed. This sigh summed up all the disillusionment, all the discouragement, all the dismay of the defeated in the world.

The hopeful one opened his mouth, and with an expression that injected confidence and dissipated the pessimism infused by the other, said:

"The people well deserve such failure for running around in search of a man who would free them from misery and tyranny. I am not going to look for a man to redeem me, but for men to redeem themselves. I do not believe in a man who grants freedom, but in men who take it for themselves. 'The emancipation of the working class should be the task of the workers themselves.'"

The hopeful one straightened his head and cast a broad glance, which appeared to encompass all things, all men, and all the events of history, a glance which perceived everything, which could contain everything, and which could comprehend all the wisdom united in science. After a short silence, he said:

"The error of humanity has consisted in wanting to be freed from misery and tyranny, allowing the cause of the wickedness to remain standing, which is the right of private property, and its natural consequences: Government and Religion. Because individual property needs a dog to guard it: the Government. And because it needs a deceiver who maintains the poor in the fear of God so they do not rebel: the priest. I am going up against Capital, Authority, and Religion. I am going towards Anarchy. I will triumph!"

The two travelers turned their backs to each other, one strong with his hopes, the other weak in his disappointments.

THE TRIUMPH OF THE SOCIAL REVOLUTION
Regeneración, *October 23, 1915*

(Translated by M.V.)

Juan is ecstatic. He has just seen a notice from Washington in a newspaper saying that the U.S. has recognized Carranza as the head of the Mexican Republic. He effusively embraces his wife Josefa, he kisses his young son, and he yells out: "Now, peace will be a reality! Misery will End! Long Live Carranza!"

Josefa stands there with her mouth open, looking at her husband. She does not understand how merely elevating a new president to power can put an end to misery. She casts a glance around the room, a room in a dead-end alleyway in the Mexico City neighborhood of Tepozán, and sighs. Everything around her is miserable. The wicker chairs are breaking apart at the bottom. The plate of the brazier does not have a sliver of coal. The miserable bed flaunts sheets that display arbitrary markings, the product of a physically suffocated child. Atop the rickety table glows a stump of paraffin in the neck of a bottle streaked with dense droplets of melted wax. Without realizing that his wife has not understood him, Juan yells: "An era of prosperity and liberty has opened before the Mexican people! Long live Carranza!"

Josefa opens her eyes insolently. Decidedly, she does not comprehend what relation there could be between the elevation of an individual to power and the death of misery. She submerges herself in profound reflections, until a louse, perhaps the hungriest among the innumerable ones that populate her head, jabs her terribly and returns her to reality. She scratches furiously, eagerly, frenetically. At the same time, with a voice enfeebled from prolonged periods of fasting, she says to her husband: "Could you tell me, Juan, what are the poor going to gain when Carranza ascends to the presidency?"

"Come on Josefa, do you still not understand these things? We are going to gain laws that benefit the worker. The ones we have favor the agricultural workers. We are going to receive lands from the hands of the government. Finally, we are going to enjoy liberty and well-being."

The outline of a grin forms on Josepha's lips, expressing the bitterness in her heart. Although poor, she has had the opportunity to read something about the history of Mexico. She remembers that all the presidents, before reaching a high public position, swore, thousands and thousands of times, to dedicate all their concerns to the well-being of the people. This was declared in the proclamations of Iturbide, the manifestos of Bustamente, the edicts of Santa Anna, and the proclamations, manifestos, songs, and circulars of Zuloaga and Comonfort, of González and of Díaz, in a word, of everyone, including Madero. All vowed to make the people happy, and the people suffered under all of them.

A bedbug walks slowly along the wall, as if killing time by going out for a stroll, as the poor people, the victims of the capitalist system, decide to go to bed. Josefa sees it, and with a prowess that demonstrates a great deal of practice, smears it with the tip of her toe, leaving a bright red footprint on the wall. The miserable woman casts an almost sympathetic glance at her husband, a glance that appears to say: "Poor slave! When will you open your eyes?"

Juan is radiant with joy, and, shaking the newspaper overhead, exclaims:

"This a constitutional order. Respect for individuals; a guarantee of the prerogatives of citizenship, without bonds; impartial administrative justice; free suffrage; no reelection; honor among public functionaries. What more could you want, my wife? Why do you make your face look so sorrowful?"

Josefa replies: "This is all a very lovely dream; but what about the bread: who will give us bread?"

"Ha, ha, ha! For that, I have arms," Juan says, laughing. He adds, "Only the lazy will die of hunger."

Discouraged, Josefa lets her arms drop. "Most certainly," she thinks, "Juan is a perfect sheep." Louse bites make her scratch herself desperately, until she begins to spout blood. Suddenly, sound peals: it is the church bells of the parish of Santa Ana. Drifting from Tezontlale comes the rumble of cries, the clatter of the firecrackers, the peal of all the bells that every church emits mixed with the triumphant notes of a military band playing a two-step. The noise winds up making Juan enthusiastic to the point of delirium. It is the supporters of Carranza who are celebrating the recognition of Carranza's government by foreign governments and the capitalists they represent. Taking off his hat, Juan marches out into the street to give free rein to his exaltation, crying at the top of his lungs: "Long Live Carranza!"

* * *

A month has passed. Juan works, but his situation has not changed. His miserable salary is just barely enough to prevent himself, Josefa, and his young son from dying of hunger. The room still has the same broken windows, the same miserable bed with its stained sheets, the poor table that they still have not been able to replace. In the brazier, they still cannot cook a decent soup: pieces of coal cost too much, as if they were made of gold. The many bloody splotches on the walls indicate that the bedbugs still have not abandoned their habit of going for a walk before eating. The louses extract the life from poor Josefa.

"How much have we gained from the elevation of Carranza?! Truly, my beloved Juan!" Josefa says with a certain sneer.

Juan scratches his head, tormented by the louses and by the deception. He believed that Carranza's ascendance to power would ensure abundance in the home. Nevertheless, he cannot accept defeat. He exclaims:

"It is impossible that a government can make the people happy in just one month. Let's give them some time so they can implement the reforms that will benefit the masses. Then we will see."

* * *

A year has passed. The conditions of Juan's life are the same as before. Certainly, the salaries are now greater. However, the owner of the house has increased the rents of the rooms; the merchants have raised the prices of primary necessities; clothes are more expensive now than they were before. Now, he works no more than eight hours a day. However, in the end, he has to do the same, exactly the same, that he did before in twelve, fourteen, and even sixteen hours.

* * *

Josefa has a copy of *Regeneración* in her hands. She reads it with marked interest, abandoning the reading for moments only when the pokings of the parasites make the intervention of her fingernails absolutely indispensable. Juan paces back and forth around the room. Visibly agitated, he holds in his hand a red booklet, whose color is the only joyous tone in this dark well of misery, filth, and sadness. It is the Manifesto of September 23, 1911.

Suddenly, Juan interrupts his pacing, and, slapping his forehead, exclaims: "What a blockhead I've been, and, along with me, all the workers who supported Carranza! We live here in misery, in the ultimate misery, even though we break our backs in work just like we did before we elevated that old scoundrel to power. Those redistributions of land wound up being the crudest deceptions. One has to bribe officials to get anything. The laws that supposedly protect the worker are actually written to protect capital. The bourgeoisie contrived to retrieve everything they had lost to us in a cunning manner. The concessions they made in their constitutional orders do not profit poor people. We continue to be, in virtue of our miserable poverty, the same pariahs as before. Death to Carranza!"

"Death to all Government!" yells Josefa, shaking the issue of *Regeneración* in her hand like a flag.

"Long live Anarchy!" Juan yells, shaking the red booklet, whose pages spout the freshness of youth, the breezes of spring, the balm of hope, and the rays of the sun for all who suffer, for all who breathe, for all who drag their existence along in the black abyss of slavery and tyranny . . .

For the first time, the sordid room is ennobled, for it serves as the haven for a pair of lions and a cub.

* * *

Several days passed. The barricades of Mexico City present a formidable front. The united neighborhoods of Merced, Curtidos, and Manzanares have erected barricades in two hours. Men, women, elders, children, and even some disabled people have taken part in the work. The ugly edifice of the Merced market has provided most of the material. Behind the barricade bristles a sea of palm hats. The leather sandals and the crude shoes of the defenders tread the black land energetically, now proud to serve as pedestals for a band of heroes. For many moments they await the attack of government forces. Everything bustles behind the barricades. The women dig trenches; the men clean their rifles; the children distribute outfits to those champions of the proletariat. A red flag, with white letters bearing the inscription "Land and Liberty" smiles in the sun at the top of a barricade, sending its salute to all the disinherited of the Earth from its peak. The proletariat is up in arms against capital, the government, and the church.

* * *

The proletarians of Rastro and San Antonio Abad are no less active. The butchers sharpen their knives, testing them with the tips of their thumbs. The streets adjacent to Rastro and the factory of Hilados and Tejidos are stripped of paving stones. All the materials have been converted into resources for the construction of the barricade. Tables, pottery, pianos, clothing, mattresses: all have been piled up in a horribly confusing heap of objects, serving to shield the noble bosoms of its defenders.

Belen and Salto del Agua; San Cosme and Santa Maria de la Rivera; San Lazaro and San Antonio Tomatlán; La Bolsa and Tepito; San Juan, Nonoalco, Santa

Maria la Redonda, La Lagunilla; all the residents of the various districts of the populous city have vacated their dwellings, emboldened by the revolutionary fire. They prepare to resist the attack of the military officers supporting Carranza. The barricades spring forth from the land in the blink of an eye. The barricades of San Lazaro and San Antonio Tomatlán show upon their summit a singular flag. It is an old petticoat, torn and grimy. It is the flag of misery! It is the brave rag defying the world of oppression and privilege. As long as the tatters are not detached from the proletariat's body, the master remains tranquil. When it appears attached to the top of a staff, the world trembles.

* * *

Whereas all the barricades are filled with enthusiasm, nothing surmounts the activity, enthusiasm, audacity, and revolutionary zeal in the united barricade of the neighborhoods of Peralvillo, Santa Anna, and Tezontlale. Juan and Josefa do not rest for a moment. Blackened with powder, they look very beautiful, sweating, panting, crossing to and fro along the barricade, communicating energy and enthusiasm to its defenders. Suddenly a formidable clamor, followed by rifle shots and bugle blasts can be heard from the direction of Concepción Tequipehuca.

"It is our comrades from Bolsa and Tepito fighting!" Juan cries, tossing his hat into the air.

A few minutes later the air resounds with the roar of cannons, the racket of rifle shots, the beating of the drums, the angry cries of the bugle, the martial airs of the military bands. They are all jumbled together in one thunderous crack throughout the entire city. All of the barricades are being attacked simultaneously by Carranza's forces.

Juan and Josefa climb to the height of the barricade where they see a dense column of Carranza supporters approaching the streets of Santo Domingo on foot.

"Finally, the enemy is closing in, comrades," they yell at the same time. "Everybody: choose the place that best suits you to defend our bastion!"

In an instant, the barricade is crowned with rifles. The enemy places two cannons at the base of Santa Catarina y Moras street, while part of the column continues advancing toward the barricade, which is situated at the base of the street.

An imperious voice emerges from the column when it is a hundred paces away from the barricade: "In the name of the supreme government, give yourselves up!" it says.

"Long live Land and Liberty!" the defenders of the barricade answer.

Rifle shots follow rapidly from both sides. The cannons direct their projectiles against the center of the barricade in order to open a breach. The smoke saturates the atmosphere until it becomes unbreathable. The attack is furious; the resistance is formidable. Carranza's officers accompany their shots with abusive words; the proletarian defenders of the barricade sing:

"Child of the people, shackles constrict you,

"but this injustice cannot continue:

"If your existence is filled with pain,

"Rather than being a slave, prefer to die."

Broadcast to the four winds like an invitation to dignity and honor are the notes of this magnificent hymn; of this hymn common to all the downtrodden of the world; of this hymn that condenses all the bitter martyrdoms of the people and the anguish of its saints who long for redemption, of this hymn that is simultaneously a complaint, a protest, and a threat.

The following day, the proletarians of Mexico city celebrate the triumph of the Social Revolution. The capitalist system has died.

JUSTICE!

Regeneración, *June 13, 1914*

(Translated by C.B.)

The ruler, the capitalist, and the priest rested that afternoon in the shadow of an ash tree whose leaves shined brightly in the mountain canyon.

The capitalist, visibly agitated, mashed a red booklet into pulp with his hands, and said between sighs:

"I've lost everything: my fields, my cattle, my mills, my factories; everything is under the power of the ragged bums."

The ruler, trembling with rage, said:

"This is the end. Nobody respects authority anymore."

And the priest raised his eyes to the sky and said remorsefully:

"Damned reason! It has killed faith!"

The three estimable persons thought, and thought, and thought . . . The previous night had seen fifty revolutionaries storm into the village, and the working people who lived there had welcomed them with open arms; and while the revolutionaries were searching for the ruler, the capitalist, and the priest to demand of them a strict account of their acts, they had fled to the canyon seeking refuge.

"Our domination of the masses has ended," said the ruler and the capitalist in a single voice.

The priest smiled and said, in an assured tone:

"Don't worry yourselves. It's certain that faith has lost ground, but I can assure you that, through the means of religion, we can recuperate everything that we've lost. At first glance, it appears that the ideas contained in this damned booklet have triumphed in the village, and they will certainly triumph if we do nothing. I don't deny that these evil ideas enjoy a certain sympathy among the common people; but others repudiate them, above all they repudiate those that attack religion, and it is among these that we can foment a reactionary movement. Fortunately, we three could escape, because if we'd have perished at the hands of the revolutionaries, the old institutions would have died with us.

The capitalist and the ruler felt as if a great weight had been lifted off their backs. The eyes of the capitalist flashed, burning with greed. How? How could it be possible for him to return to enjoying the possession of his fields, cattle, mills, and factories? Had it all been nothing but a cruel nightmare? Could he return to having all of the people of the region under his power, thanks to the good offices of religion? And, rising to his feet, he shook his fist in the direction of the village, whose country houses shined brilliantly white beneath the sun.

The ruler, emotionally, said with conviction:

"I have always believed that religion is the firmest support for authority. Religion teaches that God is the primary boss, and that we rulers are his lieutenants on Earth. Religion condemns rebellion because it holds that the rulers are above the people by the will of God. Long live religion!"

Fired up by his own words, the ruler snatched from the hands of the capitalist the red booklet, tearing it to shreds and throwing the scraps in the direction of the village, as a challenge to the noble insurrectionary workers.

"Dogs!" he cried. "Receive this along with my spit!"

"The scraps of paper flew happily away, blown by the wind, like big toy butterflies. They were the Partido Liberal Mexicano manifesto of September 23, 1911.

The first shadows of night began to fall in the valley, and in the twilight one could see waving, above one small house in the village, a red flag bearing in white letters this inscription: "Land and Liberty." The ruler, the capitalist, and the priest screamed, waving their fists at the village:

"Nest of vipers! We'll soon crush you!"

The final rays of the sun still shone in the west as it set; the frogs began their customary serenade, free, happy, ignorant of the miseries that men suffer. In the ash tree, a pair of songbirds sang their song of free love, free of judges, priests, law clerks. The peaceful beauty of the hour invited the human heart to manifest all of its tortures, and for those sentiments to materialize in a work of art.

Making even the rocks shake, a formidable cry rolled up the canyon: "Who is there?"

The ruler, the capitalist, and the cleric trembled, anticipating their end. Night had finally laid all of the rays from the sun to rest; the songbirds grew quiet; the frogs fell silent; a gust of wind agitated frighteningly the branches of the ash tree; and in the darkness, frightfully, returned the ominous cry: "Who is there?"

The three estimable persons remembered in a single second their crimes: they had enjoyed all the good things of life at the cost of the suffering of the humble; they had maintained humanity in ignorance and misery in order to satisfy their appetites.

The sound of energetic footsteps grew louder: they were those of the soldiers of the people, of the soldiers of the social revolution. A round of gunfire left rolling in the dust, without life, the representatives of the hydra with three heads: Authority, Capital, Clergy.

NEW LIFE

Regeneración, *November 13, 1915*

(Translated by C.B.)

"What can we do now?" The workers are asking themselves this question with a certain degree of uneasiness.

They've just taken the city through blood and fire. There doesn't remain in it a single capitalist, nor a priest, nor a representative of authority who isn't hanging from a telegraph pole, lying in the earth, or whose bloated corpse isn't rotting in the sun, because these brave workers understand that, if they allow a single one of these parasites to escape, they won't tarry in returning at the head of a cloud of mercenaries to stab them in the back.

"What can we do now?" And the anxious question is repeated by thousands and thousands of worried lips, because these men, who do not fear the machine gun and enthusiastically greet the roar of the enemy's cannon, which could send them to their deaths with each shot, feel timid in the presence of life, which offers itself to them, splendid, beautiful, good, and sweet.

The men scratch their heads as if shy or thoughtful; the women bite the ends of their shawls; the kids, in their innocence free of the preoccupations of their elders, take advantage of the absence of the policeman to go wherever they like, invading orchards, and for the first time in their lives satisfy, to the point of stuffing themselves, their appetites.

* * *

The multitude stirs before this spectacle. It is the children who, in their innocence, are teaching their elders what should be done. It's natural for the children, whose minds haven't been corrupted by the preoccupations or prejudices which enchain the minds of their elders, to do what is just: to take whatever is at hand. The multitude stirs itself, and in its agitation a sea of ragged hats wave. The sun, our father, upon kissing the rags of the dignified plebeians, allows to fall, generously, upon them part of its light, its gold, its beauty, and those rags are the happy banners of victory.

In the midst of this sea surges a man who appears the most virile of this ship en march to life. It's Gumersindo, the austere campesino who ended up being seen in the most dangerous places with his scythe held high, the harvester of the evildoers' heads, and the symbol, at the same time, of fertile, noble work. Gumersindo swings his sarape over his shoulder, and the crowd falls quiet; one can hear a pin drop. With emotion, Gumersindo says:

"The children are setting the example. Let us imitate them. The indispensable thing is to eat; that should be our first task. Let us take from the shops and warehouses what we need to satisfy our hunger. Comrades: let us for the first time eat whatever we want!"

In the blink of an eye, the crowd invades the shops and warehouses, with everyone taking what they need; in other parts of the city, the same thing occurs, and for the first time in the history of this people there isn't a single human being who goes hungry. A great joy reigns in the entire city. The houses are empty:

the entire world is in the streets; ad hoc groups of musicians wander the streets playing happy tunes. Everyone greets each other, and all call themselves brothers, even though they didn't know each other a few hours before. There is dancing, singing, laughing, crying, jesting in the streets. Frolicking everywhere. The tyrannical rules of the police are at an end!

Night comes, but no one thinks of sleeping. The fiesta of liberty continues, even more joyful, if that were possible. With the municipal services disorganized by the disappearance of the principle of authority, men and women of good will tend to the public lighting, haul off the dead bodies from the streets, and they do all of this with good cheer, without needing orders from above nor barracks-like rules. Now the dawn of the new day breaks, and the fiesta, the great fiesta of liberty shows no signs of ending. And why should it? The death of centuries of oppression merits celebration, not only for a few hours, not only for a day, but until the body, done in by an excess of pleasure, demands rest.

* * *

While the entire population is delivering itself to pleasures, pleasures of which it never could have dreamed, the comrades of the group The Equals, composed of men and women, work day and night.

The noble builders of the new order hardly sleep. Dirty, stubbled, exhausted by their continual vigilance, they still find themselves, nonetheless, active, enthusiastic, valiant. Upon their shoulders rests the gigantic task of constructing anew upon the rubble of a past filled with slavery and infamy. They make use of the old town hall to hold their meetings. Ramon, the railroad worker, speaks with enthusiasm. He has barely slept for five days, since the taking of the city by the proletarian forces. He is radiant. His bronzed, square face, in which can be seen honesty, resolution, audacity, sincerity, shines as if behind his dark skin burns the sun. He sweats, his eyes shine intensely, and among other things he says:

"Finally the people enjoy themselves. Finally thousands of years of pain have been thrown off. Finally, the people know the pleasures of life. Let us enjoy their happiness as a father enjoys seeing his children play. Let our brothers enjoy themselves, until it exhausts them. Meanwhile we will work: we will finish the plans of social reconstruction."

The happy notes of a waltz rise from the street, turning all heads toward the windows. The waltz ends, and then comes an explosion of shouts, whistles, laughter, and noises of all types produced by striking things together.

"The people are enjoying themselves," says Ramon; "Let us work."

And the men and women of The Equals continue with their labor.

Ten days have passed since the proletarian forces have taken the city, and the entire population rests after a week of pleasures celebrating liberty. Numerous groups of proletarians meet in the plazas asking themselves what would be good to do. The comrades of The Equals have finished their plans for social reconstruction and have put up flyers on the street corners, in which they invite the inhabitants of the various parts of the city to meet in places determined by those who live in the various parts to deal with affairs of common interest. Everyone heeds the call, since everyone is anxious to do something. For many the future is uncertain; for others the horizon is limited; there is no lack of those who believe that the wrath of heaven will soon discharge itself upon those judged by the priests; fear of the unknown is general; uneasiness commences to murmur . . .

The comrades of The Equals find themselves scattered around different parts of the city, and in simple language explain to the people the goodness of communist anarchism. The people mill around. They don't want words; they want actions. They have reason: they've been defrauded so often. But no: this time they're not dealing with a swindle, and the orators expound with clarity that which must be done immediately, without delay, on the march. The first thing which must be done is to investigate, with the greatest exactitude possible, the number of inhabitants of the city and to make an exact inventory of the articles, foodstuffs, and clothing which exists in the stores and warehouses in order to calculate how long the population can feed and cloth itself with the stocks on hand.

The problem of housing has been resolved in part during the days of the fiesta celebrating liberty by the people of the city; on their own initiative they have taken up residence in the houses of the capitalists and parasites of all descriptions, who have now disappeared forever. There are still many families occupying shacks and barrios, but upon hearing of this, the masons come forward saying that they will build as many comfortable, attractive houses as are necessary. They themselves, immediately, without the need of anyone ordering them around, name committees to take charge of seeing that the number of houses it's necessary to construct without delay corresponds to the number of people who still live in shacks and barrios.

* * *

The murmuring ceases: that which is being arranged dissipates the fears and suspicions. "This is for real," is said, and in the people's hearts confidence is reborn, with a warming light, dissipating their numbness, something which is so necessary to all human effort. More than enough men of good will lend themselves to taking the census of the population and to taking the inventory of all warehoused articles, because it's not only necessary to inventory articles related to food and clothing, but also those that are of domestic use and of use in industry.

The applause grows, not to reward the merits of the volunteers but as an indication of the expansion of the people's spirit, because these simple people understand that doing one's duty is not meritorious, and the sea of humble sombreros waves happily beneath the rays of the friendly sun. The women appear happy, dressed cleanly, in the clothes taken from the stores; the children suspend their frolics, afflicted by furious stomach aches due to their stuffing themselves; flocks of birds fly happily above the throng, leaving behind a feeling of freshness, of health, of youth, of Spring. Every dawn is beautiful, for how could a dawn of liberty and justice not be beautiful?

* * *

Meetings were suspended yesterday until two o'clock today. The voluntary committee members are all present: they have all brought with them the exact number of inhabitants of the city, as well as the inventory of the foodstuffs and other goods in the stores and warehouses.

The day is splendid, a day at the end of April in which there is light, perfume, color, youth, love. Women work voluntarily in the gardens, the flowers show off their silky petals, and the soft, warm, damp shoots of vegetables respond to the care and love.

There is animated talk in the same places that yesterday were the sites of meetings. "What good, and so quickly!, has been done when there is no intervention of authority," is said in conversations. Hearts beat excitedly. Gumersindo has no time to rest: extremely active, he goes to all the sections of the city in an expropriated automobile, now the property of the community, and his agitation is extremely necessary, because it lends unity to the resolutions made in each part of the city. He hasn't abandoned his scythe, which tied to the hood of the car lends prestige and luster to that formerly aristocratic machine. The sarape on the shoulder of the campesino is the guarantee of his lack of self-interest.

* * *

Now it is known how many inhabitants there are in the city and what there is in the way of manufactured goods. Despite not having a mathematician at hand, the time in which the existing goods will last is quickly calculated—something necessary to arranging production. Hundreds of workers' hands write out numbers with expropriated pencils.

In a few minutes these men of the hammer, the shovel, the wood chisel, and the steel chisel say that, having so many inhabitants, this much in the way of foodstuffs will be needed daily, and that, having found such a quantity of foodstuffs, the entire people can subsist for so much time.

Everyone is satisfied with this. "Damn, but this is going well!" they say. Now one doesn't hear a single murmur. "Truly, in arranging things there's no one better than the anarchists," they add, and the cheering for anarchy thunders out in the ovations that the sacred ideal justly receives. Ramon, the railroad worker, crying with emotion and waving on high a small red book, says with a voice racked by sobs: "This is our teacher!" It's the manifesto of September 23, 1911, issued by the Organizing Junta of the Partido Liberal Mexicano.

* * *

Ramon is splendid. His square face, which appears to have been chiseled from hard wood, is radiant, like that of all heroes. The hero is not a god, since anarchists don't have gods, but rather a being who by his acts raises himself above the rest of us as an example, as a great, healthy, teaching, and, like it or not, shines as a sun.

Ramon explains the necessity that exists, given the data at hand, that all the workers in the same industry unite in order to come to accord about how to organize the work in their industry, and that once this accord is reached, that delegates from the workers of all of the industries come to agreement in order to produce what the people need. Everyone approves the idea, and this agreement is conveyed by Gumersindo to the assemblies in the different parts of the city, who receive it with a great show of enthusiasm. An era of progress and prosperity opens in the redeemed city, in which production quickly adjusts itself to the necessities of the people, and not to the enrichment of a few bandits.

* * *

Volunteers in various trades have finished constructing great public warehouses in various places in the city, and other volunteers have brought to those warehouses the goods that were found in great quantities in the shops, warehouses, and other places—goods which were carefully classified and which were distributed to the places built expressly to contain them, and from which people go to take what they need. The products of the various industries are placed in these public warehouses.

* * *

The comrades of The Equals group do not rest. What an enormous task they have! What an enormous responsibility would fall on them if the new order were to fail! But they work with a great faith in success, with an intense faith born of profound conviction. However, some details preoccupy them. The city can't exist without work in the fields. It's necessary that the campesino give to the worker what he needs to eat, as well as the raw materials for industry: cotton, agave fiber, wool, wood, and many other things. In exchange, the campesino will have the right to take from the warehouses of the city whatever he needs: clothing, foodstuffs, natural or manufactured, furniture, machinery, and work tools—in a word, everything he needs. The metallurgic industries worker needs the miner to supply him with metals, obtaining in exchange, like his brother the campesino, everything that he needs.

"Yes!" cries Ramon enthusiastically, "We need the cooperation of the campesino, the miner, the quarry worker, of all who work outside the city, and we'll get it!"

A cloud of authorized volunteers spreads itself throughout the region conquered through the arms of the workers, in order to invite their brothers to cooperate in the great work of social production. Everyone accepts this with enthusiasm and promises to send to the city that which they produce, in exchange for that which the city produces.

* * *

Anarchist society is now a fact. Everyone works, everyone produces according to his aptitudes and abilities, and consumes according to his needs. The elderly and invalids do not work. Everyone lives happily, because they feel free. No one commands and no one obeys. Harmony reigns in the workplaces, without foremen, without bosses. The traffic on the streetcars, railways, highways, of carts and cars, is great, because everyone now has the right to transportation to wherever they want to go.

* * *

Less than a month has been enough to obtain this happy result. Finally humanity has regenerated itself through the adoption of the principles of communist anarchism. One needn't comment on the emotional state in which Gumersindo and Ramon find themselves upon contemplating the beautiful work to which they've contributed so much. After walking up a nearby hill they see with eyes damp from emotion the peaceful, tranquil, brotherly city. The whisper of the vast metropolis reaches them even there. Now it is isn't the whisper of fatigue nor the death rattle of agony of a population of slaves, but rather the wide, deep, healthy whisper of a city of free and happy human beings.

CHRONOLOGY

[Assembled by M.V.]

NOTE: The editors of this volume have used chronologies in David Poole's (ed) Land and Liberty, *Ethel Turner and Rey Devis'* Revolution in Baja California, *and Armando Batra's* Regeneración: 1900–1918 *to construct the following list. I was unable to contact these authors to determine how they compiled their information. Although this document provides the reader with a general overview of the history of Ricardo Flores Magón and the Partido Liberal Mexicano, I would strongly recommend that all serious scholars check primary and secondary sources before citing any events listed in this chronology.*

1810

September 16 Parish priest Miguel Hidalgo declares El Grito de Dolores, summoning his native and mixed-blood Mexican congregation to rise up against their Spanish overlords, and initiating the War for Independence.

1821

February 24 The Plan de Iguala establishes Mexico's independence from Spain.

1854

March Liberal reformers in Mexico publish the Plan de Ayutla, initating their struggle against the conservatives who control the nation.

1855

August 17 Mexican dictator General Antonio López Santa Anna flees the country for Venezuala. Shortly afterwards, liberals such as Ignacio Comonfort and Benito Juárez establish a liberal government.

1857

February 5 The liberal constitution is promulgated in Mexico. Among other reforms, this document wrests a great deal of power away from the Catholic Church.

1862

May 5 Oaxacan Brigadier General Porfirio Díaz beats back an invasion by the

French army. This day is still celebrated in Mexico as the Cinco de Mayo.

1863

Margarita Magón, Ricardo's mother, meets Teodoro Flores while carrying ammunition to Mexican soldiers at the siege of Puebla. Teodoro may be a pure blooded Zapotec Indian. Margarita has mixed Spanish/Indian blood.

1864

Librado Rivera is born in the municipality of Rayon, San Luis Potosí, son of a small landowning farmer.

1869

April 20 Chavez Lopez issues manifesto calling for the peasants to rise up against the government, the church, and the plantation owners and expropriate the lands.

September 1 Chavez Lopez is executed by firing squad, crying "Long live socialism" as the federal troops discharge their ammunition.

1871

Jesus Flores Magón is born.

1872

July 18 Mexican President Benito Juárez dies of a heart attack

1873

September 16 Ricardo Flores Magón is born in San Antonio Eloxochitlan, district of Teotitlan, Oaxaca on Mexican Independence Day.

October 4 Francisco I. Madero is born into a wealthy landowning family in the Mexican state Coahuila.

1876

October 16 Porfirio Díaz enters Mexico City after overthrowing President Lerdo. He assumes the head of a provisional government with the promise of "Effective Suffrage and No-Reelection."

1877

April 13 Enrique Flores Magón is born.

1879

Uprising in Veracruz against Díaz is suppressed with great violence.

1880

Manuel Gonzalez is elected president, but Díaz is still effectively in control.

1882

Práxedis G. Guerrero is born to a rich landowning family in the Leon of district Guanajuato.

Juan Sarabia is born in San Luis Potosí the son of a musician.

1883

Ricardo Flores Magón starts school at the Escuela Nacional Primaria in Mexico City, where his family has moved.

1884

Díaz is reelected.

1888

Librado Rivera graduates with honors from the Escuela Normal in San Luis Potosí and becomes the director of the El Montecillo School in the same town.

Díaz changes the constitution to enable him to stay in the presidency for more than one term. He is re-elected.

1892

May 16 Ricardo Flores Magón, along with his brothers Jesus and Enrique, now at the Escuela Nacional Preparatoria, joins in a demonstration against the Díaz dictatorship and is arrested. The people of Mexico protest against the arrests, saving him and many others from execution. Ricardo goes free after a short detention. His brother Jesus is sentenced to five months for sedition in Belen prison.

Díaz re-elected.

1893

February Flores Magón joins the staff of the opposition newspaper *El Democrata*. The paper lasts until April when the police surround Flores Magón's house to arrest him and other comrades working on the paper.

However, he escapes by jumping from a window. The rest of the staff is taken. Flores Magón hides with friends for three months before returning to school.

Teodoro Flores dies.

1894

El Democrata starts again with Flores Magón as a contributor. After a few weeks, the government buys out the paper.

1895

Librado Rivera returns to the Escuela Normal in San Luis Potosí where he teaches history and geography. Soon he becomes its director. One of his students is Antonio I. Villarreal.

Flores Magón is expelled from school because of his political activities.

1899

Juan Sarabia, with the financial support of Camilo Arriaga, publishes a dissident newspaper entitled *El Democrata* in San Luis Potosí.

1900

Around the turn of the century, Flores Magón reads extensively the works of anarchist writers such as Bakunin, Kropotkin, Malatesta, Reclús, Stirner, Proudhon; also Karl Marx.

In San Luis Potosí, *El Democrata* is closed. Juan Sarabia founds another newspaper, *El Porvenir* ("The Future").

August 7 Ricardo Flores Magón founds *Regeneración* with his brother Jesus and Antonio Horcasitas, both law school graduates.

A group that includes Camilo Arriaga, Librado Rivera, and Juan Sarabia founds the liberal club Ponciano Arriaga in San Luis Potosí. Sarabia is the club's secretary and the editor of its newspaper *Renacimiento*. ("Rebirth"). The liberal movement club intends to fight against the Catholic Church's influence over the government. By the end of the year, more than one hundred liberal clubs are active all over Mexico.

Díaz is reelected.

December 31 *Regeneración* changes its ideological position from being a pure law journal to that of an "Independent Journal of Combat."

1901

February 5–14. The first congress of Liberal clubs is held in the Teatro de la Paz, San Luis Potosí. Armed soldiers patrol the streets outside. While most of the delegates are content to attack only the clergy, Ricardo Flores Magón, representing the newspaper *Regeneración,* gives a speech denouncing the Díaz administration as "a den of thieves." It is here that Flores Magón first meets Librado Rivera and other prominent liberals.

May 23 Ricardo and Jesus Flores Magón are arrested and sentenced to twelve months in Belen prison for "insulting the president." However, *Regeneración* continues clandestinely with the aid of Enrique Flores Magón and Eugenio Arnoux. Flores Magón continues to write articles for the paper from his prison cell. A group of sympathetic prisoners smuggles them out.

June Diario del Hogar is suppressed because it printed the banned issue of *Regeneración.*

June 14 Margarita Magón dies. Despite their pleas, Ricardo and his brother are refused a final visit to her.

Repression of the Club Liberal de Lampazos in Nuevo Leon.

August 22 Antonio Díaz Soto y Gama sent to Belén for making a speech criticizing Díaz.

October Díaz informs Ricardo Flores Magón that if he does not stop publishing *Regeneración,* he will be shot. Flores Magón, knowing his precarious position, decides to suspend publication for a while. The government begins a general campaign of repression against all liberal clubs and the opposition press.

October 7 Last issue of *Regeneración.* The government closes down its press.

1902

January 24 Twelve days before the proposed second Liberal Congress, the army breaks up a meeting of the Liberal Club Ponciano Arriaga in San Luis Potosí. Juan Sarabia and Librado Rivera are arrested and imprisoned for twelve months.

April 6 Juan Sarabia, Camilo Arriaga, and Librado Rivera, jailed in San Luis Potosí, found the newspaper, *El Demofilo.*

April 30 Ricardo and Jesus Flores Magón are released from prison. Jesus leaves the struggle against Díaz and opens a law office in Mexico City.

July 16 Ricardo and Enrique Flores Magón, along with Santiago de la Hoz, take over the satirical anti-Díaz newspaper *El Hijo del Ahuizote* from Daniel Cabrera. The anti-Díaz weekly *Vesper*, edited by Juana B. Guiterrez de Mendoz and Elisa Acuña, publishes *The Conquest of Bread* by Peter Kropotkin in booklet form at the request of Flores Magón.

July 30 The press of *El Demofilo* is confiscated

August 10 *El Demofilo* disappears.

September 12 The editorial staff of *El Hijo del Ahuizote* is arrested and the presses and office equipment are confiscated. Ricardo and Enrique Flores Magón are held incommunicado for thirty-four days in the military prison of Santiago Tlatelolco before being sentenced by a military tribunal to four months each "for insulting the army."

September 19 Librado Rivera is released from prison in San Luis Potosí.

November 23 *El Hijo del Ahuizote* reappears under the direction of Juan Sarabia. Antonio Díaz Soto y Gama, Enrique Flores Magón, Alfonso Cravioto, Librado Rivera, and others contribute.

1903

January 23 Ricardo and Enrique Flores Magón are released from prison. They resume their work on *El Hijo del Ahuizote*. Díaz tries to buy Ricardo off by offering him a position in the government, but Ricardo declines.

El Hijo del Ahuizote is repressed again. Nevertheless, Federico Perez Fernandez continues to publish it.

February 5 Ricardo and Enrique Flores Magón, along with others, reorganize the Confederation of Liberal Clubs of the Republic.

February 5 Ricardo and the other editors of *El Hijo del Ahuizote* drape a banner saying "LA CONSTITUCION HA MUERTO" from the balcony of the newspaper's office.

March Ricardo and Enrique Flores Magón and others found the Club Liberal Rendención. He and Santiago de la Hoz found the newspaper *Excelsior.*

April 2 Troops under the command of General Reyes shoot down protesters in Monterey, Nuevo Leon demonstrating against the reelection of Reyes as state governor.

April 2 Ricardo and Enrique Flores Magón, along with members of the Club Liberal Rendención march to Díaz's palace carrying signs saying "NO REELECTION." Only the crowds around them save them from execution.

April 16 The police invade the offices of *El Hijo del Ahuizote* for the second time. As before, all the equipment is taken. Ricardo and Enrique Flores Magón

Librado Rivera, and seven others are arrested for "ridiculing public officials." A special law is passed forbidding anyone from publishing anything by the April 16 convicts. At this time, the paper had a circulation of about 24,000.

May–December *El Padre del Ahuizote*, *El Nieto del Ahuizote*, and other newspapers are founded and quickly repressed by the government.

May Alfonso Cravioto and others found *El Colmillo Publico*.

June 9 The Mexican Supreme Court bans the publication of any article by the Flores Magón brothers.

July Librado Rivera released from prison.

October Ricardo and Enrique Flores Magón are released from Belén prison. During their stay, they were held incommunicado for two and a half months. The dissidents are warned that they will not exit prison alive again. Realizing it is no longer practical to stay in Mexico, they decide to continue the struggle from the U.S.

1904

January 4 Santiago de la Hoz and Ricardo and Enrique Flores Magón arrive in Laredo, Texas almost penniless. Later, they are joined by Librado Rivera, Antonio I. Villarreal, Juan Sarabia, and Rosalio Bustamente. All find jobs as laborers.

March 22 Santiago de la Hoz drowns while swimming in the Rio Bravo.

September 22 Práxedis G. Guerrero leaves Mexico and finds work in the U.S.

November 5 *Regeneración* reappears in San Antonio, Texas, where Ricardo now lives. Enrique, Juan Sarabia, and Manuel Sarabia help publish the paper.

December A thug employed by Díaz enters Ricardo's home and attempts to stab him in the back. This attempted assassination is averted by the quick action of Enrique, who throws the man out of the house. Despite this fact, police arrest Enrique and fine him $40 for "breaking the peace." The would-be assassin goes free.

1905

February 2 *Regeneración* moves to St. Louis, Missouri and resumes publication, this time with the help of Librado Rivera.

Ricardo starts to attend meetings organized by Emma Goldman. He also becomes friendly with Florencio Bazora, a former comrade of Italian anarchist Errico Malatesta.

Díaz's dictatorship begins to monitor Ricardo's mail with the help of the U.S.

postal authorities.

February 27 Regeneración resumes publication from Saint Louis.

August Antonio de P. Araujo, Tomas R. Espinoza and Lazaro Puente found the Liberal Club Libertad in Douglas, Arizona, together with a newspaper El Democrata.

September The circulation of *Regeneración* is 20,000 and climbing, mainly in Mexico.

September 28 The Junta Organizadora del Partido Liberal Mexicano (PLM) is formed with Ricardo as President, Juan Sarabia as Vice-President, Antonio I. Villarreal as Secretary, Enrique as Treasurer and Librado Rivera, Manuel Sarabia, and Rosalio Bustamante as committee men. The motto of the Junta is "Reform, Liberty and Justice."

October Díaz sends Manuel Esperon de la Flor, a Mexican government official and landowner, to the U.S. to bring a charge of criminal libel against *Regeneración*

October Emiliano Zapata reads *Regeneración* for the first time.

October 12 Pinkerton detectives raid the *Regeneración* offices on 107 North Channing Avenue. Ricardo, Enrique and Juan Sarabia are imprisoned. All newspaper's equipment, including its printing presses, typewriters, and furniture, are stolen by the U.S. Authorities and sold.

December Ricardo, Enrique, and Sarabia are freed on bail collected by supporters both in the U.S. And Mexico. At this time, the circulation of *Regeneración* is between 20,000 and 30,000 copies.

1906

January Juan Sarabia and Ricardo and Enrique Flores Magón are released on bond

February 1 Regeneración renews publication. Circulation is now 30,000

March 20 Fearing that Díaz will arrange their extradition to Mexico through U.S. Authorities, Ricardo, Enrique and Juan Sarabia pay their bail and flee to Toronto, Canada. Rivera, Villarreal and Manuel Sarabia continue to publish *Regeneración*. However, at the request of the Mexican government, U.S. postal authorities withdraw its fourth class mailing privileges.

May Ricardo, Enrique and Sarabia move to Montreal after harassment from Díaz's agents in Toronto. The Mexican government offers a reward of $20,000 for the capture of Ricardo.

May 5 On the holiday celebrating Díaz's victory over the French, PLM clubs in Cananea hold a rally exhorting miners to form a union.

June 1–4 Copper miners in Cananea, Sonora go on strike. The strike leaders are either members of local PLM clubs or supporters. At the request of the mine owner, Colonel William C. Green, 275 armed American volunteers cross the border into Mexico. During the strike, the army massacres over 100 Mexican workers.

July 1 The Program of the Partido Liberal Mexicano (PLM) is issued from St. Louis. This program remains the platform of the PLM until it is replaced five years later by the September 23, 1911 Manifesto. Junta leaders have consulted as many PLM members throughout Mexico and the United States as possible to create this 1906 document. This declaration of principles is the basis of Mexico's present-day progressive constitution.

July 3 The PLM Club Obreros Libres is formed in Morenci, Arizona with Práxedis G. Guerrero as president.

September 2 Ricardo and Juan Sarabia arrive secretly in El Paso, Texas. They join Antonio Villarreal, Prisciliano Silva, and other liberals to complete a plan for an armed uprising in Mexico.

September 4 Arizona rangers raid the homes of PLM members in Douglas, Mowry, and Patagonia. The newspaper *El Democrata* is confiscated. Arms are found. Fifteen liberals are arrested and handed over to the Mexican authorities. They are all sent to San Juan de Ulua prison.

September 12 Librado Rivera and Aaron Lopez Manzano are arrested in St. Louis and put on a train for deportation to Mexico at the request of the Mexican authorities. They are taken as far as Ironton, Missouri when a public outcry, led by a St. Louis newspaper, forces the U.S. to stop this illegal hand-over. Instead, Rivera and Manzano are imprisoned and held incommunicado.

September 15 Pinkerton agents and U.S. officials raid *Regeneración* office, smashing its printing press.

September 24 Prisciliano Silva, now in Mexico, asks Francisco I. Madero, then an unknown landowner in Coahuila, for arms. Madero refuses, claiming that he did not want to see the spilling of Mexican blood. Madero states, "Díaz is not a tyrant, a bit rigid, but not a tyrant." He later writes to his grandfather, Evaristo, to brag about having nothing to do with any revolution.

September 26 With a force of 30 men, Juan Jose Arredondo and Trinidad Garcia seize the main plaza of Jimenez, Coahuila. They manage to hold the town for a day after cutting the telephone wires and expropriating money from the town treasury.

September 30 Hilario C. Salas and 300 men attack Acayucan, Veracruz. They nearly achieve victory, but unfortunately Salas receives a shot through the stomach. This forces the poorly armed liberals to withdraw. At the same time, groups are supposed to attack Minatitlan and Puerto Mexico. Due to bad coordination, these attacks do not occur.

September 30 Ricardo flees to Los Angeles

October 1 Román Marín attacks Pajapán. His attack is sucessful, and his troops proceed to Puerto México, but they retreat when they see a large army contingent coming to the city.

October 1 P.L.M forces take Ixhuatlán, Veracruz but federal soldiers drive them out.

October Jesus M. Rangel leads the uprising in Camargo, Tamaulipas, but is fought off by Mexican rural police.

October 19 Juan Sarabia, Cesar B. Canales, and Vicente de la Torre are arrested in Ciudad Juarez after being led into a trap by a former school friend of Sarabia.

In El Paso, U.S. Authorities raid the home of Junta leaders. Antonio I. Villarreal, Lauro Aguirre, and J. Cano are arrested. Ricardo manages to escape by jumping from a window. In addition to the arrests, officials discover the names of PLM members and groups in Mexico as well as a subscription list for *Regeneración*. These are immediately delivered to the Mexican authorities. Armed with this information, the dictatorship embarks upon the systematic repression of liberals in Mexico. Two hundred and fifty are arrested in Chihuahua alone. On their side of the border, the U.S. Authorities follow suit.

November 14 Ricardo is spotted while hiding in the house of Romulo Carmona in Los Angeles. He manages to avoid arrest.

November 30 Librado Rivera is brought to trial in St. Louis, Missouri, but is freed by the U.S. Commissioner.

December 4 Textile workers influenced by PLM propaganda strike in Veracruz, Puebla, and Tlaxcala.

1907

January 4 Porfirio Díaz calls for the end of the textile strike in Veracruz, Tlaxaca, and Puebla. He reopens all of the factories and orders all workers to return to their posts. Laborers in Rio Blanco, Veracruz remain on strike.

January The Junta sends Mayo Indian Fernando Palomarez to Baja California to organize groups for the revolution.

January 7 Sarabia, Canales, and de la Torre are brought to trial in Veracruz. All are given 7 years imprisonment, and sent to the fortress prison of San Juan de Ulua.

January 8 800 striking textile workers at the Rio Blanco mill are massacred by troops under the command of General Rosalio Martínez. Flatcars full of murdered workers are hauled to the Gulf of Mexico and fed to sharks.

January 18 Ricardo's hiding place is again discovered. This time, he escapes disguised as a woman. He flees to earthquake-devastated San Francisco.

February 26 Antonio I. Villarreal escapes as he is about to be handed over the border to the Mexican authorities in El Paso.

Ricardo, still on the run, finds refuge in Sacramento, San Francisco and finally Los Angeles. A price of $25,000 is put on his head and 100,000 wanted posters with his photograph are circulated throughout the U.S. They are hung in all post offices and other places. In Los Angeles, Ricardo is joined by Antonio I. Villarreal.

June 1 Ricardo and Villarreal issue the first issue of a new paper from Los Angeles. The name is changed from *Regeneración* to *Revolución* in an attempt to evade authorities.

June 16 Librado Rivera arrives in Los Angeles.

June 29 The Junta appoints Práxedis G. Guerrero as a Special Delegate of the Junta. He starts to organize revolutionary PLM forces along both sides of the US/Mexico border.

June 30 Manuel Sarabia, Juan's cousin, is kidnapped in Douglas, Arizona. He is forcibly taken over the border into Mexico. As he is taken from his home and before he is gagged, however, he is able to shout out his name and protest against his kidnapping. Several people hear this cry. After a campaign by concerned citizens, the labor activist Mary "Mother" Jones, and the Douglas newspaper *The Daily Examiner*, the Mexican government is forced to hand him back to the U.S on July 12.

August 23 The operatives of the Furlong Detective Agency arrest Flores Magón, Rivera, and Villarreal without a warrant. This agency's sole purpose seems to be tracking down liberal party members in general and Flores Magón in particular. During the arrest, Flores Magón is beaten unconscious when he and Sarabia try to attract the attention of passers by. They are taken to Los

Angeles county jail where they are accused of "resisting an officer." Bail is set at $5,000 each, but later withdrawn.

August 24 The "detectives" return to the offices of *Revolución*. This time, they arrest a co-worker, Modesto Díaz, and take lectures and other documents. Modesto Díaz dies later in Los Angeles jail.

September John Kenneth and Ethel Duffy Turner arrive in Los Angeles.

September 1 A protest meeting organized by the International Socialist Party is held in support of Ricardo and the others. A defense committee is formed.

September 26 Trial of Ricardo, Rivera, and Villarreal. The charge of "resisting an officer" is dropped. It is replaced with four new indictments: 1) murder and robbery committed in Mexico; 2) criminal libel; 3) the murder of an "unknown man" in Mexico; 4) the violation of the neutrality laws. The first three of these are dropped. Finally, all three men are found guilty of violating the neutrality laws. They are sentenced to be deported to Arizona where the alleged crime took place.

The American socialist lawyers, Job Harriman and A. R. Holston defend the accused Mexicans. During the trial, Thomas Furlong, head of the Furlong Detective Agency, admits that the arrests took place without a warrant and that he was paid for the work by the Mexican government.

September 27 Lazaro Gutierrez de Lara, the new editor of *Revolución*, is arrested on direct orders of the Mexican government.

November Revolución, now edited by Frederico Arizmendez and Francisco Ulíbarri publishes extracts from the works of Kropotkin. The editors are arrested for criminal libel. They are later freed on bail. After this, the paper is edited by Manuel Sarabia, Juan's cousin.

December 22 Lawyer Job Harriman applies for a writ of habeas corpus on behalf of Lazaro Guiterrez De Lara. This is refused on the grounds that charges against him were on their way from Mexico.

December 27 Ricardo, Rivera, Villarreal and De Lara write a "Manifesto to the American People" in which they explain the reasons for their persecution both in Mexico and the U.S.

1908

January Manuel Sarabia is arrested and *Revolución* is suppressed.

February The "Manifesto to the American People" is published by several socialist newspapers and by Emma Goldman's *Mother Earth*.

February 17 Díaz, in an interview with the American journalist J. Creelman, promises to retire in 1910 at the end of his presidential term. He also says he will welcome an "opposition party."

April Revolución reappears, directed by Práxedis G. Guerrero and edited by Modesto Díaz.

Sprung From the Los Angeles County Jail, Ricardo founds the newspaper, *Tierra y Libertad*. It runs for three issues

May Modesto Díaz is arrested and the press of *Revolución* is destroyed. The paper has finally been suppressed.

May The first issue of *Libertad y Trabajo* appears in Los Angeles as a successor to *Revolución*. Fernando Palomarez and Juan Olivares, respectively veterans of the Cananea and Rio Blanco strikes, edit the paper.

Junta sends delegate Francisco Manriquez to alert Liberal groups in Mexico of the revolution date, June 25.

May 8 Manuel Sarabia is extradited to Arizona.

May 30 Díaz decides to run for re-election.

June Guitterez De Lara is released from prison on a legal technicality.

June 13 In a letter to Enrique and Práxedis G. Guerrero, Ricardo expresses his anarchist ideals for the first time. However, he also states, "if we had called ourselves anarchists from the start, no one or at best a few would have listened to us. Without calling ourselves anarchists, we have fired the people's mind with hatred against the owner class and government caste."

June 18 Homes of PLM members are raided in Casas Grandes, Chihuahua after the group was infiltrated by an informer. Many important letters and documents are found.

June 23 Díaz's network of spies, assisted by U.S. postal officials, learns about the plans for the revolution. Díaz' soldiers and police nip it in the bud. Many Liberal supporters are jailed.

June 25 Prisciliano G. Silva's home in El Paso, Texas is raided by Texas Rangers. They seize 3000 rounds of ammunition and important documents, including a letter written by Ricardo to Enrique that was smuggled out of Los Angeles jail by Ricardo's companion Maria Brousse. This letter gives details about individuals and groups who are about to start an uprising against Díaz in Mexico.

June 24-25 A PLM group takes Viesca, a town in northern Coahuila. After holding the town for a day, they are forced to withdraw owing to the hostility of the local populace. Because the insurgents crossed the border from Texas, the people think they are bandits and not "real revolutionaries."

June 26 Forty PLM fighters led by Encarnación Guerra, Benjamin Canales, and Jesús M. Rangel attack Las Vacas, Coahuila. After a bloody fight with the local garrison of 100 men, the Liberals take the town. However, they decide to evacuate because of heavy losses. Jesus M. Rangel leads the retreat.

A PLM group attacks the town of Matamoros, Tamaulipas, but the army forces them to retreat.

June 30–July 1 Práxedis G. Guerrero, Ricardo's brother Enrique, and José Inez Salazar lead a small liberal group on an attack of Palomas, Chihuahua. However, after a brave fight, they are forced to withdraw.

July From about this time, U.S. left-wing journals and organizations come to the defense of the imprisoned PLM spokesmen. Articles on them and about the situation in Mexico, many spotlighting the connivance between the U.S. And Mexican authorities, appear in *Appeal to Reason*, *The New York Call*, and *The Border*. American socialists such as Eugene V. Debs, Frances and Primrose Noel, John Murray, James Roche, John Kenneth Turner, and Ethel Duffy Turner spend much time helping the PLM with their propaganda

A PLM uprising by liberals in Janos, Chihuahua is crushed when the local garrison is reinforced.

A small PLM group attacks Mexicali, but then move inland.

Yaqui Indians led by Fernando Palomarez rise up in Sonora, but Palomarez is later arrested.

In Orizaba, informers infiltrate P.L.M groups. Many members are arrested before they can begin their uprising.

At the request of the Mexican government, Ricardo Flores Magón, Rivera and Villarreal are held incommunicado in the Los Angeles county jail.

August Flores Magón, Rivera, and Villarreal are sent to the federal circuit court in Tombstone, Arizona.

August 9 Jesus M. Rangel, leading a group of guerrillas, ambushes a column of federal soldiers in the Sierra del Burro, Coahuila, killing 20 soldiers.

September 5 Hilario C. Salas, Candido Donato Padua, and three other comrades start to regroup revolutionaries in the state of Veracruz by issuing a manifesto declaring their continuing support for the aims of the PLM While Padua remains in Veracruz, Salas begins to spread PLM propaganda in Oaxaca, Puebla, and Tlaxcala.

Following the attack on Palomas, Enrique and Práxedis return to the U.S. And continue their propaganda activities along the U.S./Mexican border. Práxedis keeps in touch with the Veracruz groups through letters.

September 14 Antonio de P. Araujo is arrested in Waco Texas and his newspaper *Libertad, Reforma, y Justicia* is suppressed. Araujo is eventually tried and sentenced to 2-1/2 years imprisonment for violating the neutrality laws.

John Kenneth Turner and Gutierrez de Lara start on a journey through Mexico. The story of this journey and what Turner found is published in a series of articles in *American Magazine*. They are later published as a book entitled *Barbarous Mexico*. This book is the most damning indictment of Díaz's iniquitous regime ever published. It exposes the plantation slavery where men, women and even children are bought and sold; the poverty and starvation that exist throughout the country; the dictatorship's attempt to kill the Yaqui Indians in order to steal their land; its systematic elimination of all opposition to Díaz's rule; and finally, the financial and moral support given to the dictatorship by both the U.S. And Europe.

September 16 PLM member Fernando Palomarez tries to assasinate Porfirio Díaz on Mexican Independence Day, but the dictator's bulletproof vest deflects the shot. Palomarez escapes into the crowd.

October 300 Liberals cross the U.S./Mexican border at Eagle Pass, Texas and attack Jiménez, Coahuila. This belated attack is repulsed by a federal force of 800 soldiers.

October 16 PLM clubs are raided in Rio Grande City, Texas.

October 19 Prisciliano G. Silva and many other PLM leaders are arrested in El Paso, Texas on direct orders of the police chief of Ciudad Juarez. Authorities take stacks of letters and documents.

November 11 The US Secret Service arrests Encarnación Díaz Guerra, commander of the Las Vacas assault, fracturing his skull. He is sent to Leavenworth Penitentiary for violating the neutrality laws.

November 13 The American Federation of Labor passes a resolution pledging sympathy and soliciting support for Flores Magón, Rivera, and Villareal.

1909

January Ricardo, Rivera, and Villarreal are no longer incommunicado but still in jail pending their deportation to Arizona.

John Murray publishes an account of his meeting with Mexico City PLM clubs in *The Border.*

January 20 After getting his father's permission, Francisco I. Madero publishes *La Sucesíon Presidencial en 1910*, calling Mexicans to form an opposition to form a political party opposing Porfirio Díaz. Madero calls for "effective suffrage" and "no reelections," essentially the same reforms that Díaz himself had proposed in his Plan de Tuxtepec.

February 22 The Junta appoints Candido Donato Padua chief of the revolutionary operation in the Soteapan area. He continues with his organizational work there.

March 4 Flores Magón, Rivera, and Villareal are extradited to Arizona.

March 13 The socialist journal *Appeal to Reason* dedicates the entirety of their issue to the PLM.

April 30 *Díaz the Tzar of Mexico* is published in New York. The author, Carlos di Fornaro, is arrested for criminal defamation.

May 12 Ricardo and the others are tried in Tombstone, Arizona

May 19 The three defendants are sentenced to 18 months imprisonment for conspiracy to violate the neutrality laws. They are taken to the state penitentiary in Yuma, Arizona to serve their sentence.

August 9 Práxedis Guerrero, with the help of Enrique Flores Magón, edits and publishes the first issue of *Punto Rojo* from El Paso, Texas.

August 10 U.S. Authorities arrest Jesus M. Rangel in San Antonio Texas. They find detailed plans for future uprisings as well as lists of PLM members.

September *The American Magazine* starts to publish John Kenneth Turner's articles on Mexico.

Ricardo, Rivera and Villarreal are transferred to Florence penitentiary.

October 10 Guiterrez De Lara is arrested in Los Angeles and charged with "disturbing public order."

November 11 Guiterrez De Lara is released after a public outcry.

1910

Madero is harassed by Mexican officials and Díaz's supporters while campaigning in Mexico's cities.

Census reveals that 3,103,402 Indians have been swindled out of their lands by the Díaz regime and reduced to debt-captive serfs.

January 9 Jesus M. Rangel is sentenced to 18 months imprisonment for violating the neutrality laws.

April 17 PLM military chiefs meeting in Tlaxcala decide that, because of the general unrest through many states of Mexico, it is now time for another revolutionary uprising.

April *Punto Rojo* is suppressed and its presses are destroyed.

April Madero is elected by the Anti-Reelection Party to run against Díaz in the forthcoming presidential elections.

May–June 1500 armed peons take the town of Valladolid, Yucatan and hold it for four days after killing the district political boss.

June Díaz imprisons Madero in San Luis Potosí. Later Madero "loses" to Díaz in the unfair presidential elections. In many towns and villages, members of the Anti-Reelection Party are not allowed to vote.

Spontaneous PLM-inspired uprisings occur in Yucatán and Sinaloa.

June 4–10 John Kenneth Turner and other PLM members and supporters expose the US government's miscarriage of justice before the House Rules Committee.

June 26 300 peons in the village of Bernardino Contla, Tlaxcala take over the town hall in the name of the PLM and hold the political boss prisoner until the army disperses them.

August 3 Flores Magón, Rivera, and Villarreal are released from Florence penitentiary.

August 5 Flores Magón and the others are met by a large group of friends and supporters at the Los Angeles railroad station. In the evening, a mass meeting is held in the Labor Temple in their honor.

September 3 The first issue of *Regeneración* appears in Los Angeles. Its editorial board consists of Ricardo Flores Magón, Rivera, Villarreal, Gutierrez de Lara, Anselmo Figueroa, Ricardo's brother Enrique, and Práxedis G. Guerrero. Both Enrique and Guerrero had continued the propaganda work while Ricardo was in prison. *Regeneración* also publishes a page in English under the editorship of German socialist Alfred G. Sanftleben.

October 1 The motto of the Mexican Liberal Party is changed to "Tierra y Libertad."

In an editorial in *Regeneración*, Ricardo writes: "'The Land!' shouted Bakunin; 'The Land!' shouted Ferrer; 'The Land!' shouts the Mexican Revolution!"

October 5 Santana Rodríguez Palafox, or Santanón, the military commander of the PLM groups in Veracruz, takes the town of San Andres, Tuxtla.

October 6 Madero escapes from San Luis Potosí and flees to San Antonio, Texas.

October 10 Madero issues the Plan de San Luis Potosí, calling for a general uprising throughout Mexico on November 20.

Candido Donato Padua warns Ricardo about an article Madero has written and published in a Veracruz newspaper. This article states that Madero has assumed the title of "Provisional President" of the republic and that Ricardo is the "Vice President."

October 17 Santanón dies while fighting against federal troops.

Fall PLM agents Fernando Palomarez and Pedro Ramírez Caule, both Native Americans, go to Baja California to map the terrain and intensify revolutionary activities.

November 15 Práxedis Guerrero goes to Chihuahua to organize revolutionaries.

November 16 Ricardo issues a circular to all Liberal Party members informing them of the timing of Madero's revolt, but warning them of the difference between themselves and Madero's movement.

November 20 Madero's projected date for the Mexican Revolution. Madero crosses the border into Mexico, but there is no army for him to lead and no guns for his non-army. He returns to the United States and goes to New Orleans.

In *Regeneración*, Ricardo sums up the aim of the PLM "The Liberal Party works for the welfare of the poor classes of the Mexican people. It does not impose a candidate [in the presidential elections], because it will be up to the will of the people to settle the question. Do the people want a master? Well, let them elect one. All the PLM desires is to accomplish a change in the mind of the toiling people, so that every man and woman should know that no one has the right to exploit anybody; that we all, by the mere fact of coming to this Earth, have the right to all we need as long as we contribute to the production of things, and that no one has the right to appropriate tillable land, because it is a gift of nature of which we all have the right to reap the inherent benefits..."

December 1 Díaz sworn in for an eighth term after a dubious election.

December 9 Práxedis Guerrero crosses the Mexican border Mexico. Together with twenty-two comrades, he begins the PLM revolutionary campaign in Chihuahua.

December 10 Again explaining the difference between the PLM and Madero, Ricardo writes in *Regeneración*: "Governments have to protect the right of property above all other rights. Do not expect, then, that Madero will attack the right of property in favor of the proletariat. Open your eyes. Remember a phrase, simple and true and as truth indestructible: 'The emancipation of the workers must be the work of the workers themselves.'"

December 16 PLM forces win three army victories on this day. The Liberals are active from Sonora in the north to Tabasco in the south.

December 28 The Práxedis Guerrero group takes the town of Casas Grandes, Chihuahua.

December 30 Guerrero is killed while his group tries to take the town of Janos, Chihuahua.

December 31 Alfred Sanftleben resigns from being the editor of English-language section of *Regeneración*. Ethel Duffy Turner replaces him.

1911

January PLM forces are now active in Sonora, Tlaxcala, Veracruz, Oaxaca, Durango and Chihuahua.

January 29 PLM forces under Simon Berthold and José María Levya take Mexicali, Baja California.

February 1 Jesús M. Rangel is freed from US jail.

February 3 U.S. Cavalry units are moved to the border allegedly "for defense."

February 5 The PLM column of Prisciliano G. Silva takes Guadalupe, Chihuahua. He generously sends tons of vital supplies to Francisco Madero's beleaguered forces nearby.

February 14 Madero returns to Mexico and assumes command of all the revolutionary forces then fighting.

February 15 The troops of Díaz's political boss, General Celso Vega, are decisively beaten by a larger force of PLM defenders in Mexicali.

February 15 Gabino Cano, a PLM member who was fighting with the Madero's forces, agrees to join Silva's column with all the men under his command after he first took some of his wounded over the U.S. border for treatment. Hearing of this, Madero informs the U.S. Authorities. They promptly arrest Cano for violation of the neutrality laws.

February 16 Madero arrives at Silva's camp with a large calvalry force and repays Silva for the gift of supplies by arresting him and disarming his troops. Silva is arrested for refusing to recognize Madero as the "Provisional President."

February 17 Silva's men, who are now mixed with Madero's army, are disarmed because they also refuse to recognize Madero. Many of them are later killed.

At the same time, Gutierrez De Lara, with a small column of U.S. volunteers, joins Madero's forces.

February 21 PLM members fighting in Baja California make clear their attitude to Madero by saying that if Madero comes to Baja California to establish a provisional government, the Liberals will oppose him.

February 25 In a front page editorial of *Regeneración*, Ricardo overtly denounces Madero as a "traitor to the cause of Liberty." Ricardo vigorously denies rumors he would be the vice president in a Madero government. Because of disrupted communications, PLM forces all over Mexico are joining or being coerced into Madero's armies.

February 26 Antonio I. Villarreal deserts the Junta and joins Madero.

March President Taft sends 30,000 U.S. troops to the border.

March 6 Madero's forces are defeated at Casas Grandes, Chihuahua.

March 10 Emiliano Zapata leads an uprising in Morelos.

March 11 Flores Magón solicits aid from Samuel Gompers, president of the American Federation of Labor, but Gompers rejects his petition

March 12 Luis Rodríguez and twenty Liberals take the town of Tecate, Baja California.

March 13 Díaz's troops under Colonel Mayol disembark at Ensenada. Their mission is to guard Algodones Dam (mainly serving big American land-holders in Mexico) southeast of Mexicali, and to retake Mexicali on the way through.

March 17 Federal forces retake Tecate and kill the entire PLM defending force.

March 24 A column of liberals under Pedro Perez, a leader of the 1908 uprising, crosses the Rio Grande and takes several plantations in northern Sonora.

April The circulation of *Regeneración* reaches 30,000.

April Antonio de P. Araujo is freed from prison. He goes to Baja California as the Junta's representative.

A PLM group under Florencio Jamarillo, which includes many Yaqui Indians, takes several towns in Sonora.

Another group under Francisco I. Reián is active in Sonora's Sierra del Durazno.

A PLM group takes the town of Tlalixocoyan, Veracruz.

Ethel Duffy Turner resigns from the editorship of the English section of *Regeneración* and is replaced by the British anarchist W.C. Owen.

April 3 The PLM junta issues a "Manifesto to the Workers of the World." It is printed in leaflet form in both English and Spanish. It explains the PLM attitude towards the revolution: "The Mexican Liberal Party [Partido Liberal

Mexicano] is not fighting to destroy the dictator Porfirio Díaz in order to put in his place a new tyrant. The Mexican Liberal Party is taking part in the current insurrection with the deliberate and firm purpose of expropriating the land and means of production and handing them over to the people, that is, to each and every one of the inhabitants of Mexico without distinction of sex. This act we consider essential to open the gates for the effective emancipation of the Mexican people ..."

April 8 Mexicali insurgents with 87 men soundly trounce Mayol's 400 men and four machine guns and send them packing for Algodones.

April 10 Captain Rhys Pryce, soldier of fortune from the Boer War, is elected commander by the PLM troops.

April 13 Simon Berthold is killed in action near El Alamo, Baja California.

April 15 Like Prisciliano Silva, Lazaro Alanis and 200 of his liberal column are arrested and disarmed for refusing to recognize Madero as "Provisional President." This is after Alanis had saved Madero's life at the battle of Casas Grandes.

April 17 More Liberal commanders are disarmed by the Maderisto's armies in the field.

Late April Captain Pryce, against Junta orders and common sense, marches his troops toward Tijuana.

May The International Committee of the Mexican Liberal Party Junta is formed.

At this time, the circulation of *Regeneración* is around 27,000 copies a week.

May 8 Tijuana is taken by PLM forces. Now much of Baja California is under Liberal control.

May 13 Revolutionary troops capture Ciudad Juárez, despite General Madero's orders, counter-orders, and counter-counter-orders.

May 20 The Junta issues a manifesto, "Take Possession of the Land." This document urges PLM members and sympathizers to go to Baja California and start agricultural cooperatives and "... make a free and happy life without masters or tyrants ..."

May 21 Madero signs a peace treaty with Díaz at Ciudad Juarez. However, the PLM refuses to lay down their arms.

May 25 Díaz resigns and leaves for Paris.

Despite the overthrow of Díaz, Mexican oficials in the U.S. continue their surveillance of the Junta's activities.

Los Angeles newspapers step up their propaganda campaign against the PLM in Baja: They claim that the Liberals are setting up—maybe even selling—a separate Baja California state.

May 30 Pryce runs off with PLM army cash to team up with publicity-hound Dick Ferris.

June Juan Sarabia is released from San Juan de Ulua prison and joins pro-Madero Liberals in Mexico City.

June 6 Madero sends troops to Baja California over U.S. territory and in U.S. trains to put down the liberal revolution in that state.

June 7 Madero basks in a gala hero's welcome in Mexico City.

Twenty-eight Liberals are murdered by Madero's officers in Altar, Sonora after being made to dig their own graves.

June 13 Madero sends Juan Sarabia and Ricardo's brother Jesús to Los Angeles to induce Ricardo and Enrique Flores Magón to accept a peace treaty. Ricardo refuses, saying "... until the land is distributed to the peasants and the instruments of production are in the hands of the workers, the liberals will never lay down their arms ..."

Sarabia promises them "all the harm I can do you."

Sarabia and Jesús also try to induce Librado Rivera and Anselmo Figueroa to join Madero's cause, but are unsuccessful.

June 14 At the behest of the Mexican government, US officials arrest Ricardo and Enrique Flores Magón, Librado Rivera, and Anselmo Figueroa in the offices of *Regeneración*. All documents are confiscated. They are accused of violating the neutrality laws.

June 16 Zapata and peasant chieftains arrive in Mexico City to be given second-breakfast treatment by Madero.

P.L.M troops surrender Mexicali when their old chief, now a supporter of Madero, convinces them the revolution is over.

June 18 Madero's army captures Mexicali.

June 22 Madero recaptures Tijuana using a force made up of Díaz's old federal troops. This army outnumbers PLM forces by a ten-to-one ratio. Madero is afraid to send revolutionary troops fearing they might refuse to fight the PLM The Liberal army in Tijuana surrenders.

June 23 Ricardo is freed on bail of $2,500 that was raised by friends and comrades in Los Angeles and the surrounding area.

July 5 The socialist newspaper *The New York Call* publishes an article attacking the PLM revolutionaries in Baja California as "bandits."

August Jesus M. Rangel, Prisciliano and Rubin Silva, and other comrades are arrested by Madero's officers and imprisoned. During this incident, Rangel is shot and wounded.

August Indians in Jalisco and peasants in Veracruz take over much land and work it communally.

August A "reconstituted" Liberal Party is formed in Mexico City, together with a newspaper called *Regeneración* edited by Sarabia and Antonio I. Villarreal. Ricardo refers to this paper as "*Degeneracíon.*"

PLM groups renew their activities in Durango and Coahuila.

August 2 Juan Sarabia writes an open letter to Ricardo that is published in *The New York Call.* In it, Sarabia tells Ricardo not only that his revolutionary movement unacceptable in Mexico, but also that the people are completely unprepared for Anarchism or Socialism.

August 27 Madero talks Zapata into laying down arms. Madero's general, Huerta, massacres Zapata's supporters.

September Honore J. Jaxon, treasurer of the PLM and its representative in Europe, addresses the British Trades Union Congress in London on the Mexican situation.

September 23 The junta issues a new Manifesto to replace the PLM's 1906 program. This new manifesto is uncompromisingly anarchist in content. It urges the peasants to expropriate the land and the workers to take over the factories and mines and work them by themselves. It ends, "... Liberty and well-being are within our grasp. The same effort and the same sacrifices that are required to raise to power a governor—that is to say a tyrant—will achieve the expropriation of the fortunes the rich keep from you. It is for you, then, to choose. Either a new governor—that is to say a new yoke—or life redeeming expropriation and the abolition of all imposition: religious, political, or any other kind. "LAND AND LIBERTY!"

September 27 The anti-junta propaganda from Mexico comes to a head when Antonio I. Villarreal publishes an article in Sarabia's newspaper, *Diario del Hogar*, accusing Ricardo of being a "blackmailer, swindler, coward, and a drunken pervert and scoundrel who shared his mistresses with all men of bad taste."

September 29 PLM groups active in the state of Tamaulipas issue a proclamation urging the workers to join them.

October 1 Madero is elected president.

October Mother Jones returns from Mexico and encourages Flores Magón to make peace with Madero. Flores Magón's reaction is shocked and hostile. Mother Jones denounces him as an "unreasonable fanatic."

October 31 Francisco Vazquez Gomez, Madero's former running mate in the 1910 elections, leads a revolt against Madero. The Vazquistas plan, the "Plan of Tacubaya," whose main author was Paulino Martinez, calls for immediate agricultural reforms, similar to those in the PLM Program of 1906. Later, Martinez joins the Zapata's supporters.

November 25 Zapata rebels against Madero and issues his "Plan de Ayala" which demands the restitution of the land to the peasants.

December Yaqui Indians using the PLM motto "Tierra y Libertad" take possession of land in the Yaqui Valley, Sonora, and work it in common.

December 2 While organizing a liberal army, Los Abanderados Rojos, Fernando Palomarez and other comrades are arrested in El Paso, Texas by a force of Texas Rangers aided by the chief of Madero's secret service. Later, U.S. Authorities sentence Palomarez to 13 months imprisonment for violating the neutrality laws.

December 5 Madero states that Zapata's Plan de Ayala is crazy because it is too radical.

1912

February 26 Madero appoints Jesús Flores Magón Secretary of Governance.

March PLM groups renew their activities in Coahuila, Tamaulipas, Baja California, and Sonora.

March 2 European anarchist journals, such as *Le Libertaire* and *Freedom*, enthusiastically support the Junta and publish many articles in their favor and on the Mexican situation in general. However, R. Forment in Jean Grave's *Les Temps Nouveaux* attacks Ricardo and the PLM He accuses them of not being anarchists and that the Mexican social revolution existed in their minds only.

March 25 Pascual Orozco, with a land program similar to the PLM's, revolts against Madero. Many of his military leaders are PLM members like Cesar E. Canales, Jose Inez Salazar, and Lazaro Alanis. He is defeated in May and driven out of Ciudad Juárez on August 20.

March 29 Ricardo and Enrique Flores Magón, and W.C. Owen publish an open letter to Jean Grave in answer to the attack made on them in *Les Temps Nouveaux*.

April Peter Kropotkin defends Ricardo Flores Magón in an article published in *Les Temps Nouveaux*.

June 4–25 The Junta members are put on trial in Los Angeles. Attorneys for the prosecution bribe many witnesses to perjure themselves or threaten them with imprisonment. During the trial, most of the prosecution witnesses do perjure themselves. One of them is even a spy for the Mexican government. Despite this, the Junta spokesmen are given 10 months imprisonment each for violating the neutrality laws. When the sentence becomes known, PLM members and sympathizers lead a mass demonstration outside the courthouse. Police using their clubs violently break up the protest. Many are arrested and wounded, including Ricardo's companion and her daughter.

While the Junta are imprisoned on McNeil Island prison, *Regeneración* is run by Antonio de P. Araujo, Blas Lara, Teodoro Gaytan, Alberto Tellez, Juan Rincon, Trinidad Villarreal, and W. C. Owen.

June 22 Luís Mendez, Juan Francisco Moncaleano, and Jacinto Huitron form the Grupo Luz in Mexico City. Moncaleano, a schoolteacher and organizer of the stone cutters' union, also forms a modern school based on Spanish anarchist Francisco Ferrer's Escuela Moderna.

July 4 The prisoners are spirited out of Los Angeles jail and sent to McNeil Island, Washington for a 23 month term.

July 15 Groupo Luz founds its own newspaper *Luz* with Moncaleano as editor.

August 5 *Luz* publishes an article written by Moncaleano supporting Ricardo.

September 11 Madero expels Moncaleano from Mexico for his support of Ricardo.

September 22 The syndicalist group Casa del Obrero Mundial is founded in Mexico City. The founding members include Jacinto Huitron and Luís Mendez. Lazaro Gutierrez de Lara, Manuel Sarabia, and de la Vega, then members of the Mexican Socialist Party, also help out.

December In a rare European protest, two military units in Portugal disobey orders for 24 hours against the imprisonment of PLM Junta leaders.

Juan F. Montero, a long standing PLM member, joins the Yaqui Indians in the Yaqui Valley, Sonora after being freed from Hermosillo jail where he was being held by Madero's officers.

1913

February 3 J. F. Moncaleano and Romulo S. Carmona, Enrique Flores Magón's father-in-law, found the Casa del Obrero Internacional in Los Angeles. A Ferrer school and the editorial offices of *Regeneración* occupy the same building as the Casa. Weekly meetings are also held there.

February Jesus M. Rangel and Jose Guerra visit Zapata as special envoys of the Junta.

February 21 Madero is assassinated in Mexico City. General Huerta assumes dictatorial power.

March Several witnesses from Ricardo's trial sign affidavits reversing their testimonies for the prosecution and admitting their perjuries. These affidavits are published in *Regeneración*.

March 27 Venustiano Carranza issues his Plan de Guadalupe which refuses to recognize Huerta.

The civil war begins. Zapata and Francisco "Pancho" Villa support Carranza.

April 17 Mexican clergy contribute $20 million to help maintain dictator Huerta in power.

May 1 The first May Day demonstration ever held in Mexico City is organized by the Casa del Obrero Mundial.

May 8 Panuco, Veracruz is taken by a PLM column under Viciento Salazar.

May 24 Inspired by several affidavits, the staff of *Regeneración* appeals to President Wilson to pardon Ricardo and the other imprisoned Junta members. Wilson refuses.

June 2 The Casa del Obrero Mundial moves towards anarcho-syndicalism when its members issue a manifesto condemning any participation in political action. Instead, the group adopts "Direct Action" as its method of struggle.

August Lucio Blanco, one of Carranza's generals, starts to distribute land to the peasants in Matamoros. Carranza demands his dismissal.

September 13 Jesus M. Rangel, now living in Texas, and C. Cline, an American I.W.W. member, along with fourteen Mexican comrades, try to cross the U.S. border into Mexico to fight against Huerta. Before they reach the border, however, the local sheriff fires upon them, shooting one of the Mexicans in the back. A fight ensues. The Mexicans take the sheriff prisoner, but release him on written assurance that they will not be molested again. The following day, they are attacked again, this time by a stronger force. One U.S. sheriff and two Mexicans die. One of these Mexicans, Juan Rincon, had been on the editorial staff of *Regeneración*. The rest of the liberals are captured. Rangel and the others are held incommunicado in prison until their trial. They all receive heavy prison sentences. Rangel is given 99 years. Two comrades are later murdered in prison.

November 24 Libertarian schoolteacher and PLM member Margarita Ortega is shot by government troops in Mexicali, Baja California.

1914

January 19 Ricardo and Enrique Flores Magón, Librado Rivera and Anselmo Figueroa are freed from McNeil Island prison. Figueroa soon dies from the tuberculosis that he contracted at McNeil.

March Some members of the Casa del Obrero Mundial, including Luís Mendez, Antonio Díaz Soto y Gama, and Prudencio R. Casales, leave the group to join Zapata.

May 18 Huerta's police close down The Casa del Obrero Mundial.

May PLM groups are now active in Sonora, where Yaqui Indians aided by Juan F. Montero control several towns between the Yaqui and Mayo rivers.

In Durango, Domingo and Benjamin Arrieta give expropriated land over to the peasants.

In Chihuahua, San Luis Potosí, Zacatecas, Mexico, Michoacan, Guanajuato, Guerrero and Jalisco, PLM groups are active. In all these states, land has been expropriated to the peasants.

June 12 In a letter to A. Shapiro, the Secretary of the International Anarchist Congress, which is to be held in London from August 28–September 2, Ricardo says that international anarchists must make up their minds about the Mexican Revolution by either supporting it fully or by condemning it. He also proposes that the PLM should be represented at the Congress. In fact, the Mexican question is going to be discussed at the Congress, but the outbreak of the First World War prevents the Congress from occurring.

July Huerta is driven from power. Venustiano Carranza becomes the self-styled "First Chief" of the Constitutionalist Army.

August Ricardo and Enrique Flores Magón, and Librado Rivera arrive in Los Angeles after a west coast speaking tour to raise funds.

August The First World War breaks out in Europe. Like many other anarchists, Ricardo Flores Magón believed that the universal slaughter will result in a social revolution in all the belligerent countries. He writes: "Behind the catastrophe, Liberty smiles."

October 10 Revolutionary leaders hold a convention at Aguascalientes to unite the country after Huerta flees Mexico. Under the direction of Antonio I. Villarreal, now one of Carranza's generals, the convention elects Eulalio Gutierrez as the provisional president. Carranza, who refuses to participate in the convention, also refuses to recognize Gutierrez.

November The forces of Villa and Zapata enter Mexico City.

November 7 The Junta issues an open letter to the Workers of the United States in which they are urged to support the struggle of the Mexican working class.

December The publication of *Regeneración* is suspended because of its financial situation.

1915

January 6 Carranza issues a decree restoring the ejidos, communally worked land around each village, to the peasants.

February 17 On Carranza's behalf, General Obregon signs a pact with the Casa del Obrero Mundial. This agreement requires the Casa to organize "Red Battalions" to fight against Zapata and Villa. In return, the Casa will be free to organize branches in all the "liberated" towns.

June 14 Anselmo L. Figueroa dies in Palomas, Arizona as a result of his recent imprisonment. The day before he dies, he is handing out PLM propaganda on the streets.

Ricardo and Enrique Flores Magón, Librado Rivera, their families, and other comrades working on *Regeneración* rent a small farm in Edendale, a rural suburb of Los Angeles where they live and work communally on the land.

October 19 U.S. recognizes the bloody Carranza regime.

October 29 *Regeneración* resumes publication. It is printed on an old hand press. The editorial office is a barn on the Edendale farm.

November 30 To avoid the strikes that railroad workers call to protest being paid in depreciating paper currency, Carranza drafts them all into the Constitutionalist Army.

December 15 Ricardo's play "Tierra y Libertad" is first staged in Los Angeles.

Ricardo is too sick to attend.

1916

February 18 Ricardo and Enrique are arrested in their Edendale home. During the arrest, Enrique is so badly beaten that he has to be taken to the hospital. U.S. Postal authorities accuse them of sending material through the post that incites others to "murder, arson and treason." William C. Owen is also indicted, but he manages to escape to New York where he boards a ship to England.

The articles in question are condemnations of Carranza, including "To Carranza's soldiers" and "The Reforms of Carranza." In the former article, Ricardo tells the soldiers fighting in the Constitutionalist Army not to surrender their arms but to keep them and, if necessary, to use them against their officers.

Immediately, a defense committee is formed to raise bail money. However, the judge refuses to grant bail, despite Ricardo's poor health.

By now, Wilson has recognized the Carranza regime.

March 4 *Regeneración* Number 228 is issued.

May 1 Carranza is inaugurated as the President of Mexico.

May 21 Trial of Ricardo and Enrique. Ricardo is so ill that he is not able to go to the courthouse. Instead, Enrique has to speak for both of them. Despite this, the judge refuses Enrique the right to read a defense statement, claiming that it is a "political" document.

Due to his poor health, Ricardo is sentenced to 12 months and a fine of $1000. Enrique receives three years and a fine of $3000.

June 26 Ricardo is released on bail pending an appeal. Anarchists Emma Goldman and Alexander Berkman raise the bail.

July 1 Enrique is released on bail.

July U.S. postal authorities revoke the second-class mailing privileges of *Regeneración*, doubling the subscription cost.

July 31 Electrical workers in Mexico City declare a general strike after a promise of a pay raise and better working conditions are not fulfilled. The workers refuse to call off the strike. In retaliation, Carranza orders the closing of the Casa del Obrero Mundial and the arrest of its members.

August 1 Carranza revives an 1862 law dealing with public disorder that threatens striking workers with the death penalty. Many workers are arrested and held in prison for months on the charge of rebellion. Only one is put on trial. He is sentenced to death but is later reprieved.

August 2 The Casa del Obrero Mundial ceases to exist.

August 26 Ricardo writes his most bitter attack on Carranza in *Regeneración*:"Carranza Despoils the Sheep of its Wool."

December 16 Constitutional Convention meets. Mexico's new progressive constitution draws its most radical ideas from the PLM Program of 1906.

1917

Ricardo and Enrique Flores Magón and Librado Rivera manage to keep *Regeneración* going, but only on an irregular basis.

Ricardo Flores Magón speaks at many meetings in the Los Angeles area despite the ill health that forces him to stop writing for a time.

April 6 U.S. enters World War I.

June Enrique Flores Magón separates from *Regeneración* due to a family squabble.

June 15 Oppressive U.S. Espionage Act passed.

September Juan F. Montero heads Yaqui Indian guerrillas fighting against Carranza in Sonora.

1918

January *Regeneración* still manages to appear despite a reduced readership and the suppression of many radical newspapers. The journal no longer has an English section. Ricardo wants to restart this page under the editorship of his step-daughter Lucía Norman, but this never happens.

February 2 Lazaro Gutierrez de Lara is shot by a government firing squad on the orders of Plutarco Elias Calles during the suppression of a miners' strike in Cananea.

March 16 Ricardo Flores Magón and Librado Rivera publish a manifesto in *Regeneración* to the "Anarchists of the World and the Workers in General," saying that the social Revolution is near and that it is the duty of all anarchists to work towards this with all their strength and ability. This is the last edition of *Regeneración*.

March 21 Flores Magón and Rivera are arrested for the March 16 Manifesto, even though it was published in Spanish. The US government charges them under the Espionage Act with sedition. Bail for Ricardo is set at $50,000.

May 16 Enrique loses his appeal and is sent to Fort Leavenworth, Kansas

Penitentiary for three years.

June 13 Ricardo Flores Magón's companion María and other PLM activists are arrested for violations of the Espionage Act.

August 15 Ricardo Flores Magón and Rivera are sentenced to 20 years and 15 years respectively for sedition. During their trial, which is held in camera, the judge tells the jury "the activity of these men has been a constant violation of the law, all the laws. They have violated both the law of god and the law of man." They are taken to McNeil Island penitentiary to serve their sentence.

1919

April 10 Zapata is assassinated on the orders of Carranza.

November Because of the ill health that has afflicted him at least since 1916, Ricardo is transferred to Leavenworth prison, Kansas. His only means of expression now are the three weekly letters he is allowed to write.

1920

May 21 Carranza is assassinated by a supporter of Obregón.

August Rivera is transferred to Leavenworth.

October 28 Juan Sarabia dies.

November Largely thanks to Flores Magón and Rivera's old Liberal Party comrade, Antonio Díaz Soto y Gama, now a member of the House of Deputies, the Mexican government under President Obregón votes to give the two men a pension. Antonio I. Villarreal is a minister of agriculture in this government. Regarding the proposed pension, Ricardo writes to a comrade: "... I am an Anarchist, and could not receive without shame and remorse money that had been stolen by the government from the poor. If the money had come from the workers, I would have accepted it with pride and pleasure, because they are my brothers. But coming from the State after being demanded—according to my belief—from the people, that money would burn my hands and would fill my heart with remorse."

1921

April Ricardo's lawyer, Harry Weinberger applies for Flores Magón's release on health grounds. He is suffering from diabetes and several respiratory complaints. Worst of all he is afflicted with cataracts and is nearly blind. The U.S. Attorney General refuses this appeal, saying that there is nothing wrong with Flores Magón's health that can not be treated in prison. Yet the prison doctor does little to help him.

June The Mexican government instructs its Washington embassy to intervene on behalf of Flores Magón and Rivera.

September 13 After taking a collection, Mexico City's Union of Graphical Workers sends Flores Magón and Rivera $24.50 each.

1922

February The anarcho-syndicalist Confederacion General de Trabajadores is founded in Mexico City.

An attempt to get an independent medical examination for Flores Magón by some of his comrades is refused by the Attorney General. Yet his health gets worse.

May 1 The Confederacion General de Trabajadores demonstrates loudly before the US consulate in Mexico City against the persecution of Flores Magón and Rivera.

November Workers throughout Mexico strike and boycott all U.S. goods in an attempt to win the freedom of Flores Magón and Rivera.

November 8 Veracruz workers strike in protest against Flores Magón and Librado Rivera's imprisonment. Governor Carrillo of Yucatan urges workers to strike too. Strikes brew in Manzanillo, Mazatlán, Salina Cruz, and Tampico. The Mexican government and the corrupt Harding Administration are perturbed.

November 18 Librado Rivera is moved out of Ricardo's cell without explanation and for no apparent reason. Ricardo is ordered to sleep with head next to bars, unlike other prisoners.

November 20 Rivera talks with Flores Magón in exercise yard and finds him in unusually good spirits and health.

November 21 Flores Magón is found dead in his cell at five in the morning. The prison doctors say the cause is a heart attack. However, Flores Magón's smashed front tooth and choke marks on his throat leave ample room for another possible verdict.

Rivera, who sees Flores Magón's body soon after his death, feels sure that he was strangled. Rivera's death message to Maria Brousse is censored and altered by the warden. Prison authorities force Rivera to tell all the comrades that Flores Magón died from a heart attack.

November 22 Thanks again to Antonio Díaz Soto y Gama, a Mexican congressional resolution honors "the great Mexican revolutionary, Ricardo Flores Magón, martyr and apostle." The Mexican Chamber of Deputies votes to pay the expense of returning Flores Magón's body to Mexico. His comrades refuse this offer. Instead, the workers in the Federation of Railroad Unions offer to transport Flores Magón's body back to Mexico at their own expense.

December 3 A young Chicano prisoner, Jose Martinez, tries to avenge Ricardo Flores Magón's death by knifing the hated, brutal chief jailer, "Bull" Leonard. Martinez held the common belief that Leonard had murdered Flores Magón. Seven guards promptly murder Martinez in retaliation.

1923

January 5–15 Flores Magón's body triumphal funeral train tours Mexico from Ciudad Juárez to Mexico City. At every town where it stops on the way, it is greeted by thousands of working people with red and black flags who want to pay their last respects to Flores Magón.

January 16 In Mexico City, 10,000 workers follow the body to the Panteon Frances where it is buried. Ricardo Flores Magón's funeral becomes a huge parade with day-long ceremonies that unify Mexico's workers as never before.

March 1 Enrique Flores Magón is freed from prison and returns to Mexico, where he starts a propaganda tour with his companion Teresa. The meetings in each town are attended by thousands who stop work to attend despite official harassment.

July 20 Francisco "Pancho" Villa is assassinated.

October 2 Rivera is freed from prison and deported to Mexico where he lives in San Luis Potosí.

In Mexico, Nicolas T. Bernal forms the Grupo Cultural Ricardo Flores Magón. This group collects and publishes Flores Magón's articles, letters and plays in 10 small volumes under the title *Ricardo Flores Magón: Vida y Obra*. In volume V, *Rayos de Luz*, Librado Rivera contributes an article "The Persecution and Murder of Ricardo Flores Magón" in which he tells the terrible story of Flores Magón's last years in prison.

1924

President Calles demands the release of all Mexican political prisoners in American jails.

Librado Rivera, now living in Villa Cecilia, Tamaulipas edits a newspaper *Sagittario*, and carries out propaganda work amongst the petrol workers.

September Enrique Flores Magón is arrested by the police in Cuantitlan.

The Grupo Cultural Ricardo Flores Magón publishes the first biography of

Ricardo Flores Magón, Diego Abad de Santillan's *Ricardo Flores Magón, el apostol de la revolucíon mexicana.*

1927

April 1 Librado Rivera is arrested and imprisoned together with other comrades in Andonegui prison, Tampico. He is held for six months before being tried. Later, he is sentenced to 6 months imprisonment for "inciting the people to anarchy" and "insulting the president." While in prison, however, Rivera still contributes articles to *Sagittario* until the police suppress it and ban it from the mail.

August Jesus M. Rangel and other comrades are freed from jail in Texas.

November 4 Rivera is unconditionally released from prison. He moves to Monterrey where he starts to publish a new newspaper, *Avante*.

1928

December An American anarchist newspaper publishes an article in English by Rivera on the extermination of the Yaqui.

1929

February 19 Rivera is arrested again and the printing plant of *Avante* is completely destroyed. While in prison, Rivera is violently beaten and an attempt is made to murder him.

April Rivera is released.

June 9 William C. Owen dies in Worthing, England. After fleeing from the U.S., he returned to England and became editor of *Freedom*.

1930

Jesús Flores Magón dies.

1931

May 1 Rivera, now living in Mexico City, starts to publish a new newspaper, *Paso*.

1932

March 1 Rivera dies in Mexico City after being run down by a motor car. True to his ideals, he did not want to prosecute the driver of the car because he was a worker.

Librado Rivera is buried in an unmarked grave in the municipal cemetery.

1937

Movement begins to transfer Ricardo Flores Magón's corpse to the national heroes' cemetery.

1945

May 1 Flores Magón's body is exhumed and re-buried in the Rotunda de los Hombres Illustres.

Antonio I Villarreal dies.

1948

Ricardo Flores Magón's companion Maria dies in Ensenada, where she had founded a Peasants and Workers Cultural Club. Although she had been living in poverty, she refused a government pension offered in memory of her husband.

John Kenneth Turner dies.

1954

October 28 Enrique Flores Magón dies.

1960

Ethel Duffy Turner's book *Ricardo Flores Magón y el Partido Liberal Mexicana* is translated and published in Mexico City.

BIBLIOGRAPHY

WRITINGS OF RICARDO FLORES MAGÓN
A. IN ENGLISH OR BILINGUAL

Correspondencia. 2 vols. Jacinto Barrera Basols, ed. México: CONACULTA, 2000.

Land and liberty: anarchist influences in the Mexican revolution. David Poole, ed. London: Cienfuegos Press, 1977.

Manifesto. Los Angeles: The Junta, 1914.

Manifesto to the workers of the world. Los Angeles, 1911.

Now and then: voices of the Mexican Revolutions: Ricardo Flores Magón, EZLN, and Enrique Flores Magón. Robert Herr, ed. Los Angeles: PFAFS, 1997.

"Prison Letters of Ricardo Flores Magón to Lilly Sarnoff." Paul Avrich, ed. *International Review of Social History* 22, no. 3 (1977): 379–422.

"The Appeal of Mexico to American Labor." *Mother Earth,* April 1911, 47–49.

Tierra y Libertad: Land and Liberty. Mitchell Cowen Verter, trans. San Francisco, CA: El Libro Libre, 2001.

5. B. In Spanish

A la mujer. Oakland, California: Prensa Sembradora, 1974.

Abriendo Surco. D. F., México: Grupo Cultural "Ricardo Flores Magón," 1924.

Actividades políticas y revolucionarias de los hermanos Flores Magón. Tomo 10, Documentos históricos de la revolución mexicana. Isidro Fabela, ed. D.F., México: Editorial Jus, 1966.

Antología. Gonzalo Aguirre Beltrán, ed. D.F., México: UNAM, 1970.

Artículos de combate. Escribido con Práxedis G. Guerrero. D.F., México: Ediciones Antorcha, 1984.

Artículos políticos, 1910. D.F., México: Ediciones Antorcha, 1983.

Artículos políticos, 1911. D.F., México: Ediciones Antorcha, 1986.

Artículos políticos, 1912. D. F., México: Ediciones Antorcha, 1981.

Artículos políticos, 1914. D.F., México: Ediciones Antorcha, 1982.

Batalla a la dictadura. Escribido con Jesús Flores Magón. D.F., México: Empresas Editoriales, 1948.

Carranza contra los trabajadores: artículos políticos, 1915. D.F., México: Ediciones Antorcha, 1987.

En defensa de la revolución. D.F., México: Ediciones Antorcha, 1988.

Epistolario revolucionario e íntimo. D.F., México: Ediciones Antorcha, 1983.

Epistolario y textos. Manuel González Ramírez, ed. D.F., México: Fondo de Cultura Económica, 1964.

Fuentes para la historia de la Revolucion Mexicana. Manuel González Ramírez, ed. Vol 1, *Planes politicos y otros documentoes.* Tomo 4, Manifestos Politicos (1892-1912). Mexico: Fondo de Cultura Economica, 1954, 1957.

La primera guerra mundial y la revolución rusa. D.F., México: Ediciones Antorcha, 1983.

La Revolución Mexicana. D.F., México: Editorial Grijalbo, 1970.

La Revolución Mexicana. D.F., México: Editores Mexicanos Unidos, 1985.

1914, la intervención americana en México. D.F., México: Ediciones Antorcha, 1987.

Númenes rebeldes. Escribido con Práxedis Guerrero. D.F., México: Grupo Cultural "Ricardo Flores Magón," 1922.

Obras de teatro: "Tierra y Libertad" y "Verdugos y Victimas." D.F., México: Ediciones Antorcha, 1980.

¿Para que sirve la autoridad? y otros cuentos. D.F., México: Ediciones Antorcha, 1981.

Regeneración 1900-1918. Armando Batra, ed. D.F., México: ERA, 1980.

Ricardo Flores Magón: el sueño alternativo. Fernando Zertuche Muñoz, ed. D.F., México: Instituto Nacional de Estudios Históricos de la Revolución Mexicana, 2000.

Ricardo Flores Magón: Su Vida, Su Obra y 42 Cartas. B. Cano Ruiz, ed. D.F., México: Editores Mexicanos Unidos, 1976.

Ricardo Flores Magón, paladín de la libertad. Oaxaca: LIII Legislatura Constitucional del Estado, 1988.

Selecciones. Eduardo Blanquel, ed. D.F., México: Terra Nova, 1985.

Selecciones (Manifestó del Partido Liberal Mexicano). Georgette Emilia José Valenzuela, ed. D.F., México: Instituto Nacional de Estudios Históricos de la Revolución Mexicana, 1985.

Testimonio carcelario de Ricardo Flores Magón. Tita Valencia, ed. D.F., México: Secretaría de Gobernación, 1977.

Vida Nueva. D.F., México: Grupo Cultural "Ricardo Flores Magón," 1924.

Vida y Obra. 10 vols. (I, II: Semilla Libertaria; III: Tribuna Roja; IV: Sembrando Ideas; V: Rayos de Luz; VI: Tierra y Libertad; VII: Verdugos y Victimas; VIII, IX, X: Epistolario Revolucionario e Intimo.) D.F., México: Grupo Cultural "Ricardo Flores Magón," 1923-1925.

ABOUT RICARDO FLORES MAGÓN
A. ENGLISH

Albro, Ward S. *Always a Rebel: Ricardo Flores Magón and the Mexican Revolution*. Fort Worth: Texas Christian University Press, 1992.

Arroyo, Laura E. And José Hernandez. "Magón: Author of the Mexican Revolution." *La Gente*, May–June 1974.

Avrich, Paul. *Anarchist Portraits*. Princeton: Princeton University Press, 1988.

Cox, Glen. "Ricardo Flores Magón and the Impractical Revolution." Ph.D. diss., UCLA, spring 1971.

Gerard, David A. "Ricardo Flores Magón and the Mexican revolution." B.A. thesis, Wesleyan University, 1972.

Gómez-Quiñones, Juan. *Sembradores, Ricardo Flores Magón y el Partido Liberal Mexicano: a eulogy and critique*. Los Angeles: University of California, Chicano Studies Center, 1977.

———. "Ricardo Flores Magon." In *The American Radical*, ed. Mari Jo Buhle, Paul Buhle, and Harvey J. Kaye. New York: Routledge, 1994.

Hanlen, Charles Jacob. "Ricardo Flores Magón: Biography of a Revolutionary." M.A. thesis, UCSD, 1967.

Hollander, Fred. "Ricardo Flores Magón and the Formation of Popular Mexican Nationalism." Ph.D. diss., UCLA, winter 1967.

Howell, Ellen Douglas. "Ricardo Flores Magón: The evolution of the political ideas of a revolutionary." Ph.D. diss., University of Virginia, 1965.

Jenkins, Myra Ellen, "Ricardo Flores Magón and the Mexican Liberal Party." Ph.D. diss., University of New México, 1953.

Langham, Thomas C. *Border trials: Ricardo Flores Magón and the Mexican liberals*. El Paso: Texas Western Press, 1981.

MacLachlan, Colin M. *Anarchism and the Mexican Revolution: the political trials of Ricardo Flores Magón in the United States*. Berkeley: University of California Press, 1991.

Myers, Ellen Howell. "The Mexican Liberal Party 1903-1910." Ph.D. diss., University of Virginia, 1970.

O'Day, Gilbert. "Mexico's Martyr." The Nation 115, no. 2998 (20 December 1922): 689–690, 702.

Pinchon, Edgcomb. "Think of the Magóns." *Blast*, 1 June 1916, 1.

Rodríguez, José A., "The Unionization Activities of Ricardo Flores Magón." Ph.D. diss., UCLA, winter 1971.

Sherman, John W. "Revolution on Trial: The 1909 Tombstone Proceedings against Ricardo Flores Magon, Antonio Villarreal, and Librado Rivera." *Journal of Arizona History* 32, no 3 (1991): 173-194.f

B. SPANISH

Abad de Santillán, Diego. *Ricardo Flores Magón, el apóstol de la revolución mexicana.* D.F., México: Ediciones Antorcha, 1988.

Aguirre Beltrán, Gonzalo, "Ricardo Flores Magón." *Crítica antropológica.* Hombres e ideas. México, Universidad Veracruzana, Instituto Nacional Indigenista, Gobierno del Estado de Veracruz/Fondo de Cultura Económica, 1990.

———. *Un precursor y un realizador de la Revolución Mexicana.* México: Instituto Nacional de la Juventud Mexicana, 1972

Aguirre, Norberto. *Ricardo Flores Magón, síntesis biografía.* México: Ediciones de la Sociedad Agronómica Mexicana, 1964.

Alba Zavala, Fausto. *Discurso del Senador... LXI aniversario luctuoso de Ricardo Flores Magón.* D.F., México: Senado de la República, 1984

Aldana Rendón, Mario A. *Introducción al pensamiento político de Ricardo Flores Magón y Venustiano Carranza.* Guadalajara, Jalisco, México: Universidad de Guadalajara, Instituto de Estudios Sociales, 1977.

Amezcua, Genaro. *¿Quien es Flores Magón y cuál su obra?* D.F., México: Editorial Avance, 1943.

Araiza, Luis. *Ricardo Flores Magón en la Historia.* D.F., México: Ediciones Casa del Obrero Mundial, 1976.

Arias de la Canal, Fredo. *Flores Magón, Poeta Revolucionario, La Revolución Mexicana Fue Anarquista.* México: Gustavo de Anda, 1977.

Barrera Fuentes, Florencio. *Ricardo Flores Magón, el apóstol cautivo.* México: Patronato del Instituto Nacional de Estudios Históricos de la Revolución Mexicana, 1973.

Batra, Armando. "La Otra Revolución Mexicana." *Siempre,* 20 Diciembre 1972 Suplemento, 2-6.

Beltrán, Alberto. *Homenaje a Ricardo Flores Magón.* Guadalajara, México: H. Ayuntamiento de Guadalajara, 1974.

Bernal, Nicolás T. *Memorial enviado por el ciudadano.* N.T. Bernal desde Oakland, California, E.U.A. D.F., México: Impr. de la Cámara de Diputados, 1920.

———. Memorias. D.F., *México: Centro de Estudios Históricos del Movimiento Obrero* Mexicano, 1982.

Blanquel, Eduardo. *Ricardo Flores Magón*. D.F., México: Editorial Terra Nova, 1985.

————."El anarco-magonismo." *Historia Mexicana* 13, no.3 (Enero–Marzo 1964): 394–427.

Cadenhead, Ivie E., Jr. "Flores Magón y el periódico The Appeal to Reason." *Historia Mexicana* 13, no. 1 (Julio–Septiembre 1963): 88–93.

Carbo Darnaculleta, Margarita. *El magonismo en la revolución mexicana*. D.F., México: UNAM, 1964.

Carrillo Azpéitia, Rafael. *Ricardo Flores Magón: esbozo biográfico*. D.F., México: Centro de Estudios Históricos del Movimiento Obrero Mexicano, 1976.

Conner, Robert P. *Regeneración: el pensamiento de Ricardo Flores Magón*. Ciudad Juárez, México: Dirección de Relaciones Publicas y Comunicación, 1990.

Delgado Gonzalez, A. *El magonismo: la corriente radical y libertaria de la revolucion mexicana*. D.F., Mexico: Ediciones Quinto, 1991.

Díaz Soto y Gama, Antonio. "Ricardo y Enrique Flores Magón." *El Universal*, 10 Noviembre 1954.

Eloy, J. Jesús. *Ricardo Flores Magón: águila encarcelada*. San Luis Potosí, México: Editora Mexicana, 2000.

Escobedo Cetina, Humberto. *El pensamiento político de Ricardo Flores Magón*. Oaxaca: El Autor, 1997.

————. *Ricardo Flores Magón: semblanza biográfica*. Oaxaca, México: H. Ayuntamiento, 1997.

————. *Ricardo Flores Magón, Presente!* Oaxaca, México: EDI Oaxaquena, 1992.

Esparza Valdivia, R. C. *El fenomeno magonista en Mexico y en Estados Unidos*. Zacatecas, Mexico: Universidad Autonoma de Zacatecas, 2000.

Ferrua, Pietro. "Ricardo Flores Magón en la Revolución Mexicana." *Reconstruir*, May–Junio y Julio–Augusta, 1971.

García, Silvino M. *Vibraciones revolucionarias*. D.F., México: Impr. Victoria, 1916.

Garro, Elena. *Revolucionarios mexicanos*. D.F., México: Grupo Editorial Planeta, 1997.

Hernández Padilla, Salvador. *El magonismo: historia de una pasión libertaria, 1900-1922*. D.F., México: Ediciones Era, 1988.

————. *Nunca aprendas a morir: historias de una generación libertaria*. D.F., México: Plaza y Valdés Editores, 1995.

Hernández, Salvador. "El Magonismo 1911: La otra revolución." *Cuadernos Políticos*, no. 4 (Abril–Junio 1975).

Lajous, Alejandra. *Presencia de la mujer revolucionaria en la vida de México: memoria del ciclo de conferencias celebrado en el auditoria "Ricardo Flores Magón"* del Instituto de Capacitación Política, del 27 al 30 de enero de 1986. D.F., México: Partido Revolucionario Institucional, 1987.

List Arzubide, Armando. *Ricardo Flores Magón*. D.F., México: Secretaria de Educación Pública, 1938.

Mader, Bernice Claire. *Ricardo Flores Magón*. California: C. Acevedo Cárdenas, 1969.

Magdaleno, Mauricio. *Ricardo Flores Magón: el gran calumniado*. D.F., México: Ediciones de la Chinaca, 1964.

Maldonado Alvarado, Benjamín. *La utopía de Ricardo Flores Magón: revolución, anarquía y comunalidad india*. Oaxaca, Oax: Universidad Autónoma "Benito Juárez" de Oaxaca, Secretaría Académica, 1994.

Mijares Ramírez, Ivonne, Hortensia Moreno, y Martha Avilés. *Ricardo Flores Magón*. D.F., México: Instituto Nacional de Estudios Históricos de la Revolución Mexicana, 1996.

Muñoz Cota, José. *Corridos de Ricardo Flores Magón*. Oaxaca, México: Universidad Autónoma "Benito Juárez," 1975.

———. *La ideología de Ricardo Flores Magón*. Tesis. Universidad Nacional Autónoma de México, 1965.

———. *Ricardo Flores Magón, el sueño de una palabra*, D.F., México: Editorial Doctrimex, 1966.

———. *Ricardo Flores Magón, un sol clavado en la sombra*. D.F., México: Editores Mexicanos Unidos, 1963.

———. *Precursores de la revolución*. México: Institución Nacional de la Juventud Mexicana, 1963.

———. *Ricardo Flores Magón, "el águila ciega."* Oaxaca, Oaxaca: Instituto Oaxaqueño de las Culturas, 1998.

Muñoz Rosas, Jerónimo. *La ideología de Ricardo Flores Magón*. D.F., México: Editorial Doctrimex, 1965.

Ojeda, Abelardo y Carlos Mallen. *Ricardo Flores Magón: Su vida y su obra frente al origen y las proyecciones de la Revolución Mexicana*. D.F., México: Secretaria de Educación Pública, 1967.

Pérez Salazar de Muñoz Cota, Alicia. *Semblanza de Flores Magón*. México: Instituto Nacional de la Juventud Mexicana, 1961.

Pérez Salazar, Alicia. *Discurso a Ricardo Flores Magón*. Tribuna (D.F., México), 22 Noviembre 1963.

Pérez Velasco, Guillermo. *La tierra: Ricardo Flores Magón*. México: Secretaría de la Reforma Agraria, Carta Agraria Nacional, 1975.

Ramos G., Víctor M. *El periódico como propagador, agitador y organizador colectivo: la prensa flores magonista, 1900-1911*. México: Universidad Autónoma Metropolitana-Xochimilco, 1980.

Reyes López, Alberto. *Las doctrinas socialistas de Ricardo Flores Magón*. D.F., México: XLIX Legislatura de la Cámara de Diputados del H. Congreso de la Unión, 1974.

Romero Cervantes, Arturo. "Flores Magón: Videncia, Ira y Temura de la revolución." *Boletín Bibliográfico de la Secretariado Hacienda y Crédito Publico*, Ano 9, Época Segunda, no. 281 (15 Octubre 1963): 12-14.

———. "Madero Frente a Flores Magón" *Boletín Bibliográfico de la Secretaria de Hacienda y Crédito Publico*, Ano 10, Época Segunda, no. 284 (1 Diciembre 1963): 4-6.

Romero R., Jorge, Clara Mandujano Hidalgo, y Armando Ruiz Aguilar. *Colección revolución*. D.F., México: Dirección del Archivo Histórico Central, Archivo General de la Nación, 1985.

Salazar, Rosendo. *Ricardo Flores Magón: (El Adalid)*. México: Costa-Amic, 1963.

Sánchez de Anda, Guillermo. *Notas sobre el pensamiento político de Ricardo Flores Magón*. México: UNAM, 1960.

Sierra Partida, Alfonso. *Perfiles de grandeza en la historia de México: Miguel Hidalgo y Costilla, Ignacio Manuel Altamirano, Benito Juárez, Ricardo Flores Magón, Felipe Carrillo Puerto*. México: Delegación Benito Juárez del Departamento del Distrito Federal, 1978.

Sierra Partida, Alfonso. *Tres grandes calumniados*. México: Editorial del Magisterio, 1973.

Topete Lara, Hilario. *Ideas en movimiento*. D.F., México: Sociedad Cooperativa de Producción "Taller Abierto," 1998.

Turner, Ethel Duffy. *Ricardo Flores Magón y el Partido Liberal Mexicano*. México: Instituto Nacional de Estudios Históricos de la Revolución Mexicana, 2003.

Valadés, José C. "El hombre que desrumbó un régimen: Ricardo Flores Magón." Todo, 5 Marzo-6 Augusto 1942.

———. *El joven Ricardo Flores Magón*. México: Editorial Extemporáneos, 1986.

Varios Autores. *Por la libertad de Ricardo Flores Magón y compañeros presos en Estados Unidos del Norte*. D.F., México: Grupo Cultural "Ricardo Flores Magón", 1922.

Villanueva, Margos de. *El gran mártir Ricardo Flores Magón*. México: Instituto de Educación Obrera, 1977.

Yankelevich, Pablo. "Los Magonistas en La Protesta: Lecturas Rioplatenses Del Anarquismo En Mexico, 1906-1929." *Estudios de Historia Moderna y Contemporanea de Mexico* 19 (1999).

BY AND ABOUT LIBERAL PARTY AND PLM
CANANEA AND RIO BLANCO
ENGLISH:

Bernstein, Marvin D. *The Mexican Mining Industry 1890-1950: A Study of the Interaction of Politics, Economics, and Technology*. Albany: SUNY, 1965.

Brayer, Herbert O. "The Cananea Incident." New Mexico Historical Review 13 (Oct. 1938): 387-415.

Mignone, A. Frederick. "A Fief for Mexico: Colonel Greene's Empire Ends." *Southwest Review* 44 (Autumn 1959): 332-339.

Pletcher, David M. *Rails, Mines, and Progress: Seven American Promoters in Mexico, 1867-1911*. Ithaca, N.Y.: Cornell University Press, 1958.

Sonnichsen, C. L. *Colonel Green and the Copper Skyrocket*. Tucson: Arizona Historical Society, 1974.

SPANISH:

Aguirre, Manuel J. *Cananea: Garras del imperialismo en las entrañas de México*. D.F., México: Libro-Mex, 1958.

Calderón, Esteban B. *Juicio sobre la guerra del Yaqui y génesis de la huelga de Cananea*. D.F., México: Ediciones del Sindicato Mexicano de Electricistas, 1956.

Díaz Cárdenas, León. *Cananea, primer brote del sindicalismo en México*. D.F, México: Departamento de Bibliotecas de la Secretaria de Educación Publica, 1936.

González Navarro, Moisés. "La huelga de Río Blanco." *Historia Mexicana* 6, no. 4 (Abril-Junio 1957): 510-533.

González Ramírez, Manuel, ed. *La huelga de Cananea*. Vol. 3, Fuentes para la historia de la Revolución Mexicana. México: Fondo de Cultura Económica, 1956.

Hernández, Salvador. *Magonismo y Movimiento Obrero en México: Cananea y Rió Blanco*. D.F., México: UNAM, 1977.

List Arzubide, Germán y Armando List Arzubide. *La huelga de Río Blanco*. México: Departamento de Bibliotecas de la Secretaría de Educación Pública, 1935.

BAJA CALIFORNIA
ENGLISH:

Blaisdell, Lowell L. *The Desert Revolution: Baja California, 1911*. Madison: University of Wisconsin Press, 1962.

————. "Harry Chandler and Mexican Border Intrigue, 1914-1917." *Pacific Historical Review* 35, no. 4 (November 1966): 385-393.

————. "Rhys Price, the Reluctant Filibuster." *The Southwestern Social Science Quarterly* 38, no. 2 (September 1957): 148-161.

————. "The Consul in Crisis: Lower California, 1911." *Mid-America* 37, no. 3 (July 1955): 131-139.

————. "Was it Revolution or Filibustering? The Mystery of the Flores Magón Revolt in Baja California." *The Pacific Historical Review* 3, no. 2 (May 1954): 147-164.

Gerhard, Peter. *The Socialist Invasion of Baja California, 1911*. Berkeley: University of California Press, 1946.

Kyne, Peter B. "The Gringo as Insurecto." *Sunset Magazine* 27 (September 1911): 257-267.

McCormick, A. I. *Letter: Los Angeles, May 20, 1911*. Bloomington, IN: Indiana University, 1956, 1911.

Owen, Roger C. *Indians and revolution: the 1911 invasion of Baja California, Mexico*. Bloomington: Indiana University Press, 1963.

Turner, Ethel Duffy. *Revolution in Baja California: Ricardo Flores Magón's High Noon*. Edited and annotated by Rey Devis. Detroit, Michigan: Blaine Ethridge, 1981.

SPANISH:

Aldrete, Enrique. *Baja California heroica*. D.F., México: Frumentum, 1958.

Anónimos, "Gloriosa defensa de Baja California." *El Imparcial* (Tijuana), 22 Junio 1952.

Blaisdell, Lowell L. *Doce escritores y un tema, la Revolución Mexicana*. D.F., México: Secretaría del Trabajo y Previsión Social, Subsecretaría "B," Coordinación General de Políticas, Estudios y Estadísticas del Trabajo, 1991.

————. *Simposio de Historia : días 12-13 Junio 1992*. Mexicali, Baja California: El Instituto, 1992.

Cantu Jiménez, Esteban. *Apuntes Históricos de Baja California Norte*. D.F., México: n.p., 1957.

Cue Cánovas, Agustín. *Ricardo Flores Magón: la Baja California y los Estados Unidos*. México: Libro Mex, 1957.

Dueñas Montes, Francisco. *Datos para la historia de Baja California: el asalto a Mexicali en 1911.* Mexicali, Baja California: Talleres Gráfica de la Editorial del Magisterio, 1978.

———. *Los acontecimientos de 1911 en el Distrito Norte de la Baja California.* Mexicali, México: Instituto Regional de Investigaciones Históricas de Baja California, 1984.

Gilí, Mario, "Turner, Flores Magón y los filibusteros." *Historia Mexicana* 5, no. 4 (Abril–Junio 1956): 642–663.

González Monroy, Jesús. *Ricardo Flores Magón y su actitud en la Baja California.* México: Editorial Academia Literaria, 1962.

Martinez, Pablo L. *El magonismo en Baja California (documentos).* México: Ed. Baja California, 1958.

———. *Sobre el libro "Baja California Heroica" (contra la defensa da una falsedad histórica).* México: Ed. Baja California, 1960.

Medina Amore, Guillermo. *No fue filibusterismo la revolución magonista en la Baja California.* Mexicali, Baja California: n.p., 1956.

Melo de Remes, María Luisa. *¡Alerta Baja California!* D.F., México: Editorial Jus, 1964.

Taylor, Lawrence Douglas. *La campaña magonista de 1911 en Baja California: el apogeo de la lucha revolucionaria del Partido Liberal Mexicano.* Tijuana, Baja California: El Colegio de la Frontera Norte, 1992.

Valadés, José. *Apuntes sobre la expedición de Baja California.* D.F., México: Confederación Revolucionaria de Obreros y Campesinos, 1956.

Velasco Ceballos, Rómulo. *¿Se apoderará Estados Unidos de América de Baja California? (la invasión filibustero de 1911).* D.F., México: Imprenta Nacional, 1920.

PRÁXEDIS GUERRERO
ENGLISH:

Albro, Ward. *To Die on Your Feet: The Life, Times, and Writings of Práxedis G. Guerrero.* Fort Worth: Texas Christian University Press, 1996.

SPANISH:

Barreiro Tablada. *Práxedis G. Guerrero. Un fragmento de la Revolución.* Córdoba, México: Ediciones Norte, 1928.

Guerrero, Práxedis G. *Artículos literarios y de combate: Pensamientos, crónicas revoluciona-rias, etc.* Mexico: Grupo Cultural "Ricardo Flores Magón", 1924.

Martínez Núñez Eugenio. *La Vida Heroica de Práxedis G. Guerrero; apuntes históricos del movimiento social mexicano desde 1900 hasta 1910*. D.F., México: Biblioteca del Instituto Nacional de Estudios Históricos de la Revolución Mexicana, 1960.

ENRIQUE FLORES MAGÓN

Flores Magón, Enrique. "El Partido Liberal, acción e ideología." *El Nacional*, January 1954.

———. "Añoranzas." *El Nacional*, 3 Febrero–30 Abril 1945.

———. "Apuntes históricos para mis memorias." *Todo*, 2 Abril, 28 May, 18 Junio, 16 Julio, 13 Augusto, 20 Augusto, y 26 Noviembre 1953.

———. *En pos de la libertad*. D.F., México: Ediciones Antorcha, 1989.

———. *Frente al enemigo*. D.F., México: Ediciones Antorcha, 1987.

———. "La vida de los Flores Magón." *Todo*, 2 January–19 Junio 1934.

———. "Los genuinos precursores." *Todo*, 22 Noviembre 1945.

———. "Notas breves de un viejo revolucionario en defensa del Partido Liberal Mexicano, iniciador de la Revolución Social Mexicana." *Gráfico*, 11–24 Enero 1931.

———. "Vida y hechos de los hermanos Flores Magón." *El Nacional*, 7 January –22 Abril 1945.

Kaplan, Samuel. *Combatimos la tiranía*. D.F., México: Biblioteca del Instituto de Estudios Históricos de la Revolución Mexicana, 1958.

———. *Peleamos contra la injusticia: Enrique Flores Magón, precursor de la Revolución, cuenta su historia a Samuel Kaplan*. 2 vols. D.F., México: Libro-Mex., 1960.

OTHER MEMBERS OF THE JUNTA ORGANIZADORA DEL PARTIDO LIBERAL MEXICANO
ENGLISH:

Albro, Ward S. "A Borderlands Revolutionary: Antonio I. Villarreal and 30 Years of Revolution in Mexico, 1904–1934." *The Borderlands Journal* 10, no. 1 (Fall 1986): 51–102.

Sarabia, Manuel. "How I Was Kidnapped." *The Border*, December 1908.

———. *Case of the Mexican Prisoners*, (late 1908?).

SPANISH:

Albro, Ward S. "El secuestro de Manuel Sarabia." *Historia Mexicana* 18 (January –Marzo 1969): 400–407.

Flores Magón, Jesús, "El amparo de Juan Sarabia." *El Tiempo*, 27 May 1911.

Lozano, Fortunato. *Antonio I. Villareal: vida de un gran mexicano*. Monterrey, Nuevo León: Impresora Monterrey, 1959.

Martínez Baez, Antonio. "Sarabia en San Juan de Ulúa." *Historia Mexicana* 10, no. 2 (Oct.-Dec. 1960): 342-360.

Martínez Núñez, Eugenio. *Juan Sarabia, apóstol y mártir de la Revolución Mexicana*. D.F., México: Biblioteca del Instituto Nacional de Estudios Históricos de la Revolución Mexicana, 1965.

Monjaras, Victor A. "Librado Rivera." *El Nacional*, 11 Marzo 1932.

Perez Salazar, Alicia. *Librado Rivera, un sonador en llamas*. México: Edición de los Amigos, 1964.

Rivera, Librado, "La mano férrea de la dictadura y el Congreso Liberal de San Luís." *Gráfico*, 12-14 Diciembre 1930.

———. *¡Viva Tierra y Libertad!* D.F., México: Ediciones Antorcha, 1980.

Sánchez Azcona, Gloria. *El General Antonio I. Viíllareal. Civilista de la Revolución Mexicana*. México: Biblioteca del Instituto Nacional de Estudios Históricos de la Revolución Mexicana, 1980.

Sarabia, Juan. *Defensa del C. Juan Sarabia*. (Folleto). San Antonio, Texas, 1907.

Valades, José C. "Treinta anos de vida política: Memorias del General Antonio I. Villarreal." *La Opinión* (Los Ángeles), November 1935-Abril 1936.

OTHER MEMBERS OF THE LIBERAL PARTY AND THE PLM

ENGLISH:

De Vore, Blanche B. "The influence of Antonio Díaz Soto y Gama on the agrarian movement in México." Ph.D. diss., University of Southern California, 1963

Gutierrez de Lara, L., and Edgcomb Pinchon. *The Mexican People: Their Struggle for Freedom*. Garden City: Doubleday, Page & Co., 1914.

SPANISH:

Batalla, Diódoro. *Diódoro Batalla: Huella de su pasión y de su esfuerzo*. México: s.n., 1957.

Blas Lara, C. *La vida que yo viví, novela histórica liberal de la Revolución mexicana*. n.p., 1954.

Flores Magón, Jesús. "Qué fue y cómo se desarrolló la Revolución que encabezó Flores Magón." *Gráfico*, 22 Noviembre 1930.

Leyva, José María. *Aportaciones a la historia de la Revolución*. D.F., México: n.p., 1938.

López Alanís, Gilberto. *Nicolás T. Bernal, amistad y compromiso revolucionario*. Culiacán, México: Dirección de Investigación y Fomento de Cultura Regional, 1998.

Martínez Núñez, Eugenio. *Los Mártires de San Juan de Ulúa*. D.F., México: IN-EHRM, 1968.

———. "Precursores de la Revolución: Antonio Díaz Soto y Gama." *Boletín Bibliográfico de la Secretaría de Hacienda y Crédito Público*, 20 Noviembre 1964.

Mata, Luis I. *Filomena Mata, su vida y su labor.* México: Secretaria de Educación Publica, Biblioteca Enciclopédica Popular, No. 62, 1945.

Morales Jiménez, Alberto, "Hombres de México: Jesús M. Rangel." *El Nacional*, 24 Noviembre 1941.

Ramírez Arriaga, Manuel. "Camilo Arriaga," speech of Nov. 20, 1949. Reprinted in *Repertorio de la Revolución*, No. 4. (1960), México: Ediciones del Patronato de la Historia de Sonora, pp. 5-28.

REGIONAL STUDIES
ENGLISH:

Aguilar Camin, Hector. "The relevant tradition: Sonoran leaders in the revolution." In *Caudillo and Peasant in the Mexican Revolution*, ed. D. A. Brading. Cambridge: Cambridge University Press, 1980.

Axelrod, Bernard. "St. Louis and the Mexican revolutionaries 1905-1906." *Missouri Historical Society Bulletin* 28 (January 1972): 94-108.

Benjamin, Thomas and William McNellie, eds. *Other Mexicos: Essays on Regional Mexican History, 1876-1911*. Albuquerque: University of New Mexico Press, 1984.

Brophy, Blake A. *Foundlings on the Frontier: Racial and Religious Conflict in Arizona Territory, 1904-1905.* Tucson: University of Arizona Press, 1972.

Cumberland Charles, C. "Mexican Revolutionary Movements from Texas" *South Western Historical Quarterly* 52 (1949): 301-324.

———. "Border Raids in the Lower Rio Grande Valley—1915." *Southern Historical Quarterly*, January 1954, 285-311.

Garcia, Mario T. *Desert Immigrants: The Mexicans of El Paso, 1880-1920*. New Haven: Yale University Press, 1981.

Hansen, Niles. *The Border Economy: Regional Development in the Southwest*. Austin: University of Texas Press, 1981.

Harris, Charles H., and Louis R. Sadler. *The Border and the Revolution*. Las Cruces: New Mexico State University, 1988.

Henderson, Peter V. N. *Mexican Exiles in the Borderlands, 1910-1913*. Southwestern Studies, Monograph #58. El Paso: The University of Texas at El Paso, 1979.

Hu-De Hart, Evelyn. "Sonora: Indians and Immigrants on a Developing Frontier" In *Other Mexicos: Essays on Regional Mexican History, 1876-1911*, ed. Thomas Benjamin and William McNellie. Albuquerque: University of New Mexico Press, 1984.

Hunt, Rockwell D. *California and Californians*. 3 vols. New York: Lewis Publishing, 1926.

Johnson, Benjamin Heber. "Sedition and citizenship in South Texas, 1900-1930." Ph.D. diss., Yale University, 2001.

Meyers, William K. "La Comarca Lagunera: Work, Protest, and Popular Mobilization in North Central Mexico." In *Other Mexicos: Essays on Regional Mexican History, 1876-1911*, ed. Thomas Benjamin and William McNellie. Albuquerque: University of New Mexico Press, 1984.

Smith, Cornelius C., Jr. *Emilia Kosterlitzky: Eagle of Sonora and the Southwest Border*. Glendale, CA: A. H. Clark, 1970.

Wasserman, Mark. "The Social Origins of the 1910 Revolution in Chihuahua." *Latin American Research Review* 15, no. 1 (1980): 15-38.

SPANISH:

Agetro, Leafar. *Las luchas proletarias en Veracruz, historia y autocrítica*. Jalapa, Veracruz: Editorial "Barricada," 1942.

Aguilar Camin, Hector. *La revolución sonorense*. México: Cuadernos de Trabajo del Departamento de Investigaciones Históricas, INAH, 1975.

Aliñada, Francisco K. *La Revolución en El Estado de Chihuahua*. Chihuahua: Biblioteca del Instituto Nacional de Estudios Históricos de la Revolución Mexicana, 1964.

Donato Padúa, Cándido. *Movimiento revolucionario 1906 en Veracruz*. Tlalpan, D. F., Mexico: s.n., 1941.

Padilla Ramos, Raquel. *Yucatán, fin del sueño yaqui*. México: Gobierno del Estado de Sonora, 1995.

Ortega Noriega, Sergio. *El edén subvertido. La colonización de Topolobampo*. México: SEP/INAH, 1978.

Rodarte, Fernando. *7 de enero de 1907: Puebla-Orizaba*. México: A. del Bosque, 1940.

Singawa Montoya, Herberto. *Sinaloa, Historia y Destino*. Ed. Cahita, 1986.

Torua Cienfuegos, Alfonso. *El Magónismo en Sonora (1906-1908): Historia de una persecución*. México: Universidad de Sonora, 2003.

THE "PRECURSOR" MOVEMENT
ENGLISH:

Cadenhead, Ivie E., Jr. And Charles C. Cumberland. "Precursors of the Mexican Revolution of 1910." *Hispanic American Historical Review* 22, no. 2 (May 1942): 344-356.

Cockcroft, James D. *Intellectual Precursors of the Mexican Revolution, 1900-1913*. Austin: University of Texas Press, 1968.

SPANISH:

Anaya Ibarra, Pedro María. *Precursores de la Revolución Mexicana*. D.F., México: Secretaría de Educación Pública, 1955.

Barrera Fuentes, Florencio. *Historia de la Revolución Mexicana, la etapa precursora*. D.F., México: Biblioteca del Instituto de Estudios Históricos de la Revolución Mexicana, 1955.

Fabela, Isidro, ed. *Precursores de la Revolución Mexicana*. Tomo 9, Documentos históricos de la revolución mexicana. D.F., México: Editorial Jus, 1966.

Ferrer Mediolea, Gabriel. "Precursores de la Revolución: la rebeldía liberal." *El Nacional*, 1, 10, 16, y 25 January 1951.

Hernández Luna, Juan. "Los precursores intelectuales de la Revolución Mexicana." *Filosofía y Letras*, no. 57-59.

Hernández Teodoro. *Los precursores de la Revolución.*, D.F., México: np., 1940.

Tovar y Bueno, W. "Los precursores de la Revolución." *La Prensa* (San Antonio, Tejas), 19 Septiembre-21 Octubre 1932.

Vega, Santiago R. de la. "Los precursores de la Revolución." *El Universal*, 20 Noviembre 1932.

OTHER RESOURCES ON THE PLM AND THE LIBERAL PARTY
ENGLISH:

Braderman, Eugene Maur. "A Study of Political Parties and Polities in Mexico since 1890." Ph.D. diss., University of Illinois, 1938.

Brown, Lyle C. *The Mexican liberals and their struggle against the Díaz dictatorship, 1900-1906.* D.F., México: Mexico City College Press, 1956.

Callcott, Wilfred Hardy. *Liberalism in Mexico, 1857-1928.* Palo Alto: Stanford University Press, 1931.

Cumberland, Charles C. "An Analysis of the Program of the Mexican Liberal Party, 1906." *The Americas* 4 (January 1948): 294-301.

Escobar, Edward J. "Mexican Revolutionaries and the Los Angeles Police: Harassment of the Partido Liberal Mexicano, 1907-1910." *Aztlan,* Spring 1986, 1-46.

Furlong, Thomas. *Fifty Years a Detective.* St. Louis, MO: C. E. Barnett, 1912.

Ireland, Robert E. "The Radical Community: Mexican and American Radicalism 1900-1910." *Journal of Mexican American History* 2 (1971): 22-32

Paz, Octavio. *The Labyrinth of Solitude.* Trans. Lysander Kemp. New York: Grove Press, 1961.

Raat, W. Dirk. *Revoltosos: Mexico's Rebels in the United States, 1903-1923.* College Station: Texas A&M University Press, 1981.

Sandos, James A. *Rebellion in the Borderlands: Anarchism and the Plan of San Diego.* Norman: University of Oklahoma Press, 1992.

SPANISH:

Antuñano Maurer, Alejandro de. *Antología del liberalismo social mexicano.* México: Cambio XXI Fundación Mexicana, 1993.

Barrera Bassols, Jacinto. "El espionaje en la frontera México Estados Unidos (1905-1911)". *Eslabones* (México) 2 (Julio-Diciembre 1991).

Bustamante Vigil, Ma. Rosa. *El partido liberal magonista y su influencia en el artículo 123 constitucional, cuna del nuevo derecho social.* Oaxaca, Oaxaca: Universidad Regional del Sureste, 1984.

Chávez Orozco, Luis. *La prehistoria del socialismo en México.* D.F., México: Secretaria de Educación Pública, 1936.

Cortes, Omar y Chantal López, ed. *El programa del Partido Liberal Mexicano de 1906 y sus antecedentes.* D.F., México: Ediciones Antorcha, 1985.

———. *El Partido Liberal Mexicano (1906-1908).* D.F., México: Ediciones Antorcha, 1986.

Escovedo Acevedo, Antonio, "Periódicos Socialistas de México, 1871-1880." *El Libro y el Pueblo* 13, no. 1 (January-Febrero 1935): 3-14.

Fuentes Díaz, Vicente. *Los Partidos Políticos en México.* México: Editorial Altiplano, 1969.

García Cantú, Gastón. *El socialismo en México, Siglo XIX.* México: Ediciones Era, 1969.

González Navarro, Moisés. "La ideología de la Revolución Mexicana." *Historia Mexicana* 10, no. 4 (Abril–Junio 1961): 628–636.

Hernández, Teodoro. *La historia de la Revolución debe hacerse*. México: n.p., 1950.

Hernández, Teodoro. *Las tinajas de Ulúa*. D.F., México: Editorial "Hermida," 1943.

Martínez Núñez, Eugenio. *La revolución en el estado de San Luis Potosí (1900-1917)*. México: Instituto Nacional de Estudios Histórica de Revolución Mexicana, 1964.

Reyes Heroles, Jesús. *El liberalismo mexicano*, 3 vols. D.F., México: Facultad de Derecho, UNAM, 1957–1961.

Sariego, Juan Luis. "Anarquismo e historia social minera en el norte de México, 1906–1918." *Historias* 8-9 (Enero–Junio 1985): 111–123

Silva Herzog, Jesús. *Trayectoria ideológica de la revolución mexicana, 1910-1917; Del manifestó del Partido Liberal de 1906 a la Constitución de 1917*. México: Cuadernos Americanos, 1963.

Vasquez Carrillo, J. Eduardo. *El Partido Liberal Mexicano, Ensayo Socio-jurídico*. D.F., México: Costa-Amic, 1970.

MEXICAN REVOLUTION IMPORTANT FIGURES

PORFIRIO DIAZ
ENGLISH

Beals, Carleton. *Porfirio Diaz, Dictator of Mexico*. Philadelphia: J. B. Lippincott Company, 1932.

Fornaro, Carlo de. *Diaz, Czar of Mexico*. Philadelphia: The International Publishing Co., 1909.

Godoy, Jose F. *Porfirio Diaz, President of Mexico; the Master Builder of a Great Commonwealth*. New York: G. P. Putnam's Sons, 1910.

Hannay, David. Diaz. In *Makers of the Nineteenth Century*, ed. Basil Williams. New York: Henry Holt and Company, 1917.

Langston, William Stanley. "Coahuila in the Porfiriato, 1893–1911: A Study of Political Elites." Ph.D. diss., Tulane University, 1980.

Relyea, Pauline S. *Diplomatic Relations Between the United States and Mexico under Porfirio Diaz, 1876-1910*. Northampton, MA: Smith College Studies in History, 1924.

Tweedie (Mrs.), Alec (Ethel Brilliana). *The Maker of Modern Mexico: Porfirio Díaz*. New York: John Lane Company, 1906.

SPANISH

Bulnes, Francisco. *El verdadero Díaz y la revolución*. México: Editora Nacional Edinal, 1960.

Cosío Villegas, Daniel, "El norte de Porfirio Díaz." *Anuario de Historia* 1 (1961): 13–57.

Fernández Rojas, José, Luis Melgarejo Randolf, y Antonio Damaso Melgarejo Randolph. *La Revolución Mexicana de Porfirio Díaz a Victoriano Huerta, 1910–1913*. México: F.P. Rojas, 1913

Garcia Naranjo, Nemesio. *Porfirio Díaz*. San Antonio, Texas: Casa Editorial Lozano, 1930.

López-Portilla y Rojas, José. *Elevación y caída de Porfirio Díaz*. México: Librería Española, n.d.

Reyes, Bernardo. *El General Porfirio Díaz*. México: Editora Nacional Edinal, 1960.

Zayas Enríquez, Rafael de. *Porfirio Díaz: la evolución de su vida*. New York: D. Appleton & Co., 1908.

FRANCISCO I. MADERO

ENGLISH:

Cumberland, Charles C. *Mexican Revolution: Genesis Under Madero*. Austin: University of Texas Press, 1952.

La France, David G. *The Mexican Revolution in Puebla, 1908-1913: The Maderista Movement and the Failure of Liberal Reform*. Wilmington, Del: SR Books, 1989.

Ross, Stanley R. *Francisco I. Madero, Apostle of Mexican Democracy*. New York: Columbia University Press, 1955.

SPANISH:

Aguirre Benavides, Adrian. *Madero, El inmaculado; Historia de la revolución de 1910*. 2nd ed. México: Editorial Diana, 1962.

Amaya, Juan Gualberto. *Madero y los auténticos revolucionarios de 1910*. México: n. p., 1946.

Cortés, Omar y Chantal López, ed. *Madero y los partidos Antirreeleccionista y Constitucional Progresista*. D.F., México: Ediciones Antorcha, 1988.

List Arzubide, Germán. *El México de 1910—El Maderismo*. 2nd ed. México: Ediciones Conferencia, 1963.

Madero, Francisco I. *Archivo de Francisco I. Madero. Epistolario (1906-1909)*. México: Secretaría de Hacienda, 1963.

———. *La sucesión presidencial en 1910*. México: Ediciones "Los Insurgentes," 1960.

Taracena, Alfonso. *Madero: Vida del hombre y del político*. México: Ediciones Botas, 1937.

Valades, José C. *Imaginación y realidad de Francisco I. Madero*. 2 vols. México: Antigua Librería Robredo, 1960

———. "Los precursores de D. Francisco I. Madero," *La Opinión* (Los Ángeles), 13 December 1929-24 January 1930.

EMILIANO ZAPATA
ENGLISH:

Millón, Robert P. *Zapata: The ideology of a peasant revolutionary*. London: Central Books, 1969.

Womack, Jr., John. *Zapata and the Mexican Revolution*. New York: Alfred A. Knopf, 1969.

SPANISH:

Magaña, Gildardo. *Emiliano Zapata y el Agrarismo en México*, 5 vols. D.F., México: Editorial Ruta, 1951.

Martinez Escamilla, Ramon. *Emiliano Zapata: Escritos y Documentos*. México: Editores Mexicanos Unidos, 1980.

Zapata, Emiliano. *Cartas*. D.F., México: Ediciones Antorcha, 1987.

———. *Leyes y decretos*. D.F., México: Ediciones Antorcha, 1987.

———. *Manifiestos*. D.F., México: Ediciones Antorcha, 1986.

OTHER IMPORTANT FIGURES
ENGLISH:

Bryan, Anthony T. "Mexican Politics in Transition, 1900-1913: The Role of General Bernardo Reyes." Ph.D. diss., University of Nebraska, 1970.

Hall, Linda B. *Alvaro Obregon: Power and Revolution in Mexico, 1911-1920*. College Station: Texas A&M, 1981.

Ignasias, Charles Dennis. "Reluctant Recognition: The United States and the Recognition of Alvaro Obregon of Mexico, 1920-1924." Ph.D. diss., Michigan State University, 1967.

Meyer, Michael C. *Mexican Rebel Pascual Orozco and the Mexican Revolution*. 1910-1915. Lincoln: University of Nebraska Press, 1967.

————. *Huerta:A Political Portrait*. Lincoln: University of Nebraska Press, 1972.

Niemeyer, Vic. "Frustrated Invasion: The Revolutionary Attempt of General Bernardo Reyes from San Antonio in 1911." *Southwestern Historical Quarterly* 47 (October 1963): 213-225.

Richmond, Douglas W. *Venustiano Carranza's Nationalist Struggle, 1893-1920*. Lincoln: University of Nebraska Press, 1983.

SPANISH:

Bassols Batalla, Narciso. *El Pensamiento Político de Alvaro Obregon*. México: Ediciones "El Caballito," 1976.

De la Huerta, Adolfo. *Memorias de don Adolfo de la Huerta, según su propio dictado*. Roberta Guzmán Esparza, ed. México: Ediciones "Guzmán," 1957.

María y Campos, Armando de.*Múgica*. D.F., México: Compañía de Ediciones Populares, 1939.

Zertuche Muñoz, Fernando. *Francisco J. Múgica*. D.F., México: Consejo Nacional de Recursos para la Atención de la Juventud/Terra Nova, 1987.

US-MEXICO RELATIONS

Anderson, William Woodrow. "The Nature of the Mexican Revolution as Viewed From the United States." Ph.D. diss.,The University of Texas at Austin, 1967.

Brandenburg, Broughton. "The War Peril on the Mexican Border." *Harper's Weekly* 50 (25 August 1906): 1198-1200, 1212.

Callahan, James Morion. *American Foreign Policy in Mexican Relations*. New York:The Macmillan Company, 1932.

Carson, W. E. *Mexico, the Wonderland of the South*. New York: The Macmillan Company, 1914.

Cardoso, Lawrence A. *Mexican Emigration to the United States 1897-1931: Socio-Economic Patterns*.Tucson: University of Arizona Press, 1980.

Chamberlain, Eugene K. "Mexican Colonization versus American Interests in Lower California." *Pacific Historical Review* 20 (February 1950): 43-55.

Cline, Howard F. *The United States and Mexico*. 2nd ed., rev. Cambridge: Harvard University Press, 1961.

Conley, Edward M. "The Anti-Foreign Uprising in Mexico." *The World To-Day* 11 (October 1906): 1059-1062.

Estrada, Leobardo F., et al."Chicanos in the United States:A History of Exploitation and Resistance." *Daedalus*, Spring 1981, 103-131.

Fogel, Walter. *Mexican Illegal Alien Workers in the United States*. Los Angeles: University of California, 1978.

Gilderhus, Mark T. *Diplomacy and Revolution: U.S. Mexican Relations Under Wilson and Carranza.*Tucson: University of Arizona Press, 1977.

Gómez Quiñones, Juan. "Piedras contra la Luna, México en Aztlan y Aztlan en México: Chicano-Mexican Relations and the Mexican Consulates, 1900-1920." In *Contemporary Mexico.* IV International Congress of Mexican History, 17-21 Oct. 1973, ed. James W. Wilkie, Michael C. Meyer, and Edna Monzon de Wilkie. Los Angeles: UCLA Latin American Center, 1976.

———. "Plan de San Diego Reviewed." *Azatlan*, Spring 1970.

Grayson, George W. *The United States and Mexico: Patterns of Influence.* New York: Praeger, 1984.

Gregg, Robert D. *The Influence of Border Troubles on Relations Between the United States and México, 1876-1910.* Baltimore: John Hopkins Press, 1937.

Haley, Edward P. *Revolution and Intervention: The Diplomacy of Taft and Wilson with Mexico, 1910-1917.* Cambridge, Mass: M.I.T. Press, 1973.

Harris, Charles H., and Louis R. Sadler. "The Plan of San Diego and the Mexican-United States War Crisis of 1916: A Reexamination." *Hispanic American Historical Review,* August 1978, 381-408.

James, Daniel. *Mexico and the Americans.* New York: Frederick A. Praeger, 1963.

Kerig, Dorothy Pierson. *Luther T. Ellsworth, U.S. Consul on the Border During the Mexican Revolution.* El Paso: Texas Western Press, 1975.

Loma, Clara. "Transborder Discourse: The Articulation of Gender in the Borderlands in the Early Twentieth Century." *Frontiers* 24, no. 2, 3 (2003): 51-74.

Parlee, Lorena M. "The Impact of United States Railroad Unions on Organized Labor and Government Policy in Mexico (1880-1911)." *Hispanic American Historical Review,* August 1984, 443-475.

Raat, W. Dirk. "The Diplomacy of Suppression; Los Revoltosos, Mexico and the United States, 1906-1911." *Hispanic American Historical Review*, November 1976, 529-550.

Rathbun, Cari M. "Keeping the Peace Along the Mexican Border." *Harper's Weekly* 50 (November 17, 1906): 1632-1634, 1649.

Sandos, James A. "The Plan of San Diego: War and Diplomacy on the Texas Border." *Arizona and the West*, Spring 1972, 5-24.

Schmitt, Karl M. *Mexico and the United States, 1821-1973; Conflict and Coexistence.* New York: John Wiley & Sons, 1974.

Servin, Manuel P. "The Pre-World War II Mexican American." *California Historical Society Quarterly*, December 1966, 325-338.

———. *The Mexican Americans: An Awakening Minority*. Beverly Hills, CA: Glencoe Press, 1970.

Wilson McEven, William. "A Survey of the Mexicans in Los Angeles." M.A. thesis, University of Southern California, 1914.

SPANISH:

Rojas, Luis Manuel. *La culpa de Henry Lane Wilson en el gran desastre de México*, vol. 1. D.F., México: Compania Editora "La Verdad," S. A., 1928.

GENERAL MEXICAN REVOLUTION
ENGLISH:

Baerlein, Henry P. B. *Mexico, the Land of Unrest*. Philadelphia: J. B. Lippincott Co., 1913.

Beezley, William H. *Insurgent Governor: Abraham Gonzalez and the Mexican Revolution in Chihuahua*. Lincoln: University of Nebraska Press, 1973.

Blasco Ibanez, Vicente. *Mexico in Revolution*. New York: E.P. Dutton & Co., 1920.

Cumberland, Charles C. *The Mexican Revolution: The Constitutionalist Years*. Austin: University of Texas Press, 1972.

DeVore, Blanche B. *Land and Liberty A History of the Mexican Revolution*. New York: Pageant Press, 1966.

Dulles, John W. F. *Yesterday in Mexico: A Chronicle of the Revolution, 1919-1936*. Austin: University of Texas Press, 1961.

Gaitan, Teodoro M. *The Mexican Revolution 1906-1914, Its Progress, Causes, Purpose and Probable Results*. Vancouver B.C: Mexican Workers Association, 1914.

Galeano, Eduardo. *Century of the Wind*, Part III of Memory of Fire. Trans. Cedric Belfrage. New York: Pantheon Books, 1988.

Hanrahan, Gene Z., ed. *Documents on the Mexican Revolution*. Vols. I-IX. Chapel Hill, North Carolina: Documentary Publications, 1976-1985.

Hart, John M. *Revolutionary Mexico: The Coming and Process of the Mexican Revolution*. Berkeley: University of California Press, 1987.

Hodges, D. C. *Mexican Anarchism after the Revolution*. Austin: University of Texas, 1995.

Knight, Alan. *The Mexican Revolution*. 2 vols. London: Cambridge University Press, 1986.

Niemeyer, Jr., E. V. *Revolution at Queretaro: The Mexican Constitutional Convention of 1916-1917*. Austin: University of Texas Press, 1974.

Quirk, Robert E. *The Mexican Revolution 1914-1915 : The convention of Aguas-calientes*. New York: Citadel Press, 1963.

Reed, John. *Insurgent Mexico*. New York: D. Appleton & Co, 1914. Reprinted Berlin: Seven Seas Publishers, 1974.

Ruiz, Ramon Eduardo. *The Great Rebellion, Mexico 1905-1924*. New York: W. W. Norton & Company, 1980.

Shipman, Margaret. *Mexico's Struggle Towards Democracy. The Mexican Revolution of 1857 and 1910*. Lee, Massachusetts: Margaret Shipman, 1926.

Traven, B. The Jungle Novels [*The Carreta, Government, March to the Monteria, Trozas, The Rebellion of the Hanged, The General from the Jungle*.] Chicago: Ivan R. Dee, 1993-4.

SPANISH:

Abad De Santillan, Diego. *Historia de la Revolución Mexicana*. D.F, México: Frente de Afirmación Hispánica A.C., 1992.

Alperovich, M. S. y B. T. Rudenko. *La revolución mexicana de 1910-1917 y la política de los Estados Unidos*. D.F., México: Fondo de Cultura Popular, 1960.

Arenas Guzmán, Diego. *El periodismo en la Revolución Mexicana (de 1876 a 1908)*. D.F., México: Biblioteca del Instituto Nacional de Estudios Históricos de la Revolución Mexicana, 1966.

Beteta, Ramon. *Pensamiento y dinámica de la revolución mexicana; antología de documentos politicosociales*. 2nd ed. D.F., México: Editorial México Nuevo, 1951.

Bremauntz, Alberto. *Panorama social de las revoluciones en México*. D.F., México: Ediciones Jurídico Sociales, 1960.

Casasola, Gustavo. *Historia gráfica de la revolución, 1900-1960*. Vol. 1. México: Editorial F. Trillas, 1962.

Castaneda Batres, Oscar. *La Revolución Mexicana, Un Ensayo Crítico*. México: Ed. Porrúa, 1989.

Cue Cánovas, Agustín. "El Aspecto Social de la Revolución Mexicana." Combate, 11 Noviembre 1960, 21-26.

Fabela, Isidro. *Mis Memorias de la Revolución*. México: Editores Jus, 1977.

Ferrer de Mendiolea, Gabriel. *Historia de la Revolución Mexicana*. México: Ediciones de El Nacional, 1956.

González Ramírez, Manuel. *La Revolución Social de México*, 3 vols. D.F., México: Fondo de Cultura Económica, 1960.

Iparrea Salaia, Abelardo. *Mensajero de la Revolución*. México: Secretaria de Educación Publica, Instituto Politécnico Nacional, 1982.

List Arzubide, Armando. *Apuntes sobre la prehistoria de la Revolución*. D.F., México: n.p., 1958.

Mancisidor, José. *Historia de la Revolución Mexicana*. México: Ed. Libro Mex, 1964.

Miranda Uriostegui, Píndaro. *Testimonios del Proceso Revolucionario de México*. México: INEHRM, 1987.

Morales Jiménez, Alberto. *Historia de la revolución mexicana*. México: Instituto de Investigaciones Políticas, Económicas y Sociales del Partido Revolucionario Institucional, 1951.

Moreno, Daniel. *Los hombres de la revolución; 40 estudios biográficos*. México: Libro Mex Editores, 1960.

Naranjo, Francisco. *Diccionario biográfico revolucionario*. México: Imprenta Editorial "Cosmos," 1935.

Portes Gil, Emilio. *Autobiografía de la Revolución Mexicana*. México: Instituto Mexicano de Cultura, 1964.

Prida, Ramon. *¡De la dictadura a la anarquía!* México: Ediciones Botas, 1958.

Ramos, Roberto. *Bibliografía de la revolución mexicana*. 2nd ed., 3 vols. México: Biblioteca del Instituto Nacional, 1958–1960.

Romero Flores, Jesús. *Del porfirismo a la revolución constitucionalista. Vol. 1, Anales históricos de la revolución mexicana*. México: Libro Mex Editores, 1959.

Rudenko, B.T. *México en vísperas de la Revolución democrática-burguesa de 1910-1917*. D.F., México: Ediciones Arguial, 1958.

Silva Herzog, Jesús. *Breve historia de la Revolución Mexicana*. 2 vols. D.F., México: Fondo de Cultura Económica, 1960.

Silva, José D. *Fuente de información de la revolución mexicana*. México: Casa Ramírez Editores, 1957.

Taracena, Alfonso. *La verdadera revolución mexicana*. D.F., México; Costa-Amic, 1960.

———. *Mi vida en el vértigo de la Revolución*. México: Ediciones Botas, 1930.

Teja Zabre, Alfonso. *Panorama histórica de la revolución mexicana*. México: Ediciones Botas, 1939.

Ullóa Ortiz, Berta. *La revolución mexicana a través del Archivo de la Secretario da Relaciones Exteriores*. México: UNAM, 1963.

Valades, José C. *Historia general de la revolución mexicana. Vol. I*. México: Editores Mexicanos Unidos, 1976.

Zea, Leopoldo. *Del liberalismo a la Revolución en la educación mexicano*. D.F., México: Biblioteca del Instituto Nacional de Estudios Históricos de la Revolución Mexicana, 1956.

LABOR
ENGLISH

Anderson, Rodney D. *Outcasts in Their Own Land: Mexican Industrial Workers, 1906-1911*. DeKalb: Northern Illinois University Press, 1976.

Clark, Marjorie Ruth. *Organized Labor in Mexico*. Chapel Hill: The University of North Carolina Press, 1934.

Gomez Quinones, Juan. "The First Steps: Chicano Labor Conflict and Organizing, 1900-1920." *Azatlan*, Summer 1973, 31-36.

Hart, John M. *Anarchism and the Mexican Working Class, 1860-1931*. Austin: University of Texas Press, 1978.

Kiser, George C. "Mexican American Labor Before World War II." *Journal of Mexican American History*, Spring 1972, 122-137.

Levenstein, Harvey A. *Labor Organizations in the United States y México: A History of Their Relations*. Westport, Conn: Westport Publishing, 1971.

Schwartz, Harry. *Seasonal Farm Labor in the United States*. New York: Columbia University Press, 1945.

Snow, Sinclair. *The Pan-American Federation of Labor*. Durham: Duke University Press, 1964.

SPANISH:

Aparicio, Alfonso López. *El movimiento obrero en México: antecedentes, desarrollo y tendencias*. México: Editorial Jus, 1952.

Araiza, Luis. *Historia del movimiento obrero mexicano*. México: Casa del Obrero Mundial, 1975.

Carr, Barry. *El movimiento obrero y la político en México, 1910-1929*. 2 vols. México: Secretaria de Educación Publica, 1976.

Cerda Silva, Roberto de la. *El movimiento obrero en México*. D.F., México: UNAM, 1961.

Díaz Ramírez, Manuel. *Apuntes históricos del movimiento obrero y campesino de México, 1844-1880*. D.F., México: Fondo de Cultura Popular, 1938.

Frost, Elsa Cecelia, Michael C. Meyer, Josefina Zoraida Vasquez con la colaboración de Lilia Díaz. *El Trabajo y los Trabajadores en la Historia de México/Labor y Laborers through Mexican History.* V Reunión de Historiadores Mexicanos y

Norteamericanos Patzcuaro, 12–15 Oct 1977. México: El Colegio de México y University of Arizona Press, 1979.

Huitron, Jacinto. *Orígenes e Historia del Movimiento Obrero en México* D.F., México: Editores Mexicanos Unidos, 1974.

Ramos Pedrueza, Rafael. *La lucha de clases a través de la historia de México, revolución democrático burguesa.* 2 vols. D.F., México: Talleres Gráficos de la Nación, 1941.

Salazar, Rosendo. *La Casa del Obrero Mundial.* D.F., México: Costa-Amic, 1962.

Velasco, M.A. *Del magonismo a la fundacion de la CTM: apuntes de un militante del movimiento obrero.* D.F., Mexico: Ediciones de Cultura Popular, 1990.

AGRARIAN
ENGLISH:
Friedrich, Paul. *Agrarian Revolt in a Mexican Village.* New Jersey: Prentice-Hall, 1970.

Phipps, Helen. *Some Aspects of the Agrarian Revolution in Mexico, a Historical Study.* Austin: University of Texas, 1975.

Salamini, Heather Fowler. *Agrarian Radicalism in Veracruz, 1920–1938.* Lincoln: University of Nebraska Press, 1978.

Tannenbaum, Frank. *The Mexican Agrarian Revolution.* New York: The Macmillan Company, 1929.

SPANISH:
Azaola Garrido, Elena. *Rebelión y derrota del magonismo agrario.* D.F., México: Fondo de Cultura Económica, 1982.

Beas, Juan Carlos, Benjamín Maldonado Alvarado, y Manuel Ballesteros Gaibrois. *Magonismo y movimiento indígena en México.* Oaxaca: H. Ayuntamiento Constitucional de San Antonio Eloxochitlán, 1997

Escobedo, José G. y Rosendo Salazar. *Los valores morales e intelectuales y fallas de quienes promovieron la agremiación obrera y campesino de México-ya extintos-y actuaron en los últimos cincuenta años.* D.F., México: n.p., 1951.

Silva Herzog, Jesús. *El agrarismo mexicano y la reforma agraria; exposición y critica.* México: Fondo de Cultura Económica, 1959.

SOME POLITICAL INFLUENCES ON RICARDO FLORES MAGÓN
Archer, William. *The Life, Trial, and Death of Francisco Ferrer.* University Press of the Pacific, 2001.

Budberg, Maura, ed. *The Collected Short Stories of Maxim Gorky*. Secaucus, NJ: Citadel Trade, 1988.

Apter, Daniel E., and James Joll, eds. *Anarchism Today*. New York: Doubleday, 1972.

Bakunin, Mikhail. *God and the State*. New York: Dover, 1970.

———. *Statism and Anarchy*. Cambridge: Cambridge University Press, 1990.

Horowitz, Irving L., ed. *The Anarchists*. New York: Dell, 1963.

Joll, James. *The Anarchists*. Boston: Little, Brown and Company, 1964.

Kropotkin, Peter. *The Conquest of Bread*. New York: New York University Press, 1972.

———. *Fields, Factories, and Workshops*. London: Freedom Press, 1985.

Malatesta, Errico. *Anarchy*. London: Freedom Press, 1995.

Marx, Karl. *Economic and Philosophic Manuscripts of 1844*. Buffalo, NY: Prometheus Books, 1987.

Stirner, Max. *The Ego And Its Own*. Cambridge: Cambridge University Press, 1995.

Woodcock, George. *Anarchism: A History of Libertarian Ideas and Movements*. New York: The World Publishing Company, 1962.

Woodcock, George, and Ivan Avakuraovic. *The Anarchist Prince: A Biographical Study of Peter Kropotkin*. London: T. V. Boardman and Company, 1950.

BOOKS BY AND ABOUT MAGÓN'S SUPPORTERS IN THE US

LOS ANGELES SUPPORTERS

Dolsen, Ethel. "Mexican Revolutionist in the United States." *Miner's Magazine*, 11 June 1908, 6–10.

Mellon, Knox, Jr. "Job Harriman: The Early and Middle Years, 1861–1912." Ph.D. diss., Claremont Graduate School, 1972.

Murray, John. "San Juan de Ulua, the private prison of Diaz." *The Border*, February, 1909.

———. "The men Díaz dreads—Mexico's revolutionaries and their third uprising." *The Border*, January 1909, 1–6.

———. "Behind the Drum of Revolution, The Labor Movement in Mexico as seen by an American Trade Unionist." *The Survey*. XXXVII (2 December 1916): 237–244.

———. "Mexico's Peon-Slaves Preparing for Revolution." *The International Socialist Review* 9 (March 1909): 641–659.

Simison, Barbara V. "The Harry Weinberger Memorial Collection." *Yale University Library Gazette* 19 (January 1945): 50–52.

Trowbridge, Elizabeth Darling. *Mexico Today and Tomorrow.* New York: Macmillan, 1919.

———. "Under the Stars and Stripes." Tuscon, AZ: Elizabeth Trowbridge, 1908.

———. "Political Prisoners held in the United States." Tucson, AZ: Border Publishing Co., 1909

Turner, John Kenneth. "The Mexican Revolution." *Pacific Monthly* 25 (June 1911): 609–25.

———. "Anti-Jingoes Win an Epoch-Making Victory; Why Wilson Turns Back from Mexican War." *Appeal to Reason*, 22 July 1916, 1.

———. *Barbarous Mexico.* Chicago: Charles H. Kerr & Company, 1911. Reprinted with introduction by Sinclair Snow. Austin: University of Texas Press, 1969.

Weinberger, Harry. "Two Political Prisoners at Leavenworth." *New Republic* 31 (5 July 1922): 162.

ANARCHISM

Avrich, Paul. *An American Anarchist: The Life of Voltairine de Cleyre.* Princeton: Princeton University Press, 1978.

Berkman, Alexander. *What Is Communist Anarchism?* New York: Dover, 1972.

Cleyre, Voltairine de. "The Mexican Revolution." *Mother Earth*, December 1911, 301–306; January 1912, 335–341; February 1912, 374–380.

Drinnon, Richard. *Rebel in Paradise. A Biography of Emma Goldman.* Chicago: University of Chicago Press, 1961.

Falk, Candace. *Love, Anarchy, And Emma Goldman.* New Brunswick: Rutgers University Press, 1990.

Falk, Candace, Barry Pateman, and Jessica Moran. *Emma Goldman: A Documentary History of the American Years.* Berkeley: University of California Press, 2003.

Fine, Sidney. "Anarchism and the Assassination of McKinley." *American Historical Review*, July 1955.

Goldman, Emma. *Red Emma Speaks: An Emma Goldman Reader.* New York: Shocken Books, 1983.

———. *Anarchism and Other Essays.* New York: Dover, 1969.

Owen, William C. *The Mexican Revolution, Its Progress, Causes, Purpose and Probable Results.* Los Angeles: Regeneracion, 1912.

———. "Mexico and Socialism." *Mother Earth*, September 1911, 199–202.

———. "Mexico's Hour of Need." *Mother Earth*, June 1911, 105-107.

———. "The Death of Ricardo Flores Magón." Reprinted from *Freedom* (December 1922). *In Land and Liberty: Anarchist Influence in the Mexican Revolution-Ricardo Flores Magón*, ed. David Poole. London: Cienfuegos Press, 1977.

———. "Viva Mexico." *Mother Earth*, April 1911, 42-46.

Reichert, William O. *Partisans of Freedom: A Study in American Anarchism*. Bowling Green, Ohio: Bowling Green University Popular Press, 1976.

IWW

Brissenden, Paul F. *The Launching of the Industrial Workers of the World*. Berkeley: University of California Press, 1913.

———. *The I.W.W., A Study of American Syndicalism*. New York: Russell and Russell, 1957.

Brooks, John Graham. *American Syndicalism: the I.W.W.* New York: Macmillan, 1913.

Chaplin, Ralph. *Wobbly*. Chicago: University of Chicago, 1948.

Conlin, Joseph R. *Big Bill Haywood and the Radical Union Movement*. Syracuse: Syracuse University Press, 1969.

Dubofsky, Melvyn. *We Shall Be All: A History of the Industrial Workers of the World*. Urbana: University of Illinois, 1988.

Flynn, Elizabeth Gurley. *I Speak My Own Piece: Autobiography of the "Rebel Girl."* New York: Masses and Mainstream, 1955.

Foner, Philip S. *The Case of Joe Hill*. New York: International Publishers, 1965.

Foner, Philip S. *The Industrial Workers of the World, 1905-1917*. New York: International Publishers, 1965.

George, Harrison. *The IWW Trial: Story of the Greatest Trial in Labor's History by One of the Defendants*. New York: Arno Press, 1969.

Haywood, William D. *Bill Haywood's Book: The Autobiography of William D. Haywood*. New York: International Publishers, 1958.

Kornbluh, Joyce L. *Rebel Voices: An I.W.W. Anthology*. Ann Arbor: University of Michigan Press, 1969.

Renshaw, Patrick. *The Wobblies*. New York: Doubleday, 1967.

Smith, Gibbs M. *Labor Martyr Joe Hill*. New York: Gossett and Dunlap, 1969.

Taft, Philip. "A Note on 'General' Mosby." *Labor History* 13, no. 4 (Fall 1972).

———. "The Federal Trials of the IWW." *Labor History*, Winter 1962, 57-91.

Weintraub, Hyman. "The I.W.W. in California, 1905-1931." M.A. thesis, UCLA, 1947.

LABOR

"Letter from the Mexican Revolutionists Defense Committee." *Miners' Magazine* 9 (6 February 1908): 12.

"Los Angeles Labor Council." *Miners' Magazine* 9 (26 March 1908): 12-13.

Clark, Marjorie R. And S. Fanny Simon. *The Labor Movement in America.* New York: W. W. Norton and Company, 1938.

Dick, William H. Labor and Socialism in America: The Gompers Era. Port Washington, New York: Kennikat Press, 1972.

Daniel, Cletus E. *Bitter Harvest: A History of California Farm Workers, 1870-1941.* Ithaca: Cornell University Press, 1981.

Fetherling, Dale. *Mother Jones, the Miners' Angel: A Portrait.* Carbondale: Southern University Press, 1974.

Foner, Philip S. *History of the Labor Movement in the United States.* 5 vols. New York: International Publishers, 1947-1980.

Gómez-Quiñones, Juan. "The First Steps: Chicano Labor Conflict and Organizing, 1900-1920." *Aztlán* 3, no. 1 (Spring 1972.)

Gompers, Samuel. *Seventy Years of Life and Labor.* 2 vols. New York: E.P. Sutton and Company, 1925.

———. *The Mexican Extradition, Case for Alleged Breach of Neutrality Laws.* National Political Refugee Defense League, 1909.

———. "United States-Mexico Labor: Their Relations." *American Federationist,* August, 1916, 633–651.

———. *President Gompers Presents the Case of the Imprisoned Mexican Patriots to President Roosevelt.* Chicago, 1909.

Herrera-Sobek, Maria. *The Bracero Experience: Elite lore versus Folklore.* Los Angeles: UCLA, 1979.

Jenson, Vernon H. *Heritage of Conflict: Labor Relations in the Nonferrous Metals Industries up to 1930.* Ithaca: Cornell University Press, 1950.

Jones, Mary. *Autobiography of Mother Jones.* Chicago: Charles H. Kerr & Company, 1925.

Lingenfelter, Richard E. *The Hardrock Miners: A History of the Mining Labor Movement in the West, 1863-1893.* Berkeley: University of California, 1974.

Miller, Richard N. "American Railroad Unions and the National Railways of Mexico: An Exercise in Nineteenth-Century Proletarian Manifest Destiny." *Labor History,* Spring 1974, 239-260.

Radosh, Ronald. *American Labor and United States Foreign Policy*. New York: Random House, 1969.

Steel, Edward M., ed. *The Correspondence of Mother Jones*. Pittsburgh: University of Pittsburgh, 1985.

———. *The Speeches and Writings of Mother Jones*. Pittsburgh: University of Pittsburgh, 1988.

Stimson, Grace H. *The Rise of the Labor Movement in Los Angeles*. Berkeley: University of California Press, 1955.

SOCIALIST

Cadenhead, Ivie E., Jr. "The American Socialists and the Mexican Revolution of 1910." *The Southwestern Social Science Quarterly* 43, no. 2 (Sept. 1962): 103 -117.

Debs, Eugene V. "This plot must be foiled. Conspiracy to murder Mexican comrades now imprisoned in this country by order of Díaz." *Appeal to Reason*, 10 October 1908.

———. *Writings and Speeches of Eugene V. Debs*. New York: Hermitage Press, Inc., 1948.

———. *Walls and Bars*. New York: Socialist Press, 1973.

———. "You Will Reap the Whirlwind." *Appeal to Reason*, 6 November 1909, 4.

———. "The Crisis in México." *International Socialist Review* 12 (July 1911): 22-24.

Ginger, Ray. *Eugene V. Debs: A Biography*. New York: Collier Books, 1962.

Kipnis, Ira. *The American Socialist Movement, 1897–1912*. New York: Columbia University Press, 1952.

Shannon, David A. *The Socialist Party of America: A History*. New York: Macmillan, 1955.

GENERAL U.S. RADICALISM

Chafee, Zechariah, Jr. *Free Speech in the United States*. Cambridge: Harvard University Press, 1948.

Christopulos, Diana K. "American Radicals and the Mexican Revolution, 1900–1925." Ph.D. diss., SUNY Binghamton, 1980.

Coben, Stanley. *A. Mitchell Palmer: Politician*. New York: Columbia University Press, 1963.

————. "A Study in Nativism: The American Red Scare of 1919–1920." *Political Science Quarterly* 19 (March 1964).

Frankfurter, Marion Denman and Gardner Jackson, eds. *The Letters of Sacco and Vanzetti.* New York: Vanguard Press, 1930.

Frost, Richard H. *The Mooney Case.* Stanford: Stanford University Press, 1968.

Gartz, Kate Crane. *The Parlor Provocateur, or From Salon to Soapbox.* Pasadena, California: Mary Craig Sinclair, 1923.

Goldstein, Robert Justin. *Political Repression in Modern America from 1870 to the Present.* Cambridge: Harvard University Press, 1978.

Hyman, Harold M. *To Try Men's Souls: Loyalty Tests in American History.* Berkeley: University of California Press, 1960.

Jaife, Julian. *Crusade Against Radicalism: New York During the Red Scare, 1914–1924.* Port Washington, N.Y.: Kennikat Press, 1972.

Kennedy, David M. *Birth Control in America.* New Haven: Yale University Press, 1970.

————. *Over Here: The First World War and American Society.* New York: Oxford University Press, 1980.

Lawler, Oscar. "Oral History Interview." *Oral History Project.* Los Angeles: UCLA, 1962.

Luhan, Mabel Dodge. *Movers and Shakers.* Albuquerque: University of New Mexico Press, 1985.

Murray, Robert K. *The Red Scare: A Study in National Hysteria, 1919–1920.* Minneapolis: University of Minnesota Press, 1955.

Nicholas, William E. "World War I and Academic Dissent in Texas." *Arizona and the West,* Autumn 1972, 215–230.

Peterson, Horace C., and Gilbert C. Fate. *Opponents of War, 1917–1918.* Madison: University of Wisconsin Press, 1957.

Polenberg, Richard. *Fighting Faiths: The Abrams Case, The Supreme Court, and Free Speech.* New York: Viking, 1987.

Powers, Richard G. *Secrecy and Power: The Life of J. Edgar Hoover.* New York: Free Press, 1987.

Preston, William, Jr. *Aliens and Dissenters.* Urbana: University of Illinois Press, 1994.

Price, Lester K. *McNeil: History of a Federal Prison.* McNeil Island, Washington: Vocational Training Duplication Dept, 1972.

Stanford, Leland G. *Footprints of Justice in San Diego and Profiles of Senior Members of the Bench and Bar.* San Diego: San Diego County Law Library, 1960.

Steffens, Lincoln. *The Autobiography of Lincoln Steffens.* New York: Harcourt, Brace, and Co., 1931.

Stimson, Grace Heilman. *Rise of the Labor Movement in Los Angeles.* Berkeley: University of California Press, 1955.

NEWSPAPERS AND POPULAR MAGAZINES

Acción (D.F., Mexico), 1923.

American Federationist

Appeal to Reason

Appeal to Reason (Girard, Kansas), 1908.

The Arizona Daily Star (Tucson), 1906–1909.

The Arizona Republican (Phoenix), 1906–1909.

The Blast

The Border (Tucson, Arizona), 1908–1909.

The Citizen

El Colmillo Publico (México, D. F.), 1904–1906 .

El Correo Mexicano (Los Angeles, California), 1907.

La Crónica (Laredo, Texas), 1909–1911.

Debs Magazine

El Defensor del Pueblo (Tucson, Arizona), 1908.

El Demócrata (México, D. F.), September 1924.

El Demócrata Fronterizo (Laredo, Texas), 1904–1913.

Diario del Hogar (D.F., Mexico), 1890–1913.

El Paso Herald, 1906–1908.

El Paso Times, 2 June 1906–16 January 1909.

El Hijo del Ahuizote, Semanario, 1902–1903.

La Estrella (San Antonio), May, 1909.

International Socialist Review

El Liberal (Del Rio, Texas), 1908.

La Libertad (San Diego, Texas), 10 August–2 November 1907.

Libertad y Trabajo (Los Angeles, California), 6 June 1908.

Los Angeles Examiner (Los Angeles, California), 1907–1912.

Los Angeles Herald

Los Angeles Times (Los Angeles, California), 1907–1912.

Miner's Magazine
Mother Earth
The Nation
The New Republic
New York Call, 26 June 1908–4 November 1909.
New York Times
New York Tribune, 19 August 1906–20 September 1907.
La Prensa (San Antonio, Texas), 1913–1923.
Punto Rojo (Del Rio, Texas), 1909.
Reforma, Libertad y Justicia (Austin, Texas), 1908.
La Reforma Social (El Paso), 3-5 September 1907.
Regeneración (D.F., Mexico-Los Angeles, California), 1900–1918.
Revolución (Los Angeles, California), 1907.
Saint Louis Post-Dispatch, 17 December 1905.
San Antonio Express, 11 August 1909–7 January 1910.
Tucson Citizen
La Unión Industrial (Phoenix, Arizona), 1911.
La Voz de la Mujer (El Paso, Texas), 28 July–27 October 1907.
Why?
Wilshire's Magazine

GOVERNMENT DOCUMENTS
EXECUTIVE

Bureau of Prisons, Washington, D.C., Ricardo Flores Magón, Leavenworth file 14596.

Clark, Victor S., "Mexican Labor in the United States," U.S. Bureau of Labor, XVII, no. 78 (Washington, D.C., Government Printing Office, 1908), 466-522.

Department of Justice, Record Group 74, Files 90755, 71-1-59, 180187, 9–19–290. Washington, D.C.: National Archives.

Department of Justice. Parole Record File No. 14596 Leavenworth. Washington, D.C.: Bureau of Prisons.

Department of State, Papers Relating to the Foreign Relations of the United States, Washington, D.C.: U.S. Government Printing Office, various publication dates.

Department of State, Record Group 59, Decimal File 311.1221. Washington, D.C.: National Archives.

Department of State, Record Group 59, Dispatches from United States Consul in Nogales, 1889-1906, Vol. 4, January 2, 1903-July 26, 1906. Washington, D.C.: National Archives.

Department of State, Record Group 59, Dispatches from United States Ministers to Mexico, 1823-1906, Vol. 183, May 15-June 20, 1906. Washington, D.C.: National Archives.

Post Office Department. Annual Report for Fiscal Year Ended 30 June 1918. Washington, D.C., 1919.

Post Office Department. Annual Report for Fiscal Year Ended 30 June 1919. Washington, D.C., 1919.

LEGISLATIVE

"An Act to Amend Section 211 Federal Penal Code of 1910." U.S. Statutes at Large, 61st Congress, 1909-1911, 36: pt. 1, p. 1339.

"An Act to Define, Regulate, and Punish Trading with the Enemy, and for other Purposes." U.S. Statutes at Large, 40: pt. 1, ch. 106, pp. 411-425.

"An Act to Punish Acts of Interference with the Foreign Relations, the Neutrality, and the Foreign Commerce of the United States, to Punish Espionage, and Better to Enforce the Criminal Laws of the United States, and for other Purposes." U.S. Statutes at Large, 40: pt. 1, ch. 3, p. 219.

Alleged Persecution of Mexican Citizens by the Government of Mexico. 61st Congress, 2nd Session, Report of a Special Committee set up under H. J. Res. 201. Washington, D.C.: Government Printing Office, 1910.

Congressional Record: Appendix of Proceedings and Debates, and Session, 66th Congress. Extension of Remarks of Hon. Albert Johnson, June 3, 1920 concerning radicals. V. 59: pt. 9, pp. 9278-9280.

Congressional Record: Proceedings and Debates. 2nd Session, 66th Congress. Deportation of Alien Anarchists, December 20, 1919. 59: pt. 1, pp. 983-989.

Congressional Record: Proceedings and Debates. 4th session, 67th Congress. Remarks of Mr. Lineberger, December 11, 1922 concerning Ricardo Flores Magón. 69: pt. 1, pp. 298-300, 488.

Federal Penal Code in Force, January 1, 1910. Boston, 1910.

Investigation of Mexican Affairs. Senate Executive Document No. 285, 66th Congress, 2nd Session. 2 vols.. Washington, D.C.: Government Printing Office, 1919-1920.

Senate Documents, 66th Congress. 2d Session, 1919-1920. Investigation of Mexican Affairs. 2 vols. Washington, D.C., 1920.

U.S. House of Representatives, Hearings on House Joint Resolution 201 Providing for a Joint Committee to Investigate Alleged Persecutions of Mexican Citizens by the Government of Mexico. Hearings held before the Committee on Rules U.S. House of Representatives, June 8–14, 1910 Washington, D.C., Government Printing Office, 1910.

U.S. Senate, Investigation of Mexican Affairs, Report and Hearing pursuant to Senate Resolution 106. Hearings held before Sub-committee on Foreign Relations, U.S. Senate, 66th Congress, 1st Session, Senate Document No. 285, 2 volumes (Serial Nos. 7665 and 7666), Washington, D.C.: Government Printing Office, 1920.

United States House of Representatives. Hearing on the House Joint Resolution 210 Providing for Joint Committee to Investigate Alleged Persecution of Mexican Citizens by the Government of Mexico. Washington, D.C., 1910.

United States House of Representatives. Resolution: Requesting Information of the Attorney General Concerning the Imprisonment of Certain Persons at Florence, Arizona. Washington, D.C., 1910.

JUDICIAL

Circuit Court of Appeals. "United States v. Motion Picture Film, 'The Spirit of '76.'" Federal Reporter, 252: Series 1, pp. 946–948.

Circuit Court of Appeals. "Magón et al. v. United States." Federal Reporter, 248: Series 1, 201–205.

Circuit Court of Appeals. "Magón et al. v. United States." Federal Reporter, 260: Series 1, 811–814.

Federal Records Center, Port Worth, Texas, Department of Justice, U.S. District Court for the Western District of Texas.

Records of the United States Supreme Court. Appellate Case No. 2r i-53. The Matter of the Application of R. Flores Magón et al. for a Writ of Habeas Corpus. Washington, D.C.: National Archives.

U.S. Supreme Court, In the Matter of the Application of R. Flores Magón, Antonio I. Villarreal and Librado Rivera, for a Writ of Habeas Corpus. Transcript of Record on Appeal from the Circuit Court of the United States of America, of the Ninth Judicial Circuit, in and for the Southern District of California, Southern Division, 1908.

United States Supreme Court. "Enrique Flores Magón and Ricardo Flores Magón petitioners v. United States of America, May 5, 1919." Supreme Court Reporter, November 1918–July 1919, 39: 391.

OTHER BIBLIOGRAPHIES AND ARCHIVES

Archivo Histórico del Gobierno del Estado de Sonora

Bancroft Library, University of California, Berkeley. Silvestre Terrazas Collection.

Bancroft library. University of California, Berkeley, John Murray Collection.

Barrett, Ellen C. Baja California, 1535-1956. A bibliography of historical, geographical, and scientific literature relating to the Peninsula of Baja California and to the adjacent islands in the Gulf of California and the Pacific Ocean. Los Angeles: Bennett & Marshall, J957

Brown Lyle C. Magonista Bibliography Baylor University nd. (unpublished mimeograph)

Brown Lyle C. Magonista chronology Baylor University nd. (unpublished mimeograph)

Cosio Villegas, Daniel, "Nueva Historiografía del México Moderno," Memoria de El Colegio Nacional, Vol. 5, No. 4, pp. 11-176.

González, Luis, y otros. Fuentes de la historia conternporanea de México. Libros y folletos. 3 vols. México: El Colegio de México, 1961-1963.

González Ramírez, Manuel, ed. Fuentes para la historia de la Revolución Mexicancana. México: Fondo de Cultura Económica, 1953-7.

Maciel, R. David, "Introducción bibliográfica a la historia intelectual de México," Aztlán, Vol. 3, No.1, (Spring 1972).

Ramos, Roberto, Bibliografía de la Revolución Mexicana, 3 vols., D.F., México: Biblioteca del Instituto Nacional de Estudios Históricos de la Revolución Mexicana, 1959-1960.

Ross, Stanley R., et al. Fuentes de la historia conternporanea de México: periódicos y revistas. 2 vols. México: Colegio de México, 1965-1967.

Secretaria de Relaciones Exteriores, Archivo, D.F., México, Asunto: Flores Magón, etc. Colocación L-E-918-954, 36 tomos.

Sherman Foundation. Corona del Mar, California.

Sterling Library, Yale University, New Haven, Harry Weinberger Collection.

Theodore Perceval Gerson Collection and the Oral History Project. Special Collections, UCLA. Los Angeles, California.

INDEX

A

Abad de Santillan, Diego, 101, 370
Abanderados Rojos, 361
Acayucán, Veracruz, 52, 53, 158, 236, 287, 347
Acuña, Elisa, 342
Adams, Ansel T., 42
Aguascalientes, 364
Aguirre, Lauro, 347
Alanis, Lázaro, 358
Alfonso XIII, 264
Algodones, Baja California, 78, 356, 357
Alexander, Joseph L.B., 61
Alianza Magonista Zapatista, 101, 102
Alomo, Baja California, 358
Altar, Sonora, 359
Alvarado, Salvador, 231
American Civil Liberties Union, 98
American Federation of Labor, 72, 77, 80, 90, 352, 357
American Magazine, 71, 352
Anarchism, 13, 16-19, 23, 25, 26, 31, 33, 37, 38, 43, 46, 60, 61, 63, 64, 69, 70, 73-75, 78-82, 84-95, 99, 100, 104f, 112-116, 146, 169, 199, 200, 207, 208, 221, 224, 225, 228, 232, 233, 332-336, 360
Anarcho-syndicalism, 26, 98, 363, 368
Andonegui prison, 370
Anti-Reelection Party, 135, 353, 354
Anti-Reelectionism, 26, 27, 30, 31, 33, 35, 75, 79, 135, 156, 192, 292, 352
Appeal to Reason, 70, 351, 353
Aquinas, Thomas, 235
Araujo, Antonio P., 41, 66, 88, 220, 345, 351, 352, 357, 362
Arizmendez, Frederico, 349
Arizona, 23, 30, 37, 39, 40, 44, 47, 49, 51-53, 58, 61-63, 69, 72, 73, 202, 345, 346, 348-353, 355
Arizona rangers, 49, 51, 58, 346
Arnoux, Eugenio, 342
Arriaga, Camilo, 32-38, 82, 84, 341, 342
Arrieta, Benjamin, 364
Arrieta, Domingo, 364
Augustine, 235
Austin, Texas, 58

B

Baja California, 12, 77-81, 83, 85-88, 228, 230, 338, 348, 355-357, 359, 361, 363
Bakunin, Mikhail, 38, 341
Barbarous Mexico, 71, 352
Barcelona, 265
Barreda, Gabino, 25
Batalla, Diódoro, 33
Bazora, Florencio, 37, 38, 344
Bebel, August, 258
Belen prison, 31, 34, 35, 43, 71, 326, 340, 342, 344
Berkman, Alexander, 72, 80, 92, 93, 99, 366
Bernal, Nicolas T., 11, 59, 100, 370
Bernardino Contla, Tlaxcala, 76, 354
Berthold, Simon, 356, 358
Biblioteca Social Reconstruir, 14
Blanco, Lucio, 363
Blast, 72, 92
Bledsoe, Benjamin, 95, 96
Boletín Biográfico, 13
Bonaparte, Charles J., 57, 61
Border, 71, 352
Brousse, María, 11, 63, 68, 87, 89, 96, 99, 110, 362, 369
Brownsville, Texas, 202-204, 207
Bush, George W., 69, 94
Bustamante, Anastasio, 23
Bustamante, Rosalío, 39, 345

C

Cabrera, Daniel, 35, 342
California, 13, 23, 37, 49, 56, 58-62, 69-71, 73, 75, 77-80, 82, 83, 87-93, 99, 102f, 135, 137, 144, 202, 204, 206, 297, 224, 283, 347-351, 353, 354, 358, 359, 361, 362, 364-366
Camargo, Tamaulipas, 347, 348
Canales, Benjamin, 350
Canales, Cesar, 347, 361
Cananea, Sonora, 12, 46-51, 56-58, 61, 67, 72, 216, 321, 346, 350, 367
Cananea Consolidated Copper Company, 47
Cano, Gabino, 356
Capitalism, 18, 26, 27, 68, 69, 74 , 77, 79, 81, 84-87, 89, 93, 112, 135-139, 141, 143, 144

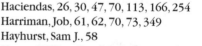

O

Oaxaca, 14, 23, 24, 30-32, 34, 42, 70, 101, 102, 102f, 140, 338, 339, 351, 356
Obregón, Alvaro, 12, 98, 365, 368
Ocampo, Melchor, 25
Olivares, Juan, 350
Orozco, Pascual, 53, 75, 252, 253, 361
Ortega, Margarita, 228 - 231, 363
Ortiz, Candelario, 218
Otis, Harrison Gray, 69, 78, 87
Owen, William C., 15, 75, 81, 92, 220, 357, 361, 362, 365, 371

P

Pachuca, Hidalgo, 32
Padre del Ahuizote, 344
Pajapán, Veracruz, 52, 347
Palma, Raul, 95
Palomarez, Fernando, 41, 67, 116, 348, 350-352, 355, 361
Palomas, Arizona, 365
Palomas, Chihuahua, 66, 76, 236, 287, 351
Panama, 198
Panama Canal, 198
Panuco, Veracruz, 363
Partido Liberal, 33, 35, 38
Partido Liberal Mexicano, 11, 15, 17, 39-41, 43-59, 61-90, 93, 98-100, 112, 113, 123-144, 156, 161, 163, 168, 169, 170, 178, 189, 195, 217, 223, 228-230, 242, 254-256, 266, 276, 277, 284, 294, 302, 304, 329, 335, 338, 345-367
　　—Junta, 13, 39-43, 47, 49-54, 56-63, 67, 69-74, 76, 77, 79-82, 84, 85, 87-89, 113, 115, 116, 123-125, 130, 134, 135, 137-139, 161, 170, 176, 186, 187, 302, 335, 345-348, 350, 353, 357, 358, 360-363, 365
　　—Program/Manifesto (1906), 43-46, 48, 50, 59, 65, 75, 84, 90, 112, 113, 124-129, 131-134, 346, 360, 361, 366
　　—1906 uprising, 12, 46, 47, 50-54, 57, 59, 76, 346, 347
　　—1908 uprising, 12, 63-68, 76, 82, 350-352, 357
Partido Revolucionario Institucional, 12, 100, 101
Partidi Socialista de México, 258

Patagonia, Arizona, 52, 346
Patriot Act, 94, 95
Perez Fernández, Federico, 343
Personalismo, 79, 86, 89, 100
Phoenix, Arizona, 58, 230
Pinkertons, 41, 42, 345, 346
Pizaña, Aniceto, 91, 203, 208
Plan de Ayala, 85, 361
Plan de Ayutla, 24, 338
Plan de Guadalupe, 363
Plan de Iguala, 23, 338
Plan de Noría, 26
Plan de San Diego, 91, 202, 204
Plan de San Luis Potosí, 75, 354
Plan de Tacubaya, 361
Plan de Tuxtelpec, 26, 27, 30, 75, 353
PLM (see Partido Liberal Mexicano)
Pochutla, Oaxaca, 42
Political Prisoners Held in the United States, 70
Political Refugee Defense League of Chicago, 61, 71
Ponciano Arriaga Liberal Club, 341
Portes Gil, Emilio, 13
Portland, Oregon, 88
Porvenir, 341
Presente, 202, 205
PRI (see Partido Revolucionario Institucional)
Proudhon, Pierre Joseph, 23, 25, 341
Pryce, Carl Rhys, 78, 358, 359
Puebla, 56, 57, 82, 140, 176, 339, 347, 351
Puente, Lazaro, 345
Puerto México, Veracruz, 40, 52, 347
Puntos Rojos, 62, 68

R

Racism, 47, 69, 74, 102f, 198-211
Ramírez Caule, Pedro, 355
Reclus, Elisee, 341
Regeneración, 11-13, 15, 32-34, 36, 37, 39-43, 48, 50, 56, 59, 73-76, 79, 81-85, 87-89, 91-94, 96, 115, 120-123, 135, 137, 190, 201, 207, 220, 221-225, 249, 255, 295, 308, 325, 326, 338, 341, 342, 344-348, 354-360, 362, 363, 365-367
Regeneración: 1900-1918, 338
Reián, Francisco I., 357

ADDITIONAL TITLES FROM AK PRESS

BOOKS:

MARTHA ACKELSBERG—*Free Women of Spain*

KATHY ACKER—*Pussycat Fever*

MICHAEL ALBERT—*Moving Forward: Program for a Participatory Economy*

JOEL ANDREAS—*Addicted to War: Why the U.S. Can't Kick Militarism*

JOEL ANDREAS—*Adicto a la Guerra: Por que EEUU no Puede LIbrarse del Militarismo*

PAUL AVRICH—*Anarchist Voices*

PAUL AVRICH—*The Modern School Movement: Anarchism and Education in the United States*

PAUL AVRICH—*Russian Anarchists, The*

ALEXANDER BERKMAN—*What is Anarchism?*

ALEXANDER BERKMAN—*The Blast: The Complete Collection*

HAKIM BEY—*Immediatism*

JANET BIEHL & PETER STAUDENMAIER—*Ecofascism: Lessons From The German Experience*

BIOTIC BAKING BRIGADE—*Pie Any Means Necessary: The Biotic Baking Brigade Cookbook*

JACK BLACK—*You Can't Win*

MURRAY BOOKCHIN—*Anarchism, Marxism, and the Future of the Left*

MURRAY BOOKCHIN—*Ecology of Freedom*

MURRAY BOOKCHIN—*Post-Scarcity Anarchism*

MURRAY BOOKCHIN—*Social Anarchism or Lifestyle Anarchism: An Unbridgeable Chasm*

MURRAY BOOKCHIN—*Spanish Anarchists: The Heroic Years 1868–1936, The*

MURRAY BOOKCHIN—*To Remember Spain: The Anarchist and Syndicalist Revolution of 1936*

MURRAY BOOKCHIN—*Which Way for the Ecology Movement?*

MAURICE BRINTON—*For Workers' Power*

DANNY BURNS—*Poll Tax Rebellion*

MAT CALLAHAN—*The Trouble With Music*

CHRIS CARLSSON—*Critical Mass: Bicycling's Defiant Celebration*

JAMES CARR—*Bad*

NOAM CHOMSKY—*At War With Asia*

NOAM CHOMSKY—*Chomsky on Anarchism*

NOAM CHOMSKY—*Language and Politics*

NOAM CHOMSKY—*Radical Priorities*

CDs

THE EX—*1936: The Spanish Revolution*
MUMIA ABU JAMAL—*175 Progress Drive*
MUMIA ABU JAMAL—*All Things Censored Vol. 1*
MUMIA ABU JAMAL—*Spoken Word*
FREEDOM ARCHIVES—*Chile: Promise of Freedom*
FREEDOM ARCHIVES—*Prisons on Fire: George Jackson, Attica & Black Liberation*
FREEDOM ARCHIVES—*Robert F. Williams: Self Respect, Self Defense, & Self Determination*
JUDI BARI—*Who Bombed Judi Bari?*
JELLO BIAFRA—*Become the Media*
JELLO BIAFRA—*Beyond The Valley of the Gift Police*
JELLO BIAFRA—*High Priest of Harmful*
JELLO BIAFRA—*I Blow Minds For A Living*
JELLO BIAFRA—*If Evolution Is Outlawed*
JELLO BIAFRA—*Machine Gun In The Clown's Hand*
JELLO BIAFRA—*No More Cocoons*
NOAM CHOMSKY—*American Addiction, An*
NOAM CHOMSKY—*Case Studies in Hypocrisy*
NOAM CHOMSKY—*Emerging Framework of World Power*
NOAM CHOMSKY—*Free Market Fantasies*
NOAM CHOMSKY—*Imperial Presidency, The*
NOAM CHOMSKY—*New War On Terrorism: Fact And Fiction*
NOAM CHOMSKY—*Propaganda and Control of the Public Mind*
NOAM CHOMSKY—*Prospects for Democracy*
NOAM CHOMSKY/CHUMBAWAMBA—*For A Free Humanity: For Anarchy*
WARD CHURCHILL—*Doing Time: The Politics of Imprisonment*
WARD CHURCHILL—*In A Pig's Eye: Reflections on the Police State, Repression, and Native America*
WARD CHURCHILL—*Life in Occupied America*
WARD CHURCHILL—*Pacifism and Pathology in the American Left*
ALEXANDER COCKBURN—*Beating the Devil: The Incendiary Rants of Alexander Cockburn*
ANGELA DAVIS—*Prison Industrial Complex, The*
NORMAN FINKELSTEIN—*An Issue of Justice*
JAMES KELMAN—*Seven Stories*
TOM LEONARD—*Nora's Place and Other Poems 1965-99*
CASEY NEILL—*Memory Against Forgetting*
CHRISTIAN PARENTI—*Taking Liberties: Policing, Prisons and Surveillance in an Age of Crisis*

UTAH PHILLIPS—*I've Got To Know*
UTAH PHILLIPS—*Starlight on the Rails CD box set*
DAVID ROVICS—*Behind the Barricades: Best of David Rovics*
ARUNDHATI ROY—*Come September*
VARIOUS—*Better Read Than Dead*
VARIOUS—*Less Rock, More Talk*
VARIOUS—*Mob Action Against the State: Collected Speeches from the Bay Area Anarchist Bookfair*
VARIOUS—*Monkeywrenching the New World Order*
VARIOUS—*Return of the Read Menace*
HOWARD ZINN—*Artists In A Time of War*
HOWARD ZINN—*Heroes and Martyrs: Emma Goldman, Sacco & Vanzetti, and the Revolutionary Struggle*
HOWARD ZINN—*People's History of the United States: A Lecture at Reed College, A*
HOWARD ZINN—*People's History Project*
HOWARD ZINN—*Stories Hollywood Never Tells*

DVDs
NOAM CHOMSKY—*Distorted Morality*
NOAM CHOMSKY—*Imperial Grand Strategy*
ARUNDHATI ROY—*Instant Mix Imperial Democracy*
HOWARD ZINN—*Readings from Voices of a People's History*

The addresses below would be delighted to provide you with the latest complete AK catalog, featuring several thousand books, pamphlets, zines, audio products, video products, and stylish apparel published & distributed by AK Press. Alternatively, check out our websites for the complete catalog, latest news and updates, events, and secure ordering.

AK Press
674-A 23rd Street
Oakland, CA 94612-1163
U.S.A
(510) 208-1700
www.akpress.org
akpress@akpress.org

AK Press
PO Box 12766
Edinburgh, EH8 9YE
Scotland
(0131) 555-5165
www.akuk.com
ak@akedin.demon.co.uk

ABOUT THE EDITORS

CHAZ BUFE is the author, co-author, compiler/editor or translator of seven other books, including *Cuban Anarchism, The Devil's Dictionaries*, and *An Understandable Guide to Music Theory*. He is currently writing an anarchist science fiction novel concerning interstellar travel, religious cults, and the blues.

MITCHELL COWEN VERTER is the author, translator, and educator responsible for the bilingual, heterodidactic edition of Ricardo Flores Magón's "Tierra y Libertad / Land and Liberty." Additionally, his essay, "Barbarous Oaxaca" details the ongoing human rights abuses in the Mexican state where Flores Magón was born. He is currently developing a book on the anarchism of the other person.